D0152823

Sovereign Soldiers

AMERICAN BUSINESS,
POLITICS, AND SOCIETY

Series editors:
Andrew Wender Cohen, Pamela Walker Laird,
Mark H. Rose, and Elizabeth Tandy Shermer

Books in the series American Business, Politics, and Society
explore the relationships over time between governmental
institutions and the creation and performance of markets,
firms, and industries, large and small. The central theme of
this series is that politics, law, and public policy—understood
broadly to embrace not only lawmaking, but also the
structuring presence of governmental institutions—has been
fundamental to the evolution of American business from
the colonial era to the present. The series aims to explore, in
particular, developments that have enduring consequences.

A complete list of books in the series
is available from the publisher.

Sovereign Soldiers

How the U.S. Military
Transformed the Global Economy
After World War II

Grant Madsen

PENN

UNIVERSITY OF PENNSYLVANIA PRESS

PHILADELPHIA

Copyright © 2018 University of Pennsylvania Press

All rights reserved.
Except for brief quotations used for purposes of review or scholarly citation,
none of this book may be reproduced in any form by any means
without written permission from the publisher.

Published by
University of Pennsylvania Press
Philadelphia, Pennsylvania 19104-4112
www.upenn.edu/pennpress

Printed in the United States of America
on acid-free paper
1 3 5 7 9 10 8 6 4 2

Library of Congress Cataloging-in-Publication Data

Names: Madsen, Grant, author.
Title: Sovereign soldiers: how the U.S. military transformed the global
economy after World War II / Grant Madsen.
Other titles: American business, politics, and society.
Description: 1st edition. | Philadelphia: University of Pennsylvania Press,
[2018] | Series: American business, politics, and society | Includes
bibliographical references and index.
Identifiers: LCCN 2017060415 | ISBN 9780812250367 (hardcover: alk. paper)
Subjects: LCSH: United States—Economic policy—1945–1960. | Economic
history—1945–1971. | United States—Armed Forces—Stability operations. |
Reconstruction (1939–1951)—Japan. | Reconstruction (1939–1951)—Germany.
| United States—Foreign economic relations—History—20th century.
Classification: LCC HC106.5 .M354 2018 | DDC 330.943/0875—dc23
LC record available at https://lccn.loc.gov/2017060415

To Carol and Gordon,
My models for being a historian,
scholar, and so much more

Contents

Abbreviations

DDEPL	Dwight D. Eisenhower Presidential Library, Abilene, KS
HSTPL	Harry S. Truman Presidential Library, Independence, MO
NA	National Archives, College Park, MD
JDP	Joseph M. Dodge Papers, Detroit Public Library, Detroit, MI
OJMS	Occupation of Japan Microfiche Series, Suitland, MD; Congressional Information Service, Washington National Records Center, Bethesda, MD
HSP	Henry Stimson Papers, Yale University Library, Microfilm Collection, New Haven, CT
GML	George C. Marshall Research Library, Lexington, VA
FRUS	*Foreign Relations of the United States,* Government Printing Office, Washington, DC
PDDE	*Papers of Dwight D. Eisenhower,* Johns Hopkins University Press, Baltimore, MD, 1970
APP	The American Presidency Project, by Gerhard Peters and John T. Woolley, http://www.presidency.ucsb.edu/index.php

rehabilitation of Germany."[2] Clay and Eisenhower worried about their orders. The orders "had to be based on the theory that there was going to be a [functioning] German government" after the war. In reality, "there wasn't any government." On top of that, "there was a real shortage of manpower" because "much of the manpower [was in prison] camps" or dead, and "our real big job was to get enough . . . agriculture going to really keep this country alive." The Germans faced "starvation and mass deaths," and all three men agreed that "Americans, of course, would never permit even their former enemies to starve."[3]

The Philippines taught Stimson that policy should never seem "vindictive." An occupied people already chafe under foreign authority, and if the occupiers complicate those resentments by undermining the local economy, the occupied people often revolt.[4] This had been his observation in the Philippines, where his efforts to bring economic growth and a modicum of welfare provisions had quickly been undone by American tariffs and punitive measures enacted at the advent of the Great Depression.[5] As a result, in regard to the orders to do nothing to help the German economy, Stimson said, "don't put too much effort in carrying them out the way they're written because you've got a job to do first which is to bring about law and order and the ability of the people in this country to live."[6] Stimson saw "no purpose in the deliberate destruction of the German economy," since "its reconstruction was essential to create an atmosphere in which it might be possible to develop a true spirit of democracy."[7] Stimson preached to the choir. Growing up in Georgia at the end of the nineteenth century, Clay had a clear sense of how occupations could lose the support of the occupied—particularly if the occupied felt exploited. Clay made the point later to reporters: he would be "damn sure there weren't any carpetbaggers in the military government."[8] Eisenhower agreed. He too had served in the Philippines where he learned the difficulties involved in governing abroad.

*   *   *

This book focuses on the concerns discussed by Stimson, Eisenhower, and Clay on that warm afternoon in Germany. On the one hand, it explains how the army found itself capable of governing a foreign people, and particularly the Germans and Japanese after World War II. In this sense, the book acts as an institutional history of military government starting after the Spanish-American War—or roughly that point at which the United

States began routinely using its military to govern non-Americans outside the continental United States.[9] The country's recent efforts in Iraq and Afghanistan highlight the fact that a history of military government is long overdue.[10] As a recent army operational guide notes, "military forces have fought only eleven wars considered conventional. . . ." while conducting "hundreds of other military operations . . . where the majority of effort consisted of stability tasks." In short, "Contrary to popular belief, the military history of the United States is one characterized by such operations, interrupted by distinct episodes of major combat."[11]

On the other hand, this book is an intellectual history of the political economy that military government created during the occupations of Germany and Japan. It explains why military government first seized on economic development as a key feature of successful "stability" operations, and how that initial interest grew into a distinct policy regime during the occupations of Germany and Japan. The book then shows how that policy regime came to dominate not only postwar Germany and Japan, but ultimately the United States in the 1950s. Because few of the people involved in its creation were economists or, in most cases, politicians, it never got a name in the American context. Eisenhower tried a variety of terms: "conservative dynamism" or "dynamic conservatism" and finally "modern Republicanism." But none of these terms fit exactly.[12]

The story is held together by the careers of the men who held positions in and around the army starting at the turn of the century. These men rose through the army's ranks and, by the 1950s, found themselves in powerful political positions. The group included most famously Generals Eisenhower, Clay, and Douglas MacArthur, along with lesser-known occupation officials such as the Detroit banker Joseph Dodge, Generals William Draper and William Marquat, and foreign leaders such as Ludwig Erhard and Hayato Ikeda. Writing in the 1950s, the sociologist and critic C. Wright Mills identified this group as part of "the power elite," the men who dominated global politics in the years after the war.[13]

By focusing on these individuals, and in an effort to remain fair to both the institutional analysis and the intellectual history, a number of important topics get a much smaller treatment than they deserve. For example, the book barely touches upon military strategy in World Wars I and II; it does not take up every military occupation, especially Korea after the Second World War; and it does not take up the causes or course of the Cold War. Instead, the book remains true to its focus on the figures who link military government as an institution with the economic policy that came out of military government and returned to the United States in the middle decades of the twentieth century.

As Stimson first intimated to Eisenhower and Clay in 1945, economic policy worked in the service of a broader democratic vision for the Germans and Japanese. More to the point, it could prevent yet another world war. Indeed, the failure to achieve a lasting peace after the First World War weighed heavily upon military government after the Second. Prosperity might provide a tangible sign to the Germans and Japanese that the future lay in partnership with the United States, rather than in opposition. At the same time, military governors understood that a giant gap existed between *wanting* economic recovery and *causing* economic recovery. If nothing else, the barely concluded Great Depression taught this fact.

The first year of occupation saw mostly failure in military government's effort to bridge that gap. Then, late in 1945 officials in Germany stumbled upon a critical insight that turned things around. On the advice of a number of German economists, they began to think more about public finance. Postwar planning had assumed that the centralized and hierarchical structure of firms in Germany and Japan enabled totalitarian political structures.[14] The initial instructions to military government included orders to break apart large conglomerates in both countries. But as time passed, military government realized that uprooting the structure of German and Japanese firms would do little to bring about economic recovery, let alone hinder future dictators.

More to the point, occupation officials concluded that both recovery and future peace depended upon integrating Germany and Japan into the global system of trade and finance imagined during the Bretton Woods Conference of 1944. They worked for more than a decade to bring the system into full operation (many countries were not ready until 1958), using their key positions in Europe, Japan, and the United States to smooth the way for its full implementation. They felt a special commitment to it as a key to preventing a future war. Yet here, again, a gap lay between wanting integration and achieving integration.

Most immediately, military government realized that integration could not occur until economic stabilization took place *within* individual economies—and particularly, the stabilization of price levels and currency values. Whenever possible they enforced balanced budgets, zero-inflation monetary policy, and investment-led growth, so as to smooth the way for free trade and international capital flows as imagined at Bretton Woods. In fact, military government in Germany and later in Japan came to conclude that the Bretton Woods system ultimately worked at odds with the Keynesian approach to public finance, then taking root within the Roosevelt and Truman administrations.[15] Military government in Germany had already become particularly suspicious of the Keynesian framework, because it seemed to resemble Nazi political economy in the 1930s a little too closely, and it left Germany in the throes of a debilitating inflation after the war. This fact also helps explain another surprising conclusion about the occupations. During the late 1940s, the United States followed *two* distinct economic policy regimes: a Keynesian framework aiming at full employment within the United States and an anti-Keynesian framework hostile to budget deficits in the occupations.

In particular, military government also worried that the Keynesian framework undermined the welfare state because of its propensity for inflation. At midcentury, most welfare states focused primarily on pensions for retirees and defined benefits for the poor. Inflation tended to reduce the real value of government benefits. As Eisenhower explained to a friend in 1953, "Every one of these [beneficiaries] will be ruined if we do not stop the deflation in the value of the dollar."[16]

*   *   *

There is a tendency among scholars to picture American governance at midcentury as a kind of three-legged stool, where one leg represents the state's commitment to the economic goals of full employment and mass consumption through Keynesian spending, the second leg represents expanded state capacities in the interest of welfare and national security, and the last, a preference for the corporate institutional form (including experts and professionals from the public and private sector).[17] Occupation officials embraced two legs of the stool (the commitment to welfare and the organizational form) while rejecting the commitment to full employment and mass consumption through Keynesian spending. More to the point, they felt that both a welfare and warfare state would prove more effective and lasting without the commitment to Keynesian spending. At the time this seemed like "conservative" or "laissez-faire" economics, and subsequently could seem like the "supply-side" approach of Reaganomics; however, it differed from both because occupation officials never opposed what today we call "big government." They did not favor tax cuts (indeed, the Eisenhower years saw some of the highest marginal rates in American history), and in some cases they favored tax increases (for example, in financing the Interstate Highway System).

Put simply, occupation officials did not see a contradiction between a muscular central state—for welfare or for warfare—and balanced budgets. Their approach has never fit comfortably within the story of American liberalism because it resists the basic "big" versus "small" government debate that has animated so much political discourse in the twentieth century. Unfortunately, the "big government–small government" debate can trap historians in categories that often obscure the many ways the American state has evolved both domestically and internationally.[18] Occupation officials asked a different question: should a vastly empowered government function (roughly speaking) on a pay-as-you-go basis? Or should it accomplish its goals on credit? From the perspective of military government, the answer to this question had enormous consequences. The occupations suggested that a pay-as-you-go approach tended to keep a balance between the interests of the state and citizenry. It also tended to *preserve* the state by avoiding the over-commitments and broken promises that could lead to political upheaval later.[19]

More recently, political scholars have focused their research on specific state institutions and how those institutions have evolved in order to accomplish an assigned task. Often an institution lacks the capacities to accomplish its task: sometimes it lacks the necessary experts; sometimes it faces legal or constitutional prohibitions; and sometimes the preexisting bureaucracy resists doing the task. This research approach, often called American Political Development, fits this story because it suggests a focus on the growing capacity of military government through the first half of the twentieth century. Occupation officials found themselves forced to expand the governing capacities of the army in response to the tasks that increasingly fell to them.[20]

At the same time, American Political Development's institutional focus sometimes misses the fact that occasionally leaders have *not* employed the capacities they possessed—whether in combination, alone, or not at all. In other words, policy also matters.[21] In simple terms, the distinction lies between what a state *can* do and what its leaders *choose* to do. The phrase "policy regime" helps get at this distinction. The term has taken on a life of its own among scholars in recent years: it has been used to describe local, federal, and even international orders where "constellations of rules, practices, institutions, and ideas [have held] together over time."[22] To better explain the occupiers' story, though, consider "policy regime" in the minimal sense often employed by economists—and specifically, Thomas Sargent—who see a policy regime as a government "strategy" that fundamentally shapes the decisions and expectations of most private economic actors. In short, to be a "regime" a policy cannot be *perceived* as temporary or a trick or a one-time effort; it must be *credible* and enduring.[23]

This distinction between capacities and policy matters because it helps clarify the overall arc of the narrative to follow. In general terms, the first half of the book explains how and why the army became a powerhouse of economic policy in the years after World War II—how it developed *capacities* as a governing institution. The last chapters of the book explain how army officials then developed a coherent *policy regime* that employed some capacities while ignoring others. In Germany, Japan, and finally the United States, occupation officials inherited state capacities they chose not to use, implementing a policy regime focused on economic restraint instead.

At the same time, American Political Development's focus on specific institutions does a better job of understanding military government than another recent development among scholars: the turn to the idea of "empire" to explain the way the United States functions in the global context.[24] While "empire" as a theoretical construct has advantages, it holds a number of disadvantages for understanding military government. The better rubric comes from the political theorist Robert Latham, who has suggested scholars focus on America's "external state"—those institutions functioning outside the formal boundaries of the United States, while still tied to it. The external state sometimes fills the space between "flag and Constitution"—what the Supreme Court (in the Insular Cases) identified as American possessions not incorporated into the United States proper.[25]

For Latham, the external state expresses more than "an external face to the state"; it refers to "the organs that are literally situated and deployed in the external realm" and distinct not only from "the internal state," but also from "those institutions which command authority over the deployment process itself, the state center."[26] Latham's terminology fits here because the military did more than simply express the desires of the American metropole. "I had too much flexibility," Clay complained later of his time in the occupation. "I had—there were many times when I would have loved to have had instructions. . . . What the hell do you do when you don't get any?"[27] Oftentimes, the external state made policy directly, for example, when Clay unilaterally stopped reparations to the Soviet Union from the American zone.[28] In that case, the external state bound the metropole, which found itself compelled to support Clay. Particularly in the aftermath of World War II, when "administrative disarray and domestic constraints" inhibited clear instructions from flowing to Germany and Japan, decision-making lodged "itself in the field,"[29] where military governments functioned as distinct institutions, developing their own policy pathways and capacities.[30]

Thinking of military government as an external state also allows for a fresh take on the vast literature already written on this topic. In general (and with exceptions), scholars have taken three broad approaches in explaining the occupations. The first approach argues that a group of American elites in government or business (or some combination of the two) pursued policies to reshape the globe in their interests. Whether in response to Soviet provocations, or "to restructure the world so that American business could trade, operate, and profit without restrictions everywhere," or to provide national security, or to impose a "corporate" reconstruction of the international economy, or to provide a New Deal for the world, or to Americanize the world (culturally or otherwise), these scholars see the United States as the hub around which the wheel of the rest of the world revolved.[31] While scholars in this group have disagreed (sometimes vehemently) over the motivations of American political and business elites, and have similarly argued over which group, ultimately, had the most influence in policymaking, they nevertheless privilege the "metropole" in telling the story of the occupations. The occupations simply expressed the broad geopolitical aims that began in Washington (or sometimes New York).

The second approach usually comes from German and Japanese scholars who have raised the possibility that Washington did not have as much power as once thought. One version of this story argues that a brief window of opportunity existed to genuinely remake the German and Japanese political economy along progressive lines; tragically, however, the advent of the Cold War shut that window as Washington essentially relinquished the reform agenda, allowing conservative German and Japanese elites to reassert their authority.[32] A different version of this story argues that the Germans and Japanese managed to cleverly undermine, thwart, or work around the occupation. Using cultural misunderstanding to their advantage, they limited the occupations' overall influence, often to their ultimate benefit.[33]

Finally, a new set of scholars has taken both a more global and a less state-centric approach. Sometimes called "transnational," "America in the world," or "New International," this group exhibits skepticism toward the idea of "the unitary state, nation, or nation-state as an ontological given," noting that states are often comprised of competing institutions with different agendas.[34] They have also looked at institutions functioning outside of official state lines (such as nongovernment organizations or the United Nations) as well as culture and cultural transmissions across borders.[35] These scholars see in the early Cold War "complex circuits of exchange" rather than a wheel revolving around Washington, D.C.[36] The idea of an "external state" fits best within this final approach because it speaks to the odd configuration of institutional power, neither national nor hegemonic, true of military government.

With the recent experience of Iraq and Afghanistan in mind, it is much easier to appreciate how precarious the entire project of rehabilitating Germany and Japan was. Both countries lay in ruins, their economies devastated by war and their people moribund from defeat. Both populations lived on the edge of starvation. Each seemed susceptible to growing resentments and (particularly in Germany) the call of communism. Moreover, each country faced rampant inflation, nonexistent financial markets, and little economic activity. For the generals who took power at the end of World War II in Germany and Japan, success seemed uncertain and failure likely. Yet they largely succeeded in bringing both countries back from the brink of chaos, a testament to the governing abilities of these soldier sovereigns.

prior agreement. General Fermín Jáudenes y Álvarez sent word through intermediaries that he would surrender the city, provided he could plausibly preserve Spanish honor. He suggested each side fire near but not *at* the other. The Spanish soldiers would make an orderly retreat into the city, abandoning their posts in succession as the American soldiers advanced. Eventually, the city would "fall" to the Americans, who could raise the American flag and take the Spanish soldiers prisoner. American guards (not Filipino insurrectionists) could then safely escort the Spanish from the city for their journey back to Spain.[9] The "battle" went as choreographed, and the garrison surrendered the city without the knowledge, input, or involvement of the Filipino rebels. As the Filipino insurrectionists looked on, the Americans advanced and the Spanish retreated. By the end of the day, American troops controlled the city, which they sealed off from the Filipinos.[10]

Military strategy in the Philippines followed President William McKinley's interest in keeping his options open. With Manila in American control, he had flexibility in negotiating peace with Spain and could also deal with the Filipinos from a position of strength. If it worked out that the United States ended up annexing some part of the archipelago, then possession avoided the problem of "retaking" the city. While not using those words exactly, McKinley ordered the military to "use any means in your judgment necessary" to maintain American authority over Manila, its bay, and the surrounding area against the Filipinos.[11]

The fateful decision to take Manila, however, created a genuine dilemma as to what to do with it along with the entire archipelago. McKinley might have simply freed the Philippines. But he worried the islands might be gobbled up by a growing German or Japanese empire (both seemed interested). He also wanted to open Asian trade and markets, and the Philippines provided a strong foothold in the Western Pacific. Finally, in an age when to the victor went the spoils, he feared a political backlash if he simply walked away from a great military victory "empty-handed." Certainly race played a part in his thinking. Whatever the motivation, in the end he decided to make the entire archipelago an American colony. The Spanish had stalled the peace negotiations in the hopes that the American people would repudiate the acquisition of the Philippines in the 1898 midterm election. They didn't. Once the election returns became known, Spanish negotiators conceded. The final treaty, signed on December 10, 1898, ceded the Philippines to the United States for a payment of $20 million. It also made Cuba independent (although still under American supervision) and added Guam and Puerto Rico to the American empire.[12]

Despite the election returns, an imperial project remained controversial if for no other reason than it seemed contrary to an American identity born out of a revolution against an imperial power.[13] Perhaps to finesse this uncomfortable historical fact, McKinley argued that Americans should take hold of the Philippines *in the interest* of the Filipinos. The Filipinos would become "Christian" and "civilized" under the supervision of their more experienced older brothers. "Bear in mind that the government which they are establishing is designed not for our satisfaction or for the expression of our theoretical views, but for the happiness, peace, and prosperity of the people of the Philippine Islands," McKinley explained.[14] American rule would be temporary and benevolent, which would distinguish it from the permanent subservience demanded by European empires.[15] More to the point, "Every step taken was in obedience to the requirements of the Constitution," McKinley liked to say of his foray into imperialism.[16] But his concern with the American Constitution and interest in distinguishing American empire from its European alternative meant that he had made little preparation for governing the Philippines once they became an American possession. In short, what entity would do the actual job of governing the Filipinos and how would that entity fit within the broader institutional framework of American governance?

The army became the default answer—at least to the question of which entity would do the actual job of governing abroad. The logic of the situation dictated as much. The army was already there, in large numbers, with clear lines of communication and a functioning command structure. No other branch of the federal government possessed these capabilities in a form that allowed for extension outside of the continental United States. In a scenario that would repeat itself in future conflicts, the army was always "there" wherever "there" happened to be.

As it turned out, in the Philippines the job of military governor fell to Arthur MacArthur, Douglas MacArthur's father. Arthur MacArthur was a career soldier and decorated veteran of the Civil War. After the treaty with Spain, he stood at the center of McKinley's effort to remake the Filipinos in an American image. Arthur MacArthur initially took this to mean using the army to restore basic services: fixing sewers and roads, sponsoring schools and markets, and generally pursuing the basic aims of "normal" civic life.[17] At the same time, he had the obligation to put down a growing insurrection as Filipinos realized the war had largely traded one colonial overlord for another. Already armed and practiced at fighting an empire, the Filipinos proved a formidable antagonist.[18] Thus, Arthur MacArthur had to make effective on the ground the contradictory orders to subdue the Filipinos in their own interest. At the same time, he had the practical task of retooling what the army does best (organized violence) for the purpose of establishing a *legitimate* governing authority among a conquered people.

In general, Arthur MacArthur took the position that aggressive violence would, over the long run, undermine American legitimacy. As a result, he issued orders offering amnesty to any Filipino willing to lay down arms and swear loyalty to the American government. He also prohibited his troops from using torture to gain information from captured guerillas (an order often difficult to enforce in practice). When a daring raid captured the rebel leader Emilio Aguinaldo alive, Arthur MacArthur spent weeks convincing him to use his influence to encourage an end to the insurrection. When Aguinaldo finally relented and agreed that the insurrection should end, Arthur Mac-Arthur wanted to release all Filipino political prisoners and send Aguinaldo on a tour of the United States, treating him as an honored diplomat. McKinley recoiled at the thought. In general, Arthur MacArthur showed a surprising lack of racism as well as a willingness to use the promise of American freedom and prosperity to pacify the Filipinos. Mostly, he wanted to get the military out of the job of governing a foreign people as quickly as possible.[19]

Perhaps his greatest challenge came not from the insurrection but from his own government. While McKinley initially relied upon military government in the Philippines, he soon afterwards decided upon a civilian version of colonial government to supplement the military. While Arthur Mac-Arthur served as military governor, McKinley sent a civilian commission headed by future president William Howard Taft to *also* function as the American government in the Philippines. Without clear lines of authority the two men never got along. In letters home Taft begged McKinley and anyone else he could in Washington to order Arthur MacArthur home. But officials in Washington worried that the insurrection might have widespread support, suggesting the army should remain in charge. Once, however, the insurrection had dwindled to a small group of incorrigibles, then a civilian government could take charge. In this regard, Arthur MacArthur and Taft sent conflicting reports: Taft insisted the rebellion had spent itself and the last remnants would melt under the heat of more aggressive military action;

Arthur MacArthur insisted that the rebellion had popular support, and aggressive military action would prove self-defeating.[20]

When rebel activity in fact began to decline, Washington officials decided to finally give Taft sole authority in the Philippines. On July 4, 1901, he relieved Arthur MacArthur and assumed all executive power in the occupation. The shift proved ironic. Taft's civilian supervision inspired the bloodiest period of the occupation, with more than two hundred thousand Filipinos dying as part of a broad-based pacification. In the end, the Filipinos were subdued, but at extraordinary cost in blood and treasure. As opponents of imperial policy liked to point out, the United States spent $20 million to buy the Philippines and another $200 million to subdue it. In the meantime more than four thousand Americans died from disease and wounds.[21]

While the conflict between Taft and Arthur MacArthur certainly involved each man's pride, it also turned on genuine questions of law and policy. Since they found themselves in a new kind of state, outside the norms of American governance, they often fought over the nature of their authority. Taft took the position that American government in the Philippines functioned under the authority of the president. Arthur MacArthur agreed. But he insisted that the president's authority came through his role as commander in chief, and, thus, it extended *only* through the military. A civilian authority (such as Taft possessed) required an "organic act" (an act of congress creating or establishing a territory of the United States).[22] Taft, a jurist and aspirant to the Supreme Court (he became chief justice in 1921), could hardly stand hearing MacArthur lecture him in areas where he saw himself as expert, even if MacArthur had a point.

The question of authority grew more complicated when it came to mundane tasks. If, for example, Taft ordered the construction of a sewer (a task that seemed civilian in nature), he needed help from the Army Corps of Engineers. To whom should an officer in the corps report, MacArthur or Taft? As it turned out, some of the nastiest fights between Taft and Arthur MacArthur turned on exactly these kinds of questions.[23]

In 1902, Congress resolved the question in the Philippine Organic Act, which "approved, ratified, and confirmed" Taft's position as civil governor. At the same time, it declared that "inhabitants of the Philippine Islands . . . shall be deemed and held to be citizens of the Philippine Islands" and that this citizenship entitled them "to the protection of the United States," but *not* American citizenship. The Act guaranteed for Filipinos the rights con-tained in the U.S. Constitution. It also provided for the creation of a Philip-pine republic able to pass its own laws, enter into treaties, and mint its own currency. However, it limited this power by declaring that "all laws passed by the Government of the Philippine Islands shall be reported to Congress, which hereby reserves the power and authority to annul the same."[24]

While the law clarified Taft's power in the Philippines, it muddied the relationship of the United States to its new territories. Ultimately, the Supreme Court tried to resolve the legal status of America's new colonial possessions (including Puerto Rico and Guam) in the Insular Cases (so called because "insular" served as a synonym for "islands"). The Supreme Court explained that the new territories were "not a foreign country" since they were "subject to the sovereignty of" and "owned by the United States." However, they were "foreign to the United States in a domestic sense" since they "had not been incorporated into the United States" as new states and were instead "merely appurtenant thereto as a posses-sion."[25] And therein lay the nature of the confusion: whether out of rac-ism, or fear of upsetting the domestic political balance, or whatever else, no branch of the federal government contemplated the eventual incorpo-ration of the new possessions into the constitutional design of the coun-try.[26] At the same time, the federal government did not create an institutional framework that looked like the kind of imperial ministries developed by the British, French, and other European powers. Indeed, in an era in which progressive Americans borrowed so many ideas from Europe, no broad effort emerged to administer the new American posses-sions through a ministry modeled on European precedents.[27] Instead, the Philippines remained in a state of semi-independence, codified in 1916 by the Jones Act, which dramatically expanded self-government and promised Filipinos that "tutelage" would eventually come to an end, while nevertheless insisting that the time had yet to come.

In a general sense, the complications that resulted from annexing the Philippines left a bad taste in the mouth of future policy makers. "If Old Dewey had just sailed away when he smashed the Spanish fleet," McKinley once observed to a friend, "what a lot of trouble that would have saved us!"[28] Indeed, after the Spanish-American War the United Stated did not attempt to duplicate the outcome of that war and colonize on a semi-permanent basis new territory. Yet it has frequently ventured abroad and conquered foes under a wide variety of circumstances. After 1900, these forays took the army to Panama, Haiti, Nicaragua, Mexico, and Europe; and with each foray, territory outside the United States came under the sovereignty of the United States without becoming a part of the United States. Elihu Root, secretary of war under William McKinley, and later Theodore Roosevelt, famously described the relationship this way: "As near as I can make out, the Constitution follows the flag, but doesn't quite catch up with it."[29] Precisely because the country refused to create a distinct and lasting bureaucracy dedicated to governing new territories as part of an American empire, the task of governing the space between flag and Constitution fell to the military. As a result, after the Spanish-American War the United States army began to grow governing capacities almost in spite of itself, out of sheer necessity.

*   *   *

If the federal government spent little time thinking about how to govern territories outside the boundaries of the U.S., it is fair to say that army leaders spent just as little time contemplating the way the army had started to expand its governing capacities into an external state. Military leaders saw counterinsurgency operations (including what today is called "nation-building") as an aberration, as something unlikely to be repeated and unnecessary to future missions. As the army intervened in Latin America, West Point added a course in Spanish but little else to note this new experience in modern warfare. The army's new War College focused on "catching up" to European powers and preparing the American army for set-piece battles against the Great Power armies. It did not plan to repeat the experience of military government.[30]

In fairness, the army had a great deal of "catching up" to do. The Spanish-American War had revealed this fact. While John Hay, secretary of state in 1898, called it a "splendid little war . . . favored by that Fortune that loves the brave," and while the Spanish-American War lasted only one summer and resulted in a total victory for the United States, the war hardly cast the army in a favorable light.[31] In reviewing the conduct of the war afterward, congressional investigators realized that the military's command structure had been deeply disorganized and unprepared. Victory had, indeed, come through "fortune" more than American military know-how.[32] Theodore Roosevelt, a firsthand witness to the disorganization, wanted a "thorough shaking up" of the War Department even before becoming president, largely to streamline the army's command structure.[33] Once in the presidency, he turned to his war secretary Elihu Root to create a centralized military leadership in a single general staff responsible for strategic planning and military preparedness (largely on the model of the Prussian military).[34] At the same time, Root spearheaded reforms to revamp education for all levels of the military. He created the Army War College and worked to coordinate its offerings with the service academies and the growing number of state colleges that emerged after the Morrill Land-Grant College Act (1862). That act required colleges to offer military training as part of their curriculum, and Root wanted to standardize the curriculum to train future officers.[35]

While much more can be said about the process by which the army professionalized at the turn of the century, for our purposes, the events that followed the Spanish-America War emphasize the fact that Douglas MacArthur, Dwight D. Eisenhower, and Lucius Clay entered military service at a time when the army itself undertook a broad transition in its capabilities and focus. In fits and starts over the next two decades it transformed from a small frontier garrison to a global projection of American power that included nation building efforts outside American borders. Thus, the careers of all three men were swept along by these broader currents of institutional change, and their ability to anticipate and lead that change in turn advanced their careers.

The oldest of the three, MacArthur entered West Point in June 1899, just as his father began to serve as military governor in the Philippines. His entry seemed predestined by the fact that his father had already become an army legend whose legacy he struggled to match. Eisenhower entered West Point in 1911 almost entirely through personal ambition. His family had little money or fame. Clay, the youngest of the three, entered West Point in 1914. He gained admittance as a political legacy: his father, Alexander Clay, had been elected to the United States Senate as a Democrat from Georgia three times before dying suddenly in 1910.

MacArthur was the best student of the three, finishing first in his class.[36] Clay had a chance to match that record, finishing first in several subjects (including English and history); however, he finished 128th in "conduct" out of about 150 plebes. Seven weeks before graduation he stood only four demerits short of expulsion. "The discipline at West Point was mainly petty," he said, "I thought it was foolish."[37] It showed. Eisenhower, in contrast to the other two, finished middle of the pack, generally more interested in athletic rather than academic competition. That said, his graduating class, the class of 1915, became famous as "the class the stars fell on." More than one-third of its 164 members went on to hold the rank of brigadier general or higher, including (obviously) Eisenhower and his longtime friend and collaborator during World War II, Omar Bradley.[38]

Unlike their counterparts in European military academics, many plebes did not plan on a life in the military. Students often attended West Point for the free college education it offered. Unfortunately, they often got what they paid for. West Point lagged far behind the new research universities popping up around the country.[39] Its curriculum had hardly changed since its creation during the presidency of James Monroe in 1817. Students memorized and regurgitated. Nothing more. Grades reflected the accuracy of the regurgitation. Nothing else. When plebes studied strategy, they consulted the battles of Robert E. Lee and Ulysses S. Grant.[40] If a plebe asked a question or wanted to understand the material he recited, the faculty cut him short: "I'm not here to answer questions," they said, "but to mark you."[41]

The absurdity of this approach nearly got Eisenhower expelled. One morning he forgot to prepare a math lecture. He stood at the board puzzling it out and, after a few tries, succeeded—but not in the prescribed way. "Mr. Eisenhower," his instructor said, "you memorized the answer, put down a lot of figures and steps that have no meaning whatsoever . . . in hope of fooling [me]." Eisenhower took this as an accusation of cheating. He became "red-necked and angry" and went right back at his professor, a clear act of insubordination. As tensions rose, a more senior faculty member happened to walk by. After looking over Eisenhower's work, the senior instruction said, "Eisenhower's solution is more logical and easier than the one we've been using. I'm surprised that none of us . . . has stumbled on it." Eisenhower survived. But so did the academy's hostility to initiative or innovation. This particular professor never forgave him.[42]

A decade earlier, in 1903, when MacArthur graduated from West Point, most plebes thought that the best assignment lay with the Corps of Engineers—probably because it led most easily to a private sector career. Promotions in this branch often came sooner than in the other branches. MacArthur, as the top of his class, obviously ended up in the corps. His first assignment took him to the Philippines, just a few years after his father had left. He took up the job of constructing roads and barracks and, eventually, a wharf. Once, while searching for timber, two Filipino insurrectionists ambushed him, shooting his hat from his head. MacArthur returned fire and killed both men. An observing sergeant, figuring that only Providence had saved MacArthur, predicted "the rest of the Loo'tenant's life is pure velvut."[43]

A year later, it seemed anything but. MacArthur had contracted malaria and the "*dhobe* itch." In October 1904, he returned to San Francisco to recover. By this point his father had become a major general, and Arthur MacArthur arranged for his recovering son to become his own aide-de-camp. As a perk, the assignment included a long tour of Japan, China, and Southeast Asia. In particular, the two MacArthurs observed the workings of the Japanese, German, French, and British colonial empires. In all, they traveled nearly twenty thousand miles, and the experience convinced the younger MacArthur that America's future was "irrevocably entwined with Asia and its island outposts."[44]

When Arthur MacArthur suddenly passed away in September 1912, his widow's health began to decline rapidly, and Douglas asked for reassignment near his mother. Secretary of War Henry Stimson felt that, "In view of the distinguished service of General Arthur MacArthur, the Secretary of War would be pleased if an arrangement could be effected" that would keep Douglas close to his widowed mother in Washington. The best way to do this was to make Douglas an assistant within the office of the newly created chief of staff.[45]

He arrived in Washington just as the dust settled following an existential struggle between Major General Leonard Wood, the new chief of staff, and Adjutant General Frederick Crayton Ainsworth. Wood represented the progressive wing of the military: he wanted centralization, professionalization, and greater executive control over the military. As adjutant general, Ainsworth headed one of the army's bureaus. He stood for the old model: independent bureaus, a more federalized organization, and congressional perks. As is often the case in institutional fights, the issue that sparked the showdown involved something minor: how to handle military paperwork more efficiently. Yet it quickly escalated to a fight over the army's future: would it fashion itself after European armies (particularly Prussia)? Or would it resemble the nineteenth-century citizen-army of the American past?

Henry Stimson, who served as secretary of war during Wood and Ainsworth's battle, ultimately favored the progressive wing of the army. An austere patrician from New York with a strong sense of duty and a clear sense of right and wrong, Stimson entered public service when President Theodore Roosevelt appointed him as U.S. Attorney for the Southern District of New York in 1906. He quickly built a strong reputation as a capable antitrust champion, which led to his appointment in 1911 as secretary of war to William Howard Taft. In the fight between Wood and Ainsworth he favored Wood generally but not decisively, hoping the two could resolve their differences despite the fact that their exchanges grew terser through 1911 and into the next year. Stimson finally felt compelled to act when Ainsworth finally sent a message that suggested Wood, as well as War Secretary Stimson, could not comprehend the "evil effects" of their paperwork "plan." Ainsworth had violated Stimson's sense of decorum. Wood wanted Stimson to initiate a court martial. But Stimson settled on simply relieving Ainsworth. In February 1912, Ainsworth "retired," indicating that the progressive wing of the military had become ascendant.

Congress, of course, did not go unaware of the bureaucratic battle. Many members understood that Ainsworth's departure called in question the old arrangement of using army bureaus to funnel appropriations back to home districts. Thus, in successive appropriations bills, Congress attached riders to remove Wood from office and to return power to the adjutant general's office. President Taft vetoed them all. He stood by his war secretary and army chief of staff. The adjutant general's office would remain under the thumb of the general staff. But congressional opponents did not go quietly; they fired a parting shot by reducing the general staff from forty-five to thirty-six officers. MacArthur got his assignment even as the staff downsized—a telling testament to the legacy of his father.[46]

As soon as he arrived in Washington, MacArthur ingratiated himself with Wood. Whether he understood it or not, his arrival *after* the bitter feud worked with his pedigree to make him a neutral arbiter with the still embittered officers throughout the army's bureaus who had come to loathe Wood but still respected the MacArthur name. Wood, however, clearly understood this dynamic, and so he utilized MacArthur extensively. Soon after becoming president, Woodrow Wilson apparently recognized the same dynamic at work and offered MacArthur a job as a White House aide in 1913. MacArthur, loyal to Wood, declined.[47] In any event, as Eisenhower and Clay still made their way at West Point, MacArthur had already managed to move to the nexus of army politics.

The outbreak of hostilities in Europe in the summer of 1914 made Mac-Arthur's position especially interesting. Initially, President Woodrow Wilson struggled to keep the United States out of the war, suspecting the motives of all the belligerents. Yet other prominent Americans feared that eventually the United States would be dragged into the conflict. In particular, Theodore Roosevelt, Stimson, and Wood—all out of office by 1914—argued that the army should actively prepare for that eventuality. Wilson would have none of it. As if to emphasize his feelings he refused to meet with his military leaders with any regularity; worse, he threatened to fire any military leaders caught making contingency plans in case war came.[48] In theory, the Joint Army and Navy Board should have allowed for some provisional discussions of American involvement in the war. Here, again, the Wilson administration remained intentionally unprepared. Assistant Secretary of War Henry Breckinridge summed up the views of the Wilson administration: he only "fooled with" the board "on hot summer afternoons when there was nothing else to do."[49]

When Germany's decision to unleash unlimited submarine warfare forced Wilson's into the war on the side of the British and French Entente, the army suddenly found itself facing a first-rate opponent on the other side of a wide ocean. Unsurprisingly, the broader national security state remained extraordinarily unprepared. When Congress declared war on April 6, 1917, the combined army and National Guard had a little over 200,000 men under arms. By comparison, at that same moment the Niville Offensive in Europe cost the Germans, British, and French more than 400,000 casualties. America's pittance of an army could not have lasted a single battle in the kind of grinding war Europeans had endured since 1914.[50]

Congress proved particularly slow to understand what it had committed the army to do. Even as it deliberated declaring war, the House Military Affairs Committee rejected the army's budget request of $3 billion for armaments and soldiers' pay. Eventually, Congress managed to provide the requested funds, but not until June 5, two months after it had declared war. A second appropriations request waited until October to wend its way through Congress.[51]

In a few aspects, though, the army anticipated the problems it would face. When Congress passed the Selective Services Act, army officials insisted that the law prohibit bounties, paid exemptions, or substitutions as part of conscription—those provisions that produced so much resentment during the Civil War.[52] More important, rather than revert to an organization built around the state militias, the army parceled out its existing soldiers to train the millions of doughboys called into service. Professional soldiers then served as the commanding officers of new combat units.[53] This way the army could best leverage its existing expertise and filter that expertise throughout the new fighting divisions.

Ironically, the decision to parcel out its regular soldiers ultimately kept Eisenhower and Clay from seeing combat. The army sent Eisenhower to Texas in the spring of 1917 as part of the newly formed Fifty-Seventh Infantry Regiment, promoting him at the same time to captain and placing him in charge of supply. He then moved to the training school at Leavenworth, Kansas, where he managed to enroll in the army's first tank school. By February 1918, he was again reassigned, this time to develop a training facility for a new tank division in Gettysburg, Pennsylvania. Just three years out of West Point, he suddenly faced the daunting task of commanding thousands of volunteers in using this new and unfamiliar weapon (for which the army had no training manuals or field guides). Eventually, he learned that he would lead his trainees into battle as part of an offensive scheduled for spring 1919, with a planned departure of November 18, 1918—as it turned out, one week after the Armistice.[54]

Having narrowly graduated in 1918, Clay requested a post in the artillery. The army assigned him to the Corps of Engineers instead. Ever the iconoclast, Clay wired the adjutant general saying, "[You] made a mistake." The adjutant general wired back telling Clay he had better show up as ordered. At Camp Lee, Virginia, Clay went through an accelerated training for engineers. No sooner had he finished that September than he got a new assignment to act as an instructor for new recruits at Camp Humphreys, Virginia, where he remained throughout the war.[55]

By contrast, MacArthur managed to use his position on the general staff to move out of the Corps of Engineers and obtain a command position within the newly formed Forty-Second Division. MacArthur named it the "Rainbow Division" because it included twenty-six different state national guards: it stretched "over the whole country like a rainbow."[56] MacArthur's reputation soared. By July of 1918, he had been promoted from colonel to brigadier general. Once the American army began to engage the Germans, MacArthur showed an almost reckless willingness to personally lead in battle. In a grinding fight that ultimately ended the war, he was twice wounded and got so close to the front that his own troops mistook him for

a German soldier and arrested him as a prisoner of war. By the time of the
Armistice, MacArthur had received seven Silver Star medals, two Distinguished Service Cross medals, two Purple Hearts, and two Croix de Guerre
awards from the French army, along with membership in France's Legion
of Honor. Second only to General John Joseph "Black Jack" Pershing, the
commander in chief of all American forces, he had become the most
famous American general in the world.[57]

Chapter 2

The War, the Economy, and the Army

By the end of the First World War, Douglas MacArthur, Dwight D. Eisenhower, and Lucius Clay were still too early in their professions to affect the subsequent peace. Yet the war had important consequences for these men as they moved forward in their careers. First, it taught them critical lessons in preparing for any subsequent wars; in particular, it focused their thoughts on the relationship between America's industrial might and its military might. Second, the army continued to professionalize as key officers recognized that the army would be an important part of America's increasing involvement in global politics. Third, individual soldiers became at least informally more informed about governing foreign people as they maintained America's interwar external state. Finally, as the peace treaty negotiated at Versailles in 1919 led within a decade to the Great Depression and then a Second World War, Eisenhower and Clay in particular began to become more involved in domestic political economy and think about what mistakes had led to depression and a Second World War.

In this last regard—the lessons that followed the Treaty of Versailles—Woodrow Wilson cast the longest shadow. In many ways, he provided the blueprint for a global order that American foreign policy has often followed since. At the same time, he ignored or misunderstood enough of his plan to almost guarantee its failure.[1] In fairness to Wilson (and the statesman he negotiated with), World War I had drastically changed the globe. It involved almost thirty nations, killed almost ten million soldiers and sailors, and introduced the world to tanks and air power. It ended three empires (the Russian, Turkish, and Austro-Hungarian) and redrew the global map—especially in Central Europe and the Middle East. It ushered in the communist takeover of Russia and sparked colonial revolts in Southeast Asia, inspiring (among others) a very young Hồ Chí Minh to dedicate himself to Vietnamese independence. In many Western countries, the war legitimized labor rights and women's suffrage, as those who bore the burdens of war became more active in shaping subsequent domestic politics. Making policy in the wake of these transitions would challenge the best of politicians.

Initially, in early 1917 and again in 1918, Wilson had defined America's war aims in broad terms. The war must produce "some definite concert of power which will make it virtually impossible that any such catastrophe should ever overwhelm us again." Indeed, only "a peace between equals can last," and so he hoped to persuade the British, French, Italians, and other belligerents away from vindictiveness toward the Germans and Austro-Hungarians. With that "right state of mind" between nations, he aimed to tackle the "vexed questions of territory [and] racial and national allegiance."[2] America would join the war, but only if the war were "the culminating and final war for human liberty," the war to end all wars.[3] "What we are striving for," he told Congress, "is a new international order based upon broad and universal principles of right and justice—no mere peace of shreds and patches."[4] Anything less would desecrate the deaths of American boys lost on French battlefields and sully America's role in international affairs.

First, he planned to tap the democratic desires of people around the world to enjoy national self-determination. "'Self-determination' is not a mere phrase. It is an imperative principle of action, which statesmen will henceforth ignore at their peril."[5] His hope, articulated in the language of democratic reform, was that ethnic and racial strife would disappear if nationalism could find an outlet within borders that reflected the ethnic and racial makeup of the people who lived there. Second, nationalism could be kept from becoming imperialism if mitigated by an international commitment to "Open Door" trade and finance. So long as every nation felt it could safely buy and sell on international markets, the justification for colonial competition might fade away.[6] Finally, a League of Nations would act as the institutional underpinning to provide security to the world. "My conception of the league of nations is just this," Wilson explained, "that it shall operate as the organized moral force of men throughout the world."[7] The league would become "the watchman of peace," it was the "main object of the peace . . . the only thing that could complete it or make it worthwhile . . . the hope of the world."[8] Behind all of these goals lay Wilson's eschatological reading of history as progressive. The future would be better than the past, and America (along with Wilson) could help history along its way.[9]

Many issues stood in the way of making those ideals reality, several of which seem obvious in retrospect. First, Wilson carried an idiosyncratic definition of self-determination that papered over the problems of implementing democracy and the "new international order" he had promised.[10] Second, the plan for economic interdependence after the war ignored the financial reality that emerged from the war. Wilson assumed individual economies would seamlessly return to a global system that rested upon the gold standard. Over the next decade, this would be the largest source of ongoing crises. Wilson also failed to consider more thoughtfully the relationship between economic performance and democratic stability. In short, Wilson did not fully think through the ways in which economic nationalism might undermine the kind of democratic institutions he hoped to see around the world, let alone economic internationalism.

The astonishing cost of World War I had driven all belligerents off the gold standard during the war. In place of gold, each had printed money with varying degrees of abandon. As a result, by war's end every country had a great deal more currency in circulation than it had held before, in some cases by multiples of ten or more. The surplus money created strong inflationary pressures that most countries tried to curb through price controls, rationing, and similar policies.[11] In addition to printing money, the belligerents borrowed from anyone who would lend. For the Allies this meant borrowing from each other and ultimately from the United States. Collectively, the Allies owed the United States about $12 billion. Britain owed $4.2 billion, France $3.4 billion, Italy $1.6 billion, and so on. Unfortunately for the French, they had loaned about $2.5 billion to Russia before the Bolshevik Revolution in 1917. The new communist regime had no intention of ever repaying this debt.[12]

After the war, Europe desperately needed capital to rebuild. Yet European currencies had lost much of their value. Only the United States had the means to make this investment because only the United States had deep reserves of the one form of money everyone trusted: gold.

All of this background helps clarify why the economic order Wilson sought not only failed to materialize, but, within a decade had wilted into the Great Depression. He insisted that the world return to an open and competitive market at a moment when the United States produced the lion's share of important products, held a huge load of the world's money,

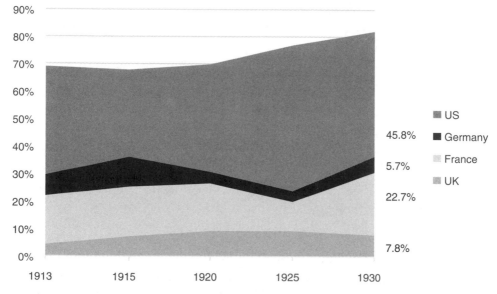

Figure 1. US, German, French, and UK gold reserves as percentage of world stock, 1913–1930. Source: World Gold Council, "Central Bank Gold Reserves, An Historical Perspective Since 1845 (November 1999)."

and also held enormous IOU's from the countries it traded with.[13] At Versailles, the French and British recognized how the arrangement tilted against them and pressed Wilson for debt forgiveness. As an incentive, they raised the question of German reparations, suggesting that Wilson forgive them their debts so that they could, in turn, forgive their debtor. After all, they reasoned, Wilson had suggested a magnanimous peace, and financial magnanimity expressed this idea as well as any other gesture. Moreover, America had come to the war late and suffered a fraction of British and French sacrifice. Debt forgiveness might equalize the American contribution to the Allied victory. Wilson's close confidant Colonel E. M. House agreed: "Should [Americans] not be asked to consider a large share of these loans as a part of our necessary war expenditures, and should not an adjustment be suggested by us and not by our debtors?"[14]

But Wilson would have none of it. He saw debt and reparations as distinct moral and legal questions. German reparations constituted a "fine"—a punishment for bad behavior. The Allies should set reparations high enough to *hurt*—to become a disincentive against future bad behavior. By contrast, Allied debts represented legal obligations entered into voluntarily. If the Allies had no interest in paying their debts, maybe they should not fight such costly wars. Besides, in a roundabout way, wouldn't debt forgiveness just encourage future war?[15]

In the end, Wilson got his way, but only to doom his ideals. America would collect on Allied debts, but the British and French passed their burden along to Germany in the form of staggering reparations totaling about 130 billion gold marks (roughly $33 billion in 1919 dollars, which, when viewed as a percentage of 2015 American GDP, amounts to $7.5 trillion).[16] Since Germany had few reserves of gold at the end of the war, it had to pay in installments out of current production, meaning it had to generate trade surpluses to created leftover reserves for reparations. Yet, as the *Economist* explained in 1921 (just prior to the first reparations payment), while Germany would likely export about 3.5 billion marks of goods that year, it would import about 4.7 billion in food and other critical materials. With no planned surplus in the coming years, where would reparations come from?[17]

The more ominous problem, though, was that the plan essentially tied the entire global financial system to the fate of the German economy. Perhaps, under the best of circumstances, this might be a good idea. But in the chaos that followed the war, with Germany perilously close to political and economic anarchy, this was a very poor choice indeed. Over the next years, the world came to the brink of financial crisis again and again as this precarious structure nearly collapsed.

For Eisenhower and Clay in particular, this history created a heavy weight when they found themselves, after the Second World War, in a position to improve on Wilson's effort after the First. They realized as quickly as any other American official that no matter how well the global financial system might be designed, it had to take into consideration the economic realities of the countries joining it. If individual countries did not enter into the global system on roughly equal grounds and with largely stable domestic economies, then the global system itself could exacerbate problems within domestic economies, creating a political backlash against the global order. Under such circumstances, the international component of Wilson's scheme would not mitigate nationalist impulses within individual countries but exacerbate those impulses.

*   *   *

Even as they observed the consequences of the peace, many army leaders worried initially about the poor American performance during the war. Much like the Spanish-American War, American victory in the First World War concealed a host of failures. Most obviously, American industry had dramatically underperformed its potential. As early as 1914, a handful of prominent figures (Theodore Roosevelt, Henry Cabot Lodge, Elihu Root, and the editors of the *New Republic*) had recognized the link between industry and war and had warned that the country remained woefully unprepared.[18] While Wilson had cited military preparation as a reason to pass the Revenue Act of 1916, he spoke only to the immediate needs of soldiers and sailors.[19] No comprehensive plan for coordinating industry ever went into effect during the war.[20]

In fact, contrary to the lore that emerged after the war, American entry had little to do with a "munitions industry" because no munitions industry really existed before it. Indeed, even after it began no munitions industry really emerged to feed it.[21] Many industrial powerhouses ignored the war altogether—most conspicuously the auto industry where neither the Dodge brothers nor Henry Ford ever converted their factories to make tanks. Each continued to turn out cars and hold onto domestic market-share rather than supply this new weapon for the war effort.[22]

The War Department made up for what couldn't be bought by ordering as much as possible of what could. The result was a predictable mess. American industry produced over thirty million 75-mm artillery shells, for example, but only twelve million fuses for those shells. Similar mismatches abounded.[23] More worrisome, American industry rarely produced what mattered most for victory. While American soldiers used about 2,250 artillery pieces during the war, only 100 of them came from the United States. With the Dodge brothers and Henry Ford setting the (unpatriotic) standard, not a single American tank made its way to the front. America was home to the Wright brothers, yet the country managed only one thousand observational airplanes (by contrast, the French produced almost sixty-nine thousand combat planes). In many cases, General Pershing chose to buy or borrow what he could from the French and British. In all, the army consumed roughly eighteen thousand ship-tons of material in the war, of which ten thousand came from continental Europe.[24]

Surprisingly, the slapdash procurement was not the army's largest logistical problem. As odd as it seems in retrospect, the country had almost no merchant marine in the early part of the century: less than 10 percent of the country's exports traveled on American ships. Thus, despite mass conscriptions and rapid mobilization, fewer than two hundred thousand troops had arrived in France during 1917. In early 1918, more than one million soldiers waited in the States for transport across the Atlantic.[25] In the end, most American soldiers made the voyage aboard British vessels (but only after the British extracted strategic concessions on the battlefield from Pershing in exchange for their ships).[26]

The chaotic procurement eventually led to inflation. Part of the price rise resulted from the influx of European gold in the first years of war. But American entry in 1917 exacerbated matters. Government propaganda encouraged Americans to borrow from banks and buy Liberty Bonds that would help fund the war. The newly created Federal Reserve flooded the banking system with liquidity (in essence printed money) to make sure banks could accommodate the demand. The expansion of the money supply had predictable results: retail prices rose 17 percent in 1916, another 17 percent the next year, and an additional 15 percent in 1918. Wilson did not attempt to impose price controls, using exhortation and patriotic appeals to encourage "fair prices" instead.[27] But prices kept rising because borrowing kept going. All together the war cost about $33 billion: new taxes generated $11 billion of that; borrowing covered the remaining $22 billion.[28]

The combination of poor coordination, haphazard purchasing, and industrial foot-dragging meant that the American economy saw almost no real economic growth between 1914 and 1920 despite the massive demand created by the war. Inflation made it appear as if the economy had doubled in size; once adjusted for inflation, that growth disappeared.

Wilson's main effort to coordinate the wartime economy came in the creation of the War Industries Board (WIB); unfortunately, the board existed as a "clearinghouse for the self-regulation of business" rather than an agency with command-and-control powers.[29] Predictably, it was ignored. Matters did not improve much until March 1918, when Wilson elevated the charismatic Bernard Baruch to be chairman of the WIB. While the WIB still struggled to control industry, it at least succeeded in launching the public career of Bernard Baruch. Already known as a genius financier, his staunch Democratic credentials—and his campaign contributions— made him a logical choice when Wilson sought a figure to run the War Industries Board. From this point forward he remained in public life, advising presidents through depression and later wars.[30]

* * *

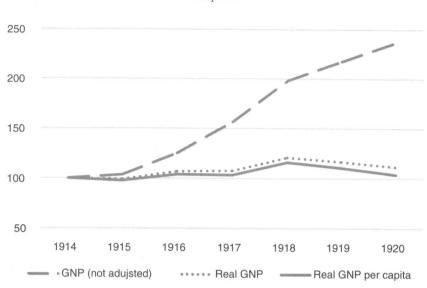

Figure 2. U.S. real and nominal growth of GNP in World War I, 1914–1920. Source: *Historical Statistics of the United States: Colonial Times to 1970*, Bicentennial Edition, Part 1 (Washington, DC: Department of Commerce), Series F 1–5. Gross National Product, Total and Per Capita, in Current and 1958 Prices: 1869 to 1970, 224.

"If not depressed, I was mad, disappointed, and resented the fact that the war had passed me by." Eisenhower had managed to find the dark lining in the silver cloud of world peace. The war had ended and, from his perspective, so had his chance to fight: he was "putting on weight in a meaningless chair-bound assignment, shuffling papers and filling out forms."[31]

Eisenhower's anxieties about missing the war mirrored the army's sense of drift in the postwar period. "Where-oh-where was that welcome they told us of?" MacArthur wrote to a friend after finally arriving home in the spring of 1919. "Where were those bright eyes, slim ankles that had been kidding us in our dreams? Nothing—nothing like that."[32] Once again, no sooner had the fighting stopped, than many Americans moved to put the war behind them. Indeed, a kind of antiwar fervor spread through the country, questioning the "real" motives for war.[33] Army leaders had hoped the war had finally made the military an acceptable part of American society. They put forward proposals for enacting universal military service, only to realize how out of step they were. Congress responded with the National

Defense Act (June 1920), which cut the army back to 280,000 men (it would be cut further to 125,000 in 1923). A future war would, Congress declared, require the same kind of sudden conscription that had marked preceding wars.

Daniel Read Anthony (R-KS), chair of the House War Department Subcommittee, hoped to reduce federal expenditures to as close to zero as possible. Specifically, he looked for "possibilities of cutting down the future development of tank, airplane and similar expensive units" for future savings.[34] He helped send the newly formed tank corps to oblivion by subsuming it under a jealous infantry determined to keep this new weapon outside of the American arsenal. Other countries would quickly jump past the United States in understanding and utilizing this critical new weapon.[35] "The peacetime Army was poor," recalled Clay. "It had no vehicles, no equipment. . . . I can remember when we didn't have our target practice for the entire year simply because we didn't have ammunition." In its place, the army had "only a certain sincerity, particularly among the younger officers, who had been the junior officers of World War I and who knew how badly we did . . . and who dedicated themselves to building a better Army."[36]

With no money and little congressional support, individual army leaders nevertheless looked to institutionalize the lessons from the world war. Often they would concede budget cuts if they came along with organizational reforms streamlining the army's command structure. Out of this came the Army Industrial College, a center to train army leaders in the economics of war (the college opened its doors in 1923).[37]

Less formally, those officers who remained in service looked for ways to improve themselves. "This was one of the reasons why the [West Point] Class of 1915 achieved such an outstanding World War II record," observed Clay years later. "They were the ones who came back from World War I thoroughly convinced that we had to be more professional, and they really introduced a spirit of professionalism into the armed services. We were amateurs in World War I. We were professionals in World War II."[38]

Despite missing combat, Eisenhower decided to do what he could to anticipate a future war, and, despite congressional cuts, he sincerely believed that tanks would be crucial. In this he found a lifelong friend and partner, George Patton. "From the beginning," Eisenhower commented later, "he and I got along famously."[39] The two men concluded that tanks could fundamentally redefine battlefield tactics. If bunched together, they could punch through enemy lines and create havoc from the rear, making trench warfare obsolete. If combined with air support, they could deliver decisive blows and race across open territory. Excited by their insights, Eisenhower and Patton submitted articles in separate military journals.

Eisenhower's contribution, "A Tank Discussion," appeared in the latter half of 1920.[40] Unfortunately, along with extolling tank warfare, it took a swipe at Congress and the infantry for shelving research into the new weapon.[41] As reward for his insight, the chief of the infantry told Eisenhower that his "ideas were not only wrong but dangerous" and that he should "not publish anything incompatible with solid infantry doctrine." If he did, he "would be hauled before a court-martial."[42] (In the meantime, German officers began experimenting with tanks and came to roughly the same conclusion, leading to the idea of blitzkrieg launched with devastating effect in World War II.)[43]

Implicit in Eisenhower's strategic vision, however, lay a basic economic reality. Military success depended upon economic might and technological innovation. Future wars would turn on domestic production at least as much as tactical cunning or courage. Thus, already in the 1920s he understood the "tendencies toward mechanization, and the acute dependence of all elements of military life upon the industrial capacity of the nation," and that led him to learn more about the way industry worked. "Large-scale motorization and mechanization and the development of air forces in unprecedented strength would characterize successful military forces of the future."[44]

*   *   *

At the end of World War I, French military leaders found an opportunity to accomplish something they had sought for years: control of the left bank of the Rhine River. The river provided a natural and formidable barrier to invasion, and holding it would guarantee against German backsliding during the peace negotiations. Thus, French leaders insisted that the Armistice of November 11, 1918, include a paragraph stating that, "The [territory] on the left bank of the Rhine shall be administered by the local troops of occupation . . . carried out by allied and United States garrisons holding the principal crossings of the Rhine."[45] Initially, the Americans and British opposed this provision but ultimately gave in. Once again, the American army found itself governing territory outside U.S. borders as part of the American external state.

By December 1, American troops marched into Germany. While in theory the Allies shared overall policy for the occupation, in reality each country had a great deal of autonomy within its zone. The French and British showed less leniency than the Americans, who followed General John Pershing's pronouncement that the Germans had a "duty . . . to regain their normal mode of life and to re-establish the schools, churches, hospitals and charitable institutions, and to continue in their regular local activities." The Germans would "not be disturbed, but rather assisted and protected," and all "existing laws and regulations, in so far as they do not interfere with the duty and security of the American troops, shall remain in force."[46]

This new form of military occupation differed from the experience of the Philippines in several important ways. First, American policy never envisioned annexing any part of Germany (indeed, American leaders had opposed the idea of occupation in the first place). In fact, since occupation had never been part of their country's postwar aims, American leaders scoured the ranks for soldiers who could at least speak German. That was all it took to become an "officer in charge of civil affairs" (OCCA), and the OCCAs made up the core of military government. Each OCCA joined a combat unit and supervised nearby towns or villages. While the combat units stood ready to back the OCCA in case of conflict, it rarely happened.[47]

Initially, the OCCAs attempted to reorganize local German government to match the organizational design of the American military. This immediately proved awkward and, as they soon realized, unwarranted. The local government already functioned with military-like efficiency. Indeed, OCCAs learned that they had gotten things entirely backward—that it would be far more efficient for the military government to mirror the civil structure of the German government. In fact, the British, French, and Belgians all took the latter approach, recognizing the inherent compatibility between the German state and their military governments.[48] Therein lay a second distinction from the Philippines. In the Philippines, the occupation had aimed to remake the Filipinos in America's republican image. In Germany, military government issued only three rules in the American zone: no public gatherings, no alcohol sales during daytime hours (a nod to Prohibition back in the United States), and no carrying of weapons.[49] On the first Sunday of the occupation, American doughboys stunned the Germans by sitting next to them at church.[50]

When it became clear that the occupation would last years rather than months, military government began promoting economic recovery. While the terms of the Armistice prohibited Germans from "military" production, the OCCAs lacked the will to enforce the rules, and the German economy in the American zone quickly improved. As the rest of Germany convulsed in political conflict, rampant inflation, and economic disorder, the American zone turned into an island of stability.[51]

Perhaps the largest misunderstanding among the Allies involved fraternization rules. The United States agreed to an anti-fraternization policy for the occupation: American soldiers should only interact with Germans over official business. For the French, the order aimed to quarantine "Bolshevism"— communist ideas that had started to sweep across Germany. By contrast and consistent with progressive ideas of virtue, American leaders hoped that soldiers would return home from Europe as sexually "pure" as they arrived. But the "anti-frat" policy (as doughboys called it) failed almost immediately, in large part because of the housing situation. The military had no place to billet troops in Germany and no interest in building barracks that it would soon vacate; thus, doughboys billeted with German families, and often enough those families included young girls. Almost immediately commanders started receiving requests from soldiers to marry their (often pregnant) German girlfriends.[52]

At the end of the war, the army ordered Douglas MacArthur to lead his Forty-Second Division into the occupation zone. He remained until spring the next year and from this experience absorbed several lessons that mattered when he became proconsul in Japan. More than Eisenhower and Clay, he saw the political realities of occupation. When he later governed postwar Japan, he mirrored the German experience by leaving much of the Japanese civil structure in place (including, quite controversially, Emperor Hirohito). He never enforced anti-fraternization rules. Most of all, he hoped to duplicate the feeling he had when he left Germany. "When we received our orders to return to the United States," he wrote years later, "the tearful departure looked more as we were leaving [home] instead of returning home."[53]

Not long after MacArthur departed Germany, Clay arrived. The army sent a number of engineers to help with the occupation. Like many soldiers, he could see the troubles affecting the rest of Germany. He, too, drew an important lesson from his experience. "I did see the inflation," he recalled later. "I did see the difficulties under which the new German [Weimar] government was attempting to establish itself."[54] As much as any American, he saw how economic chaos undermined the good intentions of democratic reforms.

*   *   *

By 1920, the Philippines had become a mostly autonomous, albeit legally anomalous, "*quasi*-sovereign."[55] The insurrection had ceased, and Congress had granted the Filipinos an elective national legislature. More than 90 percent of eligible voters cast a ballot, and the national legislature held wide latitude in determining domestic policy. However, the government remained headed by an American governor-general who acted as executive and could veto any act of the national legislature. While he had to gain the consent of the Philippine legislature for his own initiatives, he ultimately answered to the American president, who had appointed him. The arrangement had force because the United States maintained a garrison on the islands that reported to the governor-general.[56]

In 1922, the army ordered MacArthur to the Philippines as part of the garrison. His former boss Leonard Wood greeted him upon arrival (President Warren Harding had appointed Wood as governor-general the prior year). The Filipinos had "done fairly well with self-government," Wood reported, but widespread graft and corruption had led to a doubling of government expenses with no improvement in public services. The courts had become "clogged," small pox and cholera outbreaks had killed nearly sixty thousand Filipinos, and the Philippine government had used tax revenue to prop up a national bank that had gone bankrupt. Wood came to the Philippines to "clean things up."[57] For their part, many Filipinos had grown weary of Wood's "supervision." In an effort to get around him, they continually sent delegations directly to the U.S. asking for immediate independence. Harding stood by his governor-general, but it irritated Wood to no end.[58] To appease the Filipinos, Wood put MacArthur to work, heading campaigns to vaccinate livestock, organize a local ROTC, and chase away jungle bandits.[59]

While MacArthur labored in the Philippines, Eisenhower and Clay also gained experience in America's external state—mostly in Panama. Efforts to build a canal there had begun in 1850, when American and British negotiators agreed (in the Clayton-Bulwer Treaty) not to compete with each other in constructing a passageway between the oceans. Of course, in 1850 neither country had the resources or technical know-how to compete any-way. But by the turn of the century the U.S. position had changed. President Theodore Roosevelt pressed for an American effort to create the canal, which led to the Hay—Bunau-Varilla Treaty between the United States and Panama. The treaty committed the United States to defending the independence of Panama and, in turn, granted the United States in perpetuity control of a zone stretching five miles to either side of a canal to be constructed by the Americans. The "United States would possess and exercise" governance of this area as "if it were the sovereign of the territory . . . to the entire exclusion of the exercise by the Republic of Panama of any such sovereign rights, power or authority."[60] Congress followed ratification of the treaty with an act that vested in the president all "military, civil, and judicial powers as well as the power to make all rules and regulations necessary for the government of the" new territory, which Roosevelt delegated to the military.[61] The Canal Zone became, like the Philippines, a part of the country's external state, functioning in that space between flag and Constitution, administered through the military.[62]

For Eisenhower and Clay, their service in the Canal Zone turned out to be life changing because each found in Panama a mentor who finally gave him the intellectual challenge he had missed at West Point. For Eisenhower, this man was General Fox Conner, who had already concluded in the early 1920s that a second world war lay near on the horizon. On his own, Conner decided to mentor the younger generation of officers to face the next world war, focusing on three in particular: George Marshall, George Patton, and Eisenhower.[63] "In the last war we fought for an ideal. . . . This time we shall be fighting for our very lives," he told Eisenhower. "I believe that Germany and Japan will combine against us, and Russia may be with them." The Allies would include "an ebbing empire [Britain] and a republic in the last stages of a mortal illness [France]."[64] By virtue of his position on General Pershing's general staff in World War I, Conner could observe the dysfunctional command that existed between the French, British, and Americans. "When we go into [the next] war it will be in company with allies," yet Conner stressed that there must be an "individual and single responsibility" at the top.[65]

Conner had an extensive library, and Eisenhower read his way through it, covering the works of Shakespeare, Plato, Nietzsche, and (most important) the brilliant military theorist Carl von Clausewitz. Eisenhower and Conner then talked over the meaning of these works as they spent hours on horseback mapping the terrain, hacking through the jungle, or cutting roads. In retrospect, Eisenhower called it his "graduate school" in "military affairs and the humanities."[66]

Clay's experience in Panama was equally influential. "I really found myself in Panama," he later recalled. "[It] was an important assignment and you worked at being a soldier." He served under an engineer named "Goff" Caples, who (like Fox Conner) was well-read and liked talking. "He was truly an independent thinker," said Clay, particularly on questions having to do with "ethnic and political movements . . . a special tutor."[67] Clay obtained his first command in Panama, a group of soldiers he rated as the best in his military career.[68]

Clay and Eisenhower worked to do many of the same things in Panama that MacArthur did in the Philippines. They surveyed jungle, built barracks, cut roads, trained junior officers, and generally did the things that today might be called "development." They also showed the kind of skill and intelligence that allowed them to quickly climb the army's ranks.

In December of 1927, MacArthur learned that Henry Stimson, the former secretary of war, would replace Leonard Wood as governor-general of the Philippines. Stimson had returned to private life when Woodrow Wilson became president in 1912. When the U.S. entered World War I, he hoped for a military appointment based on his prior service. Wilson refused. So Stimson enlisted, quickly rising to the rank of colonel in the artillery. After the war he again returned to practicing law. But the decline of Leonard Wood's health in 1927 led President Calvin Coolidge to seek a replacement and he asked Stimson to accept the governor-generalship. Stimson had just turned sixty, but decided to accept despite his age.[69]

Unlike Wood, Stimson harbored fewer racial judgments about the Filipinos. He felt that they deserved independence. But in a hostile world, surrounded by hungry empires, they could not survive long if that independence came too soon. "The Philippines are protected from foreign submersion," Stimson wrote, "solely by . . . [the] military power of the United States." For a lasting independence, the Filipinos needed a national military capable of defending that independence, and institutionally speaking, this seemed far away. Japan, in particular, seemed eager to gobble up the islands.[70]

More worrisome, the long-term success of the Philippines depended on the development of the *internal* institutions necessary to maintain democracy. Here, the islands seemed quite unprepared to stand on their own. The country needed a strong press, civic organizations, and established political parties. The national legislature had the form of democracy, but none of the social or civil infrastructure that would help it flourish.

In a move that characterized military government in the future, Stimson saw the solution to all problems in economic development. "There has been very little accumulation of capital [in the islands]," complained Stimson, "One result of this is that the revenues possible from taxation at present are quite insufficient . . . for military and diplomatic purposes." More to the point, the lack of industrialization meant "no middle class or bourgeoisie between the educated *ilustrado* and the ignorant *tao* . . . which might serve, as it does in other countries, as the backbone of self-government." In short, entrepreneurial capitalism would foster not only national independence but also civic virtue.[71]

During his stay in the Philippines, Stimson became familiar with MacArthur. But their time together (at least in Manila) proved short lived. In March 1929, newly elected President Herbert Hoover asked Stimson to come back to Washington to serve as secretary of state. Then, in August 1930, Hoover asked MacArthur to return as the chief of staff of the army. MacArthur hesitated. He enjoyed life in the Philippines, and leading the American army from Washington seemed like more headache than opportunity. So he deliberated—until his mother learned of his hesitation. She cabled him right away: "Your father would be ashamed of your timidity."

"That settled it," MacArthur said, and he quickly sent Hoover his acceptance.[72]

*   *   *

It is hard to imagine how the 1920s could have done more to prepare Dwight Eisenhower for his future. He had instinctively understood the weaponry and tactics of the next war. Moreover, he had found a mentor in Fox Conner who would guide his career thereafter. Conner had a plan for Eisenhower. The first part of the plan sent Eisenhower to the Command and General Staff College (which served to prepare mid-level officers for future command). Eisenhower flourished there, finishing at the top of his class. After this, Conner arranged for Eisenhower to become a part of the American Battle Monuments Commission directed by General Pershing. Eisenhower had the task of writing a handbook that explained the events commemorated by the war's monuments and cemeteries. Ostensibly a guide for tourists, in reality it became a battle-by-battle summary of the war. More important, it gave Eisenhower a firsthand opportunity to walk the fields of France. By the time he had finished, Eisenhower had as clear an understanding of tactics in World War I as anyone. He also had a clear sense of the terrain Americans would travel in the next war.[73]

In 1927, Eisenhower entered the Army War College, where he studied industrial conversion. His thesis took up "the administrative and economic War Powers of the President," including the changes necessary to move the normally free economy toward a controlled war economy.[74] He considered everything from a command economy's constitutionality to the nitty-gritty of administrative coordination, and recommended that "an agency . . . be set up . . . with a man at its head in whom is centralized full responsibility and adequate authority" to direct the economy.[75] His work helped open a new door to his career when Fox Conner managed to get Eisenhower a position with Brigadier General George Van Horn Moseley within the army's planning division in Washington. The National Defense Act of 1920 instructed the army to develop an industrial conversion plan, but by the late 1920s, it remained to be written. Because of Eisenhower's work at the Army War College, Moseley wanted him to write the report.

In working through the many issues involved in that report, Eisenhower decided upon an approach that became a hallmark of his management style thereafter. He spoke with everyone who had played a hand in the last effort to create a wartime economy. While most saw the project as pointless— they would never "again [be] called on to arm and equip a mass army"— "some manufacturers . . . [were] ready to cooperate." Most important, he discovered Bernard Baruch.[76]

Baruch eagerly talked with Eisenhower, explaining all the policies and powers he wished he had had. He also took to Eisenhower, and afterwards became a mentor along the lines of Conner. "He was ready to talk to me at any time," Eisenhower noted.[77] In time of war, Baruch explained, the government needed the power to set price controls, provide central administration and public education, and hold total power to defeat inflation—in short, it needed all the powers denied the War Industries Board. While the Hoover administration seemed unlikely to embrace a report that recommended such broad government powers, Eisenhower accepted Baruch's ideas wholeheartedly and defended them to his superiors.[78]

By December 1930, Eisenhower had completed his *Plan for Industrial Mobilization* and forwarded it to Hoover (who promptly ignored it). He then wrote an accompanying article (published almost a year later in the *Cavalry Journal*), summarizing the contributions of the many people he interviewed.[79] Several themes ran throughout. First, while the "Government has wisely refrained, as far as practicable, from interfering with the operation within our own country of fundamental economic laws. . . . In war all this changes." For example, "demand becomes not only abnormal but is measured in terms of national self-preservation rather than in capacity to pay. Time is vital." In short, war reversed the natural laws of capitalism.[80]

At the same time, the "problem facing the Federal Government in war is to be prepared to minimize damaging effects of sudden changes in industrial activity," even while striving to "mobilize material, labor, and capital for the support of the fighting forces."[81] In other words, the less the state had to change, the better. Here, he adopted Baruch's views, specifically on the question of outright nationalization of industry during war. "Who would run it?" Baruch asked. "After you . . . had taken it over and installed your Government employee as manager, what greater control would you have then than now! [Through taxation] you can choke it to death, deprive it of transportation, fuel, and power, divert its business, strengthen its rivals. Could any disciplinary means be more effective?" Besides, even "if [a federal] bureau could prove adequate to the task [of running industry] . . . the mere process of change would destroy efficiency at the outset."[82]

Indeed, efficiency remained the watchword throughout the plan, and it imagined that competition between various sectors of the economy (and among departments within the government) might create frictions that would undermine industrial output. Such competition "must not exist." To overcome this, "the government must know the national needs—and by wise and conservative measures direct the efforts of the population toward meeting those needs."[83] To do this, the plan envisioned centralized coordination, but also, and crucially, "the force of public opinion." It encouraged the president to take advantage of the "unified and intensive public opinion" common at the outbreak of hostilities, because this unity, "[if] properly directed and employed under a popular leader, will make effective any reasonable, practical and efficient plan that may be adopted."[84]

The third theme, and what proved the most controversial, centered on controlling price levels during war. Here, again, Eisenhower followed Baruch, who favored widespread price controls across the entire economy. On the one hand, this solved the problem of war profiteering; on the other, it addressed an issue in terms that would prove very important for Eisenhower in the future. "Inflation enormously increases the cost of war and multiplies burdens on the backs of generations yet to come," Baruch argued. "In the inevitable post-war deflation the debt, of course, remains at the inflated figure. Thus the bonds that our Government sold in the World War for 50-cent dollars must be paid through the years by taxes levied in 100-cent dollars."[85] Altogether, Eisenhower's report provided the basis for a planned economy along with the nuts-and-bolts of how to implement it—a valuable resource for American administrators when the next war came.

Thus, by 1930, one thing could be said about MacArthur, Eisenhower, and Clay as well as Henry Stimson. Each had, during the 1920s, gained invaluable experience in the tasks that awaited them. While the nation had made little effort to institutionalize military government as a core part of America's external state, individual military leaders had gathered a great deal of experience and informal understanding of military government, political economy, and the art of governing. The initial lessons they learned came from the very practical problems of maintaining a civil society. They realized that it was already hard enough to subjugate a people and maintain some order. That task became impossible once military governments were seen as adding impoverishment to subjugation. Thus, in many cases they personally helped the local economy by cutting roads and building wharfs.

Put another way, military leaders absorbed Wilson's contention that economic cooperation might foster peace, yet realized that Wilson had missed the local dimension of that promise. He had missed the fact that local economic stability became the prerequisite for global integration. The problem of the future—as military government played a much larger role in the lives of many more people around the world—would be learning *how* to achieve local economic stability. It was one thing to govern an agrarian archipelago or a narrow strip of Panamanian jungle. It would prove quite a different thing to govern densely populated and industrialized nations suffering after terrible defeats.

Chapter 3

The Army in a Time of Depression

Lucius Clay left the United States for Panama in July 1929. When he returned in July 1931, it seemed like a different country. In the intervening years America's industrial production had dropped by more than 30 percent. "My work carried me all over," Clay recalled, ". . . and particularly along the Monongahela River—which was the region that supplied Pittsburgh with its coal. And it was a scene of shocking desolation."[1]

The Great Depression was the most important economic event of the twentieth century. It had enormous political and social consequences for nearly every nation. Although scholars debated its causes almost from the start, in the last two decades a "greater consensus" has emerged about the most likely sources of the economic collapse. Economists generally agree that the unstable arrangement coming out of Versailles finally caught up to the world and expressed itself in the form of the century's greatest economic downturn.[2]

Of course, it has taken many decades to come to the current consensus, and the current consensus is neither the first nor the most strongly held agreement among economists. A framework offered by the British economist John Maynard Keynes (discussed below) generated widespread agreement within the United States for several decades as to the cause and cure for the Great Depression—although it has fallen out of favor over the last few decades. What matters for this study, though, is the way the current consensus fits particularly well within the insights that ultimately came out of military government. Of course, economists working during the depression were familiar with the events and data that make up the current consensus—as were non-economists such as MacArthur, Eisenhower, and Clay. Nothing about the current view was hidden from past generations. But the economists working during and just after the depression saw the same events as less decisive and the same data as less relevant than recent economists feel. By contrast, military government came to see the same events and data as particularly critical to the stability of the global economy and in a way that dovetails with the current consensus. The surprising agreement between the occupiers in the late 1940s and today's economists therefore justifies a discussion of the current consensus.

While the current consensus has many subplots, one plot plays the central role: Germany could not recover from the war and pay reparations at the same time, and this fact destabilized global finance. To get around the challenge of paying reparations while trying to modernize industry and recover from the war, German officials more or less deliberately resorted to a kind of Ponzi scheme. Since the United States ended the war with surplus gold, it became Germany's largest creditor. By 1927, Americans had sent more than $1.5 billion to Germany, covering the $500 million in reparations installments along with an extra billion to buy everything from new factories to new opera houses. A new market in the United States for German municipal bonds helped funnel American savings to German municipalities, which received the lion's share of American investment. In simplified form, through the 1920s Germany borrowed heavily from the United States to pay its reparation debts to France and England (while keeping some to rebuild its infrastructure). France and England then used reparations to repay war debts to the United States (while keeping some to rebuild infrastructure). In other words, the U.S. lent the money ultimately used to repay itself, with overall global debt growing with each turn.[3]

As the scheme persisted, several German officials thought they saw an opportunity in their growing dependence on American finance. "One must simply have enough debts," explained Gustav Stresemann, the foreign minister. Indeed, "One must have so many debts that, if the debtor collapses, the creditor sees his own existence jeopardized." In his version of too-big-to-fail, Stresemann imagined that, "These economic matters build bridges of political understanding and of future political support."[4] He hoped that the bridge would reach from Berlin to New York and on to Washington so that eventually the American government would feel obligated to protect Germany's economic health in order to protect itself as creditor.

While Germany ran up its debt, many other countries worked to get back onto the gold standard. For much of the nineteenth century, the standard had facilitated global trade and economic growth. In war most countries had suspended it to have a freer hand in financing production. While

a great deal can be (and has been) said about the gold standard, two features are worth focusing on here. First, it embodied particularly well the
"invisible hand" of market relationships and, in this sense, had a kind of
legitimacy for standing outside of politics. Just about everyone could
understand how it worked since it generally followed principles of personal
finance. If a country bought more than it sold on international markets, it
experienced about the same consequences as individuals who bought more
than they earned. For individuals, the consequence was frugal living; for
nations, frugality meant less total money in circulation (what economists
label a "forced" deflation) because money (gold) now belonged to another
nation. In practical terms, when a nation ran out of gold, it usually suffered
a recession and rising unemployment. To be "on gold" meant governments
had no monetary policy as such; they followed "the market," discarding
"independent national [economic] objectives of their own."[5]

Second, the gold standard signaled an acceptance of international
norms. After World War I, norms appealed to many policymakers around
the globe.[6] More specifically, gold signaled an effort to make good on
Woodrow Wilson's vision of a global marketplace. Gold acted as a check
on "independent national objectives," which in the early twentieth century
often expressed themselves in right-wing nationalism and militarism. Gold,
in this sense, stood for peace rather than nationalist conflict.[7]

Unfortunately, returning to gold after the First World War created as
many problems as it solved—particularly for the British. The world economy had changed during the war, and the pound should have devalued
coming out of it. Yet British officials insisted on maintaining the pound's
prewar value. In reality, it forced the British economy into deflation and
chronic recession. Depreciation could have helped revive the economy,
only to make British war debt relatively larger. In the end, British officials
stuck to the higher value of the pound despite the economic hardship.[8]

The British economy would have benefited from American investment
to make its products more competitive. Indeed, nearly all of Europe needed
American investment for the same reason. German municipalities managed
to get a larger share of American loans because they promised (unrealisti-
cally) greater returns. Ultimately, though, European recovery often followed American investment, and this flow continued at least piecemeal
until 1928, when no level of return competed with what the New York
Stock Exchange offered.

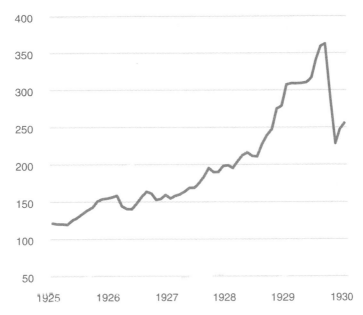

Figure 3. Dow Jones Industrial Average, 1925–1930. Source: Federal Reserve Bank of St Louis, FRED Economic Data, Dow Jones Industrial Stock Price Index for United States (M1109BUSM293NNBR).

The Dow Jones rose impressively between 1925 and 1928, going up 64 percent—a large increase, but not out of step with the growing productivity of the American economy. It then spiraled an additional 82 percent in just one year, and this increase had little to do with rising productivity. The promise of such great returns caused money to flow into Wall Street from around the globe, adding fuel to the speculative fire and draining investment from everyone else. Thus, as the American market took off, the British, German—even the Japanese economy—slipped into recession.[9]

Surveying Wall Street at the end of 1928, president-elect Herbert Hoover grew nervous. He and the governors of the Federal Reserve decided to burst "the bubble." The central bank raised interest rates from 3.5 percent at the end of 1927 to a high of 6.0 percent by the summer of 1929. The rate hike had the intended effect, and industrial output began to decline. Yet the stock market ignored the data and continued to go up until, famously, in October, it lost spectacularly.

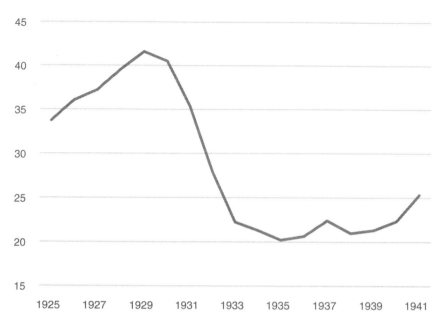

Figure 4. U.S. bank loans, 1925–1941 (billions of U.S. dollars). Source: Federal Reserve System, Banking and Monetary Statistics, 1914–1941 (Washington, DC, 1941).

European central bankers, and particularly the British and Germans, met the market crash with enthusiasm. In theory, once Wall Street stopped siphoning gold from around the world, investment would return to them. Yet their expectations were frustrated because at that moment the global financial system lay under tremendous pressure. Banks around the world had begun to fail and had stopped lending altogether. Worse, as credit collapsed, the economy in many countries slipped from recession to depression.[10]

By 1930, the moment of truth came for the German economy. In October the former German financial official Hjalmar Schacht made a trip to the United States. He pleaded with the American people to accept a revision of reparations and forgive war debts. "Never before," asserted Schacht, had "a conquering force first taken from the vanquished all that they had in colonies . . . and then demanded the conquered people . . . to pay still more."[11] If America took the lead in debt and reparations forgiveness, Woodrow Wilson's ideal might get one last chance to succeed. But the American press wanted to talk instead about the upstart Nazi Party. They wanted a sense of who Adolf Hitler was and how he had become so popular so quickly. Frustrated, Schacht explained, "You must not think that if you treat a people for ten years as the German people have been treated they will continue to smile. . . . If the German people are going to starve, there are going to be many more Hitlers."[12]

Without American loans, German authorities announced they could not make the next installment of reparations. Without reparations, the British and French could not repay their debts to America. Seeing that the global system lay on the brink of collapse, Herbert Hoover declared a one-year moratorium on reparations and war debts, finally acknowledging what European authorities had argued since 1919. Hoover hoped that with time the Germans, British, and the rest of Europe might turn their economies around. None did.

Unfortunately, reparations represented only part of the problem. German municipalities also started defaulting on their loans, causing additional shocks to the global banking system. To slow the financial crisis, Berlin applied exchange controls to prevent gold from leaving its banks, as did nearly all Central European countries (Czechoslovakia, Bulgaria, Romania, and Yugoslavia).[13] By the end of summer, 1931, the Bank of London was near panic as gold drained from it as well. Seeing no other alternative, on September 20, the British left the gold standard. "The struggle to bring the British pound back to par after the World War," wrote the New York Times, "will rank among the epic contests of world finance. That struggle has failed."[14] The value of the pound finally dropped, losing 20 percent against the dollar. Almost immediately Sweden, Norway, and Egypt followed England off of gold. Many countries began to negotiate exchange rates bilaterally. In response, the United States suffered a new wave of bank failures corresponding to the financial crises in Europe, killing what had looked like a modest recovery in the first part of 1931.

The combination of Hoover's moratorium and Britian's move off of gold seemed to indicate the time had finally arrived to rethink the whole issue of reparations and war debt. In the summer of 1932, in Lausanne, Switzerland, leaders from the principal European countries gathered and, in a "gentlemen's agreement," decided that they would set aside German reparations once the British and French had "satisfied" their obligations to the United States. "We are still ready to cancel all debts due us," explained Neville Chamberlain, then chancellor of the exchequer, "If the United States should decide to cancel all debts due her."[15]

The gentlemen's agreement launched an intense debate within the Hoover administration. On one side sat President Hoover, who considered his moratorium strictly a temporary "depression measure." By contrast, his secretary of state, Henry Stimson, felt forgiveness "might really be the beginning of a recovery." In a long conversation, he urged Hoover to accept it "without fear or rancor." The two argued back and forth until Hoover exploded. "The European nations [are] all in an iniquitous combine against us!"

A frustrated Stimson did not know what more to say. "If [you really feel] that way, we [are] indeed on such different ground that I . . . ought not to be [your] adviser."[16] He tried to resign.

In the end, Hoover refused to accept the resignation. But he also refused Stimson's advice. The moratorium remained temporary, and the disagreement strained the two men's relationship thereafter.

Ultimately, Europe settled the issue on its own. Germany defaulted on reparations, and when the 1932 war debt came due only the British paid in full. The next year another payment came due, and this time no one paid. American loans to Europe, whether for war or peace, had been a cause of, and ultimately a casualty of the depression.

As he often did in his long career, the journalist Walter Lippmann captured succinctly the transition that had occurred between 1919 and 1933. "The theory was," wrote Lippmann of the thinking in 1919, "under free trade, national frontiers would mark off cultural and local interests, but that economic opportunity would not be determined by political boundaries." Ideally, once "there were no great barriers to trade at the frontiers, the problem of the frontiers would cease to be so troublesome." By 1933, that charter had failed. Rather than cooperate economically, the victors had "insisted upon payments from the defeated powers and upon payments from one another," with "a destructive and deflationary effect upon world commerce." Now, in the face of depression, all nations seemed to agree that governments "must organize industry and agriculture and finance to a much greater degree than they have ever been organized before." To do this "it follows inevitably that the system must be protected against external forces that cannot be controlled"—that is, the domestic economy had to be shielded from the vicissitudes of global competition. Thus, the world had entered into a new phase, a "Second Reconstruction" that combined political nationalism with economic nationalism. "Along these general lines the Second Reconstruction is now being carried out," he concluded. "Will it bring that peace and that prosperity which the First failed to establish? Who can say?"[17]

*   *   *

At the end of 1932, Franklin Roosevelt beat Herbert Hoover handily in the presidential election. As it turned out, MacArthur, Eisenhower, Clay, and Stimson all had front-row seats to the unfolding drama of the Roosevelt administration. MacArthur and Eisenhower had been in Washington for several years before the election. "He had greatly changed and matured since our former days in Washington," MacArthur said of Roosevelt in 1933.[18] Clay had coincidentally received orders to report to Washington almost immediately after Roosevelt's inaugural. He would supervise all river and harbor projects for the Army Corps of Engineers. For the first time (but not the last), all three future proconsuls found themselves together in the same place. Stimson ultimately joined the Roosevelt administration for a second stint as secretary of war in 1940.

In solving the Great Depression, Roosevelt tended to play to his strengths. He was first and foremost a politician, not an economist, and he tended to answer economic questions in political rather than technical terms. "If I read the temper of our people correctly," he explained in his inaugural, "we now realize as we have never realized before our interdependence on each other; that we cannot merely take but we must give as well; that if we are to go forward, we must move as a trained and loyal army willing to sacrifice for the good of a common discipline."[19]

Roosevelt's choice of metaphor, suggesting that the country must become a "trained and loyal army," became embodied in the National Industrial Recovery and Agricultural Adjustment Acts. Each aimed to create giant cartels in every segment of the economy as a means to rid it of "ruinous" competition. "The jig is up. The cat is out of the bag. There is no invisible hand. There never was," wrote Rexford Tugwell, a member of Roosevelt's "Brains Trust" and later an official in the agriculture department. "Time was when the anarchy of the competitive struggle was not too costly. Today it is tragically wasteful. It leads to disaster. We must now supply a real and visible guiding hand to do the task which that mythical, nonexistent, invisible agency was supposed to perform, but never did."[20]

For their part, Eisenhower and Clay both held high hopes that Roosevelt could end the depression. Clay had "followed the election very closely, and

I can remember sitting up election night listening to the returns. . . . I was thrilled at the election results."[21] For Eisenhower, the early New Deal's rhetoric proved intoxicating. "Congress met and gave the Pres. extraordinary powers over banking," Eisenhower wrote in 1933. "Now if they'll just do the same with respect to law enforcement, federal expenditures, trans. systems, there will be such a revival of confidence that things will begin to move."[22] Later that year he noted, "The purpose of the [National Recovery Administration] is to establish codes of business practice among our various trades associations, with the idea of . . . raising prices . . . and wages for labor. As in all other ideas of the President's that have been translated into actual national effort—the announced objective is a most desirable one."[23]

In large measure, Eisenhower embraced the early New Deal because its intellectual genealogy included a common progenitor of his own—the War Industries Board headed by Bernard Baruch. Indeed, Baruch and other members of that board proved deeply influential in the design of the National Recovery Administration (NRA) and in the general thinking about the economy that permeated Washington in Roosevelt's first years.[24] Eisenhower sensed the way these ideas had come of age. As he noted, "a course that three years ago would have been unquestioned, either by the govt. or by any private citizen" had fallen out of favor. Now "unity of action is essential to success in the current struggle." Indeed, Eisenhower felt that "individual right must be subordinated to public good"—that "we *must* conform to the President's program. . . . Otherwise dissension, confusion and partisan politics will ruin us."[25]

Yet for all the talk of American society functioning like an army, Roosevelt had little interest in helping the actual army. Looking to make good on promises to eliminate waste in the federal government, he sought to trim two-fifths of the army's appropriation, requiring the dismissal of about twelve thousand men. He also sought to "furlough at half-pay any army officers the President may select."[26]

MacArthur felt compelled to speak up. In a meeting soon after the inauguration he confronted Roosevelt. "The world situation [has] become too dangerous to allow a weakening of our defense." Japan, Germany, and Italy all showed signs of rearming. The American army had already been cut to the bone. "The country's safety [is] at stake," MacArthur said bluntly.

Roosevelt dug in. He ridiculed MacArthur's concerns and mocked his tone. Roosevelt had no interest in sparing the army, and did not appreciate MacArthur's second-guessing.

The two went back and forth for a few minutes until MacArthur finally lost his cool: "When we [have] lost the next war, and an American boy, lying in the mud with an enemy bayonet through his belly and an enemy foot on his dying throat, [has] spat out his last curse, I [want] the name not to be MacArthur, but Roosevelt."

"You *must* not talk that way to the President!" Roosevelt boomed.

The room went silent. MacArthur knew he had overstepped.

"I'm sorry," he said. "[You have] my resignation as Chief of Staff." His career, he assumed, had come to an end.

As he turned to leave, he heard a conciliating voice: "Don't be foolish, Douglas; you and the budget must get together on this." Roosevelt blinked first. Both men took deep breaths and agreed to work together. Then MacArthur left the president's office, went to the White House steps, and threw up.[27]

The underlying message, though, quickly became clear To protect itself, the army needed to become relevant to the New Deal. Perhaps because his father had served for years in Congress, Clay intuited the political reality more quickly than anyone else. He saw in the proliferating New Deal relief agencies—the Public Works Administration (PWA) and the Works Progress Administration (WPA)—an opportunity. None of these had a bureaucratic infrastructure or list of potential projects to employ relief workers. The "Corps of Engineers was going to have to expand and take on a great deal of this work," he explained, "because we were the only ones . . . that had programs and projects on the drawing board." Given time, the New Deal agencies could figure this out, and when they did, they might eventually replace the corps as the federal government's construction agency. Clay decided to approach Harry Hopkins, head of WPA, about involving the corps in its projects. "We would like to lend to you, in each of your regions, a capable, competent Engineer officer who would bring with him a capable and competent chief clerk who knows how to disperse and set up public funds, just to get you going."

Hopkins was suspicious: To whom would these people report? Did the corps aim to steal the role just given to the WPA?

"No," Clay explained. "These people would be reporting directly to [you]. They would be [your] people."[28]

In the end, Hopkins warmed to the idea. In particular, he liked Clay. As the corps became involved in the WPA, the Public Works Administration began to look to the army for talent to take on its projects. Eventually, it found Eisenhower, who jumped at the idea of joining the relief agency, calling it a "marvelous" opportunity. But MacArthur killed it. He had come to depend upon Eisenhower, and, so long as MacArthur had a voice, Eisenhower would work for no one else. Yet MacArthur recognized Clay's insight that the more the military helped the New Deal, the safer its appropriations. He allowed Eisenhower the task of overseeing Civilian Conservation Corps camps from time to time.[29]

As the New Deal unfolded, Clay became increasingly enmeshed in its politics. Because of his father, he had both Democratic Party connections and a sense of how Congress functioned, and so he often testified on behalf of the Corps of Engineers before congressional committees. Eventually, he took charge of specific relief projects. Between lobbying and testifying he became the main liaison between the military, Congress, and the National Emergency Council, (a kind of clearinghouse for New Deal domestic policy). On the council he became close to many of the big names in Roosevelt's administration: Chester Davis, General Hugh Johnson, Harold Ickes, Donald Richberg, and Frances Perkins.[30]

In the meantime, Roosevelt and MacArthur also managed a working relationship. To MacArthur's surprise, Roosevelt asked his thoughts on the many social programs emerging from the New Deal. Eventually, MacArthur asked, "Why is it, Mr. President, that you frequently inquire my opinion regarding the social reforms under consideration, matters about which I am certainly no authority, but pay little attention to my views on the military?"

"Douglas," Roosevelt replied, "I don't bring these questions up for your advice but for your reactions."[31]

By the time the Supreme Court invalidated large parts of the New Deal in the spring of 1935, MacArthur and Eisenhower's destiny lay elsewhere. The Philippine Independence Act (often called the Tydings-McDuffie Act of 1934) instructed Filipinos to draft their own constitution, "republican in form," containing "a bill of rights" and "submitted to the people of the Philippine Islands for their ratification or rejection."[32] Once drafted, and after a ten-year "commonwealth period," the new constitution would go into full effect and the Philippines would become fully independent. Many Filipinos went to work immediately and established their own constitution at the end of 1935.

Congress wanted to give the Philippines independence, but worried for the islands' safety as Japan aggressively expanded its empire into China. "Can we suppose that Japan, suffering from a lack of raw materials and from excessive over-population will not be interested in the fate of these islands eventually?" asked an observer in 1935.[33] The "commonwealth period" aimed to provide cover while the Filipinos developed a capable self-defense. When Manuel Quezon became the first president of the commonwealth government, he turned to Douglas MacArthur for advice. "General," he asked, "in your professional opinion, can the Philippine Islands defend themselves in an independent status?"

"I know they can," MacArthur replied.

"If the matter can be arranged with the President of the United States," he continued, "will you accept the post as Military Adviser, taking charge of all defensive preparation in the Islands?"

MacArthur answered "in the enthusiastic affirmative."[34]

No sooner had MacArthur agreed to move to Manila than he made Eisenhower part of his team. "You and I have worked together a long time," he explained. "I don't want to bring in someone new."[35]

The Philippine assignment held several advantages for American soldiers. Most important, in a time of depression they could draw two salaries: one from the Philippine commonwealth, the other their regular American pay. In fact, MacArthur's combined salary from the United States and the Philippines made him the highest-paid military leader in the world (at about $4,000 a year).[36] The assignment also allowed MacArthur to hold the rank of field marshal (a unique opportunity since the American military did not offer this option).

MacArthur landed in Manila, hoping to build an elaborate army of thirty divisions (the American army at that time consisted of three). Eisenhower's job quickly became finding the means to build MacArthur's army from the limited resources available to a poor nation in the midst of a global depression. It proved impossible. "The General is more and more indulging in a habit of damning everybody," Eisenhower confided, "who disagrees with him over any detail, in extravagant, sometimes almost hysterical fashion." He "now . . . seems to consider that the combined use of his rank, a stream of malapropos, and a refusal to permit the presentation of opposing opinion will, by silencing his subordinates, establish also the validity of his contentions." However, as Eisenhower observed, the Philippines lacked everything from ammunition to training facilities. "He makes nasty cracks about 'technicians' and 'small-minded people' when we try and show that we are simply arguing from the standpoint of the amount of money available. I'm coming to believe," he concluded, "that the 30 Div.

Plan is adopted, not because he believes there is any honest possibility of attaining it, but to justify [his] early appointment [as] Field Marshal."[37]

Complicating matters, pleas for more resources fell on deaf ears in Washington. Even simple requests, such as obtaining obsolete rifles from the U.S. Army, stalled in a bureaucratic limbo. Eisenhower pressed MacArthur to return to the United States to lobby for weaponry and anything else that would help train the Filipino army. But MacArthur resisted.[38] Instead, through much of 1936 he instructed his staff to plan for a grand Philippine army whereupon Eisenhower would explain that the Philippines could not afford it. "I argue these points with more heat and persistency" observed Eisenhower, "consequently I come in for the more severe criticism," usually in the form of "regular shouting tirades" from MacArthur.[39]

With Quezon in tow, MacArthur finally traveled to the United States to plead the cause of Philippine preparedness in early 1937. The trip went badly. Roosevelt had grown cool toward MacArthur after he left Washington and avoided MacArthur's requests to meet. He refused to see Quezon at all. Eventually, MacArthur convinced Roosevelt to hold a short interview with Quezon only to be horrified as Quezon harangued the president for five hours, demanding immediate independence. Roosevelt refused. Worse, MacArthur failed to get any promises on matériel for the Philippines.[40]

Yet when he returned to Manila, MacArthur announced success. First, he explained that the Army Corps of Engineers had given him several engineers to assess the archipelago's suitability for hydroelectric dams. As it turned out, Clay belonged to the group. It "looked like an ideal opportunity," he explained.[41] By this point a fixture in the Washington social scene, the *Washington Post* covered Clay's plans to depart on its "social page."[42]

Second, MacArthur announced that, while no additional funds would come from Washington, he had obtained a different windfall. Quezon had just promised him "oil money" (revenue generated from a tax on coconut oil) that would allow a tripling of the equipment budget. It also provided for the constructing of new office space for the "use of engineers that are to come over in October [that is, Clay]." He then revealed that his "real purpose in having [the engineers] here under my thumb is that, though paid by funds of the [Philippine] Power Development Corporation, I can use them to help us out whenever they are not busy on other work."[43] With this new information in mind, Eisenhower went to work on a revised budget for submission to the Philippine National Assembly with more army appropriations. He submitted it in August 1937.

Things went badly from there. Eisenhower began to hear, to his surprise, that Quezon had perhaps not promised MacArthur any "oil money" and therefore did not anticipate a revised budget calling for an expanded equipment appropriation. In fact, by October Quezon had called MacArthur on the carpet. He could not understand why the budget ultimately came to so much more than MacArthur had apparently initially promised.[44]

MacArthur responded that he had "never approved" of the plan for thirty divisions "or even suggested it except as an expression of his hopes and ambitions." Indeed, "all portions of the plan that exceed the" original estimate were "nothing but the products of [his staff] . . . without approval from him." If the obvious dissembling were not enough, MacArthur then called together his staff (including Eisenhower) and reprimanded them for sending the budget without his approval, despite (in Eisenhower's words) every "scrap of auxiliary evidence, letters, partial plans presented to the Gen., requisitions, and the direct testimony," indicating the literal opposite of his claim.

Eisenhower could not take it. He "challenged" MacArthur "to show that I'd done anything not calculated to further his plans." MacArthur moderated. He made clear "his 'personal' confidence in" his staff. He even "accepted much of the blame for the misunderstanding" even while he "'shouted down' any real explanation" of the situation—to which Eisenhower wrote in his journal, "But it was not a misunderstanding! It is a deliberate scuttling of one plan . . . while he *adopts* another one, which in its concrete expression, at least, I've never even heard of before."

The episode finally broke the relationship between the two men. Eisenhower confided that he must "decide soon whether I can go much further with a person who, either consciously or unconsciously, deceives his boss [Quezon], his subordinates and himself (probably) so incessantly as he does." In reality, Eisenhower had "remained on this job, not because of the Gen.—but in spite of him. I've got interested in this riddle of whether or not we can develop a [Philippine War Department] and an army capable of running itself. . . . But now I'm at a cross road."[45]

Just as Eisenhower debated whether to demand a transfer away from MacArthur, Clay arrived in Manila and took up residence in the same hotel as the Eisenhowers and MacArthurs. For the next year, the three future military governors lived in the same building. Quickly, Clay developed a working relationship with MacArthur ("General MacArthur never came to the office but about an hour a day," he recalled, but every "once in a while, he'd call me up and we would go to a prize fight. He loved prize fights").[46] More important, he connected with Eisenhower. "We were great friends," Clay said. [47] "I had known Eisenhower socially in Washington, but it was not until the Philippines that I came in close contact with him. And I became very close to [him] and remained so until his death."[48] Together, they organized maneuvers for U.S. and Filipino soldiers, developed an engineering school, and did their best to create a modern Philippine army. Ultimately, both men concluded the Philippines needed many things, new dams being the least important of them.

At the same time, Quezon appeared to have realized the truth about the budget. Through 1937 he reached out to Eisenhower and treated him as an informal presidential adviser, asking his thoughts on everything from "taxes [to] education, honesty in government, and other [policy] subjects." He "seemed to enjoy" the discussions. "Certainly I did," recalled Eisenhower.[49] While the difficulties with MacArthur remained, Eisenhower's growing responsibilities and friendships made the work interesting enough that he decided to stay in the Philippines after all.

In many ways, though, his growing involvement in Philippine politics led to the final break with MacArthur. A "group of Filipino legislators," recalled Clay, "felt that they could turn over [MacArthur's] job of military advisor to Colonel Eisenhower and save the Philippine government a great deal of money." Eisenhower earned much less and paid his own rent (unlike MacArthur who lived in the penthouse of the Manila Hotel at government expense). "I know that . . . Colonel Eisenhower had no part in this, and that he told these Filipino legislators that if they proceeded any further he would just have to ask to be sent home." But their ideas did not remain secret. When it finally came to "General MacArthur's attention . . . he just couldn't believe that this could have happened . . . unless it had been instigated by Colonel Eisenhower."[50]

While Eisenhower left on a long-deserved vacation, MacArthur demoted him, prohibited him from contact with Quezon, and relegated him to work that kept him away from the National Assembly. Upon his return Eisenhower learned of these new restrictions, and attributed the matter to MacArthur's jealousy and thin skin. "He'd like to occupy a throne room surrounded by experts in flattery," he wrote in his journal.[51] Recognizing that his career had come to a standstill, Eisenhower once again reached out to Fox Conner, and once again Conner provided. Within a few months, Eisenhower received orders taking him back to the States. Quezon begged him to stay. But at that point, he told Quezon, "No amount of money can make me change my mind."[52]

Clay also returned to the States about this time. Congress had approved construction of the Denison Dam along the Red River between Texas and Oklahoma. When completed, it would be the world's largest rolled earth–filled dam, and something Clay had wanted to work on "for a long, long time."[53] In the summer of 1938, when he learned of the opportunity to build the dam, he jumped at it.[54]

In retrospect, the saga of Clay, Eisenhower, and MacArthur in Manila reads like so much court intrigue involving men who, in the near future, would hold the fates of millions in their hands. Certainly, the personality conflict revealed a lot about the character of Eisenhower and MacArthur as well as Clay, who managed to become a confidant of both men. But to focus on personality, tempting as it is, masks the important substantive dispute that first brought them into conflict.

For his part, MacArthur revealed an approach to military service driven by a sense of mission and a burning desire for success, and he could take great risks to accomplish that mission. This instinct led him to bravely challenge President Roosevelt's planned cut of army personnel in 1933, but it led just as easily to his ham-fisted effort to sneak a bigger military budget past Manuel Quezon. At times, his willingness to treat every mission as a pivotal moment in world history reduced him almost to caricature; yet his instinct to succeed at all costs and seek almost apocalyptic tests of his character fit a kind of military ethos and as often as not ended with stunning victories.

By contrast, Eisenhower brought a sensibility to his work deeply attuned to the limits of his environment. He coupled this sensibility with a willingness to consider what military theorists subsequently called "grand strategy"—namely, the use of all the resources available to a nation (economic, moral, political) along with military might—and the way that all resources could be deployed directly or indirectly.[55] The eminent nineteenth-century German military theorist Carl von Clausewitz famously argued that "war is merely the continuation of politics by other means."[56] The eminent nineteenth-century German statesman Otto von Bismarck famously noted that "politics is the art of the possible." Eisenhower absorbed both insights in thinking of war as the art of the possible.

In the postwar years, these two Americans—MacArthur and Eisenhower —would embody contrasting visions of how America should fight the Cold

War. Their personal inclinations would result in a political rivalry that would ultimately shape more than their increasingly strained friendship. But in the meantime, while Clay began work on his dam and Eisenhower traveled home, war erupted in Europe. Most Americans wanted to stay free of the conflict, but Roosevelt began to see American entry as inevitable. In foreign policy he tended to gather information informally through anecdote and conversation, assuming this gave him a better sense of a country than he could receive from his own State Department.[57] His feelings toward Japan proved a telling example. While Roosevelt attended Harvard in 1902, a Japanese student showed him a map outlining a twelve-step plan for annexing Korea, Manchuria, Australia, and New Zealand, and eventually all Asian people. Roosevelt related the story years later, as if to show that he learned more in one afternoon than what his own state department had discovered through the decade of the 1930s.[58]

In June 1940, he surprised many by announcing a shakeup in both the Navy and War Departments. The Republican Frank Knox would become secretary of the navy. Roosevelt then turned to another Republican, Henry Stimson to become the secretary of war for the second time. Stimson had just turned seventy-two and with Roosevelt in office assumed he had finished his public career. Yet here he was, again, in the executive branch—working for a Democrat, no less. Roosevelt made the appointments "in behalf of national defense" and as a means to create "national solidarity in a time of world crisis."[59] Americans generally liked the approach: over 70 percent approved Stimson's appointment in a Gallup poll taken just after his nomination.[60]

Chapter 4

The Army, the New Deal, and
the Planning for the Postwar

Because of their duties in the Philippines and later in World War II, Mac-Arthur, Eisenhower, and Clay missed what came to be called the Keynesian Revolution. In 1936, John Maynard Keynes wrote *The General Theory of Employment, Interest and Money.*[1] Prior to Keynes, most economists saw savings as the key to economic growth, where the more parsimoniously a people lived, the wealthier they would become. As Adam Smith argued, "Whatever a person saves from his revenue he adds to his capital." What was true for one proved true for all: "As the capital of an individual can be increased only by what he saves . . . so the capital of society . . . can be increased in the same manner."[2] In short, savings did not disappear from the economy; they made economic growth possible.

Among the many arguments in his enigmatic book, Keynes reversed Smith's argument by pressing precisely on the question of what happened to savings.[3] Nothing guaranteed their automatic conversion into investment Keynes believed. Entrepreneurs invested based on the expectations of future profits. If, for some reason (Keynes posited "animal spirits"), they lost confidence in the future, they would hold their money rather than invest. "With the separation between ownership and management which prevails to-day," he explained, "and with the development of organised investment markets, a new factor of great importance has entered in." A well-developed and efficient financial system "sometimes facilitates investment," but just as often, it "adds greatly to the instability of the system."[4] In short, the creation of capital markets lent itself to a kind of "mass psychology of the market," which could "change violently as the result of a sudden fluctuation of opinion."[5] Investment depended on the mood of the investors, not the supply of savings, interest rates, or thrift. In pessimistic times money sat idly, waiting for investors to feel courageous again. Economists ultimately called the phenomena a "liquidity trap"—a term meant to contradict Adam Smith's claim that savings easily made their way back into circulation. Thus, "the equilibrium level of employment, i.e. the level at which there is no inducement to employers as a whole either to expand or to contract employment, will *depend* on the amount of current investment."[6]

Keynes showed how, ironically, a high savings rate could kill growth. It could facilitate depression. He argued that a perfect balance of savings and investment was rare, "an optimum relationship" that "can only exist . . . by accident or design," but hardly in the natural state of the economy.[7] Put in simplest terms, Keynes argued that the economy's vulnerability came from the investor class—rich capitalists and their hired guns—who could, in their flightiness and timidity, choke the economy into depression.

But an alternative existed. Government could "compensate" for the investor class by spending those idle savings when investors lost their nerve. It could "prime the pump" and return the economy to full employment. Indeed, only government could pursue the public interest over the narrow anxieties of the investor class and restore the economy to a full employment equilibrium.[8]

While it took time and developed piecemeal, eventually the Keynesian approach came to dominate the thinking of the New Dealers. For New Dealers, monopolists and reckless bankers—whose hatred Roosevelt had "welcomed" in 1936—need not be evil.[9] Keynes showed they were just as dangerous by being timid, flighty, and narrow. They could effectively ruin the economy either way. The Keynesian approach had the additional advantage of showing that difficult and often controversial efforts to regulate and reorganize business were unnecessary. Rather, government simply needed to spend, and spend enough to restore the economy to full employment.[10] Indeed, as spending on World War II ramped up, Keynes appeared to be a prophet: the American economy grew dramatically and unemployment disappeared.

By the mid-1930s, Roosevelt began to worry that he had prioritized the domestic economy at the expense of the international. His secretary of state, Cordell Hull, prevailed upon him to embrace the cause of free trade. While Hull never gained Roosevelt's full confidence, Roosevelt did support the Reciprocal Trade Agreement Act of 1934, which gave him authority to grant "most favored nation status" and unilaterally reduce tariffs with a particular country. Then came a 1938 U.S.-British trade agreement, lowering tariffs on a handful of goods. Roosevelt's interest in the global economy accelerated as war seemed inevitable. Starting with his "Good Neighbor" policy toward Latin America, Roosevelt increasingly saw economic diplomacy laying the foundation for security.[11]

As Hull also began to think of war as inevitable, he initiated a Committee on Problems of Peace and Reconstruction, staffed largely with veterans of Woodrow Wilson's administration. This group tried to divine "out of the experiences of the interwar years and out of the experiences of the [First World] war itself" what had gone so terribly wrong. They concluded that Wilson's efforts had focused too narrowly on political reconstruction alone. "No program of constructive economic and social action agreed upon among all the victor powers of 1918 had come into being." As a result, when "insecurity had grown" because of "problems left by the war," and because of "the lag between national and international economic, social, and political policy on the one hand and swift technological development and desires for a higher standard of living on the other," the precepts of "Christianity and democracy" had collapsed.[12]

By 1940, the committee made economic reconstruction, rather than political reconstruction, its starting point since "the common interests of nations were more generally recognized in the economic than in the political field." This seemed a particularly good starting point because "the experiences of the interwar period"—that is, the global Depression—had "focused [policymakers'] attention on the effects of economic policies on international relations." Echoing Walter Lippmann's 1933 essay, the committee argued that a collapse of international trade would be followed by nationalist economic and political policies. Lack of global economic cooperation created an "important source of friction between nations and [was] a basic factor contributing to stability or instability within states."[13]

But trade remained a particularly thorny issue, particularly with the British. When Roosevelt met with Winston Churchill to craft what became the Atlantic Charter in 1941 (the Charter stood as the fundamental document outlining American and British war aims), the State Department inserted a clause that the United States and Britain would "strive to promote mutually advantageous economic relations . . . through the elimination of any discrimination . . . against the importation of any product originating in the other country." Churchill balked at this. The British, former champions of free trade, had since the depression realized the value of a preferential system of trade within their vast empire.

"Time being of the essence," Roosevelt thought it best to compromise with Churchill. He rewrote the passage to say only that the two countries would "endeavor to further the enjoyment by all peoples of access, without discrimination and on equal terms to the markets and to the raw materials of the world which are needed for their economic prosperity." Churchill reluctantly supported this broad, vague aim.[14]

By 1943, the idea of creating a global economic order had become fundamental to American postwar planning. In testimony before Congress, Hull explained that "when the day of victory comes, we and other nations will have before us a choice . . . as it was in 1918." On the one hand, the world could choose "extreme nationalism, growing rivalries, jealousies and hatreds"; or it could choose "increased international cooperation in a wide variety of fields" and a chance at peace. "Of the various necessary fields of international collaboration one of the most essential is the field of economic life." In what became almost a mantra in the postwar period, Hull said, "The political and social instability caused by economic distress is a fertile breeding ground of agitators and dictators, ready to plunge the peoples over whom they seize control into adventure and war." Avoiding this outcome required "mutual willingness to cooperate in the fundamental business of earning a living."[15]

Hull had placed his analytic eggs in the basket of economic determinism. Of course, on the surface, this did not distinguish his views from Roosevelt and the rest of the New Dealers. They, too, saw the political consequences of economic downturns. "Democracy has disappeared in several other great nations," Roosevelt argued, "not because the people of those nations disliked democracy, but because they had grown tired of unemployment and insecurity." After "seeing their children hungry while they sat helpless in the face of government confusion" they eventually settled for the security offered by authoritarian leaders such as Hitler.[16]

For Hull, however, the causal flow moved from the international to the domestic. Democracy had disappeared in other nations because the people in those nations sought a way to assert nationalist claims on the international stage. The collapse of an open economic system after World War I had left Germany and Japan, for example, in economic distress. As the Council of Foreign Relations explained in one of its *Studies of American Interests*, "high and discriminatory tariffs and colonial quotas were already limiting the possibilities of Japanese trade expansion by 1935." The Japanese acted in a predictable way. "People in extreme economic distress have [often] turned to some new form of authoritative government."[17]

In fairness, "I do not mean, of course, that flourishing international commerce is of itself a guarantee of peaceful international relations," Hull explained.[18] Still, he assumed that economic breakdown did more than provoke armed conflict; it produced distinctly illiberal regimes within countries cut off from the global market. As Dean Acheson (Hull's assistant secretary of state) explained, "If you wish to control the entire trade and income of the United States . . . you could probably fix it so that everything produced here would be consumed here." But this approach ignored the way law, politics, and trade had evolved together in the industrialization process. To cut off trade "would completely change our Constitution, our relations to property, human liberty, our very conceptions of law."[19]

Hull found a combination of support and rivalry in Roosevelt's treasury secretary, Henry Morgenthau, who became Hull's "frenemy" (to apply a contemporary term). While Morgenthau may not have been the smartest or most innovative policymaker among the New Dealers, he knew how to make the bureaucracy work in his favor. Mostly, he understood how he could sway Roosevelt and keep the president's attention on issues he cared about. In the freewheeling atmosphere of the Roosevelt administration, where lines of authority meant less than a relationship to the president, Morgenthau's genius shined.

Morgenthau wanted a role in the postwar period and saw the effort to rebuild global finance as a natural fit for the Treasury Department, in part because his trusted adviser, Harry Dexter White, had already begun work on the problem. White recognized that under "the gold standard, exchange rates were fixed, so that the balance of payments had to adjust through domestic deflation," and domestic deflations had run amok in the early 1930s, eventually sinking into global depression.[20] Keynes had shown how these deflationary recessions could become a vicious circle in which timid investors reinforced the very economic decline they feared. But how to prevent the gold standard from triggering a depression?

The obvious answer lay in getting rid of the gold standard. This would prevent nations from suffering "forced" deflations. Nations could simply devalue their currency anytime they got out of balance with their trading partners. Yet letting exchange rates fluctuate created two potential problems. First, it might discourage trade because merchants could never know for certain what the exchange rate would be—a phenomenon commonly known as "exchange risk." International commerce had enough unknowns without adding the risk of profits evaporating because a country decided to suddenly depreciate its currency. The gold standard at least brought certainty to international trade.

Second, during the 1930s, American officials noted that as "many countries . . . played the game of artificially manipulating the exchange rates of their currencies in order to gain advantage in the international market place." Countries would intentionally "depreciate their currencies in order to sell their exports more cheaply in external markets." Global economics became a "kind of 'beggar my neighbor'" game that led to a currency war "with everybody trying to depreciate against everybody else in order to gain trading advantage. This was a pretty chaotic system."[21] White tried to find a way to make exchange rates more flexible without letting them become capricious.

After some deliberation White struck on a solution that fit the general tenor of the New Deal. In place of the gold standard, he wanted an *agency* to actively manage, in the global interest, the world's currencies. Initially called the International Stabilization Fund, this agency would act as an umpire for global finance. In the short term, it would have a reserve that it could use to provide loans for countries that found themselves (for whatever reason) temporarily low on foreign exchange. Thus, a country caught in a short-term crunch could avoid drastic measures to pay its foreign debts. In the long term, if a country suffered chronic deficits, the agency could give permission for a currency devaluation. Devaluations could happen, but not in the "beggar my neighbor" approach common in the interwar years.

By the spring of 1942 White gave Morgenthau a copy of his plan, titled "United Nations Stabilization Fund and a Bank for Reconstruction and Development of the United and Associated Nations." In particular, Morgenthau appreciated that White's plan shifted the postwar discussion from trade to finance—which meant that the Treasury could move into the heart of postwar policy. As White explained, "if the Treasury doesn't initiate a conference on the subject it almost certainly will be initiated elsewhere, and it should be preeminently Treasury responsibility."[22]

It worked. Roosevelt gave Morgenthau the green light to proceed, but wanted consensus within the administration before going to the Allies. Through the following months representatives from Treasury, State, Commerce, the Federal Reserve, and the Board of Economic Warfare worked out the details.[23]

Coincidentally, John Maynard Keynes had started work on a British plan to accomplish many of the same things entailed in White's plan. He, too, sought an exchange rate regulated by an international agency. Yet his plan went well beyond White's in that the International Clearing Union (his proposed agency) would have its own currency (the bancor) that it would substitute for gold. In simplest terms, Keynes proposed the construction of a central bank for the world, working something like the Federal Reserve, but with a global currency.

Under Keynes' plan all global trade would be financed in bancor and serviced through the International Clearing Union. If a country ran too much of a trade deficit, the Clearing Union would penalize it by taxing it a small amount. But the same would be true for a country running perpetual surpluses: it, too, would be penalized. In the short term, deficit countries could make up their shortfall by borrowing from the surplus countries. As Keynes explained, "each country is allowed a certain margin of resources and a certain interval of time within which to effect a balance in its economic relations with the rest of the world."[24]

Keynes' plan for an International Clearing Union remained consistent with his ideas about domestic depressions. In each case, his diagnosis suggested that unused money ("liquidity traps" again) caused a vicious cycle of deflation, ending in a permanently depressed global economy. Within a domestic economy, government could force this money back into circulation through borrowing and spending. Keynes aimed to accomplish the same thing on the international level through the clearing union.

Most important for the British, at its creation the International Clearing Union would create accounts in bancor for its member countries proportionate to their participation in global trade. Thus, from the get-go each country would have, in essence, start-up capital with which to trade. As Keynes understood, the British would end World War II as they had the First World War, in desperate need of investment capital with which to buy products from the world (and especially America). The overall arrangement made perfect sense for the British, who, at war's end, would be heavily in debt again to the United States and would have little gold to buy internationally. Indeed, the plan made sense for just about every country *not* the United States because just about every country (particularly in Europe) would be in the same position as the British.

Unfortunately for Keynes, both Harry Dexter White and Henry Morgenthau harbored resentments toward their British allies, stemming from

the war debt crisis of the previous decade. In their view, Britain had abandoned the gold standard to welch on its debts and used its imperial system to
block American exports during the worst part of the Depression. Both men
saw their plan fatally wounding the British Empire in the name of a globally
open economy.[25] As a result, as Keynes and White brought their two plans
together at Bretton Woods, New Hampshire, in the summer of 1944, Morgenthau's stated claim—"We can accomplish [our] task only if we approach it
not as bargainers but as partners"—was consistently undermined by White,
who did his best to assert American over British interests whenever possible.[26]

For example, where Keynes wanted an International Clearing Union
with its own money, White insisted on an International Monetary Fund
(IMF) using only dollars and controlled largely by the United States. Keynes
hoped to have extensive start-up capital provided to debtor countries at the
end of the war; the IMF had relatively small reserves. Keynes wanted to
penalize both trade surplus and deficit countries to achieve balance; White
managed to see the burden fall largely upon deficit nations. Keynes sought
to disconnect international trade entirely from the gold standard through
use of the bancor; White managed to ensure all global trade used dollars.
But here, White made a decision that troubled American policymaking for
decades after the war. Making the dollar the global trading currency allowed
the United States to, in essence, force the rest of the world to follow its
monetary policy: the United States could add or remove dollars from the
world supply according to its needs. Ultimately, White agreed to peg the
dollar to gold (at the rate of $35 an ounce). Foreign countries could redeem
dollars at that rate from the "gold window" (as it came to be called). "To
all intents and purposes," *Congressional Quarterly* summed up, "the American gold bullion standard of $35 an ounce amounts to an international
dollar standard with the U.S. Treasury in the role of central banker."[27]
White had essentially let the problems of the gold standard back into global
finance through the back door.

The Bretton Woods Conference ultimately produced the Bretton Woods
agreement, a treaty signed by forty-four nations, leading to what has subsequently been called (no surprise) the Bretton Woods system. Had Keynes
gotten his way, the new global order would have more seamlessly matched
the Keynesian approach to domestic economic management, something
White did not realize at the time. Indeed, in advancing American interests
over British, he unintentionally created a global system that would ultimately work at odds with the New Deal's domestic political economy.[28] He

also learned the wrong lessons of global finance coming out of World War I. Then European countries were deep in debt and faced staggering inflation. That was the disease. The symptoms had been the debt defaults, currency devaluations, and the turn to bilateral trade agreements. As American policymakers quickly realized, the same was true after World War II.

Morgenthau had not finished shaping the postwar order though. Around the same time White was negotiating with Keynes over the future of global finance, Morgenthau became increasingly interested in making postwar policy for the occupations of Germany and Japan.[29] Throughout 1943 and into 1944, State Department planners had included Germany within a broad framework for trade and international economic cooperation. A typical memo from 1943 felt "no illusions as to the difficulties in . . . creating an effective democracy" in Germany because it would be tempting to punish the Germans for the war. But the lessons of World War I offered instruction: "A minimum of bitterness against the peace terms is in order," the drafters argued, "to avoid an appealing program for future nationalistic upheavals at home and disturbances abroad." Moreover, "in the interest of fostering moderate government in Germany," the drafters recommended "a program looking to the economic recovery of Germany . . . and to the assimilation of Germany . . . into the projected international order."[30] In short, economic revival and a position within the new global system would foster a "moderate" German electorate willing to maintain the peace.

When Morgenthau learned of the State Department's plans to include Germany in the international order, he recoiled in horror. He got hold of a draft of these plans and handed them privately to Roosevelt with a covering memo suggesting that the policies contradicted Roosevelt's stated views on Germany.[31] After reading several pages, Roosevelt threw the memo down on his desk. "Feed the Germans!" he said, "I'll give them three bowls of soup a day, with nothing in them. Control inflation!" he continued, "Let them have all the inflation they want. I should worry. Control industry," he concluded, "There's not going to be any industry in Germany to control."[32] As Morgenthau knew, Roosevelt had expressed deep cynicism about the Germans throughout the war. They were "hopeless to retrain," he told his assistant George Elsey one day. "We could do nothing with them."[33] To Morgenthau, he had been blunter and cruder. "We either have to castrate the German people or you have got to treat them in such manner so they can't just go on reproducing people who want to continue the way they have in the past."[34]

A lot can be and has been said about the debate that followed over a "hard" or "soft" peace for Germany.[35] In the briefest terms, Morgenthau found bureaucratic support for the "hard" peace from the most devoted of New Dealers (such as Harry Hopkins), who blended their frustration at big business with their moral outrage over Hitler's genocide of Europe's Jews. Morgenthau, Roosevelt's only Jewish cabinet member, had become increasingly alarmed at the reports of atrocities and, by late 1943, had begun actively involving himself in persuading Roosevelt to do more to save Europe's Jewry.[36] When it came to the postwar period, Morgenthau felt that nothing could be done about the German people's *desire* to enslave the world. The only solution lay in devastating Germany's *ability* to enslave the world. As he summarized in a memo to Roosevelt: "(1) The German people have the will to try [to conquer the world] again. (2) Programs for democracy, reeducation and kindness cannot destroy this will within any brief time. (3) Heavy industry is the core of Germany's warmaking potential." Thus, "We are more convinced than ever that if we really mean to deprive Germany of the ability to make war again . . . it is absolutely essential that she be deprived of her chemical, metallurgical and electrical industries. We don't think that this alone will guarantee peace, but that it is one of the steps we must take now."[37]

Here, the New Deal's antagonism toward "monopolists and reckless bankers" overlapped with Morgenthau's prescription for postwar Germany. As if to symbolize the connection, soon after Congress concluded hearings into domestic monopolies (before the Temporary National Economic Committee), it began hearings on "the effects of . . . international cartels to the problem of national defense and the establishment of world peace" (before Committee on Military Affairs, Cartels, and National Security).[38] The investigation concluded that "our Axis enemies engaged in systematic economic warfare against the United States." Indeed, as defeat approached, "German aggressors . . . are already deploying their economic reserves throughout the world in preparation for a third attempt at world domination."[39] Within the context of the newly concluded Bretton Woods agreements, a "real cooperation of sovereign nations" meant "the end of the cartel system, which has in the past proven an insuperable barrier to international harmony," a cartel system mastered by the Germans. Roosevelt agreed. "The history of the I.G. Farben trust by the Nazis reads like a detective story," he wrote. "Defeat of the Nazi armies will have to be followed by the eradication of these weapons of economic warfare."[40] Roosevelt seemed to suggest a neutering of the Germany economy. Morgenthau couldn't agree more.

Morgenthau's opposition came largely from Henry Stimson, the most vocal advocate for a "soft" peace within the administration. He felt Morgenthau missed the main lesson coming out of World War I. "The question is not whether we want Germans to suffer for their sins." Stimson, as much as anyone else, "would like to see them suffer the tortures they have inflicted on others." The only real "question is whether over the years a group of seventy million educated, efficient and imaginative people can be kept within bounds on such a low level of subsistence." No matter how justified, Stimson asserted, it "would be very difficult, if not impossible, for them to understand any purpose or cause for such revolutionary changes other than mere vengeance of their enemies and this alone would strongly tend towards the most bitter reactions."[41] In short, in focusing on the question of the Germans' *ability* to start another war, Stimson saw Morgenthau guaranteeing their *desire* for that war.

More immediately, enforcing poverty would be incredibly difficult. "I do not believe that is humanly possible," Stimson told Roosevelt. "Even if you could do this," he asked, is it "good for the rest of the world either economically or spiritually?"[42] Stimson drew support from the British who agreed that "an indefinitely continued coercion of [millions of] . . . technically advanced people . . . would at best be an expensive undertaking" and would never guarantee "real security." The British added that "there exists no convincing reason to anticipate that the victor powers would be willing and able indefinitely to apply coercion." In fact, "the best guarantee of security, and the least expensive, would be the German people's repudiation of militaristic ambitions and their assimilation, as an equal partner, into a cooperative world society."[43]

Roosevelt listened to the various viewpoints throughout 1944 and zigzagged back and forth without making up his mind. He favored Morgenthau's position initially, only to slowly come around to Stimson's. In the meantime, his health began to fail. He found it harder to make difficult decisions. In his last real conversation about postwar policy for Germany, Roosevelt explained to Morgenthau and representatives from State and the army that he "did not hold extremist views on the subject." He "would let the Germans retain such industries as machine tools and locomotives manufacture." At the same time, he felt "we should not be responsible for maintaining a minimum standard of living in Germany." Of course, "we should feed the German people to prevent them from starving"; perhaps we could develop "soup kitchens for feeding the German people." An army representative asked if Roosevelt would accept the idea that the occupation should take measures to prevent "disease and unrest," and Roosevelt said he had no objection.

In general, though, he remained uncertain. "We [have] to get into the country first and take a look and see what [is] possible and impossible."[44]

With Roosevelt fading, Morgenthau pressed his views aggressively forward. In the end, he managed to include in the official instructions for military government much of what he wanted (even if the instructions often contained caveats based on maintaining security and civil order). True to his own bureaucratic expertise, he also knew that a lot depended on which military officer would run the occupation. It was a foregone conclusion that Eisenhower would be in charge initially. So, in August of 1944, Morgenthau went to Europe to try and commit Eisenhower to a "hard" peace.[45] As it turned out, he found a receptive listener. Eisenhower told Morgenthau that "following the conclusion of hostilities . . . the German people must not be allowed to escape a sense of guilt, of complicity in the tragedy that has engulfed the world. . . . The warmaking power of the country should be eliminated."[46] Eisenhower "was perfectly willing to let them stew in their own juices"—a phrase Morgenthau often quoted in arguing his point with War Department officials.[47]

Still, everyone in Washington also knew that Eisenhower did not want to be military governor. Indeed, he did not want military government.[48] So the question turned to who would replace him in that role. Initially, both Harry Hopkins and the head of the War Mobilization Office, James Byrnes, looked like possibilities, but both opted out.[49] A number of other names floated to the top of the list. Roosevelt ultimately approached John J. "Jack" McCloy, Stimson's assistant secretary of war. But McCloy thought someone who had come up through the army might command more respect from the troops and other Allied military leaders. He also thought the person should have experience in logistics. He suggested Lucius Clay. Roosevelt agreed.[50]

Clay fit all the right criteria. Politically, Clay had made friends with all the right people. He was an able administrator. Still, Morgenthau wanted to know where Clay stood. So before Clay left for Germany, the two men spoke. "You know that our attitude is pretty tough towards Germany," Morgenthau said.

"Yes," Clay replied.

"Well, are we together?"

"I think we are," said Clay, much to Morgenthau's approval.[51]

Confident that Clay would be tough on the Germans, Morgenthau finally "felt good" about the future of Germany.[52] Indeed, as victory over Germany neared, Morgenthau had managed two very important achievements in shaping the postwar: he had crafted a new global framework for postwar finance and a tough policy for postwar Germany.

Fresh on the heels of these victories and just weeks after Germany's surrender, Morgenthau appeared before the Senate Committee on Banking and Currency, where Robert Taft, the son of William Howard Taft, decided to ask about these two victories. Taft had joined the Senate in 1939 and had subsequently become one of the Roosevelt administration's chief Republican antagonists. He assumed, based on the Bretton Woods agreements, that the administration wanted to "increase international trade." But, he asked, "Is the purpose affected by the fact that Japan and Germany are practically out of international trade? Didn't they have a very large volume of international trade before the war?"

"No," Morgenthau replied. "That is a general misunderstanding, if you don't mind my saying it. . . . continental Europe can so easily pick up Germany's export and import trade that the disappearance of it will never be noticed."

Taft seemed unsure. "Well, it seems to me—I don't know—I have no particular view as to what ought to be done with Germany or Japan, but it seems . . . that whatever increase we might get in international trade by [the Bretton Woods agreements] . . . is going to be more than balanced by what we lose in international trade figures after completely eliminating Germany and Japan." In short, "we say we have to make these people prosperous so they can buy our goods, but in Germany we say that we must make them absolutely flat so that they cannot buy our goods. It seems to me the two policies are practically contradictory."

"If Germany is to be deindustrialized, as I hope she will," Morgenthau explained, "all of the studies which we have made show that her former position in world trade, in the export and import fields, could so readily be absorbed by just continental Europe."

Taft was confused. "I cannot see how you can take 150,000,000 people of the most highly industrialized nations in the world . . . and just bar them . . . from all international trade without substantially contradicting and to a large extent nullifying any good that may come from the other agreements."

"If you had the time to spend an afternoon or an evening I would be very glad to come to your office and put all these figures before you," Morgenthau said.[53]

Taft thanked Morgenthau for the offer but did not follow up. Still, he spotted a central paradox in the postwar strategy coming out of the Roosevelt administration. Morgenthau found himself arguing that this new global economic framework would protect the United States from precisely those nations that had not attacked it, while the two nations responsible for the war would be excluded from it.

In the meantime, Clay prepared to leave for Germany to become Eisenhower's successor as military governor of the U.S. zone. On the last day of March 1945, he went to see Roosevelt to get the president's "blessing" before leaving for Europe. At the meeting, Roosevelt suggested that Clay think about "a giant TVA for Germany and all of Europe," as "something that would have great meaning, great significance."[54] But otherwise, Roosevelt did not ask any questions, nor did Clay. The meeting seemed somber and a bit awkward. As Clay left the president's office, he turned to James Byrnes (who had accompanied him) and said, "Mr. Byrnes, we've been talking to a dying man."[55] Byrnes didn't believe it. He had spent a great deal of time with Roosevelt over the preceding months and saw no reason for worry. But less than two weeks later Roosevelt had passed away.

Chapter 5

"This Thing Was Assembled by Economic Idiots"

"Lucius, come on up here to Reims."

General Walter Bedell Smith, Eisenhower's chief of staff, had just tracked down Lucius Clay in Paris on a busy May afternoon in 1945. "There's something interesting going to take place." Reims had become the temporary headquarters for the Allies; a commandeered technical college provided offices for Eisenhower, Smith, and the other tactical commanders, along with Clay and a few military government officials.

"Bedell, I've got all sorts of appointments for tomorrow," he complained.

"Lucius, you'll be sorry all your life if you don't come up."

Wondering what could be so important, Clay eventually scrounged up a "liaison airplane" (a small aircraft that could land on almost anything) and flew himself to Reims. Arriving between six and seven o'clock, he went directly to his office. When he opened the door, there was a "very immaculately dressed German General behind my desk." He couldn't believe it. He couldn't believe Smith had dragged him back from Paris just to play a prank.

"What's going on in my office," he barked at the first officer he saw.

"That's General Jodl," the officer said to a disbelieving Clay. "He's here to surrender." Clay was stunned. "Jodl can't sign until he gets permission," the officer added. They had no place to put Jodl while he waited—except in Clay's empty office. Jodl watched awkwardly as Clay made sense of the situation.

After hours of waiting, General Alfred Jodl signed the surrender. It went quickly while Clay and the others witnessed. The one person not in the room was Eisenhower. Ever since he had seen the concentration camps,

Eisenhower refused to meet with any Germans. Even upon becoming military governor, he avoided them, taking many years to overcome his horror at becoming a witness of the Holocaust.[1]

Nearly everyone in Washington assumed Eisenhower would become the military governor of the American zone in Germany. The only exception to that rule was Eisenhower himself, who consistently argued that civilians should control the military even in an occupation government. He expressed his views to Roosevelt as early as December 1942, as the American army struggled to govern the newly liberated parts of North Africa.[2] By January 1944 he had become emphatic. In a private meeting he "urged, again, that occupied territories be turned over, as quickly as possible, to civil authority." He also expressed his "objection to dividing Germany into 'national sectors.'" He worried that a divided Germany might lend itself to dividing the Allies.[3]

Eisenhower wanted to avoid the responsibility in large measure because his experience abroad with America's external state had taught him how much could go wrong in an occupation. Indeed, something of a consensus existed on this point within the army which sought to avoid the obligations of military government after the war.[4] Yet Roosevelt, while sympathetic, had few options. For one thing, Cordell Hull insisted that the State Department (the other logical choice) couldn't handle the responsibility.[5] No other bureaucracy had emerged in the first decades of the century to govern territory outside the United States. Moreover, the other Allies planned on using military government in their occupation zones. Thus, upon German surrender, Eisenhower found himself "demoted," as it were, from supreme allied commander in charge of French, British, and American troops to one military governor among four.

Eisenhower and Clay both worried that whoever served as military governor would get blamed no matter what. "If he tried to help [the Germans], he was going to be damned for too much sympathy for an enemy; and if he didn't and it [became] . . . the vacuum that would help to destroy all of Europe, then he would be equally damned." No one could "win on this." Clay at least supported Eisenhower's wish to go back to the States as early as possible. "I couldn't see where [Eisenhower] could get any additional appreciation of his work and his services by remaining in this disaster-stricken chaotic country."[6]

Yet Eisenhower and Clay also agreed that military government had an opportunity to bridge the divide between the two emergent superpowers.

Clay called postwar Germany an "experiment in international cooperation," and Eisenhower thought it a "laboratory for the development of international accord."[7] In that spirit in August 1945, Clay and Eisenhower traveled to the Soviet Union as special guests of Joseph Stalin. On the flight to Moscow, the pilot flew close to the ground, navigating by landmarks. "I did not see a house standing between the western borders of the country and the area around Moscow," Eisenhower wrote. Everything had been destroyed.[8] Because they could see the damage done in Russia, both Eisenhower and Clay always doubted that the Soviets would initiate war with the West over the next decades. "Throughout my stay in Germany I had scoffed at the possibility of war with Russia and had been one of the principal supporters of the viewpoint that war, if not impossible, was most unlikely," explained Clay.[9]

Despite their hopes of working constructively with the Soviets, they often worked at loggerheads. The first misunderstanding had to do with money. Throughout the war the army struggled to find a simple solution to the problem of currency in liberated areas. "Within a few days or weeks after invasion of any enemy occupied territory," the occupation "authorities would have to administer . . . a sound monetary, banking and fiscal order" in that territory.[10] On the one hand, the army wanted to have a currency it could use to buy supplies from the locals. On the other, "if the unfortunate should happen, and we should be defeated in the invasion and thrown out, we didn't want a usable large stock of U.S. currency to fall into German hands." Military planners wanted to ensure that the United States could "repudiate the [currency] without damaging the circulation of regular U.S. currency."[11] Eventually, Treasury worked out a system for using military scrip at easily converted exchange rates for use in occupied territory.[12]

The planning for Germany was more complicated for two reasons: first, it would be occupied rather than liberated (meaning the scrip would probably be used for an extended period); second, all the occupying armies would need to use the same scrip, including the British, French and Soviets. The British and French assented to letting the Americans print and distribute scrip in their zones. The Soviets, however, insisted on having their own printing plates for use in their own zone. Treasury officials felt "it would have a very nice effect upon the German people if we all used the same type of currency" and would show "evidence of cooperation between the [Allied] nations." More to the point, American officials realized that in the absence of the American plates, the Soviets would simply "embark upon a currency of their own . . . and establish a rate of exchange of their own and also establish monetary and financial programs of their own." The result would jeopardize "the likelihood of developing a uniform and coordinated Allied pattern of action towards Germany."[13] Thus, on April 18, 1944, "the Soviet Ambassador was furnished with glass negatives and positives of plates for the use of the Soviet Government in the printing of Allied military marks."[14] By the time the American army stood ready to enter Germany, the Treasury Department told Eisenhower that "for the purposes of pay of troops and your internal accounting . . . you will use a rate of 10 [German Reichsmarks] to the dollar and 40 marks to the pound sterling."[15]

By spring 1945, American and Soviet troops began to bump into each other as they advanced upon the collapsing German Wehrmacht. One surprising result of this contact came in the generosity the Soviet soldiers showed the Americans. Eisenhower radioed home that the "Russians, using their printings of identical AM [Allied military] marks, [are] giving same to United States troops . . . as gifts." Unfortunately, the generosity created a "new problem." Eisenhower noted the "amounts involved" and worried that the Soviets had been "issuing AM marks to their troops in large quantities" since "they place little value on them."[16] After lengthy discussions, the Treasury, State, and War Departments agreed that the matter could become problematic and recommended that it be resolved through the Allied Control Council (or ACC—the official policymaking forum for the four occupying powers).[17]

Upon further investigation, it became apparent that the Soviets had promised to pay their soldiers only *after* they reached Germany. Once in the country, the Soviets had provided all back pay in allied military marks. Complicating matters, they also told their troops that the marks could not be converted into rubles. In other words, Soviet soldiers had to spend their entire accumulated pay in Germany before they went home.

Eisenhower's instructions to coordinate with the Soviets ignored the reality that the Soviets never kept track of how many military marks they had distributed or planned to distribute. In the meantime, throughout Germany—and especially in Berlin, where troops from each power had a garrison—mini bazaars sprang up. Russian soldiers, flush with military scrip and short on goods, arrived with "bags and suitcases [of Allied military marks]," while American "GIs and Germans [did] the selling and trading." The GIs reaped a whirlwind profit, selling cigarettes for 1,500 marks, cameras at 2,500 to 5,000 marks, and watches for 5,000 to 10,000 marks.[18]

By August 1945, the bazaars had become newsworthy—as had the implications for the Treasury, which had to convert the military marks into dollars. *Stars and Stripes* ran an article noting that American troops in Berlin had sent home roughly $4 million in July despite the fact that "during the same period . . . the soldiers in the U.S. Berlin garrison were paid a total of only about $1 million."[19] The situation became more absurd as time passed. One morning, a Russian officer arrived at the American headquarters in Berlin with a bag containing one hundred thousand military marks. He explained that he was willing to give the entire amount for a course of penicillin to help cure his syphilis. The Americans declined the money and gave the officer his medicine anyway.[20]

Eventually, Smith informed Eisenhower, "Obviously there is no real limit being placed on the exchange of these 'Russian' marks." They appeared to be distributing the marks hot off the presses. He worried that it could get out of hand: "I really think we will have to [limit] it."

"The story is exaggerated," Eisenhower replied, "but is still bad enough" and agreed he should do something.[21] In the absence of Soviet cooperation on monetary policy, however, Eisenhower had few options for slowing the money flowing back into the United States. On August 7, 1945, he sent an order to all theater commanders, prohibiting "the transmission by military personnel of funds . . . in excess of the sender's unencumbered pay plus 10 per cent."[22] But this measure backfired. The problem lay in the arbitrariness of the 10 percent figure coming at the same time as massive military downsizing occurred throughout Germany. Hundreds of thousands of GIs received their discharges from military service throughout 1945 and into 1946, and many soldiers had "accumulations of many months' pay and allowances" as well as bonuses. It struck many, and eventually Eisenhower, as cruel and unfair to deprive good soldiers of their legitimate pay to stop the behavior of bad soldiers earning from the black market. But "no means existed of distinguishing currency properly acquired from that illegally acquired."[23]

Finally, Eisenhower fell back on an appeal to the soldiers' honor and patriotism. In September 1945, he ordered "all field grade officers and all civilians" hoping to exchange military marks into dollars to take a written oath that stated: "I certify that these funds . . . were derived only from United States official sources." Enlisted men had to do the same.[24] It had no effect.

Through the end of 1945, Eisenhower and Clay searched for means to stop American soldiers from converting military marks into dollars, while continuing to respect the idea of four-party cooperation on the currency. By August 1946, Eisenhower (at this point back in Washington as army chief of staff) officially disallowed the exchange. "Disbursing officers of the United States Army and their agents, wherever stationed, will no longer acquire indigenous currencies of the areas in which military payment certificates are in use."[25] The only solution lay in total withdrawal from the shared currency. The Soviets continued to use the military marks, but American soldiers could not convert them into dollars.

Altogether, American military personnel had sent home at least $250 million (adjusted for inflation, roughly $3 billion) more in money orders than they had earned, which the Treasury had to underwrite from taxpayers.[26] The entire episode created a scandal with an accompanying congressional investigation and proved a lasting lesson in the dangers of loose monetary policy.

It also proved a lesson in the challenges of maintaining a stable currency without a firm commitment from all the parties involved. "If [the Soviets] want to spend more money in Russia, they just issue more money," concluded Clay. The Soviet state "was used to using money as they want to, to meet their government aims." By contrast, "we have to value money as the *property* of an individual." In short, "it's an entirely different concept of money."[27]

The experience with the military marks foreshadowed the challenges lurking within postwar Germany. When Clay called Germany a "disaster-stricken chaotic country," he dramatically understated conditions. *Time* magazine called Berlin a "city of death": "Death stared from the cadavers of mighty buildings; the smashed, charred bones of the Reichstag," it reported. "The battle-broken Chancellery . . . the ruins of the Propaganda Ministry, Foreign Office, Kroll Opera House and almost every other notable Berlin edifice. The stench of death rose too from corpses still rotting under debris, from the corpse-clogged Lützow Canal, from hasty, shallow graves dug in every park and Platz."[28] The *Economist* noted that, "[Germans] sitting in their wrecked houses beside their ruined factories, cold, hungry and parting daily with their last possessions to buy essential needs in a soaring black market, are losing hope." In dark tones, it noted that "this picture of breakdown and collapse is not exaggerated. If anything, it understates the ruin, the misery and the gloom."[29] Clay reported that "the progress of the war in Germany has accomplished, at least on the surface, very much more destruction than most people at home realize."[30]

An American survey done just after the war concluded that Allied bombing had "made 7,500,000 people homeless, killed some 300,000 and wounded 780,000."[31] Subsequent estimates suggest that a little over three million civilians died from the war—from bombing, artillery, crossfire, or murder (although some of these died at the hands of the Nazis themselves).[32] Moreover, during the Yalta Conference, Stalin, Churchill, and Roosevelt had agreed to the "removal" of all Germans south and east of the new German borders. In all, a little over fourteen million Germans were forced to flee, of which two million died in flight, leaving the twelve million survivors homeless and destitute (and largely residing in the American zone).[33] According to the census of 1951, more than 20 percent of Germans in western Germany were refugees.[34]

More than anything, the vast destruction unnerved both Eisenhower and Clay. Eisenhower preferred to avoid Berlin and its constant smell of death. Clay, knowing he would soon be responsible for governing, began to have second thoughts about his promise to Morgenthau. Most important, both realized that they could not, in clear conscience, watch as the Germans died from starvation. As Eisenhower explained, "Germany would soon be starving [and] Americans, of course, would never permit even their former enemies to starve and would voluntarily assume the costly task of feeding them." Clay concurred: "We couldn't let starvation and mass deaths take place, where we were responsible." Indeed, shortly after the surrender, Clay noted that "my exultation in victory was diminished as I witnessed this degradation of [the Germans]. I decided then and there never to forget that we were responsible for the government of human beings."[35]

Finding a way to feed the Germans presented only one of a wide range of critical problems facing the occupation. Because nearly every official in the German state had some Nazi connection, the Allied effort to *denazify* the country created a massive manpower problem. The army found itself forced to take on all kinds of government duties it had not anticipated. "I think that too much of our planning at home has envisaged a Germany in which an existing government has surrendered with a large part of the country intact," Clay wrote in April of 1945. "In point of fact, it looks as if every foot of ground will have to be occupied. Destruction will be widespread, and government as we know it will be non-existent."[36] The problem went beyond government. Clay "quickly began to realize that . . . much of the manpower that had been working [during the war] was now in [prison] camps," and so "our real big job was to get enough work [and] agriculture going to really keep this country alive."[37]

Clay, in particular, hoped to get some guidance from Washington, knowing that Eisenhower would soon return to the States, leaving him in charge. Initially, that meant making sense of JCS 1067 (Joint Chiefs of Staff order 1067), titled, "Directive to Commander in Chief of United States Forces of Occupation Regarding the Military Government of Germany."[38] JCS 1067 provided instructions for military government and embodied Morgenthau's interest in punishing the Germans. It "should be brought home to the Germans that Germany's ruthless warfare and the fanatical Nazi resistance have destroyed the German economy and made chaos and suffering inevitable and that the Germans cannot escape responsibility for what they have brought upon themselves." Of more importance to Morgenthau, military government should "take no steps (a) looking toward the economic rehabilitation of Germany, or (b) designed to maintain or strengthen the German economy." As if to bring the point home, Morgenthau insisted that military government should "take appropriate measures to ensure that basic living standards of the German people are *not* higher than those existing in any one of the neighboring United Nations."[39] The orders did not explain exactly how to deliberately maintain such a specific standard of living for an entire nation.

At the same time, and possibly in contradiction, the occupation should "prevent starvation or widespread disease or such civil unrest as would endanger the occupying forces." Moreover, military government must "assure that German resources are fully utilized"—although the Germans should not see the benefit of this utilization. The occupation should remain certain that "consumption [is] held to the minimum in order that imports may be strictly limited and that surpluses may be made available for the occupying forces." The Germans would pay for their own occupation.

JCS 1067 also called for the decentralization of the political, administrative, and industrial structure of the country. Military government should not only remove or destroy Germany's industrial plant, it should fundamentally restructure the organization of German firms.[40] JCS 1067 therefore gave clear instructions to outlaw "cartels or other [similar] private business arrangements" and "to effect a dispersion of the ownership and control of German industry."[41]

When he finally got his hands on these orders, Clay gathered together his senior staff to look it over. Lewis Douglas, the former director of the

Bureau of Budget under Roosevelt had come to Germany to act as the director of Clay's Finance Division. Douglas had built a strong reputation administering the Lend-Lease program. Clay recruited him almost as soon as he learned of the assignment.[42] The same was true for another member of the inner circle: William H. Draper, Jr. Draper had gone to New York early in life to work as an investment banker but had interrupted his career to fight in World War I. After the Armistice, he returned to banking but decided to remain in the Army Reserve. When World War II broke out, he went back into combat as a regimental commander, serving in the Pacific theater until ordered back to Washington to work in the vast army procurement bureaucracy, where he remained until Clay asked him to go to Germany. Draper possessed both financial and military experience, a rarity that Clay wanted to take advantage of in military government.[43] Draper served as the director of the Economics Division.

The last member of the circle, Robert Murphy, came from the State Department. A career diplomat, he joined the Foreign Service in 1921, and his first assignment took him to Munich, Germany, in the tumultuous years just after the First World War. He arrived at the peak of the economic upheaval caused by the massive inflation after the war—the central event of his first years on the job. He also had what he considered a minor assignment at the time: he was to track the progress of a fringe right-wing candidate named Adolf Hitler. While he met Hitler several times, Murphy did not, of course, realize the impact Hitler would later have. He viewed Hitler as a product of his environment and time. The massive "inflation, more than any other factor, had created a national state of mind which made Hitlerism possible."[44] Murphy functioned as Clay's political adviser.

As the group went through JCS 1067, they were shocked. Douglas, in particular, was perplexed. "This thing was assembled by economic idiots," he said. "It makes no sense."[45] The others agreed. The instructions seemed utterly divorced from the experience of Germany in the 1920s—an experience shared by Clay and Murphy. "Actually, after World War I, Germany was a democratic country in the sense that its officials were truly elected by the German people and were held responsive to an elected parliament," Clay explained. "On the other hand, there was no effort made at that time to bring about any kind of an economic recovery." Indeed, Germany's "first venture, after World War I, into democracy took place at a time of economic want," Clay recalled, "and it therefore appeared to be a failure to the very people who had established it. This enabled the power-grabbing political leaders of the period to come in and take over, to forget about democracy, using the economic chaos as their reasoning."[46] JCS 1067 seemed to ignore all of these lessons.

As they learned more about German life after surrender, their concerns about JCS 1067 grew. By late May, Draper concluded a preliminary survey of German industry and determined that surrender had "brought about a virtually complete stoppage of production as a whole." In the short term, he explained, the goal should be "to get enough production going to avoid chaos, while developing long-range policy to prevent the revival of war production." Already it was clear that "the food and agriculture program is the most vital."[47] As spring turned to summer, the situation became more acute. "The food situation is serious," he reported, "average caloric ration [is] at 927, a starvation diet."[48] Clay ordered military government to draw on the American supplies designated for soldiers to help feed the Germans. But this provided only temporary relief.

At war's end, the agrarian parts of the old German Empire either fell within the Soviet zone or were incorporated into Poland. The Soviets directed any food surpluses in these regions eastward, to feed their own starving population. Western Germany had lost roughly a quarter of the German Empire's arable land, at the same time its population swelled with German refugees. Famine conditions set in. The Allies aimed to provide the population with 2,800 calories per person per day. In reality, they came closer to 1,550.[49] Food riots and strikes consistently broke out in the west, and particularly in the British zone, which had even less arable land and a large, industrial population.[50] On top of that, a large portion of the population had little to do. As Clay worried, "We are carefully studying the potential political danger which exists [in the] fact that people in urban areas are largely idle." The "absence or low level of industrial activity" because of the "war and [policy] directives" meant that most working-class Germans spent their day pondering their empty stomachs.[51]

While Clay focused on the food crisis, others on his staff pursued JCS' instructions to deindustrialize the German economy. In particular, Bernard Bernstein, a former member of Morgenthau's Treasury Department, conducted extensive investigations into German cartels and business. Bernstein had completed his law degree at Columbia University in 1930 and had become counsel in a big New York firm, only to decide during Roosevelt's run for the presidency that he wanted to help the New Deal. He contacted a former professor, Herman Oliphant, who had just become counsel to

Henry Morgenthau in Treasury, about a job. Oliphant obliged, and soon afterwards Bernstein began working in Treasury under Oliphant.

By 1938, Bernstein had become assistant general counsel, working on international monetary affairs. As Morgenthau became increasingly concerned with the growing aggression of Germany and Japan, Bernstein found himself involved in what officials called "economic warfare"—namely, the use of sanctions and other incentives to aid American allies and undermine Nazi and Japanese ambitions. Perhaps his best work came when he conceived of a means for identifying and blocking the assets of foreigners who lived in countries conquered by the Nazis.[52]

Because of his expertise, Bernstein was reassigned to work on currency policy for newly liberated areas.[53] When the North African invasion took place, Eisenhower contacted Treasury to find someone who could be on site to administer the use of the scrip. Morgenthau sent Bernstein, getting him a commission as a lieutenant colonel in the process. As Bernstein flew to England, he struck up a conversation with a superior officer. "You know, this is quite an experience for me," he said. "I've never had any military training whatsoever, never ROTC of any form, I don't even know how to salute."

The officer turned to Bernstein and saluted. "Now, you salute me back," he said. Bernstein did as told. "Now you've had your basic training."[54]

Over the following years, Bernstein continued in Eisenhower's entourage, although everyone knew "Bernstein is recognized throughout the theater as representing [Morgenthau's] viewpoint."[55] As Morgenthau became more involved in postwar planning, he came to rely increasingly on Bernstein to provide information about the military's preparations for governing Germany. In fact, as the postwar planning began in earnest toward the end of 1944, Morgenthau recalled Bernstein briefly to help craft JCS 1067, where Bernstein stiffened the wording in the interest of punishing Germany.[56]

Clay initially appreciated Bernstein's expertise and folded him into the Finance Division, where he began immediately to investigate Germany's large industries as preparation for dismantling them. But soon Clay's growing doubts about the wisdom of a tough peace began to put them in conflict. On a summer afternoon, as they flew over the Ruhr (Germany's industrial center), they surveyed the destruction below. Clay decided to make his point. Pointing downward he observed, "You don't have to worry about Germany ever reviving its industrial power."

"General," Bernstein responded, "I fear that Germany will not only revive its industrial power but it will do it with new plants and new equipment and be far greater industrially than before."[57]

*   *   *

As military government had just begun to take charge, Eisenhower, Clay and the others learned that Harry Truman, Winston Churchill, and Joseph Stalin decided to work out the details for postwar Germany in Germany—at Potsdam, a town just outside of Berlin—from July 17 to August 2, 1945. Having the foreign policy apparatus of the Allies so close gave Eisenhower and Clay a chance to get revisions to JCS 1067. As they met with Truman and his senior officials, they began to warn of the potential for starvation and rioting in Germany. Truman, overwhelmed since becoming president, largely deferred occupation questions to the State Department, now headed by James Byrnes, the former senator and Supreme Court justice who had worked closely with Clay in the Office of War Mobilization. Eisenhower and Clay also raised concerns about the cost of the occupation if Germany could not provide more support for it.[58]

Thus, just months after the war ended, the occupation had already come to a crossroads. Within military government, Clay, Douglas, Draper, and Murphy had concluded that they needed to foster some rehabilitation of German industry and economic power, largely to keep the Germans from starving or at least to reduce the burden on the American taxpayer to pay for the food that would keep the Germans from starving. On the other side stood Bernard Bernstein and his patron Henry Morgenthau, who wanted to dismantle German industry and bring home to the Germans the consequences of their atrocities.

Soon after the conference began, Secretary of War Stimson arrived. His appearance surprised Eisenhower and the others because he was not a part of the official delegation. Unbeknownst to them, scientists in Los Alamos, New Mexico, had successfully detonated the first atomic bomb. Stimson had come to deliver the news personally to President Truman. After he had privately delivered this world-changing message, Stimson had nothing more to do. So Eisenhower invited him to lunch one afternoon and decided to include Clay. Together, on a terrace in Bad Homburg, they spent the afternoon talking over the occupation. Stimson was sympathetic to Eisenhower and Clay's concerns. He referred to his experience as governor-general of the Philippines. He worried that JCS 1067 refused to learn from the military's experiences in the Philippines and in the Rhineland after World War I.[59] In talking over JCS 1067, Stimson "could see no purpose in the deliberate destruction of the German economy," since "he was convinced that its reconstruction was essential to create an atmosphere in which it might be possible to develop a true spirit of democracy."[60] He summarized by saying, "Don't put too much effort in carrying out [your orders] the way they're written . . . you've got a job to do first which is to bring about law and order and the ability of the people in this country to live."[61]

To help give Eisenhower and Clay room to maneuver against Morgenthau, Stimson followed up the conversation by crafting a memo for Truman: "I . . . urge . . . that Germany shall be given an opportunity to live and work; that controls be exercised over the German people only in so far as our basic objectives absolutely require." After viewing the country, Stimson was "satisfied that [Germany cannot survive] unless there is a flow of commerce, establishment of transportation systems, and stable currency." Stimson concluded that the "Russian policy on booty in eastern Germany, if it is as I have heard it reported, is rather oriental. It is bound to force us to preserve the economy in western Germany in close co-operation with the British, so as to avoid conditions in our areas which, in the last analysis, neither British nor American public opinion would long tolerate."[62] In short, the more resources the Soviets took out of Germany, the more the United States would have to pour in. Yet Truman, overwhelmed and distracted by the domestic problems that followed the end of war, filed the memo away.[63]

Clay took Truman's distraction as an opportunity. If Washington could not focus long enough to reverse policy, it would likely not notice if Clay began to take the initiative on his own. As J. Burke Knapp, the economic adviser to Robert Murphy, summarized it, "[Clay] began talking about getting the Ruhr coal mines back to work, getting steel production up, getting the railways running again, getting agricultural supplies so the Germans could start growing their own food instead of relying upon a handout from the occupying forces." Clay also spoke to the basic security needs of the occupation. "You had to put people back to work, because if people weren't back to work they were rioting in the streets, and then you'd have to bring in GI's to knock heads and keep people quiet." As a result, over the coming months, "the Morgenthau plan just faded, because it had been totally impractical for an occupying power to be in a country and try to govern it in the state of disorder that would have resulted."[64]

Still, if the Great Depression taught nothing else, it demonstrated the yawning gap between *wanting* economic recovery and *causing* economic recovery. While Clay could talk about bringing industry back, he had no clear plan for affecting the kind of recovery he wanted. He consulted his advisers, and Lewis Douglas pointed to one issue that quickly rose to the top: "the seriousness of the public debt problem." Essentially all of Germany's "financial institutions" held all their assets "in the form of Reich obligations"—that is, they held bonds issued by a government that had ceased to exist. "The entire credit structure is, therefore, in danger."[65]

Clay asked Douglas to work on a way out of the problem, but, at this point, Douglas had become disillusioned. He did not like the way JCS 1067 seemed limited in focus or, especially, how Bernstein peered over his shoulder, ready to correct him when he did not sufficiently follow the instructions. Eventually he talked it over with Clay. "I've got to go back home and see if we can get these changed," he said. Clay consented. But when Douglas failed to get the changes in Washington he wanted, he quit. Clay needed a new finance director.[66]

The second almost intractable problem had to do with coal. All of Europe needed coal, and Germany had the mines to provide it. But the French hoped to take Germany's coal as reparations, meaning little could be used to offset the costs of importing food. "The Combined Food Committee has estimated an annual shortage of between three and four million tons of wheat for the US, British, and French zones," Draper reported in August. "The immediate problem is to finance the import of about 1,000,000 tons of wheat by selling coal for dollars and not charging it against the reparations account." While the "British have accepted the principle of export from the three zones to finance food imports [the] French are 'reluctant' (but offer no alternative solution)."[67] Murphy tried to help by insisting to his counterparts "that the United States will not finance German reparations as they did after the last war." The default on all those loans to Germany in the 1920s still stung. In short, "food imports to Germany will be financed by exports."[68]

As the summer of 1945 wore on, Clay found some hope of progress. Despite the widespread destruction, military government soon realized that many manufacturing plants in Germany had survived "virtually intact." They remained moribund not because of Allied bombing but because "of coal and transport shortages." Once again, coal became the central issue. "It will be difficult to produce even for the minimum needs of the civilian economy such articles as textiles and shoes, which require coal," Clay's staff reported. "Coal will likewise be required for certain essential food processing."[69]

For his part, Clay could not see making progress on the coal question without making progress on the basic questions of German government. "There can be no real start on restoring the German economy until governmental machinery has been re-established." This included "the levying of taxes, the servicing of the public debt, the re-creation of a sound banking system and restoration of credit." Indeed, he feared that "through it all there stalks the fear of inflation, freezing cold, inadequate housing, and food shortage during the coming winter."[70] Without some form of genuine government, he could not imagine how to tackle these problems.

In the meantime, he still faced problems within his own organization. When Morgenthau learned that Douglas had quit, he pressured Clay to appoint Bernstein as the new finance director. Clay would have none of it. He forestalled the secretary. "[Bernstein] is busy as a bird dog and most useful and most helpful," Clay reported, "but [I] don't think he can handle the big affair."[71] So, over the next months military government remained divided. "[W]e had to wiggle here and waggle there and do the best we could without openly breaking our directive to permit the German economy to begin to function," recalled Draper. "We argued with this one and argued with that one . . . in Washington and in Germany, wherever we had the chance, and bit by bit, we recouped or revised the situation so that it became possible" to work.[72] Clay found some support back in Washington through Assistant Secretary of War John McCloy. "Live with [JCS] 1067," he advised, "but don't live it to the extent that you let [Germany] starve to death or break down with the lack of opportunity for economic life."[73] Still, the efforts remained piecemeal and divided.

Clay finally struck upon a solution when he found someone to replace Douglas. Clay had wanted, from the beginning, to bring another one of his subordinates from War Contracts to Germany: that man was Joseph Dodge. Dodge came from Detroit. Born in 1891, the son of a dirt-poor Quaker artist, Dodge had scrounged for work, tried his hand at everything (including boxing) before he landed a job as a bank messenger. He never attended college; nevertheless, he managed to make his way up the ladder at the bank, moving from messenger to clerical and then bookkeeping positions. After a stint working as a bank regulator, he was asked by the founder of the Bank of Detroit to become an operating officer. At the beginning of the Depression, Dodge steered his bank through a series of mergers and reorganizations that saved it from the widespread panic sweeping the nation. Becoming president of the bank in 1933, he somehow increased its assets and profits despite the economic struggles plaguing the rest of the country. When war erupted, he felt the patriotic tug and went to work for Roosevelt's War Department in 1942, despite being a Republican. He eventually assisted Clay in War Contracts.[74] Dodge was shy. He hated the limelight and felt particularly awkward around those who grew up with privilege and education—ironically, precisely the people his success forced him to circulate with more and more. The *New York Times* later described him as "the man most likely to get lost in a crowd."[75]

Clay had reached out to Dodge almost as soon as he arrived in Germany. "I suppose it would be useless to try to persuade you to get away from your bank [but] if you were interested in the slightest and felt you could take another leave, you could be of great help to us here in determining the extent and conditions under which banking should be resumed in Germany."[76] While Dodge resisted initially, Clay eventually prevailed upon his friend to help in the reconstruction effort. By late summer, 1945, Dodge decided to come to Europe. By the first of September, he had arrived and met the staff.[77]

When Clay appointed Dodge to head the Finance Division, he made clear that he wanted the division reorganized and its direction changed. Clay would be using Dodge to solve "his Bernstein problem," frankly saying that Bernstein "runs a one-man show, all his acts [are] slanted in one direction, no one could work with him, or could follow him."[78] On September 12, 1945, Dodge took action. He reorganized the division to include matters of trade and removed responsibility for dismantling German industry, creating a new section of the legal division for researching the concentration of German industry. Because Bernstein's training was in the law, he seemed the perfect fit. More important, this moved Bernstein out of policymaking and into investigation. Bernstein headed a new "Division of Investigation of Cartels and External Assets" under the Legal Division, which could investigate all it wanted, but held no power to affect industry.[79]

Dodge's reorganization dramatically changed the dynamics, direction, and focus of military government.[80] For one thing, Dodge's loyalty went to Clay alone. In joining the occupation, he solidified Clay's vision among the senior staff working on economic questions. In addition, Dodge was (like Clay) a pragmatist when it came to politics, and he admitted repeatedly in his journal that he had a great deal to learn about Germany, government, and global finance. He "felt like a schoolboy who had been pulled off the street to bat for the Tigers against the Yanks."[81] Like Clay, Dodge had initially felt vindictive toward the Germans ("The recent revelations of what has gone on in German prison camps have shocked the country and I believe they have convinced everyone that the Germans are entitled to little consideration of any kind," he wrote).[82] But also like Clay, after he saw the widespread destruction inflicted upon the Germans, he modified his views. "Try to guess how long it will take to supply common necessities with the complete destruction which has taken place here and its collateral effects on the population," he wrote home. "With the help of a solvent Government, insurance payments, and every other agency, it took 15 years to cover the damage to San Francisco after the earthquake and fire [in 1906]." Meantime, "every city in Germany has the same situation, no Government and no insurance payments or outside help." He then considered some of the very practical problems he saw. "The cost of removing debris alone will be astronomical and take years of non-productive labor for hundreds of thousands of workers. Then what will be the cost of reconstruction and how will that be met? . . . And what type of a generation (physical) will take its place? Now 170 women to 100 men, but the men are old men or boys."[83] After only a few weeks in the country, Dodge had started to think like Clay about reconstructing a decimated nation.

But in accepting the finance directorate, Dodge reoriented economic reform. Dodge was a banker; Bernstein an attorney. This meant, ultimately, that Bernstein saw political economy as a matter of legal constructions that affected business organization. He thought in terms of cartels, trusts, corporate charters, and the laws that enabled these organizations. By contrast, Dodge thought in terms of money, how it flowed, who held it, and how it was used.

Bernstein had cut his policy teeth in the Treasury Department during the 1930s, investigating big industry. Like many New Dealers, he tended to think of the concentration of industry as a threat to democracy.[84] Bernstein accepted the New Deal claim that "as a consequence of this unholy alliance between Hitler and the cartelists, Germany's plans for economic warfare, aimed at ultimate world domination, were expanded." The Germans had used cartels to "penetrate the economy of other nations . . . [which] impaired the production of other nations [and] gathered intelligence and spread Nazi propaganda."[85] Bernstein saw "a conspiracy [in Germany] dating back to some of its Junker and Prussian traditions." This conspiracy included "German heavy industry and German finance." Moreover, he believed that cartels had "helped to a considerable extent in financing the Nazi Party before it came into power."[86]

Dodge was not so sure. He wanted to know for himself how the German economy worked without bringing with him the scars of political fights from the United States. Washington planners had largely ignored questions of finance and left instructions for Clay to work within the existing German banking structure (after seizing Nazi accounts and dismissing Nazi employees).[87] Clay had only asked Dodge to consider the military government's banking policy as a lure to get him to come to Germany.[88] Mostly, Clay wanted a loyal aid. But once he arrived, Dodge decided to put his expertise in banking to work.

Chapter 6

The Army Creates a Plan for Germany

By December 1945, Eisenhower had returned to Washington to become chief of staff of the army. There, he hoped to "shout from the housetops what we are doing to ourselves in the international world and in the occupied areas."[1] Lucius Clay had an ally in Washington and, as it turned out, in London as well. "London is worried over the notion that the [occupation] will result in impoverishment of Germany to a point where German economy and population will become a burden to England," Robert Murphy reported to Clay in January 1946. From the British perspective, Clay had not pursued economic recovery enough. "You people don't seem to mind [economic chaos]," they complained to Murphy. "You are going more and more in Morgenthau's direction."[2]

In the meantime, Congress voiced a different concern. In hearings over appropriations for the German occupation, various congressmen worried that the United States kept Germany alive while the other Allies looted it. "I think it is absolutely inconsistent," argued Albert Engel (R-MI), "to . . . take all the equipment out of the American area and make it unable for [Germans] to support themselves, and then ask us to go and tax our people to feed these people."[3] Clay began sending Draper back to the States to protect the occupation from Congress whenever it considered appropriations. "We managed to wiggle through during the first eight or ten months because our own Army had been bringing with it a food reserve. . . . Those things helped that first . . . ten months."[4] Fortunately, the first postwar winter proved relatively mild. Thus, the first year of occupation did not require large appropriations. But military government could already recognize coming problems with Congress. The sooner Germany could return to self-sufficiency, the better—a fact brought home the next frigid winter when the army had no surplus food. Because American agriculture survived the war intact, the American farmer largely kept Europe alive during the critical shortages of 1946–1947.[5] Food riots and strikes consistently broke out in the west and particularly in the British zone.[6]

As military government actively sought to revive the German economy, the problem of the German currency continually arose to thwart it. The Germans had largely given up on their own money. Farmers would not sell their produce because they didn't want money in return. The same was true for manufacturers. The basic function of money—to foster exchange within the market—had ceased.[7] At the same time, the more military government investigated Germany, the more it discovered that Germany's capital stock had actually grown in efficiency and sophistication between 1936 and 1945.[8] Clay and Draper came to realize that coal only represented one reason industry remained idle; "in view of the fact that you were paying people to work in currency that was depreciating all the time," Clay explained, "there was a very little . . . incentive for people to work."[9]

Charles Kindleberger, a State Department economist assigned to Germany, concluded that, "Everybody had a lot of money. What they really wanted was to be paid in kind." In short, the country fell into a kind of barter system centered on coal. "[The] so-called *Deputat-Kohl* was a truck system in which workers got paid in goods [instead of wages]. A coal mine needing cement would take a truck full of coal and wander around looking for a cement factory. . . . The whole system of orderly exchange broke down."[10] German workers still appeared each day at the factory; they received a paycheck each month; but they produced nothing and could buy nothing with their wages. Of course, the fiasco with the military marks only added to the monetary confusion. In November 1945, Clay asked Dodge to do additional research and formulate a solution.[11]

Dodge began with what he knew: banking. With the help of researchers within his division, he learned that German banks could hold stock in the same companies they lent money to, and that a few large banks held a great deal of equity in German companies. Roosevelt ended this practice in the U.S. with the 1933 Banking Act because it magnified the effects of the Great Depression: as companies went bankrupt their partner banks also failed. The banks could not sustain the double loss of defaulted loans and stock devaluations. Better, it was thought, to keep the two practices— lending and investment—separate.[12] Dodge worked from the same assumption. But as he learned more, he discovered a new reason to worry about German banks. Nazi officials learned to control the banking system. As banks lent and invested in industry, the Nazis used bank finance to determine which companies thrived and which folded. On the surface, the Nazis had not officially nationalized industry, and a capitalist class remained in place. Yet the Nazis controlled their economy just as effectively through the banking structure as if they had nationalized industry.[13]

As he dug deeper, Dodge learned that the commercial banks had secretly also supported Nazi rearmament. When Hitler came to power in 1933, he promised to reverse the depression and revive German economic vitality. He had already rejected reparations as a political matter, as a constant reminder of the "injustice" of the Versailles treaty. Once in power, though, the Nazis turned to Hjalmar Schacht, the central banker in the 1920s, to devise a policy to reinflate the economy. Schacht hoped to initiate significant public spending (in a policy precursor to Keynesian theory). Yet he feared setting off an "inflationary psychosis" that would duplicate the kind of hyperinflation Germany experienced after the First World War.[14]

What evolved came to be called "silent financing." It aimed at expanding business and industrial activity by increasing the money supply, but doing so without letting the public know what was happening. In the short term, this meant circumventing German laws put in place to prohibit inflation, such as a 1926 law that prohibited Germany's central bank, the Reichsbank, from lending more than 400 million reichmarks to the government. From the Nazi perspective, the key lay in manipulating commercial banks to ensure that that they made state finance their priority without revealing their activities.[15] Among other ploys, the Nazis invented an "employment creation bill" that acted like a bond. The government issued it and allowed it to be deposited with a commercial bank. But Schacht then had the central bank buy up the employment creation bills held by the commercial banks. Ostensibly, the central bank had on its books commercial paper (that is, notes from the commercial banks), when in reality it had just underwritten government debt.

Over time, the Nazis instructed commercial banks to buy government debt whenever called upon (although they could turn around and sell this debt to the Reichsbank in most cases). The government never called upon the public for a bond drive or pursued public offerings of bonds. Commercial banks could sell government bonds to individual customers if asked, but were instructed not to make large sales. By the end of the war, a little less than 10 percent of government debt was held by the public; the rest resided in banks.[16]

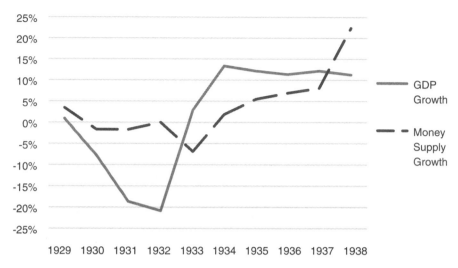

Figure 5. Growth of German GDP and cash in circulation, 1929–1938. Source: "The German Mark," (unpublished), Edward A. Tennenbaum Papers, subject file, box 2, the German Mark, HSTPL, 1: 4–11.

As a result, by 1938, 75 percent of the Reichsbank's holdings and 80 percent of commercial bank deposits were government debt. All of this money creation started to have inflationary effects. In response, the Nazis launched a "second four year plan" that rationed consumer goods and instituted price controls. It also, in essence, set the timeline for war, since the banks could not hide silent financing much longer.[17] When the banks finally ran out of savings, the Nazis passed a further law in June 1939, which placed the Führer at the head of the Reichsbank. From this point forward, the Reichsbank purchased any debt the other banks could not handle, again by printing money. As a result, nearly all the assets sitting in the Reichsbank at the end of the war came in the form of government securities.[18]

But that was not all. To continue the rapid conversion of savings into government securities, the Nazis outlawed hoarding of cash, insisting that Germans immediately deposit any excess cash in the bank. The Nazis also instructed industry, when possible, to use a rudimentary form of direct deposit. Thus, wages could quickly become bank deposits (that would in turn be recycled into government debt). In the meantime, the Nazis passed an additional law that prohibited corporations from hoarding money.

German corporations had to pay profits as dividends immediately or invest the surplus in—no surprise here—government debt.

By 1940, all banks and insurance companies had come under secret government control. In fact, without ever having to publicly offer a bond, the Nazi government managed to redirect nearly all excess cash back to itself to fund a program of massive deficit spending, none of which it ever had to acknowledge publicly. Indeed, even at the end of 1944, when many Germans began to realize defeat had become imminent, inflation did not begin to erupt nor were bank runs common. Once the Allies began crossing Germany's borders, however, the financial system finally broke down. Bank runs became pandemic, and a barter economy emerged in which cigarettes had become the most reliable currency.[19]

In broad terms, the volume of currency in circulation rose by ten times while that in savings multiplied five times. By contrast, the total real volume of wealth in the country plummeted by nearly 70 percent, and the overall productive capacity of the country fell in half, largely as a result of the bombing, shelling, and destruction of German infrastructure. In short, the ratio of wealth to currency dropped from roughly ten to one in 1935, to just over one to one by 1945.[20]

JCS 1067 assumed a compatibility between Nazism and the way German firms organized themselves. Dodge had come to learn that the centralization or decentralization of business had mattered relatively little to actual Nazi power. The banks were the heart of the issue. The Nazis had forced them into collusion and used them to rebuild the German economy and control industry. Ultimately, they held the key role in building the Nazi warfare state. Moreover, the Nazi approach to finance had also *guaranteed* economic chaos at war's end. The illusion of Nazi economic power rested on the "silent" part of "silent financing." Like so much about the Nazi effort, its economic policies had relied upon a lie. By 1938, the lie had already started to leak out, and this fact as much as any other prompted the Nazis fateful decision to become increasingly aggressive in its foreign policy.[21] The dramatic increase in debt and credit fostered by the Nazi government only had positive effects in the short term and as a response to the ravages of depression. Once depression conditions abated, the continued monetary expansion ensured a day of reckoning that would be increasingly catastrophic the longer the policies lasted. By 1945 the reckoning had come.

"I have introduced for consideration of the Finance Directorate several papers which would eliminate the excessive concentration of economic

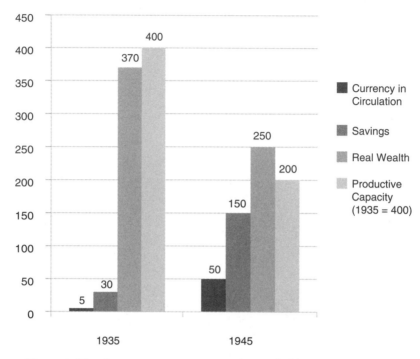

Figure 6. The German economy, 1935 and 1945 (billions of Reichsmarks). Source: Appendix A, Record Group 260 (Finance Division), Box: 909, Appendixes to Colm-Goldsmith Plan, NA.

power in banking and destroy the intimate relationship between German banks and large corporations," Dodge wrote Clay not long after uncovering the system of "silent financing." These "proposals are an integral part of our program to ensure that the German financial hierarchy will never again play any part in disturbing the peace of the world."[22]

Clay responded enthusiastically to Dodge's plan and then circulated it among the other Allies as well as German financiers and bankers.[23] Preventing collusion between banks, the state, and industry seemed far easier than dismantling German industry generally, and (according to Dodge) might achieve the same goal of separating industry from militarist policies. Clay instructed Dodge to work with the financial experts from the other zones. Initially, the Soviets seemed very interested; but the British opposed it, arguing that it contradicted the Potsdam agreement, which stated that Germany should be governed as a single economic entity. Behind this claim, however, lay the British fear that breaking up the Reichsbank might create too much financial chaos at a time when they needed a smooth flow of German money to help pay the costs of their own occupying army. The British had maintained the Nazi system of financial domination but co-opted it to their own purposes. The French liked the plan precisely because they thought it would fail, and supported anything guaranteed to continue economic chaos in Germany.[24]

To break up the centralized banking structure, Dodge hoped to implement a federalized system roughly based on the American Federal Reserve. He wanted each *Land* (the equivalent of a U.S. state) to have its own "head office . . . in the *Land* (no Nation-wide branches)." He wanted to "take bank supervision away from the *Reichsbank*" and create in its place "a coordinating Banking Council of . . . Chairmen . . . and the 'Banking Commissioners.'" While he acknowledged that a unified banking structure had "practical advantages," still he thought it "not good policy" because he aimed to "decentralize a highly centralized banking structure formerly run nationally by the *Reichsbank* and a few big commercial banks which also dominated and actually controlled industry."[25] In short, Dodge hoped to implement the American Federal Reserve system in Germany in order to minimize German industry's vulnerability to domination by the state.

Throughout 1946 the Allies debated the banking plan. By late 1946, Clay managed to get it enacted in the American zone by newly elected German assemblies.[26] The French soon enacted the plan in their zone as well, which led the British to conclude that Dodge's reforms had become inevitable. Thus, in March of 1948, they closed all the remaining branches of the Reichsbank and established their own *Land* banks.[27] The new Bank deutscher Länder proved more centralized than Dodge had initially hoped, in part because even Clay saw advantages in having a national (as opposed to regional) banking structure.[28] However, in most critical aspects it retained Dodge's initial vision. Most important, the new banking system remained independent from the national government (indeed, more so than the American Federal Reserve Banks at that time).[29] In this respect, Dodge closed the "backdoor" that the Nazis had used to dominate industry through the power of finance.

But this still left the monumental problem of inflation, and here Dodge needed help.[30] While he understood banking, he did not have a great deal of experience working in monetary theory or, frankly, macroeconomic policy. He felt out of his depth. Importantly, he decided to reach out to

German experts, not simply because they were available, but also because the United States had never faced such a massive expansion of its currency, whereas Germany (after World War I) had.

His initial efforts led him to Adolf Weber, the brother of the famous sociologist Max. Alfred served as a professor of economics at Munich University. He was generally associated with the Austrian School of Economics and remained a longtime friend of Ludwig von Mises (arguably the most prominent member of that school). Among other things, Austrian School economists emphasized the role of money in the *political* economy. *Economically* speaking, they argued that money only acted as a simple medium of exchange if the overall money supply remained largely constant. However, any state effort that shrank or expanded the overall money supply ended up having unintended and often negative economic consequences. *Politically* speaking, money represented a contract between state and citizen. Inflation, in particular, violated the contract because it devalued the wealth of some, while making it easier for government to pay its debts.

Dodge traveled to Munich on November 21, 1945, where he eventually located Weber in a small apartment, a short distance from campus. Weber was seventy-five years old "but very alert and intelligent." Dodge wanted to talk, but Weber was running late for a lecture. Dodge offered to drive him, Weber accepted, and they both agreed to meet when Weber was finished. When they finally had a chance to talk, Weber recommended a near-total repudiation of the German national debt (the Reichschuld). Germany should, in Weber's view, start over fresh. He also suggested several books that Dodge might consult on the question of government debt and monetary policy, which included a discussion of the Bolshevik refutation of Russia's national debt after the 1918 revolution.[31] Dodge apparently followed up on Weber's suggestion since he had his staff track down an English translation of the Soviet Decree of 1918.[32] "I met the Dr. at noon and talked to him for an hour," Dodge reported. "Asked him to write me his views on what should be done which he agreed to do." Weber "understands English very readily but does not speak it fluently." Dodge told Weber he "was looking for some economists who were also realists" that he, Dodge, might also speak with. Maybe Weber could help?[33]

Over the next weeks Dodge and his staff met with a variety of German experts, some recommended by Weber and others they had found on their own.[34] In general they learned that many non-Nazi Germans had already begun to consider the economic future of the country and, in particular, what to do about the massive volume of currency, price controls, and the lack of production.[35]

Knowing that eventually his research would result in a reform plan not considered by JCS 1067, Dodge returned to the States and made the rounds of the foreign policy establishment in December 1945. At the same time back in Germany, his staff researched how the other military governments viewed German financial reform. "We have made good progress on the lesser financial problems," they concluded. Unfortunately, "No one of the four powers have yet been ready to go to the mat on the basic problems."[36] Dodge hoped to advance on all fronts simultaneously: with Washington, the Germans, and the other Allies.

Eventually, the State and War Departments informed Clay, on January 25, 1946, that he would receive a "mission of not more than four experts, if possible, consisting of representatives of War, State, Treasury, Federal Reserve Board but acting for Military Government."[37] Clay demurred. "I am not enthusiastic over a special mission of technical experts on anti-inflationary measures." Clay's "experience with missions to date is that they do not fit into our Military Government organization and as a result are apt to create misunderstandings." Given the difficulties he had finally overcome with Bernstein, Clay worried that a mission's "loyalty . . . is not to Military Government but to the respective agencies and points of view which they represent." By contrast, he had "every confidence in Dodge's ability to solve this problem insofar as developing a program is concerned, if he can obtain a few experts to continue with Military Government for its implementation."[38]

Washington insisted. A mission was on its way. Importantly, though, Clay's instructions reiterated Dodge's approach. The mission should "analyze programs and results of anti-inflationary action taken by other European countries as well as analyze the German situation."[39] On this point Clay agreed; it helped move the eventual solution outside of the confines of JCS 1067.

Ultimately, Washington sent two experts: Gerhard Colm from the Budget Bureau and Raymond Goldsmith from the Planning Division of the War Production Board. Clay managed to ensure that Dodge remained in command of the mission. As it turned out, Colm and Goldsmith proved able assistants. Each served as an economist within the administration, but, more important, each had fled Germany in 1933 when Hitler took power. While they had since become American citizens, they of course retained their language skills and, particularly in Colm's case, maintained contacts within the academic world within Germany.

In a very broad sense the task of reforming Germany's monetary regime involved two distinct but related tasks: (1) solving the immediate problem of the vast amount of currency; and (2) devising a new policy regime that could ensure that the solution to the first problem endured. Generally speaking, Colm and Goldsmith focused on the first problem; Dodge, Clay, and the staff of the Finance Division on the second.

Colm and Goldsmith arrived in Germany on Ash Wednesday, March 6, 1946. They had made productive use of their time. "[We] really had the plan in essence when we came over on the plane," explained Goldsmith.[40] Having said that, the trip also had a profound emotional meaning for both men. Having lived in exile for thirteen years, they returned to a country they hardly recognized. "The roads are still littered with rubble," Colm wrote his wife. "Everywhere are burnt-out tanks. Iron and steel is twisted into fantastic sculptures." Surveying the scene, Colm couldn't help but "think of the phrase 'God's judgment.'"[41]

Quickly, former friends and colleagues reached out to the two men, sometimes to ask favors, sometimes to offer advice. "We talked to everybody we thought could give us ideas including some well-known professors," explained Goldsmith. They reached out again to Alfred Weber as well as other senior economics professors.[42] In retrospect, the list of people they spoke with became a kind of who's who in German economic policy in the future West German republic. The most famous was probably Ludwig Erhard, the future economics minister and later prime minister of the German Republic, whom they met as they made their way through Bavaria. Perhaps the most interesting trip came around Easter, 1946, when Dodge, Colm, and Goldsmith traveled into the Soviet zone, where they discovered the Soviet approach to finance and budgeting. They were surprised to learn that nearly every locality had started to run a budget surplus under the Soviets, a feat accomplished through heavy taxation and "drastically reduced expenditures"—particularly for welfare benefits. They were all surprised to learn that the Soviets had given the local president a "bonus of 100,000 marks" for bringing the budget into surplus. In the end, though, they realized that the Soviets had essentially siphoned off most of the overhang of currency and placed it in a central fund for use by the occupation.[43]

Despite all the feedback they received, Colm and Goldsmith remained loyal to the plan they had devised on the plane to Germany. The fact-finding missions mostly allowed them "to see whether there was any hitch [in their plan] and whether there couldn't be something done better. Some things, of course, we did do better," Goldsmith explained. "Nobody knew at that time how much currency was around to make close estimates. So we had sample surveys, which our military government introduced into Germany, along the line it had been done by Michigan University during the war."[44] But in essence, their part of the plan remained about the same.

By contrast, the missions had a deep impact on Dodge and the rest of the Finance Division. While Colm and Goldsmith worked together on the details of a currency reform, Dodge paid special attention to the broader policy. As the mission concluded, Dodge had been exposed to roughly thirty distinct policy plans for reforming the monetary situation in Germany. In general, all of the plans focused on three specific issues: "the elimination of the monetary overhang; the solution of the public debt problem; and the equalization of the financial burden."[45] With few exceptions, the Germans they spoke with wanted a broad and permanent (rather than piecemeal) solution. The Germans also hoped that financial reform would allow for an end to price control and rationing, a largely free market (Alfred Weber in particular advocated this point), and an adjustment of exchange rates that would allow Germany to take advantage of international free trade and the Bretton Woods agreements. Most of the planners also felt that no plan would work until after a central government and a central bank could be established (although they conceded this could work at a zonal level if necessary). Finally, each hoped that the plan would include provisions to help those who had suffered most from the war.[46]

Colm and Goldsmith decided on a dramatic currency devaluation as the best way to solve the first problem. They wanted to switch the old currency for a new currency at a ten-to-one ratio. Dodge supported the idea. "One of the objectives," he explained to Clay, was to "reestablish what is known technically as the 'store of value' to money." That is, money had "two values—one as a medium of exchange, and another as a store of value in future purchasing power." The problem was that "under the present situation in Germany . . . any form of goods had more value than money."[47] Echoing Weber, Dodge argued that a stable currency did more than keep prices level. "When money is made scarce, people are willing to receive and to hold money for what it will buy in the future. Like the goods themselves, scarcity adds to its value."[48] When the Nazis flooded the economy with reichsmarks, they undermined this store of value and with it undermined the Germans' willingness to think to the future. It shifted the focus to the immediate rather than the long term, and it undermined the productive power of the economy. "The abundance of money or bank deposits in the hands of many individuals greatly reduces the incentive to work," he explained. "Workers with abundant supplies of cash are reluctant to work merely in order to obtain more cash." In fact, "there are reports of labor scarcities throughout [Germany] despite the fact that productive employment is at a low level."[49]

Colm, Goldsmith, and Dodge agreed that Germany's national debt should be repudiated. The Weimar Republic had labored through the 1920s under the heavy debt burden of war and reparations—a major reason it had collapsed to the Nazis.

This left the really difficult question of how to equalize the consequences of the currency conversion. Colm and Goldsmith feared the way it would unfairly redistribute German wealth. They considered, for example, the consequences on two Germans who had an identical net worth, but one held his wealth in cash and the other in land. A ten-to-one currency devaluation would reduce the wealth of the cash-holding German by 90 percent. By contrast, the land-holding German would not be affected. It seemed unfair to disadvantage cash holders alone.

A Plan for the Liquidation of War Finance and the Financial Rehabilitation of Germany, usually just called the Colm-Dodge-Goldsmith (CDG) plan, eventually landed on Clay's desk in June of 1946. It followed Colm and Goldsmith in calling for a 90 percent reduction in the volume of German currency; the old Reichsmark would be replaced by a new Deutschmark.[50] The plan dealt with the equalization issue in two parts. First, it placed a mandatory mortgage on all real assets (for instance, land, buildings, factories, equipment) so that Germans who held their wealth in real property would suffer along with those who saw their cash holdings reduced. The proceeds of these mortgages would then equalize war losses—that is, support German refugees from areas that now belonged to Poland and the Soviet Union.[51] Second, it placed a capital levy on those who, despite the currency conversion, still had large cash reserves (largely from war profits). Here, again, the money generated would help pay for those Germans suffering from the war.[52] The report allowed for the end of controls on the economy, but chose to leave the timing up to the German government (assuming there was one).

No sooner did Dodge, Colm, and Goldsmith submit their plan to Clay than they left for home (Dodge to his bank in Detroit, Colm and Goldsmith to Washington). Colm accepted a position with the newly created Council of Economic Advisers, established by the 1946 Employment Act. With Colm now close to the president, Clay enthusiastically forwarded the CDG plan to Washington hoping for quick action. He was wrong. The joint State-War-Navy Coordinating Committee (SWNCC—often called "swink") objected to the plan's mortgage and capital levy. In August, the SWNCC informed Clay that he could proceed on the 90 percent reduction in currency, but it asked him to wait on the mortgage and capital levy for a future German government to work out.[53]

Clay was predictably frustrated with SWNCC's compromise. "If we are truly interested in democracy in Germany," he lamented, "and really expect to have free enterprise, then we must face fiscal reform courageously to create a stable fiscal condition which will be conducive to democracy and free enterprise." To him, Washington's inability to approve the plan amounted to a kind of cowardice. "Our failure to act now is a relegation of the leadership which we have exercised in this field and is certain to result in the loss of confidence of our [Allied and German] colleagues. In point of fact, it may well result in our own plan being presented by others. We have now lost four months of study and effort."[54]

The SWNCC wouldn't budge. In particular, the secretary of war, Kenneth Royall, feared that the CDG plan's mortgage and capital levy went beyond economic questions and into social engineering.[55] On some level, Royall had a point. Colm and Goldsmith never denied their interest in social justice through the currency conversion. Dodge, however, came at the matter from a different perspective. In a long letter to Draper, he explained that he had "no disposition to fight for this Plan as against any other which can be proposed and which may be better." The problem was that his plan seemed so much better than "the other half-baked, incomplete, and ineffective operations which have been initiated or attempted in other European Nations." By mid-1946, he had learned a lot about European monetary policy. He had also observed how the rest of Europe dealt with the inflation after the war. "So far they have all left out some essential ingredient which places them in the position of having to do the same kind of thing a number of times."

He shared particular frustration toward the French. "In my talks with the French Financial and Economic Ministries' . . . you will [not] be surprised to know a proposal was made that a controlled inflation in Germany was the proper corrective." The French proposal for Germany followed

Table 1. Recent foreign experiences with monetary and financial reform.

	Austria (billions of shillings)	Czechoslovakia (billions of korunas)	Belgium (billions of francs)	Netherlands (billions of guilder)	Denmark (billions of kroner)
Pre-war level	1	10	30	1.3	0.5
Before Conversion	9	120	100	5.5	1.25
After Conversion	2.5	20	42	1	0.87
Present Level (June '46)	4.2	40	70	2	1.5

Source: Appendix O, Record Group 260 (Finance Division), Box: 909, Appendix to Colm-Goldsmith Plan, NA.

"along the line of meeting their own problems by inflationary means." Dodge wondered "how could you announce [inflation] as a policy [and] control it; if you did not announce it, how could you tie the resulting penalty on the German people directly to the war and avoid the Allies being charged with the responsibility as a result of mismanaging the economy."

More to the point, he told Draper to read a section of the CDG plan that captured Dodge's observations directly. "I suggest that pages 1 to 7, covering Section 1—General Considerations—of Appendix O, may be worth while because they tell why the other plans used in Europe have not provided any satisfactory solutions and why the plan we proposed included what it did."[56] In fact, the CDG plan came in two parts. The first part outlined the blueprint for conversion and equalization. It provided the plan for action. The second part consisted of seventeen appendixes (labeled "A" through "Q"), summarizing the reasoning for the plan. It gave statistical and theoretical bases along with summaries of the various European approaches to inflation. "Appendix O" assessed recent currency conversions in "Belgium, the Netherlands, Denmark, Austria, Czechoslovakia, and Italy." It turned out that as the Nazis had invaded and subdued each of those countries in the early 1940s, they had exported silent financing. As a result, all of those countries faced similar problems with their currency once their economies were liberated from German domination. To solve the problem, each country had undergone a currency conversion that massively devalued its money soon after liberation.[57]

Dodge emphasized to Draper that, "In most of the countries studied, currency and deposits increased to a considerable extent *after* the currency conversion." The reason was simple: "the continuation of budget deficit on current account and the financing of such deficits by borrowing from the banks." In short, a repetition of the basic features of silent financing. This rapidly brought the volume of currency back to where it stood before the conversion.[58]

Germany would almost certainly repeat this pattern in the absence of a broad reform to public finance. Indeed, deficit finance was sure to return because Germany already possessed an established welfare state. "Undoubtedly there are many types of claims which will be made against the German Government as a result of the war," Dodge explained. The equalization parts of the CDG plan aimed to make it easier for a new German government to meet those aims. "We felt obliged to provide a machinery for recognizing these claims and permitting some means of reimbursement," as a principle of good government. However, he wanted this charge to be "an exclusion from [the normal] budgetary operation," because if the new government faced too many obligations, it might resort again to deficit financing and the inflationary approach practiced by the Nazi regime. Repudiating the Nazi war debt followed the same logic. The entire calculus of the debt "had to be considered in relation to the budgetary situation in Germany and the fact that it is practically a welfare economy with a tremendous reconstruction problem to be internally financed.[59]

"We laid great stress on the internal financing required in Germany to meet their problems, including welfare, cleanup costs, rehabilitation, occupations costs, and reparations," Dodge reiterated to Draper. In short, precisely because the German government would have important welfare and war-related obligations moving forward, it needed to capture as much revenue as possible early on and as part of the Allied inspired currency conversion. This way the Allies, not the new German government, would feel any public backlash over the large levies assessed to fund the demands of the welfare state.[60]

While Dodge vented his frustrations to Draper, helping him understand the underlying logic to his approach, it is easy to miss the fact that neither man ever questioned the wisdom of the German welfare state. They took it as a given and largely only worried about how to pay for it in the long run. This aspect remained a hallmark of their political economy moving forward. The question was not *whether* to have a welfare state or large government expenditures. The central question was *how* to pay for it.

*   *   *

"When I said goodbye to Gen. Clay he expressed the hope that you, Ray, and I would talk here [in Washington] to the various people concerned in order to straighten them out on their questions," Colm wrote Dodge soon after taking up his position on the Council of Economic Advisers. "I found that they were looking at the plan as if it were proposed for the United States. They do not realize here the whole background and climate of the European scene."[61]

Dodge agreed. "I talked to both Ray Goldsmith and Ken Galbraith on the telephone and they explained the situation in Washington," Dodge replied. "I will arrange to come down [to Washington] and see what I can do to help it along." By late summer, he made the trip to lobby on behalf of the plan, shuffling from office to office, explaining his reasoning for each of the plan's measures. In the process he gained the support of John Kenneth Galbraith, the well-respected Truman administration economist, who helped champion the plan and move it through the federal bureaucracy.[62]

Still, the plan stalled. Washington officials could not get behind the equalization parts of the plan no matter how much Dodge, Colm, and Galbraith insisted that it would not rebound on American politics. Dodge tried to help by eliminating "the use of the expression 'capital levy' in our proposal," he wrote Clay. He began "using the phrase 'War Lots Equalization Tax.' Of course this is semantics, but in public affairs semantics has its place."[63] As the summer wore on, however, they made little progress.

As the reform plan continued to occupy Dodge and Colm back in Washington, Clay advanced along a different path. He reached out to the British to merge the British and American sectors into a single "Bizonia." Taking effect at the end of July 1946, Bizonia finally created a means for an Anglo-American Joint Export-Import Agency (JEIA). In short, Germany (at least the British and American zones) could (tentatively) enter into global trade again. German businessmen could even leave the country for business purposes (although the first to do so did not leave until November 5, 1947).[64]

"I am sure you have seen the terms of the unification of the British zone and that you will agree it is a real step forward in making possible an earlier restoration of some kind of an economy in Germany," Clay wrote to Dodge in December 1946. "It does not provide sufficient working capital to do the job at maximum speed. However, it makes available for the first time some working capital and that alone gives us confidence in moving ahead."[65]

As Clay saw some progress in Germany, the rest of Europe struggled to recover. As had been true at the end of World War I, the continent desperately needed "working capital" rather than currency. Specifically, Europe needed the goods and materials in short supply everywhere except the United States. Yet few in the United States had an interest in trading for inflated European currency. As a result, economic progress remained piecemeal in Europe and especially in Germany. When the whole continent experienced an unusually cold winter and shortages of every kind at the end of 1946, coal again became the focus of Europe's concern. Germany could provide the coal if the German coal mines could once again become productive.[66]

Yet once again dynamics within Germany followed their own logic. "Railroad engineers would take a trainload of coal and tear into a curve going like hell then slam on the brakes as they rounded the curve so that the stuff would spill out," explained Charles Kindleberger. "Or they'd slow down going through a town and people with shovels would climb aboard and shovel like mad as they'd creep through the town. They'd come out the other end with a train half empty."[67] In other words, the Germans behaved just as Henry Stimson had warned when he talked with Clay and Eisenhower the year before. As soon as they felt that the occupations aimed to exploit them economically, they began to cleverly resist.

Surveying Europe from the Vatican, Pope Pius XII found it difficult to offer hope in his Christmas message to the faithful. "Humanity has barely come from the horrors of a cruel war, the results of which fill her still with anguish," he observed, "and she now gazes with amazement on the yawning abyss between the hopes of yesterday and the realizations of today, an abyss which the most persistent efforts can bridge over only with difficulty." Barely a year later, the "joyous and exuberant intoxication has vanished." In its place remained an awareness of the "inevitable difficulties . . . in all their crudity."[68]

Chapter 7

A German "Miracle"

While restoring Germany's domestic economy remained a top priority for Lucius Clay and Joseph Dodge through 1946, this effort raised a second important question: how would Germany, in turn, fit into the global economy? The Bretton Woods conference had aimed to establish "a stable and orderly system of international currency relationships."[1] Yet Henry Morgenthau had operated from the same assumptions at Bretton Woods that he used for JCS 1067. In each case, he assumed (following his adviser Harry Dexter White) that European countries (and especially Germany) would be in a much better economic position after the war than, in fact, they were. Moreover, he assumed that Europe (and particularly Germany) would likely exploit American generosity, and so he remained guarded.[2]

Almost as soon as the war ended the world experienced what came to be called "the dollar gap." Global demand for American goods exceeded American demand for global goods to the tune of $7.8 billion in 1946 and $11.6 billion in 1947. By running trade deficits with the United States, other countries could never earn extra dollars to build a safe reserve. As a consequence, European countries were forced to ignore the Bretton Woods agreements and impose exactly the kind of import and exchange controls the agreements had hoped to make obsolete.[3] The Bretton Woods agreements had unintentionally recreated the same unstable dynamic that existed at the end of World War I, where Europe once again could only get working capital by borrowing or begging from the United States. Increasingly, Washington officials realized that American aid, grants, and loans would have to continue for some time, a realization that came to its apotheosis in the Marshall Plan.[4]

Harry Truman appointed George Marshall as his secretary of state in January 1947, at the moment Europe's economy had reached its nadir. Inflation ravaged nearly every nation there. Production lagged. The continent increasingly divided between the Soviet Union and America. The brutally cold winter that stretched from the end of 1946 and into 1947 added to the misery. Over the next months, Marshall saw for himself the situation as he traveled to Russia and back, stopping along the way to meet with leaders across the continent. He also spent six grueling weeks in Moscow negotiating with the Soviets over Germany, European borders, and a host of other issues—none of which he managed to resolve. On his return trip, he stopped in Berlin to talk again with Clay. What ultimately emerged from this experience was the outline of the Marshall Plan for rebuilding Europe.

While a great deal can be (and has been) said of the Marshall Plan, from Clay's perspective Marshall largely took the lessons learned by military government and applied them broadly to Europe as a whole.[5] We "had already started a Marshall Plan for Germany," Clay explained.[6] Two particular lessons seemed to impress Marshall.

The first had to do with the way regions of Germany had specialized in the German economy. When the country was divided into zones, the American zone suffered particularly because it depended on the resources from the other zones. Thus, an early focus for Clay came in getting the other Allies to treat Germany as an "economic unit." The Marshall Plan largely applied the dilemma of the German zones to all of Europe. Those countries that accepted American aid had to think of the continent (or at least the western half, as it turned out) as an "economic unit" and open up trade between themselves. Most important, this meant including Germany in future trade patterns.[7] The plan caused a "structural adjustment" between the nations of Europe, allowing each to take advantage of its trade specialties.[8]

Second, the financing of the Marshall Plan also followed the experience of the occupation. As Dodge pointed out in a radio address in support of the plan on CBS radio: "We are not sending so much of our money abroad as we are sending our goods." Aid to Europe consisted of American products paid for by the U.S. government. European governments then received the goods and sold them to their own public for their own currency. Our "money is being spent here and the goods are going abroad" explained Dodge. European governments could then take the proceeds of the sales and invest their own currency in their own economies.[9]

But the central point, shared by Marshall and Clay, was that recovery in Europe meant access to goods abroad, not more spending by the governments of Europe. "Monetary stimulations within Germany are of no help, for the goods the extra money would buy, no matter how soundly based or tightly controlled the money might be, are simply not available," Clay explained. What was true of Germany proved true of Europe generally. Currency and inflation remained closely tied to access to American goods. Without access, or at least the promise of access, currency reform would not provide for industrial recovery. "No new German currency which we might introduce," he explained, "would serve as a full stimulation unless there were either goods immediately available for which that money could be spent or unless there were a sound political structure to inspire a confidence in the holder of the money that government will make sure he will one day be able to buy at an agreed value the things he needs now, but which are not now available."[10]

This form of financing had the advantage of relieving European countries of the need to deficit finance. Indeed, with this in mind, Marshall Plan aid required countries to balance their budgets as a precondition of aid. It therefore acted to reduce inflation while relieving European countries of some of the difficult spending decisions they might otherwise have faced under a balanced budget. The Marshall Plan was "actually . . . not a plan," explained Dodge, "and it is not a formula." Rather, much as military government had come to approach Germany, the plan was "a statement of fundamental principles which should control our attempt to aid Europe." It hoped to solve "the most serious obstacles to an effective reconstruction . . . in the internal [that is, domestic] economic, financial, and political conditions of the foreign Nations which seek our aid." In essence, Dodge wanted America to understand how the Marshall Plan fit into a broad understanding coming out of the occupation, that global reconstruction after the Second World War needed to reverse the order of reform that had followed the First World War. Woodrow Wilson had hoped for political reconstruction ahead of economic reconstruction. Now, policy would preference the restructuring of internal economies to facilitate global economic integration. Marshall aid simply encouraged the rest of Europe to do what military government aimed to accomplish within Germany.[11] It helped overcome "a universal reluctance and delay . . . in applying completely obvious and necessary remedies . . . [to] inflation; nationalization programs, and their growing bureaucracies; large budget unbalances; constantly depreciating currencies; black markets; low production efficiency; loss of incentive; exchange restrictions; and unrealistic currency exchange rates." In short, all of the things Dodge saw in Germany, he saw in the rest of Europe, and the Marshall Plan gave the incentive to end them, not just for Germany, but for the continent. "What Europe needs is better Government housekeeping; increased production; the maximum, efficient use of its own resources; and the modification or elimination of those factors which inhibit enterprise and investment, discourage working effort, and multiply frustration."[12]

* * *

As the development and implementation of the Marshall Plan occupied foreign policy officials, the need for currency reform became increasingly obvious to Clay and, because of Marshall aid, easier to implement. German currency remained essentially worthless; until the basic problems identified in the CDG plan had been addressed, the Marshall Plan could not accomplish the central aim of integrating the German economy with that of the rest of Europe. Clay continued to press for the reform, meeting surprising support from the Soviets, who remained open to a currency conversion since its early suggestion—provided they had a copy of the printing plates. "Soviet representatives have now offered . . . to place the proposed printing in Leipzig [in their zone] under a quadripartite committee composed of one representative of each of the occupying powers," Clay informed Washington. "In theory, it is difficult to argue against this proposal as printing in Leipzig would simplify and expedite the entire printing problem." Yet, once burned, twice shy. The "experience with Allied military marks makes me doubt the advisability of accepting Soviet proposal. In spite of Allied Control Council agreements, we have never received any information as to the total amount of Allied military marks printed and/or issued in the Soviet zone." He feared that even "a quadripartite committee could not in fact check the printing of money in Leipzig."[13] Taking a page from the Soviet playbook, Clay made the same offer in reverse. He offered to make the Staatsdruckerei (the German government printing office) into a quadripartite enclave. The Staatsdruckerei lay just inside the American zone in Berlin. But the Soviets declined, insisting that any new currency must be printed in the Soviet zone if Clay wanted the Soviets to participate.[14]

The French also remained wary of the currency conversion. "The French have always liked your plan," Clay wrote Dodge early in 1947, "their only worry being that it is too good a plan for Germany."[15] In general, they saw no reason to relieve the Germans from the problem of inflation at a time when their own economy suffered from it. They also disliked the part of the CDG plan that would relieve the German government of its war debts, hoping once again to financially burden future generations of Germans as had been the case after the First World War. Through 1947 they declined to move forward on a currency plan.[16]

Yet with the Marshall Plan moving forward, Clay understood that the "need for new currency becomes more urgent each day" so that Germany could take part in the plan to integrate into the European economic community. In August 1947, he cabled to Washington that "Present economic controls which have miraculously held in the face of a worthless currency are now being undermined at an accelerated pace. The dam may break at any time." So long as the Germans had nothing to buy, maintaining controls remained relatively easy; once American goods flowed into Europe, the economy would become entirely illicit. The problem took on added urgency because once the United States committed to the currency conversion, it would "still take several months to complete currency printing." The CDG plan estimated that having enough new deutsche marks would take four to six months (in reality it took almost nine).[17] Despite Marshall aid, "we can still make only token progress toward industrial revival and self-sufficiency until a respected currency medium can restore incentive to worker and manufacturer alike."[18]

The SWNCC agreed and quietly began printing the new currency back in the United States. Designated "Operation Bird Dog," the presses ran day and night to churn out enough new deutsche marks to cover one-tenth of existing Reichsmarks. While Clay hoped to keep the operation secret, eventually word leaked. By December, the Soviets began to ask about American plans.[19] In the spring of 1948, a stack of crates marked for Barcelona via Bremen, Germany, left New York. In reality, the crates were destined for vaults of the Reichsbank in Frankfurt. They contained 23,000 steel cases, weighed 1,035 tons, and contained billions of new deutsche marks. It took eight hundred army trucks to deliver the cash. And it all happened without anyone taking notice.[20]

Around Christmas, 1947, Marshall, Clay, and Robert Murphy (Clay's political adviser) met in the home of Lewis Douglas who, after leaving military government, became the American ambassador in London. The meeting included their British counterparts: Ernest Bevin, the British foreign secretary, and Brian Robertson, the British military governor in Germany.

Clay and Murphy urged action on the currency reform in Bizonia. Further delay made little sense from their perspective.

Marshall and Bevin hesitated. Perhaps they should give the Soviets and French one last chance to join the American plan? Clay and Murphy consented, but only on condition that if they could not get agreement soon, the currency reform could go ahead in Bizonia by summer. Marshall and Bevin concurred.[21]

In January 1948, Clay made a final offer on currency reform to his counterparts in military government. This began a lengthy negotiation over the details of the reform that showed initial hope for consensus. The French finally seemed ready to move forward, and it appeared that currency reform would soon take place at least in the three western zones. By the spring, it became clear that the Soviets would not join in the plan. The other three Allies decided to move forward on their own, a move that proved the final straw in creating a lasting division of Germany into two nations.[22]

Western Germans, of course, had a deep interest in these plans. Soon after the creation of Bizonia, the Americans and British authorized a German Wirtschaftsrat (economic council) to advise military government and, on a limited basis, provide economic policy for the Bizone. By June 1947, the council created the Sonderstelle Geld und Kredit (Special Office for Money and Credit) with the express purpose of influencing the currency conversion. The group began meeting near Frankfurt in October 1947, where it developed its own ideas about currency conversion. Most important, it became a platform for the ambitious Ludwig Erhard.[23]

Born near Nuremberg in 1897, Erhard had aspired to become a symphony conductor, only to realize he was at best a mediocre pianist. His family owned a textile shop, and it seemed more likely he would end up continuing in the family business, until World War I took him into action in Ypres, where he was severely wounded. To pass the time during a long convalescence, he studied economics. Eventually, he earned an appointment as the head of the Nuremberg Economic Research Institute, only to be dismissed when the Nazis seized power in 1933 (Erhard refused to join the party). In the last months of the war, he began work on creating a path for the postwar economy, distinct from the Nazi aberration. His background and freedom from Nazi association made him ideal for work in the occupation. This work in turn led to a long public career in Germany after the occupation ended. Later in life, he admitted the value of his work in the occupation by explaining, "I am an American discovery."[24]

Many of the same issues raised by Colm, Dodge, and Goldsmith reemerged in the Sonderstelle. As had been true for the CDG plan, currency devaluation remained the least controversial of the issues. Rather, what to do in addition to the conversion ended up occupying much of the discussion. In particular, Erhard had grown deeply fatigued with price controls. The continuing instruction from the Allies to hold the line on prices left a feeling that anything that interfered with the normal role of prices in a market economy smacked of totalitarianism.[25] The key lay in getting markets to function again, not simply for economic but also for political reasons. One "can argue that the decisive moment is not the quantitative reduction in the amount of currency, but rather the restoration of the money function," wrote a member of the economic council. By early 1948, a growing number of Germans began to argue that prices should be decontrolled along with the currency conversion.[26]

In the meantime, as rumors began to swirl of an imminent currency conversion, German businesses began to repair factories and machinery and bring back to work their most skilled employees. In addition, they began to hoard raw materials and semi-finished products. Their strategy fit the logic of the moment. Knowing that the old currency would soon be devalued, it made no sense to sell goods for the old currency; instead, the goal became to stand ready to rush to market as many goods as possible immediately after the new currency was introduced. That way firms could capture market share.[27]

Erhard began to use his position on the Sonderstelle to push the Allies into moving faster toward currency reform. In a meeting with military governors on March 15, 1948, he urged them to go ahead with currency reform with or without the Soviets. He explained that currency reform was only a first step in the larger project of returning a functioning market to Germany. The Soviets, he reasoned, could perform a currency conversion, but would not return the economy to a free market. Erhard wanted Germans to see a clear distinction between ideologies; only with a comparison could they stop thinking salvation lay in the fully planned economy of the east.[28]

In April 1948, Erhard moved from the Sonderstelle Geld und Kredit to become the chairman of the Wirtschaftsrat. From his new position, Erhard had a more powerful bully pulpit from which to pursue his plan for freeing the market at the earliest possible moment.[29] With that in mind, he drafted a proposal to end the price controls which he brought to the next bizonal administration meeting. There, he demanded that military government implement his proposal at the same time as currency reform. Again, he reiterated his views that currency reform represented only a first step. Price controls needed to end so a fully free market might return. Anything that interfered with the normal operation of prices not only slowed economic growth, but also violated the implicit agreement between the state and citizenry.[30]

To a large extent Erhard preached to the choir when he spoke to Clay. The CDG plan had recommended decontrol of the economy soon after the currency conversion. If Clay could have found a way out of the controls, he already would have. The problem, from Clay's perspective, was the British. In 1948, their economy also remained under price controls and involved rationing. It would be particularly embarrassing for the British to see Germany's economy return to normal before its own. Out "of sympathy with Great Britain, operating under controls and a victor in the war, I would have found it very difficult to have tried to force approval" for removing them.[31]

Erhard also preached to his fellow Germans. The "need is urgent . . . [for] the restoration of sound monetary conditions," he explained in April 1948. For too long "our economy has been deprived of any standards of value and comparison . . . [we] are living in a world of fiction." When the conversion came, it would undoubtedly "expose the stark realities of our social and economic life clearly and, if you like, brutally." Yet, this "process also has its own healing qualities." After the currency reform had taken place, "we must again provide more scope for the human will and human activity both in production and consumption and then automatically allow the competitive spirit to develop." The system of price controls, what he called the Nazi "price freeze," had really just "provided a cover for a state policy that was deliberately creating chaos. . . . [It] was the logical forerunner of a state-controlled economy." By contrast, market price-making "is absolutely essential if there is to be a free exchange of goods with the rest of the world on a firm currency-exchange basis."[32]

Based on his position, Erhard assumed he would play an active part in executing the currency conversion. In reality, Clay kept him in the dark and out of the decision-making process. He wanted to keep the exact day of the exchange as secret as possible. On the morning of June 15, Clay and his counterpart Brian Robertson, the British military governor, called Erhard to their office. Erhard waited while they talked. And talked. They finally emerged at two o'clock that afternoon. They had been fighting with the French. But the matter was now resolved. Currency conversion would be announced on the 18th of June. It would be implemented on the 20th.[33]

Erhard was deeply upset. Why had they waited so long to tell him? Why hadn't they given him more time? The next day, Erhard and other German economic leaders learned more details. Then on the 18th the reform was announced. Erhard made a decision. He had a regularly scheduled radio show that afternoon. On his own, without telling military government, he took to the airwaves and claimed credit for the currency conversion, announcing the end of all price controls at the same time.[34] "We were well on the way to regimenting democracy to death and reducing the fundamental democratic rights of our people to a mere shadow," Erhard explained. "Only when these rights find expression again in a free choice of occupation, in the freedom to change jobs and, above all, in freedom for the consumer, can we expect the German people to play the same active part in political affairs as before."[35]

Erhard understood that his move put Clay in a difficult bind. If he reversed Erhard's policy, it would undermine the credibility of the fledgling German state. But leaving it in place put the British in a very awkward position. Most of all, Erhard had been insubordinate. Clay called Erhard to his office immediately and gave him a severe tongue lashing. But he did not ask Erhard to rescind his statement. Despite official protests, the British never tried to restore the controls in their zone either. Years later, and in retrospect, Clay mused that "the way it happened was the very best way for it to happen."[36] In reality, much had gone as military government anticipated. Near the end of 1947, the Finance Division had realized that Germans would "engage themselves in work and planning that may be fruitless" since Clay planned to act unilaterally. Still, the Finance Division felt "Germans engaged in these studies should be able to produce quite independent ideas on the subject. We can then use such of their proposals as seem logically to fit in with our ideas of the requirements."[37]

When currency conversion finally came, military government still worried that the Germans might not embrace it. In particular, the Finance Division worried that moving forward with currency reform without taking up the question of "equalization"—that is, ensuring a bit of social justice—might undermine the reform efforts. Still, "if Military Government must choose between the two objectives," concluded the Finance Division, "it is obvious that the former must have primacy. Without economic recovery, without elimination of inflation, concessions to equity as regards the past will be of little weight as against the inequities which will spring up currently [and] in the future." Indeed, while failure to perform equalization "may lead to weakness of future governments," failure to achieve economic recovery "leads to strikes and riots, and may lead to the downfall of present governments. The former can be ameliorated by equalization schemes and property levies. The latter can be cured only by eliminating inflation. Thus, apart from our immediate obligation to prevent waste of the taxpayer's money, we have an immediate coterminous obligation to prevent chaos."[38]

Indeed, in the months leading to the currency reform, military government began looking nervously to the postconversion policy regime. "History is full of unsuccessful currency reforms," the Finance Division warned Clay. "The first currency reform, the exchange of *assignats* for *mandats* during the French Revolution, was unsuccessful. More recently, both in Japan and in Austria, an exchange of currency brought no lasting benefits. New pieces of paper went the way of old pieces of paper, the new currency came into as much disrepute as the old." Currency reform functioned like the Marshall Plan. It could reset the economy and help get rid of the consequences of bad decisions in the past. But only "the introduction of sound monetary policies in the future" could guarantee lasting stability and steady growth.[39]

The key lay in two policy measures "generally recognised [sic] to be the foundation of a sound monetary policy." First, "government expenditures must be balanced by revenue from taxation"—in short, governments must run balanced budgets. Second, "money created by the banking system must go solely into short-term financing of production, not into long-term investment"—and especially government bonds.[40] The Finance Division worried that facts "lead to some pessimism as to the prospects of a successful financial reform." Much as Dodge's original survey of currency conversions had shown, "fiscal policy will for the first months be a danger rather than a possible means of overcoming inflation." With less currency, tax "revenue will decline substantially," while occupation costs, "the biggest element in the budget, will be more or less inflexible." In the meantime, "the pressure on the government to provide money which can no longer be found easily elsewhere will grow to an extent not yet experienced," especially in "the British and French Zone (by no means counterbalanced by the surpluses in the U.S. Zone)."[41] Despite the overall pessimistic assessment, there remained some reason for hope. "Dr. Ludwig Erhard, the new Director . . . for Economics . . . has come to very similar conclusions."

Indeed, "Military Government would be well advised to agree with the general line followed by [Erhard and] the German Bizonal Economic authorities."[42]

When currency conversion finally occurred, what followed surprised everyone. Previously empty shelves suddenly filled. Manufacturers began to finish their semi-finished products and rush them to market. The combination of a new, stable currency and decontrolled prices signaled to firms across West Germany that the economy had returned to normal. "The immediate benefits of currency reform have been unbelievable," Clay wrote in September 1948. "The result is that Germany is going back to work, and in western Germany particularly the people on the street visibly have taken a new hold on life."[43]

Soon afterward, a sudden rise in prices tempered some of Clay's enthusiasm. Between June and October, prices in the American zone rose at an annualized rate of 33 percent, and producer prices rose even faster, at roughly 45 percent.[44] As predicted, the short-term pressure to open up government spending became intense. By mid-October Erhard in particular faced growing criticism. His own party called for his resignation. But at precisely that moment prices stabilized.[45] For his part, Clay decided to trust Erhard's views that price controls remained unnecessary as long as the volume of money did not increase. "Of course an immediate buying spree resulted" from the currency reform as the "consumer-starved population rushed to spend its new marks." But while his "own staff became apprehensive of runaway inflation," Clay remained convinced that there "was insufficient money in circulation" to allow it to last long. Moreover, "raw materials were arriving regularly, production was increasing rapidly, and I was certain that with the exhaustion of the initial issue of currency the buying spree would stop."[46]

The French, however, continued with a controlled economy in their zone, despite participating in the currency reform. As a result, policymakers had a clear comparison of the effects that followed the removal of price controls. The results were unambiguous. As the months passed, a large productivity gap appeared between the Bizone area and the French zone, prompting French officials to bring their zone's policies in line with the British and Americans within the year.[47]

The "economic miracle," as it came to be called, did not dominate the headlines through the middle of 1948. As the plan for currency conversion advanced, the Soviet Union informed Clay that rail traffic in and out of

Berlin needed permission from the Soviets. In early April, they began to stop all traffic, only to allow it again later that month. When the Allies announced the currency conversion in June, the Soviets made a critical announcement. "Citizens of Germany!" declared the Soviet military governor, Marshal Vasily Sokolovsky, "the American, British and French monopolies . . . are dismembering Germany and striving to weaken her by subordinating her economy to their domination." As a result, currency "issued in the Western zones . . . will not be permitted to circulate in the Soviet zone." To prevent the mingling of currencies, "the Soviet Military Administration in Germany will take . . . necessary measures."[48] In short, the blockade had returned. The British, French, and mostly the Americans responded with a massive airlift to supply western Berlin with food, coal, and other staples. The blockade lasted until the following April, when the Soviets again allowed rail supplies to enter West Berlin.[49] Thus, currency conversion marked the end of any hope for a united Germany. For the duration of the Cold War, the country would be the symbol of the division between East and West.[50]

The experience in Germany profoundly affected Clay, Dodge, Draper, Murphy, and by extension Eisenhower, who was watching from Washington. Collectively, they developed an approach to political economy that linked deficit spending and inflation to a moral conviction that both perpetuated a lie. Government deficits provided a short-term economic boost (perhaps necessary in depression) but at the expense of long-term stability. Moreover, they also associated deficit spending with the slippery slope of state encroachment into private life. The disease of inflation led to a series of government steps to treat its symptoms: price controls, rationing, economic planning, domination of the country's central bank, and ultimately, militarism. The state took each step in an effort to help consumers, yet in the long run it enslaved them. The Nazi experience with silent financing warned of this eventuality.

One of Clay's economists back in Germany summarized the views of the occupation. "Keynes and others proclaimed the virtues of the printing press as a solution to unemployment. At first their arguments seemed heretical, then paradoxically true, and finally commonplace verities." By 1949, "most economists abandoned the nineteenth century's blind faith in monetary stability for an up-to-date but equally blind faith that monetary stability did not matter." Germany proved the potential folly of embracing Keynesian economics.[51]

When Clay left Germany in May 1949, he returned to the United States to near universal acclaim. "The United States may well be proud," wrote the *Washington Post*, "that it can produce at this critical moment . . . soldiers of the stamp of General Clay."[52] The *New York Times* concurred. Clay "never wavered in his own belief that our first aim is democracy." He impressed upon the Germans "the idea for which we fought."[53] For most observers, his departure marked an ending: an end to occupation, an end to military government, an end to the view that Germans were incapable of democracy. A year after returning home, Clay published his memoir, *Decision in Germany*. "We had much advice from those who professed to know the so-called German mind," he wrote, recalling the orders he had received soon after arriving in Germany. "If it did exist, we never found it; German minds seemed to us to be remarkably like those elsewhere."[54]

About that same time, the journalist Walter Lippmann summarized the situation in Germany. The "policy of the United States in Germany has not been formed or managed by [Secretary] Byrnes, [his successor Secretary] Marshall, or the State Department, but in fact by General Clay." This was not to say that Clay had "usurped" their power. "If he has acquired power . . . it is because there has been no one in Washington . . . who knew enough about Germany to argue with General Clay." In short, "Our German policy is so intimately bound up with General Clay . . . it would be a rash man indeed who thought he could carry on what General Clay has begun."[55]

Chapter 8

Political Progress in Japan— and Economic Decline

In broad terms Japan had closed itself off from the external world starting in the late 1500s for fear that Europeans might introduce muskets, cannons, and Christianity, upsetting its existing power structure and culture. The ruling Tokugawa shoguns issued a series of decrees—eventually termed *sakoku* (or "closed country")—that sealed the island kingdom from the rest of the world. While total isolation never occurred, the decrees nevertheless managed to work as intended, secluding Japan from its surrounding world for centuries.[1]

Sakoku, however, could not last forever in an age of growing globalization. The cataclysmic event happened on July 8, 1853, when the American commodore Matthew Perry arrived in Tokyo harbor with two steamer gunboats and two sailing vessels. From his bridge aboard the *Susquehanna*, Perry delivered a message from President Millard Fillmore to the emperor, proposing "that the United States and Japan should live in friendship and have commercial intercourse with each other." Fillmore promised that the "Constitution and laws of the United States forbid all interference with the religious or political concerns of other nations." Instead, "I have sent Commodore Perry, with a powerful squadron, to pay a visit to your imperial majesty's renowned city of Edo [asking] friendship, commerce, a supply of coal and provisions, and protection for our shipwrecked people."[2]

The word "religion" created the greatest difficulty for the translators. For outsiders, the Japanese practiced something they recognized as religion. But to the Japanese, these practices did not include the competition for souls (among other things) indicative of Western faith. They simply had no equivalent term, a fact that, as much as anything, symbolized the gap between Japanese life and the Western world.[3]

The Japanese did, however, understand the meaning of "powerful squadron." When Perry entered the harbor, the Japanese fired warning shots and made signs they might engage the Americans. Perry needed only to brandish his superior firepower to get the Japanese to back down. Quickly, the ruling shoguns realized that they had little choice in becoming trading partners and signed what came to be called "unequal treaties" with the United States—and later Great Britain, Russia, and France. These agreements had little mutuality: the Western powers set the tariff rates going *into* Japan, prohibited the Japanese from legal action against Westerners for crimes committed in Japan, and reserved the right to build and own warehouses and other dwellings in Japanese ports.[4]

The humiliating encounter created massive political upheaval; yet Japan managed to avoid a total social breakdown through a remarkable political realignment known as "the Meiji restoration"—a term that explains both the "restoration" of the emperor to the center of political power, as well as a period of revolutionary reforms that sped Japan into modernity. By 1890, Japan had a new constitution, based roughly on the Prussian model, including a bicameral parliament (the Diet). At the same time, the emperor remained the head of state and embodiment of Japanese cultural identity. Over the next decades Japan managed to shed itself of the unequal treaties and rapidly industrialized its economy into the "workshop of Asia" (surpassing America's growth rate—but not size—by the early 1900s). It also mimicked Europe's great powers by building a nascent colonial empire in East Asia. Beatrice Webb, the British Socialist, said what many thought when noting how, by 1911, the Japanese had surpassed the West—they "shame our administrative capacity . . . shame our inventiveness . . . shame our leadership."[5]

While much can be said of the dramatic events of this critical episode in Japanese history, several elements of the restoration mattered more for the occupation that followed World War II. While the Meiji Constitution created a kind of parliamentarian government, the military remained accountable only to the emperor. As a result, it increasingly acted in its own interests and became, in a sense, the tail that wagged the dog. The advent of the Great Depression exacerbated this tendency because it discredited the military's potential rivals for political influence: the business class and political leaders, both of whom had bet on the success of Woodrow Wilson's vision of free and open competition along with democratic reforms. As Japan fell into depression and watched as the United States and

Britain—the models of democracy and free trade—erected trade barriers seen as lethal to Japan's economic survival, right-wing militarists argued with some justification that Wilson's vision had been a sham.[6]

A group of sailors assassinated Prime Minister Inukai Tsuyoshi in 1932 in a failed coup attempt; soldiers assassinated two former prime ministers in 1936 in another bloody but failed coup attempt. While the emperor and general staff did not support the rebels, Emperor Hirohito (typically called Emperor Shōwa in Japan) failed to act decisively against his military, and as a result militarism gained political power. While the emperor complained at each critical moment and prodded his advisers about how to slow the militarists, he refused to directly confront them. Whether he feared that he too might fall to assassins or whether he felt the emperor should not second-guess his own army, until he finally forced the nation to surrender in 1945, he remained largely a bystander to the disastrous events that ended in Hiroshima and Nagasaki.[7]

The Japanese intellectual Masao Maruyama captured this curious dynamic by suggesting that while Japan seemed like "ideal soil for the concept of dictatorship . . . in fact it was hard for this concept to take root," since "the essential premise of a dictatorship is the existence of a free, decision-making agent [as the dictator], and this is precisely what was lacking in our country: from the apex of the hierarchy to the very bottom it was virtually impossible for a truly free, unregulated individual to exist."[8] Instead, Japan experienced a "system of irresponsibility"—a system in which all policymakers felt constrained regardless of their role in the hierarchy; a system that followed "a vast accumulation of illogical decisions" ultimately leading to war. At almost every turn in the policymaking process, all were "driven ahead, as if by some invisible force."[9]

*   *   *

Back in the United States, plans for postwar Japan began just three months after the attack on Pearl Harbor. The planners included the few people who had expertise in Japan's history and culture—former State Department officials, academics, and Americans who had spent time there. Some of the group saw Japan's attack in racial terms, arguing that the Japanese had no rational war aims beyond a thirst for blood. Others saw the advent of war as a tragedy in which militarists hijacked a promising young democracy. In general, though, the group tried to take seriously the potential economic and political causes of the war in thinking about what to do after the war.[10]

Once Treasury Secretary Henry Morgenthau had successfully forced a revision of America's postwar German policy, however, it became increasingly apparent that Japan could not receive better treatment than Germany. As the planners for postwar Germany redrafted their instructions based on Morgenthau's directions (resulting in JCS 1067), the planners for postwar Japan felt obligated to follow their lead.[11] Various army and State officials "came over" to the Japan planners "and tried to persuade us, 'Look, all you need to do is to cross out Nazi and put in Japanese and you can use this directive.'"[12]

At the same time, Japan started to have an appeal for a number of young New Dealers who saw in postwar Japan a chance to reengineer that society along New Deal lines. Thus, planning for postwar Japan shifted from an initial interest in the distinct historical and cultural factors that led Japan into war toward the Treasury's vision of a hard peace for Germany, along with the young New Dealers' vision of Japan as a tabula rasa awaiting their particular reformist vision.[13]

A particular sticking point had to do with the organization of Japanese firms. Just as Treasury officials felt certain that cartels had facilitated Nazi aggression, they assumed a similar business interest existed in Japan. They soon focused their ire on the large family-owned conglomerates called *zaibatsu* (from *zai*, which means wealth, and *batsu*, which means person of influence or powerful clique—something akin to "robber baron").[14] Some of these large firms had existed since the mid-nineteenth century and through overlapping stock ownership they had a hand in a wide variety of related industries. The largest—Mitsui, Mitsubishi, Yasuda, and Sumitomo—played a role in shipping, mining, currency exchange, and banking.[15] One young New Dealer, Corwin Edwards, summarized the thinking about the zaibatsu by arguing that whether or not the zaibatsu had supported the war in fact made little difference; rather, the whole "zaibatsu type of industrial organization" inevitably served "the purposes of aggression." Taking a broad structural approach to reform, American policy should therefore focus on ways "to break the system."[16]

By the time Douglas MacArthur had accepted the Japanese surrender and assumed control as supreme commander of the allied powers, or SCAP (an acronym that stood for him personally and for military government generally), he had received three separate documents that detailed the aims of military government. While many Japanese believed that MacArthur made the occupation rules on his own authority (a misunderstanding he did not discourage), in reality he did his best to follow the written policy he received.[17]

The Potsdam declaration of July 26, 1945, set the broad framework for the occupation. The Allies demanded unconditional surrender and the right to eliminate "for all time the authority and influence of those who have deceived and misled the people of Japan into embarking on world conquest." But the declaration went further: it concluded that militarism *as an ideology* needed purging from Japan: "for we insist that a new order of peace, security and justice will be impossible until irresponsible militarism is driven from the world." As a result, the Allies demanded that "the Japanese Government . . . remove all obstacles to the revival and strengthening of democratic tendencies among the Japanese people," including protections for "freedom of speech, of religion, and of thought, as well as respect for the fundamental human rights," but also a reform of Japanese industry that would "sustain her economy and permit the exaction of just reparations in kind, but not [industry] which would enable her to rearm for war."[18]

The selection of MacArthur as proconsul served political purposes. Since he had left for the Philippines in the 1930s, he had feuded with official Washington and soured on Franklin Roosevelt. Upon learning of Roosevelt's death, MacArthur said of him: "He never resorted to the truth when a lie would suffice." He had even less patience with his successor, Harry Truman: "We're even worse off with that Jew in the White House." He had apparently determined Truman's ethnicity by looking "at his face."[19] The feeling was mutual. In his journal, Truman called MacArthur, "Mr. Prima Donna, Brass Hat, Five Star MacArthur. He's worse than the Cabots and the Lodges—they at least talked with one another before they told God what to do. Mac tells God right off. It is a very great pity we have to have stuffed Shirts like that in key positions."[20] Yet his own dislike for MacArthur explained why MacArthur got the appointment. No one wanted him back in Washington. Better to leave him in Japan and far away where he would not make trouble for Truman.[21]

For MacArthur, however, the opportunity to serve in Japan might allow for a triumphant return to Washington. Already a legend before World War II began, by its end MacArthur had accomplished about all that a military man could hope for except, perhaps, serving as president of the United

States. That idea had certainly crossed his mind before the war began, and it became a real likelihood even before the fighting ended. In April 1943, Henry Stimson had reiterated an old army directive that "no member of the military forces on active duty will hereafter become a candidate for or seek or accept election to any public office not held by him when he entered upon active duty." At a time when Republicans in Congress had started to see weakness in the Roosevelt juggernaut, the "immediate question . . . was: 'Is this designed to head off the nomination for President of Gen. Douglas MacArthur?'"[22] At that point MacArthur was probably the most admired Republican in the country. As speculation grew, Stimson backtracked, explaining "I can tell you with great explicitness that I did not have General MacArthur in mind at all, or any other individual."[23]

Of course, the unintended consequence of Stimson's announcement was to make MacArthur the topic on everyone's mind as a potential opponent for Roosevelt in 1944. In particular, Arthur Vandenberg, the seasoned Republican senator from Michigan, began to publicly support MacArthur, who reciprocated, telling the senator of the "absolute confidence I would feel in your experienced and wise mentorship."[24] A series of polls conducted through 1943 showed MacArthur trailing Thomas Dewey (the governor of New York) and Wendell Willkie (the nominee in 1940) among Republicans, but not by a prohibitive amount. Moreover, in the Midwestern farm belt, he polled better than Roosevelt, leading the president by as much as sixteen points.[25]

For his part, MacArthur understood that actively campaigning for the presidency while leading troops in battle showed bad form. In a strategy he would repeat, he publicly focused on his duties as general; privately, surrogates manipulated events in the states on his behalf. If support became a groundswell, he would return and accept the nomination to general acclaim. If not, he had publicly risked nothing and therefore lost nothing. By April of 1944, the first primaries suggested that the strategy had played itself out, and Dewey had become the frontrunner for the Republican nomination. MacArthur, realizing that he would not get the nomination, professed not to want it. He announced that he "felt it necessary" to "make my position entirely unequivocal, I request that no action be taken that would link my name in any way with the nomination. I do not covet it nor would I accept it."[26]

If the political whirlwind around MacArthur's non-nomination amounted to little in the short term, it seems to have had two effects over the longer term. First, it repaired the Arthur MacArthur and William Howard Taft feud—at least for the next generation. Taft's son Robert had won election to the Senate in 1938 and had quickly become a leading Republican. When MacArthur's name began to float as a presidential candidate, friends assumed Taft would be opposed. He set the record straight: "I don't know just what . . . you may have seen, but I have nothing against MacArthur," he told one.[27] By 1945, he openly praised MacArthur to friends. "I think General MacArthur has made a wonderful beginning in Japan. His . . . statements were excellent, a good deal better than those of the President [Truman]."[28]

Second, the episode appears to have boosted MacArthur's appetite for this last accomplishment, an appetite whetted by public opinion polls conducted in the spring of 1945, which indicated that Americans considered him the nation's greatest general, with 43 percent naming him over Eisenhower (31 percent) and Patton (17 percent).[29] In fact, while he never stated it definitively, he hinted that his interest in becoming military governor for Japan lay in part in providing him a record of domestic accomplishments for the 1948 presidential election. If he could turn Japan's occupation into a demonstrable success, he could plausibly portray himself as an able chief executive.[30]

In accepting the challenge, he showed serene confidence. "Military occupation was not new to me," he explained. Indeed, in a sense, he had grown up within it along the American frontier. His father, Arthur, had overseen a regiment at Fort Wingate, New Mexico, through the 1880s. The outpost kept order and protected white settlers from marauders, bandits, and Indians, including William Bonney (Billy "the Kid") and the Apache leader Geronimo. For much of his youth, Douglas lived on the stories of soldiers who fought famous outlaws and Indian chiefs in battles to establish civil society over "lawlessness."[31]

More recently, "I had garrisoned the west bank of the Rhine as commander of the Rainbow Division at the end of World War I." There he saw the "basic and fundamental weaknesses" of an occupation: "the substitution of civil by military authority . . . the lowering of the spiritual and moral tone of a population controlled by foreign bayonets . . . deterioration in the occupying forces . . . as the disease of power infiltrated their ranks and bred a sort of race superiority." In a telling insight, he noted, "If any occupation lasts too long, or is not carefully watched from the start, one party becomes slaves and the other masters."[32]

At the same time, he planned to accomplish a radical transformation of Japanese society. "From the moment of my appointment as supreme commander, I had formulated the policies," he explained. He intended to "destroy the military power. Punish war criminals. Build the structure of representative government. Modernize the constitution. Hold free elections. Enfranchise the women. Release the political prisoners. Liberate the farmers. Establish a free labor movement. Encourage a free economy. Abolish police oppression. Develop a free and responsible press. Liberalize education. Decentralize political power. Separate church from state."[33]

Not coincidentally, the orders he had already received from Washington told him to do the same thing. Titled JCS 1380/15, the "Basic Initial Post-Surrender Directive to Supreme Commander for the Allied Powers for the Occupation and Control of Japan," it remained top secret until the end of the 1940s and spelled out in detail Japan's rehabilitation. While reiterating the reforms MacArthur wanted, it added that MacArthur held "supreme authority" extending to "all matters in the economic sphere." He should, to whatever extent possible, "use the services of the Emperor and the machinery of the Japanese Government to accomplish" his objectives. Specifically, in a phrase that echoed directions given to Eisenhower in Germany, the order told MacArthur that he should "not assume any responsibility for the economic rehabilitation of Japan or the strengthening of the Japanese economy" and that he should make this fact "clear to the Japanese people." In short, Japan's "standard of living will depend upon the thoroughness with which Japan rids itself of all militaristic ambitions . . . and cooperates with the occupying forces and the governments they represent."[34]

While JCS 1380 mirrored JCS 1067, the two occupations differed from the get-go. For one thing, the Allies divided Germany and liquidated the Nazi state. By contrast, Japan remained intact under American supervision with a functioning state. The occupation of Japan looked much more like the provisional government of the Philippines than the quadripartite control of Germany.[35]

In addition, Japan had a very different American leadership in MacArthur. In Germany, Eisenhower quickly deferred occupation policy to Lucius Clay. Clay had extensive experience working within government and so quickly took control of the policymaking process. This meant he began to weed out those staffers he saw conflicting with his own aims (such as Bernard Bernstein). More important, Clay imported experts wherever he could (Dodge and Draper, for example).

By contrast, MacArthur placed military men as directors of the various government divisions.[36] Brigadier General Courtney Whitney, a former attorney and MacArthur's closest confidant, ran the Government Section. Major General William Marquat, a former journalist and anti-aircraft expert headed the Economic and Science Section. While he had no college degree or background in education, Brigadier General Ken R. Dyke headed the education system, the press, and cultural affairs. Finally, Major General Charles Willoughby, an expatriate of German aristocratic stock, headed up domestic security and supervised both the Japanese and military police (and tended to see leftist conspiracies within SCAP as well as in the Japanese government).[37] Each demonstrated total loyalty to MacArthur.

By contrast, the majority of the staff serving MacArthur's generals came from the State or Treasury Department. These were often young, bright, and dedicated New Dealers. Moreover, this group quickly discovered how to direct policy. Their power stemmed from their location in the policy-making process. To put things visually, if political power in Japan were arranged as a pyramid, Japanese government occupied the bottom row (it had the least power but the most expansive reach). At the pinnacle sat MacArthur and his confidants. They had total power but little expertise. This allowed the middle of the pyramid, that part occupied by young American bureaucrats, to take the strongest position in influencing policy in both directions. They knew more about governing than MacArthur's inner sanctum, and they held more power than the Japanese government. Moreover, because MacArthur's instructions included provisions that he should work through the Japanese state, the New Dealers stood in a perfect position to filter information and instructions in either direction, a fact magnified by MacArthur's preference to remain aloof at all times from the day-to-day activities of the occupation. Quite quickly they developed a working relationship with their Japanese counterparts. As a result of these dynamics, and whether or not MacArthur or the Japanese knew it, the occupation began as an effort to remake Japan in the image of the New Deal.[38]

The triple challenge of reform, relief, and recovery that organized the early New Deal applied equally to the occupation of Japan. MacArthur started with reform. Within weeks of assuming control, he abolished the Japanese system of censorship, ordered all political prisoners released, instituted universal female suffrage, legalized labor unions, and abolished child labor. By November, he had ordered the dissolution of the four largest zaibatsu holding companies, redistributed property to tenant farmers, and

begun to arrest war criminals. Then in January, SCAP began to purge all
men of influence from political and economic positions of power. Finally,
in February, MacArthur personally rejected the Japanese attempt at drafting
a new constitution. Instead, he assigned twenty-four Americans to draft it
for them. The group included four women and twenty men, some in uniform but none professional military, some staunch Republicans but most
Democrats. They had one week. When completed, he insisted the Japanese
accept it as written. It included the famous Article 9, renouncing war as a
sovereign right and prohibiting Japan from maintaining standing military
forces.[39] Militarism no longer functioned as the expression of Japanese civic
virtue. Whitney, in explaining the draft to MacArthur, said it "constitutes
a sharp swing from the extreme right in political thinking—yet yields nothing to the radical concept of the extreme left."[40]

In advancing these reforms, MacArthur followed both the spirit and
letter of the orders sent from Washington. He put political reform ahead
of economic recovery, and quickly found himself stuck with a persistent
problem of relief. "In politics the interest of the Japanese is much less
than it is in solving their economic problems," a State Department memo
from early 1946 warned. "To achieve these ultimate [political] objectives
and to avoid the dangers [to political reform]," it continued, "it is essential to prevent economic distress for the Japanese." Summing up, "a sane
democracy cannot rest on an empty stomach. Economic distress normally
leads to an attempt to change the existing government to one which
promises relief—either an extreme right wing or an extreme left wing
movement."[41]

Like Germany, Japan ended the war in desolation. "As far as we could
see lay miles of rubble," wrote an American journalist. "The people looked
ragged and distraught. They dug into the debris, to clear space for new
shacks." The Japanese used hand carts "piled high with brick and lumber.
But so vast was the destruction that all this effort seemed unproductive.
There were no new buildings in sight. The skeletons of railway cars and
locomotives remained untouched on the tracks."[42] Between 1942 and surrender, Japan lost roughly one-quarter of its total wealth, or the equivalent
of everything it made after 1935. American forces had annihilated the life-
blood of the island nation—its commercial shipping. At the time of Pearl
Harbor, Japan held almost six million tons in ships and added an additional
four million during the war, but almost nine million of those tons lay rust-
ing on the seafloor by the time the occupation began, thanks to American

air and naval power. Roughly two and one-half million Japanese died as a result of the conflict (three-quarters as soldiers, the rest as victims of bombing or during the Okinawa campaign). In addition, millions of Japanese living throughout the empire had been expelled and forced to return to the Japanese mainland. Japan also lost its rights to fishing waters. In 1942, Japan's catch surpassed one million tons; even by 1950 it had only recovered to roughly one-third that total.[43]

Like Clay and Eisenhower in Germany, MacArthur realized that his immediate problem lay in feeding the Japanese. Because the Japanese had prepared for invasion in 1945, they had not planted a rice crop, and rice production dropped to one-third of the typical harvest.[44] As condition of its surrender, Japan had to forgo any empire, and this cut the island off from its main sources of food on the Asian mainland. "One of the first things I did," MacArthur recalled, "was to set up our army kitchens to help feed the people. Had this not been done, they would have died by the thousands."[45] SCAP took additional measures to increase food production, such as converting unused airfields into farms. "We must not lose sight of . . . the inescapable relationship of politics and economics," wrote political adviser George Atcheson to President Truman. "In the dire straits of the Japanese people today, political development depends upon solution of the problems of food, shelter and clothing. Today political education and experience in the practice of democracy are impeded by the preoccupation of the people with their economic distress."[46]

MacArthur swung into action and helped convince Congress to make Government and Relief in Occupied Areas (GARIOA) funds available to Japan. He put the matter bluntly to Herbert Hoover, visiting on a food mission in May 1946: "Send us food or send us soldiers."[47] Over the next five years, GARIOA grants to Japan amounted to about $2.2 billion.[48] MacArthur put the grants to great political use, making public announcements as each food shipment arrived in Yokohama or Kobe, implying personal responsibility for saving the Japanese people. American officials realized even sooner for Japan than Germany that Japan needed economic recovery quickly to survive. In a follow-up directive to MacArthur of January 1946, the SWNCC told him that it "should be borne in mind that a process of reorientation will only be effective as it goes hand in hand with some gradual improvement in the economic condition of the ordinary Japanese toward whom it is directed." Thus, it became "essential that the economic policies of our occupation . . . be integrated as a part of the entire process of reorientation of the Japanese." Most important, SCAP's entire program "should be designed so that it can be carried on by the Japanese themselves following withdrawal of controls."[49] But a year into the occupation, American officials worried that recovery seemed far away. "Democracy cannot be beaten into the mind nor can it be absorbed on an empty stomach," George Atcheson wrote Truman in January 1947. "I do not think that the importance of the economic considerations can be over-emphasized. The Japanese economy is bankrupt and whether we like it or not Japan has become an economic responsibility of the United States." If Japan could not become self-sufficient soon, "grave dangers" loomed ahead.[50]

Still, SCAP did relatively little through 1947 to bring about recovery. In this, MacArthur simply followed his original orders which said that recovery should come from Japanese initiative.[51] Besides, many in SCAP thought that democratizing the economy would largely foster, not hinder, Japanese recovery.

When many of Japan's experienced policymakers were purged for war crimes, a cadre of heterodox policymakers filled the political vacuum, particularly an influential group of Marxist economists organized as the Ministry of Foreign Affairs Special Survey Committee. Over time, many of the group's members played important roles in Japan's economic policymaking. Initially, the group sought to develop a "third way" of economic democracy, distinct from American capitalism and Soviet communism and unique to Japan. The "mechanical application to Japan of either [Soviet or American type] of democracy" would be inappropriate, they felt; the Japanese should "create a new type of democracy by itself, together with those countries such as China and other Asian countries which have rather similar basic conditions."[52]

In broad terms, this group of Japanese economists focused on three problems plaguing the economy: low production, unemployment, and inflation.[53] In addition, Japan stood outside the global economy; it had lost all international trade as a condition of the peace. Thus, the Japanese Marxists searched for a domestic resource that might become the basis of future growth. One committee member, Hiromi Arisawa devised a "priority production system" that left intact the industrial organization of war production but focused on coal production (rather than armaments). When Shigeru Yoshida became prime minister in 1946, he adopted Arisawa's suggestion and convinced MacArthur to use the GARIOA program to obtain American products that facilitated coal production.[54]

At the same time that Yoshida embraced Arisawa's "priority production," he appointed Tanzan Ishibashi as finance minister. Ishibashi called himself Japan's "first Keynesian" and believed strongly that Japan's industry could only recover through massive government stimulus. In a nationwide radio broadcast, he explained that, "The goal of national finance, particularly in situations like that of our country today, is first, more than anything else, to give people jobs, to revive industry, to aim for full employment, and so to propel the national economy forward." Citing Keynes as his authority, he told the country that "in order to achieve the goal of resuming production, there is no harm if, for example, government deficits occur, or if, as a result, an increased issue of currency is induced."[55] To facilitate the Keynesian approach to "priority production," the Japanese Diet created the Reconstruction Finance Bank (RFB) in August of 1946. New regulations followed in March 1947, giving the Ministry of Finance control over its loans. The ministry divided industry into three groups and instructed banks to prioritize lending to the "priority production group," namely coal, steel, and fertilizer.[56]

The priority production system helped with the first two of Japan's postwar economic problems, employment and industrial recovery. But it exacerbated the third problem: inflation. Japan had already started to see inflation as early as 1942; the end of the war saw a great surge in prices as Japan's government escalated the use of newly printed money to pay its bills. Between January 1945 and 1946, retail prices nearly tripled, and in the following six months nearly tripled again.[57]

In February of 1946, SCAP helped the Japanese put into effect a currency reform that mirrored the CDG plan for Germany. But the plan did not involve the restructuring of the banks, the end of price controls, or a postreform policy of balanced budgets. Japan's central bank and the RFB continued to support priority production and soon after the reform prices climbed again.[58] Indeed, even with a freeze on personal and corporate accounts, prices continued to skyrocket. In the eighteen months that *followed* the currency reform, prices went up nearly five-fold.[59]

MacArthur's initial orders included a provision requiring the Japanese to enforce price controls and initiate anti-inflationary policies.[60] The Yoshida administration made only gestures in this direction. "The type of inflation we are experiencing is not inflation in the usual sense," Ishibashi explained. "Starvation prices can only be cured by the production and flow of goods onto the market."[61] This required continued spending and monetary expansion to stimulate production. Unfortunately for Ishibashi, his

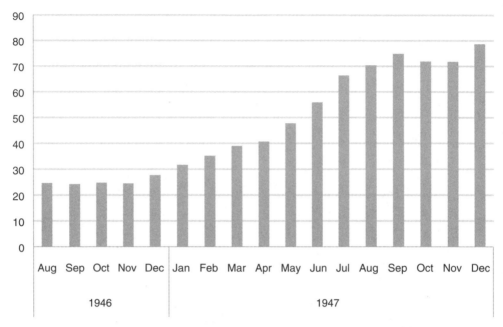

Figure 7. Japan's consumer price index (August 1946–December 1947).
Source: Programs and Statistics Division, Economic and Scientific Section,
GHQ, SCAP, Japanese Economic Statistics, 39, 3:18, February 15, Mainichi
1950.

refusal to listen to SCAP's instructions on any front—including his refusal
to cancel war contracts—made him too many enemies. SCAP purged him
in mid-1947, forcing Yoshida to find a new finance minister.[62] Ishibashi's
approach continued, however, without pause.

As SCAP officials became concerned with the persistent inflation, they
simply berated Japanese officials for not doing more. "Unless determined
measures are undertaken at once by the Japanese Government, the inflationary condition of the economy . . . will become increasingly serious,"
MacArthur warned Yoshida in March of 1947. Referencing his initial
orders, he explained that "this directive made it the responsibility of the
Japanese Government to maintain a firm control over wages and prices and
to initiate and maintain a strict rationing program for essential commodi-
ties in short supply." Indeed, "it is imperative that the Japanese Government carry out this responsibility to the Japanese people." Finally, in an

ominous warning, he observed, "the Allied Powers, of course, are under no obligation . . . to import foodstuffs." Yoshida needed to solve the problem or else.[63]

For the most part, however, these threats fell on deaf ears. Yoshida knew that MacArthur had no desire to starve the Japanese. Besides, despite SCAP's efforts to censor reports about economic conditions in the United States, Japanese officials knew that the U.S. also suffered from postwar inflation. They understood that Washington had no clearer idea for solving these problems.[64] "The generals 'lectured' the finance ministers, particularly Ishibashi . . . on the need for economy," explained one SCAP economist, "but . . . the ministers found these lectures as confusing as I did." Moreover, inflation remained a secondary concern. The main task was political—"the purge, the *zaibatsu*-liquidation program." SCAP's economists did not focus on "broad monetary and fiscal developments;" they instead worked through organizational charts of the country's largest firms. In short, they "knew too little about what was really going on inside or outside the government of Japan to be able to impose timely and effective checks on monetary and fiscal excesses."[65]

By the fall of 1947, with inflation running at 163 percent annually, with SCAP focused on its zaibatsu dissolution program, and with Washington receiving warnings that economic conditions might unravel the whole occupation, MacArthur released a statement upon the "Second Anniversary of Surrender." Trying to quell Washington's growing anxiety, he explained, "There need be no concern over fears recently expressed of imminent economic collapse." He had inherited a moribund economy. "The actual collapse of [the] Japanese economy, which was a major Allied war aim, occurred prior to the surrender as a result of . . . the crushing force of Allied arms." Besides, even if the economy failed to recover, he saw no danger to the political reforms. "It is furthermore a false concept which contends that democracy can only thrive if maintained in plenty," MacArthur told the Japanese (and Washington). "On the contrary, history shows that it springs from hardship and struggle and toil, to flourish naturally in the hearts of men who cherish individual freedom and dignity—or not at all." Democracy stood above vulgar materialism. "A spiritual commodity, it is neither for purchase nor for sale."[66]

*　*　*

At roughly the same moment MacArthur delivered his speech, William Draper became the new undersecretary of the army, supervising all occupations. Clay had sent Draper to Washington in the spring of 1947 to negotiate a new coal production agreement with the British. Near the conclusion of the negotiations in August, Army Undersecretary Kenneth Royall shared a stunning piece of news. Earlier that day Robert Patterson, the army secretary, had revealed he was resigning. His "money had run out completely, he had borrowed all he could on his life insurance policies, and he had to go back to work in order to be able to support his family." Patterson thought it likely that Royall would replace him. "If this happened," Royall told Draper, could Draper "be good enough for three or four days to just cover [my] desk and handle what papers [you] could?"

"I shouldn't," replied Draper, "because I [am] in uniform and this [is] a civilian job."

"Well," Royall said, "you'll be just doing this on my behalf, so don't worry about that."

Truman, in fact, named Royall as the new secretary of the army as predicted. Royall then turned around and not only had Draper cover his desk, but also offered him his old job. Draper was stunned. The new position would reverse his relationship with Clay. Up to that moment Draper had been "reporting to [Clay], and this was going to twist the relationship all the way around." Royall told Draper to call Clay, and when Draper had explained the situation, Clay said, "Sure, go ahead." Thus, Draper became undersecretary.[67] By the end of August, Truman had made it official.[68]

Royall wanted Draper because of his German experience. The occupations had taken on a new dimension with the rivalry growing between the United States and the Soviet Union. While Draper had no close relationship with MacArthur and knew relatively little about Japan, his experience in Germany gave him a sense of what the occupation should accomplish and that he needed to "get right over there and come to terms with General MacArthur."[69] For his part, MacArthur rolled out the red carpet, taking the unusual step of greeting Draper personally at the airport. For the next few days Draper stayed with the MacArthurs. At the end of his trip, Draper held a press conference and announced two critical, related points. First, he assured the Japanese that a "proper provision" guaranteeing Japan's protection against foreign aggression would be included in a peace treaty. That is, he implied that since MacArthur had stripped Japan of its ability to defend itself, the United States would defend Japan from the Soviets. Second, he suggested that Japan needed to climb off the backs of American taxpayers: "Japan must promptly begin to stand on her own feet, revive her own economy and pay her own way."[70] Put simply, American aid in the future would come in the form of military defense and not economic relief.

The New Dealers within SCAP found Draper's announcement puzzling. Initially, they hoped he would recognize their efforts to rehabilitate the Japanese economy. But they quickly realized he saw reform in different terms and recovery coming from different sources. In particular, he had no intention of following through on the zaibatsu dissolution and had every intention of dramatically intruding into Japan's economic affairs. "While it wasn't called the Morgenthau Plan, the economic order to MacArthur very closely paralleled those that went to Germany," Draper explained. "Because I had become convinced from what I'd known in Germany," he decided that "the orders concerning the economy of Japan had to be changed." In essence, he planned to reverse SCAP's approach, leaving zaibatsu dissolution to Japanese initiative and making fiscal and monetary policy the new focus for SCAP. From Draper's perspective, the Japanese had no real room to revive their economy as long as zaibatsu dissolution hung over their heads. The uncertainty made business plans untenable. "So the thing was just falling between two stools."[71]

Despite the priority production system, American aid to Japan had grown larger over time. The issue remained food, a problem that the priority production system failed to recognize. To buy food on the international market, the Japanese needed to produce something other nations wanted. Draper concluded that only through the "restoration of mutually profitable commercial relations between Japan and the rest of the world" could it achieve genuine "self-support"—that is, feed itself.[72]

Draper decided to recommend that SWNCC revise MacArthur's initial orders. The State Department was in "full agreement with the desire of the Department of the Army to make it known . . . that the United States Government desires to accelerate the processes of economic recovery in Japan." State only worried that "any statement of U.S. policy on this subject . . . should be so worded as to minimize fears that this 'shift of emphasis' implies in any way reversal or repudiation of the broad principles and policies which have underlain long term occupation objectives."[73]

In November 1947, Washington sent MacArthur SWNCC 384, which stated that "the first two years of the occupation of Japan" had shown "exceptional progress . . . in establishing political and economic institutions

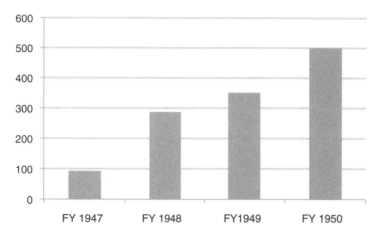

Figure 8. GARIOA Aid (FY 1947–FY 1950) (millions of U.S. dollars). Source: Programs and Statistics Division, Economic and Scientific Section, GHQ, SCAP, Japanese Economic Statistics, 39, 3:18. February 15, Mainichi 1950.

which will permit the development of a democratic and peaceful Japan." However, SCAP still needed to establish "a self-supporting economy in Japan." If it could not, "the achievements of the occupation cannot be consolidated." In short, "economic chaos in Japan has been prevented only at the expense of the American people who have financed the importation of vital food and other materials required to prevent widespread disease and unrest." Should this support end without a rehabilitated Japan, the efforts of the prior years would evaporate.[74]

Again, the staff in SCAP felt confused. They saw the new directive as consistent with their efforts. Why reiterate the point? They soon learned, however, that they were becoming marginalized. To "buttress" his "own recommendations to the President and the Secretary of State and the Congress," Draper began organizing economic missions to devise specific policy recommendations.[75] In March of 1948, he selected a group of businessmen (including the future head of the Marshall Plan, Paul Hoffman) to join him for a Japanese fact-finding trip. A later group headed by the Federal Reserve governor Robert Young went to Japan in May. Together, these two missions confirmed Draper's intuition: Japan needed price stability more than zaibatsu reform before any real industrial investment and recovery could take place. The missions criticized the Japanese government's "policy of maintaining full employment in plants regardless of their production" as "wasteful and uneconomic" and recommended the country balance its budget.[76] They suggested curbs on union activity, better trade with Japan's former enemies, and better integration with Asian markets. Young's group in particular emphasized these points.[77] As these reports rolled in, Draper became a bête noire within SCAP. He seemed like the typical investment banker who had no "empathy with the ordinary Japanese," and probably not "much empathy for working-class Americans either."[78] SCAP's staff offered a "negative, almost vitriolic, reaction" to the idea that the Japanese should balance their budget and restrain credit.[79]

Their vitriol notwithstanding, events increasingly went against them. The economic success that followed currency reform in Germany in June 1948 strengthened Draper's hand by demonstrating what Dodge had taught him: currency conversion only worked if accompanied by policies of fiscal restraint. As Germany recovered economically, Japan seemed to get worse. Charles Saltzman, the assistant secretary of state for occupied areas, once again warned in April 1948 that, "Unless [the Japanese] have . . . economic interests which give them a stake in the maintenance of a free government they will inevitably, and probably sooner rather than later, be seduced by one or another of the dynamic concepts of fascism or communism which will promise them great economic gains."[80]

The whole matter dramatically intensified as a communist victory in China's civil war grew more likely. Here, the diplomat George Kennan played an increasingly important role in moving Japan to the center of America's overall defense plan in the Far East.[81] While a great deal can be (and has been) said about the way Japan's economic recovery fit within the unfolding Cold War, the critical point for Draper was the way American policy largely added force to conclusions he had already made during his time in Germany. In March of 1948, Kennan told MacArthur that "to many of us in Washington," it appeared that "the developing world situation" should make "occupational policy" focus "from here on out . . . in the achievement of maximum stability of Japanese society, in order that Japan may best be able to stand on her own feet when the protecting hand is withdrawn." A focus on social stability implied that "the accent should now be placed on . . . an intensive program of economic recovery . . . and a relaxation in occupational control." If done correctly, this might "stimulate a greater sense of direct responsibility on the part of the Japanese Government and [might] give the Japanese people greater opportunity to assimilate in their own way the reform measures already introduced."[82] Kennan's strategic framework fit Draper's economic judgments.[83]

Worse for the SCAP staff, MacArthur had started to question their wisdom as well. As Japan's economic situation worsened, MacArthur asked Draper, "Could you find me somebody that knows something about running the economy of Japan, because I don't. And my military officers who are responsible for it don't either."[84] He voiced a similar concern to Kennan. He had concluded "that to some extent . . . occupational policies had been influenced by academic theorizers of a left-wing variety, at home and in Tokyo." He planned "soon to cut down on the SCAP section . . . concerned." He hoped "the problem would be adequately taken care of" soon.[85]

In reality, though, MacArthur was in a bind. He knew that Japan had to recover economically for the sake of his legacy. "The job of occupation is to restore Japan's production to self-sufficiency," he explained. To the press he opined: "I once read a statement Winston Churchill made in one of his moments of profound inspiration. Speaking of Germany, he said, 'The problem is not to keep Germany down, but to keep it up.' I didn't understand it then, but I do now. Our problem is to keep Japan up."[86] Left-leaning intellectuals in Japan subsequently labeled MacArthur's turn a "reverse course" (*gyaku kōsu*)—the moment the New Deal–inspired democratic reforms at the beginning of the occupation gave way to growing concern that Japan's economy should become the focus of American reform efforts.[87]

*   *   *

Perhaps to escape the shift in policy and growing concern with Japan's economy, MacArthur began to focus on running for president in 1948. In the years leading to the election, his close advisers often painted a picture of broad support among the Republican establishment. "Everywhere I go," wrote one, "people tell me what a grand job they think you are doing. . . . Often they refer to incidents or situations elsewhere and say: 'I wish we had MacArthur in command of that situation, too.'"[88] As he had in 1944, MacArthur preferred to let surrogates do most of the campaigning while he maintained a dignified aloofness. If the Republican Party seemed enthused, he would return to accept the nomination at the convention, but not before. Premature campaigning would disrupt the appearance that he had been "drafted" by the party. It "would instantly project me actively into the political arena, regardless of how scrupulously I sought to avoid political implications." Yet if "selected as the standard bearer of the Republican Party by the National Convention, I should, of course, look upon it as a mandate." Only with a mandate would he "campaign to win the election."[89]

As his surrogates maneuvered to win him the Republican nomination, MacArthur went about sizing up the man he saw as his primary rival: Eisenhower. In 1946, Eisenhower went through Tokyo on a tour of the Far East. MacArthur "kept me in his study from dinner 'til 1:00 A.M. trying to persuade me to run for president in 1948," Eisenhower recalled. "When I suggested that he was the one to be a candidate, he merely dismissed the notion with the remark that he was too old for the job." Yet Eisenhower knew his old boss too well and saw the conversation as a feint to get Eisenhower to show whether he also wanted to become president.[90]

As MacArthur's surrogates maneuvered to get him the nomination in January of 1948, a different group entered Eisenhower's name in the New Hampshire primary. Eisenhower would have none of it. In a letter published in the Manchester, New Hampshire, *Union Leader*, he disavowed any interest in the presidency and added: "It is my conviction that the necessary and wise subordination of the military to civil power will be best sustained . . . when lifelong professional soldiers . . . abstain from seeking high political office." To make the point especially clear, he added, "nothing in the international or domestic situation especially qualifies for the most important office in the world a man whose adult years have been spent in the country's military forces."[91]

When MacArthur learned of Eisenhower's letter, he grew irate. It was a "slur on the army," he told the British ambassador, and became "the reason I [feel] obliged to offer my own candidacy."[92] In March he made it official: "While it seems unnecessary for me to repeat that I do not actively seek or covet any office," yet "I can say, and with due humility, that I would be recreant to all my concepts of good citizenship were I to shrink . . . from accepting any public duty to which I might be called by the American people."[93] He wanted to be president, but only if the party gave him its nomination by acclamation.

"Consensus of the MacArthur chiefs," wrote the *Chicago Tribune*, "is that the only effect of Gen. Eisenhower's withdrawal . . . will be to increase

MacArthur's lead over what he would get if Eisenhower ran."[94] Meanwhile, Eisenhower felt obligated to deny that he had tried to forestall MacArthur's candidacy. He "resented implications" that "he may have had Gen. Douglas MacArthur in mind when he said professional soldiers should not seek the presidency." Really, "I would do nothing knowingly to damage him."[95] In reality, though, he aimed exactly to derail MacArthur's presidential ambitions, and his insistence that soldiers should not seek the job while still soldiering tended to burnish his own bona fides. Of course, in public Eisenhower would never criticize a fellow general. Yet in private he expressed to friends his deep reservations about MacArthur's leadership, going back to their days in the Philippines. He recalled standing there, next to MacArthur and thinking, "I just can't understand how such a damn fool could have gotten to be a General."[96]

To have any chance of winning the nomination, MacArthur had to carry the Wisconsin primary—technically his home state and an early contest in 1948. Going into the vote, MacArthur, the "favorite son," was favored by as much as "5 to 1."[97] Surprisingly, though, he lost. Harold Stassen, the former governor of Minnesota, took the state and earned nineteen delegates to MacArthur's eight. While MacArthur did well in the popular vote (Stassen took 40 percent, MacArthur 36), MacArthur needed a mandate. Without it, he could not sustain the narrative that he ran "as a public duty." As the journalist Arthur Krock ruminated, the "great proconsul in Tokyo" may have "dominated an Emperor 'divinity' who seems thankful for the domination," but "he did not come to Wisconsin." Without his personal effort on the campaign trail, "neither the magic of his deed nor his ancestral name was effective in this anti-militarist state." The result was now clear: "his Presidential boom is now fatally deflated."[98] Back in Tokyo, MacArthur felt the deflation. The day following the election returns, he refused visitors. "The General is as low as a rug and very disappointed," explained his chief of staff.[99]

Chapter 9

"Recovery Without Fiction"

In October, 1948, the newly constituted National Security Council issued NSC 13/2, which told MacArthur to stop "further reform legislation."[1] Moreover, he should reduce his personnel and accept an "ambassador" to spearhead economic reforms. Specifically, SCAP should "make it clear to the Japanese Government" that recovery depended upon "high export levels . . . a minimum of work stoppages, internal austerity measures and the stern combating of inflationary trends including efforts to achieve a balanced . . . budget as rapidly as possible."[2]

Draper concluded that making these new orders work depended upon finding the right "economic ambassador." Draper had exactly the person in mind: Joseph Dodge. But it was no easy task to get Dodge to agree to the assignment. After he had finished his work in Germany in 1946, Dodge vowed to leave government service and settle into his role as president of the Bank of Detroit. But in April of 1947, Secretary of State George Marshall asked him to create a "special committee of experts . . . to discuss all questions regarding the Austrian" peace treaty, and specifically to settle the question of "German assets in Austria and Austrian property in Allied countries." Marshall wanted Dodge "to serve as the American member of the Special Commission." Indeed, he "urged" Dodge "to undertake this task."[3] Dodge reluctantly agreed.

Then, no sooner had he returned to the States in 1947, than his fellow bankers elected him president of the American Bankers Association. As *Fortune* magazine wrote, the bankers wanted someone "obviously . . . not a Wall Streeter," whom they felt "would get along with 'those people in Washington.' "[4] Dodge accepted the election and toured the nation telling his fellow bankers to practice "selective inaction" to fight American inflation. While his campaign had limited effect on prices, it did keep Truman from promulgating new anti-inflationary controls on the banks, which made Dodge a bit of a celebrity within financial circles.[5]

Thus, in 1948 when Draper begged Dodge "to go to Japan as a kind of economic czar," Dodge "wouldn't go."[6] So Draper did the next best thing and asked Dodge to informally advise on policy. Dodge agreed and helped in the writing of NSC 13/2.[7] But Dodge could see the "obvious difficulties" facing Japan and "the possibility of ultimate failure" for anyone taking on its economy.[8] In particular, he couldn't see how an outsider would prevail over MacArthur and his SCAP staff.

With Truman's support, "the rules were changed," retorted Draper, "there was a chance to win, for the economy to recover—but it took somebody with a lot of knowledge and a lot of guts to do it."[9] Draper really wanted Dodge, but it would take a hard sell to get him.

In December 1948, Dodge discovered that "a telegram had been dispatched . . . from the White House and they were standing by with a plane to pick me up at such time as I determined I wanted to use it."[10] The president had summoned Dodge for a personal meeting in the Oval Office and had sent his own plane to bring him. Dodge boarded the plane that night and flew to Washington. The next morning, knowing what might be coming, he met Draper and explained "he wasn't going to take the job."[11] Then, at a little after 11:00, Dodge "called on President Truman" in his office.

Truman "expressed appreciation" that Dodge came "on such short notice, but stated the reason for it was that he had a very important problem to discuss," specifically "the economic situation in Japan and its relation to what [had] been happening in China."[12] The president "had taken a personal interest in [Japan's economy], and was completely informed about it." Over the previous days the situation had been discussed "by the Joint Chiefs of Staff, the National Advisory Council, and the National Security Council." Truman then mentioned NSC 13/2 and said he approved the "course of action and policy decision . . . taken by the National Security Council [and] implemented by action of the Joint Chiefs of Staff." Summing everything up, he told Dodge "it was the unanimous opinion of the Members of the National Security Council, without qualification or dissent of any kind" that Dodge take the assignment. Truman wanted to "personally ask . . . and plead" with Dodge to take the job.[13]

Dodge asked about MacArthur; Truman explained at length that Dodge would have the "support of the top Government levels where the present situation and the difficulties related to it [i.e. MacArthur] . . . are fully recognized." In short, he had the president's full backing. Dodge replied that he had already performed a great deal for the country. His board of directors at the bank were "disposed to think . . . that I had done my share." Truman agreed. He "knew all about" the board and admitted that "he could understand" their views "and did not blame them." Still, the *country* needed Dodge. "After all," argued Truman, "if when the Government was in trouble and could not depend on men like [you] to assist it, it was in a bad way." Dodge was stuck. He could say no to a friend like Draper, but not so easily to the president—especially not when called upon as a matter of patriotic duty. By the time he left the Oval Office, he had accepted the call.[14]

Dodge would have authority over any matter affecting the Japanese economy. After an initial trip to Tokyo, he would leave behind a small staff to complete the mission. The total assignment should not last more than a year. Truman then formalized matters in a letter. "The necessity for stabilizing the economic life of Japan and of combating present inflationary influences . . . is a prerequisite to the gradual achievement of self-support" he explained. "Recovery rather than relief must be our aim in order that a sound economic basis be laid for democratic self-government."[15] In writing the letter, Truman had given his imprimatur to Dodge's policy, and Dodge had a trump to play should he face opposition from SCAP.

On December 14, General MacArthur received a cleverly worded cable from Secretary of War Kenneth Royall. "The president is taking a strong personal interest in supporting you in the difficult stabilization of the Japanese economy," he wrote, phrasing as assistance what amounted to a vote of no confidence. "Secretary Draper discussed with you in Tokyo the possibility of enlisting the help of Mister Joseph Dodge, president of the Detroit Bank" to stabilize the Japanese economy. Earlier that day "the president personally asked Mister Dodge to undertake important responsibility assisting you with the whole economic and financial program in Japan."[16] Dodge would have the rank of minister and would "advise" MacArthur. But he answered to Truman.[17] He remained outside SCAP's command structure. As a correspondent for the *Economist* noted when learning of the arrangement, "The expert has finally taken over from the soldier in Japan." While Dodge crinkled "his eyes behind his rimless spectacles" and explained that "he is only 'financial adviser' . . . no one is really in any doubt of the new power behind the throne in Tokyo."[18]

On March 8, 1949, Joseph Dodge held his first press conference in Tokyo. Both Japanese and American reporters hoped to understand the nature of his assignment and what changes he hoped to effect on the Japanese economy. Would he remove price controls? "I cannot say at this time."

Would he change any of the social and political reforms already affected? "This comes under SCAP's policy. Sorry." What about wage controls? "It is our objective to make them unnecessary." Finally, one of the reporters asked the central question that had plagued Japanese economists over the last two years: "Do you believe in stabilization or recovery first?" Dodge thought for a moment: "I believe in recovery without fiction."[19]

The reporters came away confused and unimpressed. Among other misunderstandings, they reported that he had said *friction* instead of *fiction*.[20] In reality, though, Dodge's arrival signaled a dramatic turn in occupation policy and proved the last significant imposition of American will upon Japan's political culture. Moreover, by this point Dodge embodied a growing consensus within the high-level army bureaucracy on political economy—specifically how to build a stable economic base on which to rest a fragile democratic order.

While Japan's inflation rate had receded from a ridiculous level of nearly 200 percent in 1947, it still remained alarmingly high through 1948 (around 50 percent). Just about everything Draper had asked him to read about Japan worried Dodge, particularly a huge political scandal that involved the Reconstruction Finance Bank (RFB) and the Showa-Denko fertilizer company. Showa-Denko executives had bribed government officials to obtain loans from the bank. As the scandal unfolded, it implicated nearly every important member of the government, including the Socialist prime minister Histoshi Ashida.[21] Worse, it pointed to a culture of lawlessness endemic to a society riddled with inflation. As the *Oriental Economist* wrote soon after the arrests became public. "When this problem is pursued to its source we are brought up against the fact that we are living under abnormal conditions necessitating almost universal infringement of some law or other in order to exist." For example, "unless black market transactions are indulged in we are liable to go hungry or cold; and under such circumstances the public is unknowingly tending toward disregard for laws and regulations." Thus, "this numbing of the conscience is inducing insensitivity to corruption"—a fact "strikingly demonstrated by the general apathy of the public." Precisely "in such an atmosphere . . . unscrupulous officials turn to wrongdoing, and such scandal cases as the Showa Denko affair are fostered into full-fledged growth."[22]

A State Department report from late 1948 agreed about the general malaise of Japan's political culture. It found that "many in the Japanese government" had learned to "pit one American official against another," to

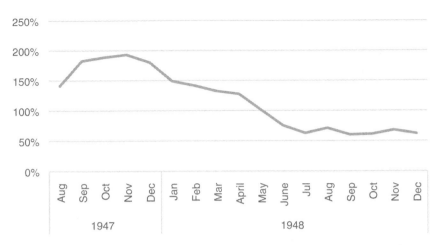

Figure 9. Japan's annual inflation rate (August 1947–December 1948). Source: Programs and Statistics Division, Economic and Scientific Section, GHQ, SCAP, Japanese Economic Statistics, 39, 3:18, February 15, Mainichi 1950.

manipulate military government and hide individual agendas. As a result, "even General MacArthur has lost his aura of sanctity." Ironically, "the growing Japanese dissatisfaction with the occupation is a sign of the success of our first lesson in democracy," since "an attitude of criticism is an inherent feature of any democracy." But this critical attitude had grown perilously close to "outright hostility toward the occupation and its objectives." In fact, "almost everyone seemed to sense that the present moment is the crisis." Given these impressions, the State Department felt amazed when it "discovered a deep-rooted sense of complacency and of permanency on the part of American officials of the occupation." Indeed, it concluded that "the lower echelons and working levels . . . in the SCAP organization felt almost a smug isolation from the troubled events of the outside world."[23]

Initially, MacArthur proved cordial toward Dodge. Knowing that the political winds had changed, he followed his usual practice: he positioned himself to take credit for what appeared to be inevitable. The two men started awkwardly. MacArthur was a legend by that point. He seemed regal, aloof, and accomplished. Everyone in America knew his name and lauded his success. By contrast, outside of the banking community and official Washington, few people knew Dodge. Nevertheless, Dodge had two significant advantages in dealing with MacArthur. First, he had the backing of the upper bureaucracy of the army and, most important, of the president, all of which MacArthur knew. Second, MacArthur needed Japan to look like a success as a matter of legacy.

Once Dodge arrived, he and MacArthur met alone each evening, "pacing around [MacArthur's] office exchanging views and arguments about problems." Dodge concluded that MacArthur was a "very unusual individual. Unquestionably brilliant, honest, and sincere. Instinctively a dramatizer of everything." For his part, MacArthur struggled to know how to treat Dodge. At times he accidentally called him "Colonel." Then he started calling him "Mr. Advisor" or "Mr. Minister." But Dodge ultimately prevailed upon MacArthur to treat him as a friend. MacArthur "finally promoted me to 'Joe,'" he wrote his wife.[24] As he would do again and again, Dodge managed to tame the great egos he encountered by making himself less and less of a threat. Indeed, the more actual power he held, the more informal he kept his relationships. Eventually, MacArthur told Dodge he would back him "whether you are wrong or right."[25] Along with MacArthur's loyalty came the loyalty of Major General William Marquat, the general responsible for economic and financial policy.

With MacArthur in his corner, Dodge worked to understand the SCAP bureaucracy. As he met with staffers he discovered that while "Japanese budgets require the final approval of the Supreme Commander and in this respect SCAP holds the veto power," he found no "evidence . . . of coordination of policies and programs [within SCAP] as they may affect the Japanese budget." Instead, "SCAP programs get under way without any measurement of their financial implications, or perhaps go ahead irrespective of the financial implications." Worse, he found "no procedure for raising [budgetary] questions specifically with respect to each [SCAP] proposal." Moreover, "while the Japanese budgets are essentially Japanese and not SCAP budgets," he realized that "there is a certain amount of cross firing between SCAP staff sections and comparable Japanese Government sections in the preparation and development of projects." Dodge quickly gathered that this "cross firing" went "on at the lower level" of the SCAP ranks, below MacArthur's and Marquat's awareness. "The result is financial management from the lower rather than the higher level."[26]

For SCAP officials who had worked in the New Deal, this level of "cross firing" and/or flexibility (depending on one's perspective) felt comfortable. It mirrored Franklin Roosevelt's love of experimentalism in government. Dodge hated it. Moreover, he began to understand how Japanese officials could use the ambiguity of authority within SCAP to their advantage.[27] Dodge therefore sent MacArthur and Marquat a memo instructing them to change SCAP's organizational flow. "Effective economic stabilization . . . requires relating the effect of policy decisions directly to the Governmental Budget, as the *principal instrument* of financial policy." Any demands "thrust on the Japanese Budget should have the same internal control and coordination as those of the Military Budget." No longer could SCAP officials pursue independent goals or allow themselves to become pawns of capable Japanese bureaucrats. All "the staff sections of SCAP [shall] be required to determine clearly, *within* the SCAP organization, the financial requirements, availability of funds and financial effects of all such proposals *before* discussion with the appropriate sections of the Japanese Government."[28] That is, Dodge required all instructions to the Japanese government to go through Marquat and MacArthur, and then himself, as the filter between SCAP and the Japanese government on all budgetary questions.[29]

SCAP staff pushed back, refusing to go along with Dodge's plan. Eventually, Dodge found himself back in MacArthur's office. "We're having trouble," he told MacArthur. "I just want to make sure we are both traveling on the same train . . . SCAP keeps ordering the Japanese to make large expenditures that unbalance the budget. Somebody is going to have to say 'no' to the military and I'm willing to do it if you give the word. I'll take the kicks in the pants." MacArthur asked for details and then "walked to the window and stood looking out of it for quite a while."

Eventually, he turned and pointed his finger at Dodge. "Remember what I told you when you arrived?"

"Yes," replied Dodge, wondering if MacArthur would renege on his promised support. "Well," MacArthur continued, "it happens you are right. . . . Go ahead." After that, whenever SCAP staff threatened to go over Dodge's head to MacArthur, Dodge said, "I invite you to do so."[30]

With SCAP under his supervision, Dodge turned to Japan's Ministry of Finance. Officials arrived at his office with briefcases full of figures and charts, which Dodge pored over.[31] What he learned troubled him. As he explained to Draper in his first radio, all "original estimates" from government's ministries turned out to be "unreliable, unrealistic and substantially unsupported." The problem lay in the way the Japanese government did its accounting. Whereas Americans preferred to use budgets to guide spending in the future, Japanese used them to keep track of actions taken in the past. Each ministry spent what it wanted and only kept a record at the "time of actual payment." The Japanese government had gone through the motions of creating budgets American style to appease SCAP officials, but they did so without ever accepting the underlying principle. As a result, it became impossible for Dodge to "relate new budget to former budget or determine over or under expenditures." This allowed the government to "predicate budget on past circumstances rather than future." In other words, the government would estimate expenditures for SCAP based on the past year or two even while making commitments that obviously expanded future outlays. Summing up, the budget became a "product of last minute emergency decisions" rather than "[an] instrument of administration or control."[32]

But the official budget represented only a small part of the problem. As Dodge soon realized, the budget largely obscured rather than clarified the government's role in the economy. This stemmed from the fact that Japan's priority production system operated largely off the books. In theory, priority production represented a kind of targeted Keynesianism. The government classified Japan's industries "into three categories, namely A, B and C." The "A" category included "the most essential industries such as coal, fertilizer, iron and steel . . . and banks are expected to meet the needs of A industries." The criteria for success, importantly, lay in whether the "A" companies received the funding *they* considered adequate. A SCAP memo sent to Dodge concluded happily that "while some complaint has been received from industries substantially shut off from funds, there has actually been a minimum of dissatisfaction with the system as established, indicating that the classification has been well worked out." Dodge thought this was crazy. In the margins next to this paragraph he wrote, "How about ability to repay?"[33]

As Dodge further investigated Japanese finance, he realized that commercial banks played a relatively small role in priority production. As had been true in Germany, government and war industry bonds accounted for nearly all the assets in Japan's banks. They were probably worthless.[34] As one SCAP official explained, the banks only survived because "apparently it never entered [the Japanese] minds that the banks were insolvent."[35] Indeed, in the early stages of occupation, SCAP had encouraged the creation of the Reconstruction Finance Bank (RFB) as a way to get around the paralyzed banking system. It had even been modeled (loosely) on the Reconstruction Finance Corporation developed in the United States in the early years of the Depression.[36] In Japan, the RFB played the central role in the priority production system. It financed the "A" category business while also recapitalizing the commercial banks by buying their worthless bonds at par.[37] Initially, the Japanese government had created the RFB through annual appropriations and at modest levels. But Finance Minister Tanzan Ishibashi worried that industry needed more capital to bring about full employment. Ishibashi called himself a Keynesian, but in many ways he went further than Keynes would have dared to go.[38]

Ishibashi eagerly grabbed control of the RFB out of the hands of legislators by convincing the Bank of Japan to buy bonds and securities from the RFB and use RFB loans as collateral. This complicated scheme boiled down to a simple, clever practice: whenever necessary, the Bank of Japan would print as much money as the RFB wanted to loan. And Ishibashi largely determined how much that would be and who got what.[39] The procedure had the added perk (from Ishibashi's perspective) that the loans never appeared in a government budget.[40] When a socialist government came to power after elections in 1947, it only extended and amplified his approach. The RFB quickly became a political instrument. Initially, this meant saving those industries that (the party claimed) had suffered most from "the cancellation of war indemnities."[41] After that, the RFB began to compensate anyone who felt disadvantaged by SCAP.[42] For example, if SCAP required the Japanese to enforce price controls on a certain set of products, the RFB quickly provided "loans" to cover "operating deficits of private industry pending the establishment of a new price level."[43]

For Dodge, these practices not only made the Showa-Denko scandal inevitable, but guaranteed that they would be repeated. In mid-February 1949, he wrote a cable to Washington about the RFB so full of vitriol that he thought it "should have distorted the radio waves."[44] His "preliminary investigation" revealed the RFB to be a "major source of inflation," full of "unsound policies, practices and highly political motivation of activities." Its assets had "questionable value." As far as Dodge could see, most industry recipients were "inclined to assume loans are gifts." In short, the government had largely "used [the RFB] to avoid difficult political decisions." His "immediate recommendations" included "freezing borrowing power" and the "elimination of subsidies and deficit financing," and better "terms of repayment [and] aggressive loan-collection."[45] In the end, he put the RFB out of business.

By the end of his first month, Dodge felt he had gained a good understanding of the politics and economics of the budget. On February 26, he wrote Draper, "Our investigations to date indicate most Japanese economic programs . . . are keyed to wage, price and subsidy increases." Each segment of the economy, "government, management and labor," worked to "break [the] price-wage line" to its advantage. "These demands" came from a "previous dependence on these solutions," but especially from consistent "government weakness in facing [these] problems." Dodge lamented in particular the cycle in which "industrial management" demanded a "wage freeze and direct controls," which brought out the predictable response from "certain political leadership" that industry planned to "return workers to slavery." Both industry and labor had political champions who solved their problems by raiding the RFB and, in doing so, spurring inflation.[46]

From Dodge's perspective the occupation had reached a moment of truth. Knowing that breaking this cycle involved potentially severe political and economic costs, he wanted to move forward with open eyes. Things would get worse before they got better. He was "inclined to believe it may be necessary [to] accept some retrogression in production and export indices" in the "immediate future in order to ensure [a] sounder long-range program."[47] But "regardless of Japanese protests to [the] contrary," he concluded that the "present trend is not likely to be stopped short of our readiness to accept shocks and disturbances certain to result from rigorous application" of stabilization. If the Americans proved utterly unbending and made the "appropriate examples" to show the the occupation's "determination to have results," the economy might recover.[48] Privately, he summed up his feelings by writing, "Oriental politics is a devious business."[49]

MacArthur and Marquat stood by Dodge. In an adjoining memo to Draper, Marquat acknowledged that success required that "the Japanese Government, industry and labor be prevented from combining forces to defeat" Dodge's work. Already he had planned "basic conferences on this subject between" the Dodge Group and SCAP.[50] But on the whole, he agreed with Dodge's approach. Despite any warnings, Washington gave the go-ahead. Dodge's February fact-finding gave way to March policymaking.

*   *   *

On March 4, 1949, Dodge began his policy push with the first of a series of meetings with Hayato Ikeda, the new finance minister. Ikeda's path to power was perhaps more improbable than Dodge's. Ikeda had belonged to the so-called "Yoshida school" of mid-level bureaucrats suddenly advanced to leadership when SCAP purged all the top-tier politicians in 1946. Shigeru Yoshida, who became prime minister that year, saw a talent for finance in Ikeda and placed him under the tutelage of Tanzan Ishibashi as part of his cabinet.

When the Showa-Denka scandal ultimately brought down the Socialist government, Yoshida returned to power. Ishibashi should have returned to his position as finance minister except that SCAP became aware in the meantime of some pro-militarist articles he had written during the war. He was blackballed. Thus, when Yoshida became prime minister again in 1949, he appointed Ishibashi's understudy Ikeda as finance minister. Ikeda owed his political rise almost entirely to SCAP purges, yet his loyalties went to Yoshida and his intellectual mentor, Ishibashi, whose policies he aimed to continue.

At the same time, Ikeda knew that Ishibashi's framework did not differ significantly from the economic program Harry Truman outlined in the United States in his State of the Union address given at roughly the same moment. While the Japanese and American economies obviously differed in the degree of inflation each suffered (Japan had much more) and the size of the economy (the United States was much bigger), the ideological differences between Ikeda and Truman's primary economic adviser, Leon Keyserling, were minimal. Both the Truman and Yoshida administrations feared unemployment more than inflation. Each feared that economic slowdowns could easily result in depression; each aimed to combat inflation by driving up production; each felt that production jumps provided the best cure to inflation (as supply caught up to demand). Truman said as much: "Production is the greatest weapon against inflation."[51]

In Japan, the influential economist Hiromi Arisawa echoed Truman. He argued that attacking inflation *before* production revived would result in a "stabilization panic" and "many bankruptcies." Even if government succeeded in halting inflation, "production may still decline and the streets will be full of the unemployed."[52] He embraced, instead, an approach called "stopgap stabilization": "Stopgap stabilization does not require the policy reversal implicit in a deflation." Rather than halting inflation suddenly, the stopgap approach aimed to create a "feeling of stability" that would eventually result in price stability.[53] Ideally, inflation would resolve itself as production caught up to prices.[54]

In the United States, the opposition to Keynesian approaches came from the political right; in Japan, the opposition came from the left. The

Marxist economist Kihachirō Kimura launched a series of challenges to the stopgap approach, sparking what Japanese intellectuals called the Arisawa-Kimura debate.[55] Kimura argued that inflation undermined savings and forced wage earners to consume immediately. Since investment came out of savings, a declining savings rate forced the state to step in. This meant that the more the state financed industry, the more it would have to finance industry in a growing cycle of deficit spending. Whereas Ikeda saw "stopgap stabilization" protecting the working class, Kimura saw it as saving the capitalist class. Thus, he advocated an "at-one-stroke" approach to ending inflation.[56] The Arisawa-Kimura debate became the central economic question through 1948 and into 1949, and it all boiled down to the question asked of Dodge in his first press conference: whether to favor stability or recovery first. The Yoshida government sought recovery before stabilization. Kimura favored stability.

Dodge's first meeting with Ikeda thus provided more than a little irony. Dodge, acting on explicit instructions from Truman, took a position on the Japanese economy that aligned him with the Marxist Kimura and against Ikeda—but also against Truman's domestic policies, which coincided with Ikeda's position, a fact not lost on Japanese officials who complained that they planned to implement in Japan only what Truman sought back in the United States. Between America and Japan, ideology had turned upside down.[57]

As the two men staked out their positions, Ikeda said he agreed in principle to stabilization, but noted his party's "political commitment to repeal the Transactions Tax [national sales tax]." He explained, "This tax [is] unpopular and repulsive and its repeal politically necessary." It was, in Ikeda's view, good politics and good economics. People hated the tax, and once repealed, the increase in pocket money might boost the economy. Ikeda expected Dodge to support his party's pledge in order for the party to support Dodge's broader reform package. Ikeda stressed that he wanted to remain consistent with SCAP's past policies.

"No," Dodge replied. The tax "revenue was necessary." Besides, why "give up this established tax" only to have to "impose new taxes and create new sources of revenue," if it caused a budget deficit. Given the challenges involved in bringing the budget into balance, it seemed an "unnecessary complication to the present tax collection process."[58]

The two men parted ways, choosing to meet again a week later to take up the same theme. When they got back together, Ikeda tried once again to

persuade Dodge about the tax. The Yoshida cabinet considered three campaign promises essential, and Ikeda needed Dodge to help him to live up
to each: (1) a "reduction in government personnel," offset by (2) "more
public works," and finally (3) "the reduction of the income tax and repeal
of the transactions tax." Ikeda explained that these polices needed to be
implemented if Japan's economy were to survive without American aid. He
compared the Japanese economy to an "old jalopy (automobile) which was
expected to be supplied with oil and gas from the U.S. but which never is
repaired." American subsidies kept it moving, but the "entire effort of the
present administration was going to be on the repairs." Of course, he would
"continue to expect to be supplied with gas and oil" in the meantime.

Ikeda's comments left Dodge perplexed. He agreed that the government
had far too large a workforce, but he saw no advantage in firing government
workers on the one hand, only to rehire them for public works on the
other. "It would serve merely to transfer the individual from one government payroll to another," he argued. Ikeda's plan failed to create any
"incentive to the individual to answer his own problem by seeking other
employment," and the economy needed more entrepreneurs, not more
relief work. Besides, Dodge had already rejected the idea of tax cuts in the
last conversation. What had changed?

"The Communists [are] gaining ground," responded Ikeda, "by using
the tax burden as a basis of propaganda."

Dodge ignored Ikeda's threat. "The basic comparison should be with
what the tax burden might be if U.S. aid were to be less," he warned.
Besides, "if inflation is not checked and proceeds as it has in the past, one
sure result would be that the communists would win anyhow." More to the
point, "No one can afford to be black-mailed by the communists." (Privately, Dodge noted, "Intelligence reports emphasize . . . that the trouble
[with the communists] is caused not so much by the amount of the tax as
the inequities in tax administration.")

Ikeda paused. Finally, seeming to understand Dodge's position, he
returned to the news reports of Dodge's first press conference. Is this what
Dodge meant, Ikeda asked, when he said he wanted "recovery without
fiction?"

"Yes," Dodge replied. "What bothers the United States is the fiction."[59]

Throughout March, Dodge's team continued work on the Japanese
budget. Much as MacArthur had grown frustrated with Japanese efforts to
write a new constitution and had therefore written one for them, so too

Dodge decided to craft his own budget and require the Japanese to implement it. Indeed, in many ways the two documents stood as the American view on how to create and maintain a democracy in Japan. The first provided the basic institutional framework; the second sustained those institutions through the mechanism of the budget (which Dodge called a statement of "the national purpose"). If the first provided an outline for democracy, the second filled in the material details.

In several radios to Washington, Dodge outlined the principles that informed the budget he had prepared for Japan. He wanted it to be transparent. It needed to clearly show all government revenues, costs, and activities. "U.S. aid should be included in [the] national budget," he explained. "Subsidies should be clearly revealed," as should "government agencies, including government corporations" and all workers on government payrolls. Once he had accomplished this, he felt a "progressive and effective rationalization program" would follow—meaning markets would again punish the inefficient and reward the innovative. The Reconstruction Finance Bank would only collect "presently outstanding industrial loans"; he stripped it of the ability to generate new loans. The state had to rid itself of all "shadow personnel" and reduce subsidies, particularly for transportation. He wanted "railway and communications operations" (both state utilities) placed on a "self-supporting basis" and saw no reason for expanding their "current facilities" through public works.[60]

Transparency and rationalization served multiple, overlapping purposes. They strengthened Japan's fledgling democracy by informing the public of Japan's real economic situation. They also disciplined firms and workers into practicing efficiency and thrift. Finally, they prepared Japan for entering the global marketplace, where it would need to dramatically improve its products to compete successfully with other nations. By accomplishing these ends Japan could effectively gain "admission as a responsible and peaceful member of the family of nations."[61] These were tall orders, however, and Dodge concluded that four budget items created the biggest obstacles for their accomplishment.

First: Accounting for U.S. aid. While measured in dollars, in practice the aid followed a circuitous route that hid the actual impact of the program. As was true with Marshall aid, when the U.S. Congress appropriated funds for foreign aid, it did not simply write a check. Instead, it used the appropriation to purchase American products (usually staple foods), which it then shipped to Japan. Once the goods arrived, the Japanese government took possession and sold the products. The proceeds fell into a kind of slush fund not part of the official budget. The opportunity for graft was obvious. Dodge wanted to end this practice by putting the proceeds on the books and creating a "counterpart fund" with SCAP in "complete control" of disbursement. Any disbursal remained "conditional upon" agreements from the "Japanese Government and banking institutions" as to the impact on the "budget, monetary and credit control," as well as some demonstrated "achievement by [the] recipients of funds."[62]

Second: Exchange rates. Like much else in the Japanese economy, trade ran a circuitous route. The Japanese government channeled "all foreign trade . . . through the *Boeki Cho* (Board of Trade)." The Boeki Cho purchased any item going into foreign trade "at a yen price sufficient to cover the cost of production plus a fair profit," and then sold those goods "at world price levels." For imports, it did the same thing in reverse. Political pressure worked on both sides of the exchange: the Boeki Cho tended to buy domestic products above world prices and sell world products back to Japanese consumers below world prices.[63] Officially, it accounted for these differences by listing thousands of different exchange rates for specific items. In reality, though, the government simply subsidized both sides of the exchange. This had the practical effect of hiding from the public the reality of Japan's meager export situation. Officially, the government could claim increasing levels of exports; but since the government underwrote the sale abroad, in reality, the more Japan exported, the more money it lost. Moreover, the practice created a disincentive for Japanese firms to innovate. Dodge solved this problem by unilaterally setting the exchange rate at 360 yen to the dollar (a rate that stayed in place for more than two decades) and scrapping the Boeki Cho system.[64]

Third: Price subsidies. The Japanese government used "special accounts" to subsidize nearly all aspects of economic life. The accounts rarely appeared as an official part of the budget so that on paper the Japanese government had never run a deficit. The "final budget as recommended by SCAP," Dodge declared, "will . . . transfer to [the] General Account all previously hidden subsidies."[65] As for subsidies themselves, they "must be reduced to barest necessary minimum at once and be progressively and rapidly eliminated." The "resulting cost pressures plus careful raw materials allocation should be used to force more rapid rationalization [of] production methods and schedules." Specifically, he wanted "inefficient high cost producers . . . foreclosed from using critical scarce materials."[66] He did not, however, demand an end to all subsidies. "Consumer price increases should be minimized," he explained, recognizing the legitimate need for providing relief through some staple goods. Instead, he targeted the "reduction and elimination [of any] subsidies" on those items "which cannot be absorbed by [the] rationalization program."[67]

Fourth (and finally): Labor. From Dodge's perspective, the regime of subsidies created too many rent-seeking incentives for the workforce, particularly for workers in the public sector. He wanted to "separate projects to relieve unemployment from [a] regular public works program."[68] Too many public works projects had been "designed [for the] purpose [of] subsidizing individuals," and government agencies and monopolies ran massive losses largely by employing "shadow workers." Dodge wanted all government monopolies (such as the railways) "reorganized and conducted so as [to] realize maximum possible net revenue" with the goal of becoming "self-supporting." He required that government work projects "not be approved unless local government can meet its share of costs from revenues or without increasing total debt."[69]

With the outline of his budget complete, Dodge knew he needed the support of SCAP's bureaucrats to help enforce it, in large part because he planned to return to the States, leaving them behind to "tend the shop." In a lengthy meeting on March 14, 1949, he argued his proposals, explaining his thoughts and responding to questions. SCAP's junior officials raised an immediate concern. "We must consider the political implications of any policy which will depress the standard of living of the Japanese worker," they pointed out. Citing estimates that Dodge's budget would cut 20 to 30 percent of the government workforce alone, they pressed him: "If [significant] unemployment results from rationalization something must be done."

Dodge hoped "separation allowances [i.e., severance pay] and unemployment insurance" might provide enough temporary relief.

"[Do you have] a reserve for this purpose?" asked an official.

"We contemplate a surplus [officially designated] for debt reduction [but] which is also a contingency fund [for this purpose]."

"How about relief to people who are not covered by unemployment insurance?"

"We intend to provide enough to meet this problem," Dodge concluded.

In short, Dodge planned to run a small surplus so that he had options for any contingencies that might arise (most likely significant unemployment). But in reality, the new budget was a gamble. The whole occupation effort could come undone if rationalization led to political disintegration.

Many of the SCAP staff thought exactly that would happen. Dodge's approach seemed brazenly harsh and his answers to their concerns too glib. But they had little wiggle room at this point because MacArthur and Marquat had committed. "Under an austerity program," General Marquat told his staff, "everyone must take some curtailment." MacArthur had made a career out of bold ventures. The Dodge budget would be no exception. "Everything . . . of a drastic nature should be done as a 'one-shot' proposition," he explained, "with easing off thereafter."[70] The SCAP staff did not like it and with good reason feared the worst. But the Dodge Line (as the Japanese were to call his budget principles) had become SCAP's new law.

Chapter 10

Implementing the "Dodge Line"

With Washington informed and SCAP on board, Dodge finally presented his budget to Ikeda with the understanding that Ikeda would see that it passed through the Japanese legislature (the Diet) without amendment. Ikeda was horrified. On March 25, 1949, he came to question Dodge about it. Raising the question of tax reduction once again, Ikeda hoped to get at least a "token reduction in the income tax by increasing exemptions." He needed some political cover in order to pass the budget.

Dodge refused. The budget had "no leeway."

But the "projected increase in the cost of rice and the tax would cut too heavily into the subsistence" of many Japanese workers, Ikeda complained.

"It is true," Dodge replied "that the tax burden [is] heavy." But "it [is] heavy in the United States and even heavier in some other countries." More to the point, "It *should* be heavy under the circumstances; and in principle the time [has] come for [the Japanese] to pay for some of their past mistakes."

But "the higher cost of rice and commuter railway fare costs could be partially offset by a token reduction in the tax" without breaking the budget, Ikeda retorted.

Dodge decided to appeal to the budgetary principle underlying his position. "[I] believe a heavy tax burden [is] *necessary.* . . . There should be an end to answering all problems from the budget." Indeed, "the more complaints there [are] about taxes, the more incentive there [will] be for the government to accomplish reduction of expenditures because everything the Japanese Government has done to date has contributed to the high taxes."

"There is no question but what the patient [is] ill and needs a doctor" Ikeda agreed. However, "a token reduction in the tax would serve as a sedative to relieve the shock and permit carrying out of the budget and provide support to the budget."

It is "time to stop ducking the issues," Dodge responded in frustration. Recent history in Japan "showed a continued series of concessions made on promises which had not been performed." America "wanted . . . a record of performance." Generalizing the problem, Dodge said that this "was not a reflection on [Prime Minister] Yoshida or [Ikeda], but on the practice of the Japanese Government." Indeed, "if the United States had been as lax in meeting its obligations with respect to Japanese aid as the Japanese [have] been in meeting their obligations to the United States, there would have been even more serious difficulties."

"[I] want only this [one] concession," Ikeda replied. "It [is] understood that . . . there [will] be no other claim or dispute about the budget." Ikeda "could give every assurance that this was true." He then warned, "this single thing would be paving the road for the budget and [I am] not sure of carrying it out without this concession."

Dodge tried to contain his frustration. He had "every sympathy" for Ikeda's position, but "even more sympathy for the United States." Ikeda "did not realize what an easy time" he had had compared to *other* "occupied areas" Dodge knew of.

Ikeda fell silent. Perhaps "it might be necessary . . . to turn over to someone else the carrying out of the budget." He threatened to resign.

"Strike and resignation proposals [seem] to be the usual answer when the Japanese [do] not get what they want," Dodge said coldly.

Would "a request from Mr. Yoshida . . . be more effective?"

No. Mr. Ikeda's "request had as much weight as that of anyone."

Out of options, Ikeda paused. He "hoped Mr. Dodge was not offended." Dodge "assured" him "he was not." Ikeda left.[1]

Over the next several weeks, Ikeda and other party leaders continued to meet with Dodge and seek concessions on the budget. When it became clear that Dodge would not give on taxes, they sought better control of the counterpart fund. Again Dodge refused. Finally, they decided that since it was Dodge's budget, he ought to be the one to speak publicly for it. They pressed Dodge to make a public statement taking responsibility for the budget, hoping thereby to avoid political blame for a budget they thought would be widely unpopular. To their surprise, Dodge agreed.

His press statement of April 15, 1949, was unprecedented. Until this point most occupation officials had followed MacArthur's conciliating messages to the Japanese. The problems of occupation were "by no means due to fault of yours . . . but rather to events and circumstances elsewhere beyond your capacity to influence or control."² By contrast, Dodge threw down the gauntlet. The blame for all Japanese problems rested upon the Japanese themselves. "There seems to be astonishingly little comprehension among the Japanese people of the real situation of their country," he explained. "Nothing should have been expected as the result of the war but a long term of hardship and self-denial." Instead, "the nation continuously has been living beyond its means." The government was the foremost offender. "There has been a general disposition in the Japanese government to accede to any demand to spend more and more." But this proved self-defeating. "Governments only spend other people's money." In short, "wealth must be created before it can be divided."

In explaining the new budget, he emphasized its moral clarity. "The general use of subsidies is abnormal and undesirable." Worse, subsidies created "fictitious and unnatural price relationships." The new budget brought everything hidden to light and put before the Japanese the true cost of their policies. More to the point, a balanced, consolidated budget "should have been made an integral part of each party platform." It rose above politics and amounted to "a Japanese national problem, not a political party problem." Indeed, "the Japanese people should demand a balanced budget and should then direct their attention to the elimination of excessive expenditures, wastefulness, subsidies, over employment and the general dependence on government instead of individual or group accomplishment."³

The next morning all across Japan newspapers responded. The *Nippon Times* declared that "the [Yoshida] Administration . . . [has] been anxious for some official statement from the SCAP authorities which it could use to silence the discontent in certain quarters." However, Dodge's statement was "undoubtedly more than the Administration bargained for." Dodge had gone far in "pointing out how unsound Japan's fiscal policy has been during the past several years." More important, Dodge showed "how this unsound fiscal policy has been hidden from the knowledge of the people by a highly complicated and incomprehensible budget which served to deceive the average citizen regarding the state of the Government's finances." The *Nippon Times* largely endorsed the budgetary changes despite the temporary pain and heartily supported the underlying ideology Dodge expressed. "The greatest effect of Mr. Dodge's statement will go far beyond the matter of this year's budget alone" because it "will inevitably help spur a necessary fundamental reform in the government's budgetary practices so that in the future the taxpayers will nevermore be fooled as they were in the past."[4]

Echoing the *Times,* the *Tokyo Shimbun* wrote, "It is regrettable that the Government's explanations of the budget bill to the *Diet* were not so plain and detailed as Minister Dodge's statement." By contrast, "discussions in the *Diet* are being carried out brazenly, as though the fact that Japan is a defeated nation has been forgotten. . . . Minister Dodge's statement on the draft budget must have been like a bucket of water poured on those dreaming after taking a narcotic."[5] The *Jiji Shimpo* wrote approvingly, "In the past the Government met the requirements of industry for working capital . . . by means of the central bank's credit backed by national power." In other words, "the past formula was political rather than purely economical." Under Dodge's budget, "industrial funds will flow according to purely economic value—at least with economic value as a center." They would "reflect the actual conditions of economy."[6] The *Sekai Keizai* also agreed. "A sizable portion of the people are intoxicated with inflation, and many have lost the will to work and are living on what they have accumulated in the past," it wrote. "It is time we take stock of ourselves, bearing in mind that inflation has virtually crippled national finance, enterprise, and management, and has plunged the national economy into disorder."[7] *Yomiuri* summed up the entire situation: "Now is the time for the nation to face stern reality bravely." No longer could the Japanese hope for perpetual aid "in order to prevent Japan from going communistic." Rather, "it is necessary to realize that [the] US aims to help the Japanese regain their independence through their own efforts, rather than to give them relief."[8]

A few papers dissented. The *Oriental Economist,* where Tanzan Ishibashi had served as editor in chief for years before becoming finance minister, wanted to remind "Minister Dodge" that the Japanese knew all too well the "hardship and self-denial" that had followed the war. They "experienced in marked degrees the results of war damages, direct and indirect, in their daily mode of living." Moreover, echoing Ikeda's arguments with Dodge, the magazine worried that the budget made "no revision of the taxation system" in the face of "the austerity living which is being forced upon the people." It worried that Dodge had thrown "economic circles into confusion."[9]

The London *Economist* took a position between them all. "For four years MacArthur . . . has said much the same thing [as Dodge] in loftier terms and windier sentences," but "without successful result." It remained "to be seen whether Dodge, the banker, can achieve better results." Surveying the political scene, the *Economist* noted that the "Communists certainly will wish him luck part of the way in the hope of thwarting him ultimately all the way." More ominous, "in the background, smoothly exploiting these Communist hopes, will still be lined up the bland, bowing ranks of the old-style Japanese bureaucrats and permanent officials, who baffled and bemused the soldiers, and who, in the event of overhardening of the American heart, will inevitably murmur to the expert: 'So sorry, plis [*sic*], but if no American money, maybe Japan go Communist.' "[10]

As he saw Dodge off for the United States in early May, MacArthur told him how profoundly he had affected the Japanese political culture. "[You have] been of inestimable value and should have a lasting influence upon Japanese thought." Once Dodge had boarded the plane for home, MacArthur returned to his office and radioed Washington. He offered his "sincere hope that [President Truman] will lend his hearty support to my own efforts to convince [Dodge] that he should return to Japan just as soon as practicable."[11] MacArthur had decided aligning himself with Dodge had the best chance of brightening his own light.

Once he was back in Detroit, Dodge became entrenched at his bank. Still, he continued to monitor the situation in Japan, reading daily news reports and cables throughout the summer. Ikeda began to implement Dodge's budget and start the rationalization process, moving away from "priority production" and toward an export-driven economy. As it turned out, the move could not have come at a worse time. In late 1948, the United States slowly moved into a recession that lasted until October 1949, leading to a global economic slowdown. The effect on the British economy proved particularly harsh, creating a currency crisis and a devaluation of the pound (and the broader sterling area), which made Japanese exports (particularly in Britain's Asian colonial markets) relatively more expensive. Japan's economy struggled through the summer of 1949.

As the Japanese felt the immediate effects of the Dodge Line, some revolted. The most vociferous protests involved government monopolies, where price rises and layoffs went hand in hand. About 126,000 railway workers lost their jobs; at the same time, commuters saw rates jump 50 percent. Unhappy workers took part in strikes, sabotaged lines, and seized cars while riders protested.[12] Two incidents in July proved particularly troubling. Officials found the body of Shimoyama Sadanori, president of Japan's National Railways, along a rail line outside Tokyo. Many saw it as a sign of more violence to come. That same month a sabotaged car plunged into a crowd in western Tokyo, killing a number of waiting commuters. [13]

Japan's National Personnel Authority estimated that the Dodge budget resulted in a quarter of a million central government employees losing their jobs, with another quarter million losing local government jobs. The Yoshida government seized the opportunity to rid the bureaucracy of employees it considered "disloyal"—whether Communist or simple supporters of the "wrong" candidates (about twenty-two thousand in all). Yoshida blamed Dodge for the dismissals.[14] Yoshida also revised SCAP's initial labor laws to give the state more power to resolve labor disputes, a reform that might have aided labor unions under different circumstances but which Yoshida used to discipline them instead.[15] The *Oriental Economist*, which by mid-summer 1949 had joined Communist papers in leading the criticism of the Dodge Line, argued that "unless basic economic remedies are administered, it will be difficult to avoid a crisis which, once encountered, may prove fatal."[16] A panicked State Department memo agreed: "The economic stabilization program has met with widespread opposition from the major segments of Japanese society—opposition that is having adverse political repercussions and is a potential threat to the successful implementation of the stabilization program and to the prestige of the United States occupation."[17]

At the same time, officials within SCAP became perplexed. True, politically speaking Japan seemed in an uproar. But economically speaking, matters seemed to be going better than even the most optimistic expectations. "The fundamental fear which appears to dominate the thinking of those opposed to the Dodge Mission," wrote the Chief of SCAP's Price and Distribution Division, "is that mass unemployment will occur" or that a "political atmosphere will develop" that favored the Communists. However, "thus far major unemployment has not occurred."[18] Indeed, Walter Le-Count, SCAP's chief economist, concluded that "an analysis of various indicators of economic activity" demonstrated that Japanese "statements [about] . . . the existence and strength of deflationary forces are greatly exaggerated and that . . . nothing in the current situation [should] require changing present financial and economic policy."[19]

LeCount was right: all the official statistics suggested that rationalizing and reorienting the Japanese economy cost far less than anyone had anticipated. Over the eighteen months after the Dodge Line's implementation, unemployment surpassed the pre-line level in just two months. It never

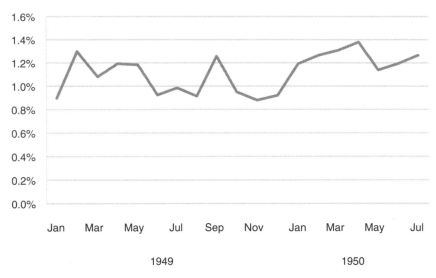

Figure 10. Japan's unemployment (January 1949–July 1950). Source: Programs and Statistics Division, Economic and Scientific Section, GHQ, SCAP, Japanese Economic Statistics, 39, 3:18, February 15, Mainichi 1950.

broke above the 2 percent line, an astonishingly low number even in a climate of economic expansion. Real wages grew, and, most important, the inflation rate dropped dramatically. By January 1950, it hit zero. "It's a textbook example of how a budget can stop an inflation cold," he said with a little awe to a group of SCAP officers.[20]

Thus, the persistent criticism grated on Dodge. "Practically every adverse circumstance is alleged to be caused by the Stabilization Program," he complained to Ikeda in August 1949.[21] In a lengthy follow-up, he warned Ikeda there was "no surprise that exaggerations and alarms should arise from [interests that] encouraged the road of inflation." Ikeda should anticipate that "the internal enemies of the country" would "attempt to restore inflation" by plunging "the country into a crisis." They would do this "by spreading unwarranted seeds of fear." He encouraged Ikeda to think of 1949 and 1950 as a time for Japan "to prepare itself . . . to engage in . . . intense world competition on an effective and self-sustaining basis." He worried that the nation could "not provide for itself as a high cost, low quality producer." In hopes of genuinely converting Ikeda to his views, he preached that "an effective stabilization . . . should encourage saving,

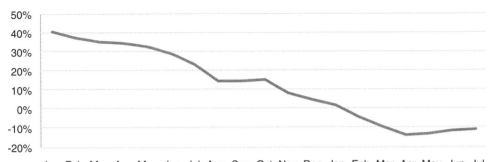

Figure 11. Japan's inflation rate (January 1949–July 1950) (year-over-year). Source: Programs and Statistics Division, Economic and Scientific Section, GHQ, SCAP, Japanese Economic Statistics, 39, 3:18, February 15, Mainichi 1950.

reduce or eliminate the black market, increase production efficiency, and further lower prices." This had more than economic virtues. "Inflation, black market activities, and a continual rise in prices destroy both monetary and moral values. It is time that money reacquires some of its practical values."[22]

*   *   *

While the Dodge Line remained the principle domestic news item throughout the summer of 1949 in Japan, it obscured an important follow-up mission sent from Washington to investigate the Japanese tax system. Japanese taxes had not changed substantially since the war and the mission, headed by the economist Carl Shoup, spent several months over the summer on "field trips" conducting "extensive interviews" around the country to understand the Japanese method of tax collection.[23] By the end of the year, the mission recommended a number of revisions for a fairer tax burden. It also recommended that "personal income taxes should be put at levels where the moderately well-to-do will have incentive to invest and work"; whereas for "the extremely wealthy, the tax rates should be kept high enough to avoid concentration of economic power in the hands of a few persons."[24] From Dodge's perspective, Shoup's research revealed something more important. Specifically, it revealed that, once again, a whole approach to state finances had gone lost in translation.[25]

Shoup revealed that Japanese tax collectors worked on a quota system, where each office needed to collect a certain amount within a year's time. Thus, the collectors focused on meeting their quota. "Many tax offices simply stopped collecting when they reached their 'goal,'" Dodge learned. Recognizing the situation, taxpayers and especially corporations procrastinated their taxes as long as possible in the hopes of avoiding taxation altogether, knowing that if they could wait long enough, the collector might reach his quota without ever coming back around. This approach made sense if the goal lay in generating a specific amount of revenue within a year's time. It made no sense if the goal lay in spreading the tax burden equitably across the entire population.[26]

When Dodge and SCAP officials realized taxes worked this way, they simply required tax collectors to collect the legal amount required from everyone each year. The new approach to taxes combined with Dodge's budget suddenly generated a 260 billion yen surplus. "There was jubilation in GHQ," a SCAP economist wrote Dodge late in 1949.[27] SCAP officials had anticipated widespread unemployment and a tiny surplus. They had not prepared for low unemployment and a sudden tax bounty.

Of course, Ikeda noticed the sudden surplus as well. He immediately called for tax relief, returning to his central concern from earlier that year. Feeling the pressure to undo the budget because of the windfall, MacArthur worked behind the scenes to get Dodge to return to Japan. "The No. 1 [Mac-Arthur] begged the [Under] Secretary [of the Army, Tracy Voorhees] to have you return here," Marquat wrote Dodge in the fall of 1949. "I really don't know who admired and praised you more, MacArthur or Voorhees," but "there was definitely a *fear* that you might not be able to make it."[28] Dodge reluctantly agreed. "Of course, the real reason [MacArthur and Marquat] want me there," he wrote a colleague, was that "I stand for certain principles and objectives which have been made clear to the Japanese Government, the Japanese people, and the SCAP organization." With Dodge in Tokyo, it served "mostly to make it easier to accomplish what has to be done. . . . It is a form of insurance of another year's continuation of the established policies." He had become a symbol and that "should be my principal contribution" during his second Japan trip. [29] He arrived the day before Halloween, 1949.

"We were able to approve a supplementary budget," Dodge announced soon after arriving, "which included not only increased expenditures over the original budget of last March, but also a tax reduction [along with] substantial provisions for debt retirement." He felt comfortable relenting because he "noted a marked improvement in the Japanese situation despite the complaints of the vested interests in inflation." Indeed, he felt pride in the fact that "Japan is somewhat ahead of most of the countries of the world which are attempting to get their own fiscal houses in order." In fact, in every measurable way, he saw success. "The wage and price situation . . . has apparently been stabilized. Black market prices are coming down. The food situation is improving. The overall government fiscal position has been completely reversed."[30] SCAP officials agreed. William Reed, SCAP's chief of public finance, reported in mid-February 1950, that "economic prospects over the next year appear to be very good." Among other things, "the index of industrial production . . . has remained stable" despite the "heavy reductions in the government public works program, the program of employee and public housing . . , and in the face of the complete elimination of . . . the RFB." Indeed, the economy's stability in spite of the layoffs suggested just how many laborers did no productive work.[31]

Despite the growing signs of success, many Japanese remained deeply pessimistic about the Dodge Line and continued to argue against it. A popular approach involved pitting Truman's domestic policy against Dodge. "A very sound basis of stabilization is being accomplished although it is meeting increasing pressures from various groups," MacArthur complained to Dodge. "One of the greatest difficulties I have to overcome, and a growing one," he continued, "is the basic difference in the policies we are imposing here and the policies being followed in the United States." The Japanese had become aware of the basic contradiction between Dodge's and Truman's policies. Truman, in his second term, had grown more Keynesian and began to favor deficit spending as a means to economic growth. As Japanese officials used Truman's words against Dodge's plan, MacArthur found his position quite awkward. The Japanese had some justification for asking "why we do not practice what we preach."[32]

In the meantime, the *Oriental Economist* continued to worry that "the expectations [of recovery] may fail to materialize." While the slow "increase in trade volume offers some hope . . . this alone will not suffice to mitigate the depression" Japan suffered.[33] The *Nippon Times* echoed the judgment: "Finance Minister Ikeda should personally contact Minister Joseph M. Dodge to ask him for a revision of the Dodge Line, because the Japanese

Government has recently come to a blind alley in regard to small business, agrarian village and labor wage questions."[34]

The persistent disconnect between the official statistics and press accounts of economic life perplexed Dodge and others in SCAP. Initially, they responded with frustration. But frustration began to give way to paranoia. Citing the continued bad press, Dodge asked Ikeda if he saw "a substantial effort to sabotage the program."[35] Throughout the spring, Japanese Communists became more confrontational toward the occupation and, in doing so, provoked greater distrust from SCAP. "It is an open secret," wrote the *Economist* "that . . . many purged Japanese military officers have joined the [Communist] Party—officially or unofficially."[36] Japan's left-of-center parties and labor groups also began to openly criticize the occupation.[37] From SCAP's perspective, stabilization remained a national problem standing above partisan politics. But Japan's Social Democrats complained that Dodge's "super-balanced budget" had led to deflation. "A conflict between the balanced budget and the decrease of purchasing power" needed resolving in favor of "lightening of the income tax burden and raising of the wage base for public servants." The Social Democrats also sought easier access to the Counterpart Fund.[38]

Because SCAP saw little statistical evidence in the critics' concerns, they began to view opposition as so many "vested interests" profiting from inflation. The Japanese chose to "sound alarms," wrote one SCAP official, rather than face the "necessity for rationalization."[39] Marquat concluded that pro-inflationary forces had "widely publicized their viewpoints with the idea of pressurizing us" into freeing up the Counterpart Fund.[40] Another SCAP economist noted that "many forces are at work to unbalance a budget and few forces at work to keep it in balance."[41] From SCAP's perspective, the strength of the opposition demonstrated how far Japan stood from the political maturity necessary to become an independent democracy.

Still, for all the difficulties involved in stabilization, the program had clearly begun to produce results. The predicted depression never materialized. Exports, and particularly contracts committing Japanese firms for future deliveries, had grown quickly through the end of 1949 and into 1950.[42]

And then it happened. On June 25, 1950, North Korean military forces crossed into South Korea. President Truman, supported by the Joint Chiefs

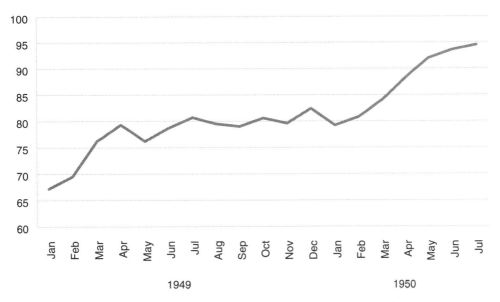

Figure 12. Japan's industrial production (January 1949–July 1950). Source: Programs and Statistics Division, Economic and Scientific Section, GHQ, SCAP, Japanese Economic Statistics, 39, 3:18. February 15, Mainichi 1950.

of Staff as well as the State Department (headed by Secretary of State Dean Acheson), decided to defend South Korea. As Acheson explained, the invasion "struck a blow at the foundation" of collective security and represented a "dagger thrust" from Joseph Stalin, which "pinned a warning notice to the wall [and] said: 'Give up or be conquered!' "[43] Two days later, the United Nations voted to join the conflict. On July 8, Truman named MacArthur to the United Nations Command in South Korea, a position he held in addition to remaining military governor in Japan. Korea would be his last war and last chance at glory.[44] Japan suddenly became the forward staging base for the Korean War, which meant a sudden influx of capital and demand for supplies. Yoshida called the war a "gift of the gods" (obviously ignoring the impact it had on those fighting).[45]

By contrast, Dodge experienced the war as nothing less than a complete disaster. Almost from the moment of its outbreak, in June 1950, his influence declined. Yoshida recognized perfectly Japan's importance in George Kennan's "Great Crescent" defense perimeter.[46] As the *Economist* noted, the

Yoshida government was "smugly anticipating bigger and better peace treaty rewards from the United States and Britain for continued Japanese democratic loyalty."[47] With its economy suddenly booming and Washington consumed with fear of global communism, the political winds had shifted again, and Yoshida knew it.

As soon as the war started, SCAP economists feared an inflationary outbreak. Ralph Reid, the army's chief of Far Eastern affairs, noted, "The problems at immediate issue are . . . how to cushion the inflationary impact on Japan of expenditures for items required in Korea." Reid felt that "the budget and the stabilization program represent the keys to the entire Japanese economic situation and, in turn, to the entire Japanese position in the world today."[48] Marquat and MacArthur both wanted Dodge to return to Japan a third time to navigate the Japanese economy through this new challenge.[49] "There is nothing remotely comparable to the stabilization program as the outstanding accomplishment in Japan to date," Marquat wrote Dodge. "The success of this program is largely attributable to your willingness to follow its progress from afar and to return to battle for its continuation on the ground."[50]

Again, Dodge relented and agreed to return. As soon as he arrived in October 1950, he announced to the press a theme he returned to again and again over the next year. "Japan has not yet answered its need and proved its ability to earn its own living with normal exports in increasingly competitive world markets," he said. "To do this the export effort has to be accelerated and strengthened and not weakened by the unexpected windfall" coming from the war. War created an abnormal situation, another fiction. "The standard of living in Japan depends on the expansion of *normal* exports," he argued.[51] Privately, in meetings with Ikeda, Dodge explained that neither man wanted "such a sudden rise in the standard of living that it has to come down later on. You want it to rise gradually and on a firm basis that can be maintained." In particular, this meant ensuring that "consumption *not* expand . . . to an abnormal degree."[52] Ikeda listened politely. But he knew that the clock had started to wind down on Dodge's influence, and that Japan could soon chart its own course.

While SCAP officials tried to fight a rearguard action against inflation in Japan, United Nations forces similarly retreated in the face of North Korean troops who had largely overrun South Korean forces. By the end of August, they held only a toehold around Pusan near the southern tip of the peninsula. On September 15, however, a risky but successful amphibious attack led by American troops at Inch'on, just west of Seoul, completely reversed the strategic situation on the peninsula.[53] As the North Korean army rapidly retreated over the next month, the war seemed to have become a United Nations rout. The momentum reversal, however, left Truman at a crossroads: should MacArthur's surprise victory at Inch'on simply restore the borders of four months earlier, or reunite the Korean people under American guardianship. On September 27, MacArthur received orders that his "military objective is the destruction of the North Korean Armed Forces." The orders authorized him to "conduct military operations, including amphibious and airborne landings or ground operations north of the 38th parallel in Korea [that is, into North Korea]." However, MacArthur should only cross into North Korea "provided that at the time of such operation there has been no entry into North Korea by major Soviet or Chinese Communist Forces, no announcement of intended entry, nor a threat to counter our operations militarily in North Korea." The orders also indicated that, "Under no circumstances . . . will your forces cross the Manchurian or USSR borders of Korea." This included "Air or Naval action against Manchuria or against USSR territory."[54] In short, he could proceed north, but only in a limited fashion and only in the interest of destroying the North's army. Implicitly, the orders hoped to prevent the Korean conflict from expanding into a general war with the Soviet Union.

In early October, MacArthur called for an unconditional surrender from the North. When the North refused, he sent United Nations troops across the original border. In the United States, the State Department began planning an occupation of the North that would end with a rebuilt and reunited Korea.[55] By mid-October, however, warning signs of a Chinese entry into the conflict came from many directions. For one thing, Chinese officials (working through Indian intermediaries) openly warned the United States that China "did not intend to sit back with folded hands and let the Americans come up to [our] border."[56] Initially, Truman thought China was bluffing. By the end of that month, United Nations troops began bumping into small Chinese contingents and, perhaps more ominously, supply caches designed for a much larger Chinese assault to come. As it turned out, on October 18, Mao Zedong had ordered two hundred thousand troops to cross into North Korea and await the unsuspecting United Nations advance. Most important, by marching only at night and covering themselves with camouflage during the day, the Chinese troops evaded American aerial reconnaissance.[57]

Truman directly broached the subject of Chinese intervention during a meeting with MacArthur on Wake Island (a U.S territory in the mid-Pacific) in November. He asked MacArthur "what the chances are of Chinese or Soviet interference?"

MacArthur did not hesitate. "Very little," he said confidently.

Thus, when the Chinese launched a full counteroffensive at the end of November, they caught United Nations troops unaware and unprepared. The momentum of war again swung dramatically in the other direction. Soon, the United Nations forces retreated south faster than they had advanced north, reaching the original North-South border in less than a month, and continuing further south into January.[58] The optimism of October had vanished in the face of what now appeared an unwinnable war. Truman began to search for "peace without victory," in part because America's United Nations allies began to lose interest in a long war of attrition.[59]

The reversal in Korea also set off a search for scapegoats. In reality, all parts of the foreign policy establishment could take blame. While Truman and his advisers thought Chinese intervention possible, they deferred to MacArthur far too easily, never challenging his assumptions. Perhaps because of this, Truman did not publicly blame MacArthur in the wake of China's military advances in Korea.

By contrast, MacArthur began to hint that Truman was responsible for the reverses on the battlefield. Specifically, he focused on his orders of September 27 and their basic premise—not to expand the war into China or the Soviet Union—as the real cause for China's success. At a press conference on December 1, he told a reporter that these orders put United Nations forces under "an enormous handicap, without precedent in military history." He went on to suggest that he had known all along China would enter the conflict, characterizing his drive to the Chinese border as "preemptive"—he hoped to take the fight to them, to "beat the Chinese communists to the punch."[60]

Back in Washington, a stunned Truman simply issued a directive to MacArthur that he "refrain from direct communications on military or foreign policy with newspapers, magazines, and other publicity media." A gag order.[61] Truman understood that MacArthur wanted to save face and, at this critical juncture, did not want to embarrass him or create controversy for United Nations forces. But for the same reasons, he did not want MacArthur to pursue his face-saving campaign in public, either.[62]

Undaunted, MacArthur turned to his longtime assistant General Courtney Whitney and asked him, in Whitney's role as legal adviser, to review the directive. Whitney provided the counsel MacArthur wanted: Truman's directive applied only to official press statements. It did not cover "communiqués, correspondence or personal conversations."[63] MacArthur continued to rewrite history, albeit through personal letters rather than in the press.

In the meantime, United Nations forces suffered one defeat after another in a long retreat down the peninsula. As if to symbolize the bad fortune, on December 23, 1950, General Walton Walker, the commanding general of the United States Eighth Army (the main American fighting force in Korea) died in a car crash. MacArthur replaced him with General Matthew Ridgway, a charismatic leader and brilliant tactician whom MacArthur saw as a protégé and the man who could help launch another surprise attack, this time into mainland China using Chinese Nationalist troops provided by Chiang Kai-shek.[64]

While Walker's death was tragic, it probably saved the United Nations' cause and stopped Truman from resorting to desperate measures (such as the use of an atomic bomb) in order to prevent the complete annihilation of the United Nations forces.[65] At least in the short term, Ridgway ignored MacArthur's plan for invading mainland China and focused instead on halting the North's advance. Much to his surprise, the Chinese were, by January, a spent fighting force. Cautiously but quickly, the Eighth Army began to advance north. By February 1951, Ridgway managed to reverse the momentum one more time so that, by March of 1951, the battle line stabilized within the general vicinity of the original North-South border.[66]

Ridgway's initial success, however, tended to contradict MacArthur's ongoing argument that no American commander could prevail under the guidelines coming from Washington. It also contradicted MacArthur's argument that "limited war" constituted an oxymoron. Ridgway showed that a military strategy of stalemate allowed, potentially, for a diplomatic strategy of negotiated peace. In so many ways, though, Ridgway's achievements increasingly picked at MacArthur's insecurities, especially as the press began to sense that Ridgway had not only taken the initiative from China but from MacArthur as well. "The fact remains," wrote the *Christian Science Monitor* in February 1951, "that the legend of General MacArthur's military infallibility . . . ended in the bleak cold of Korea's northern mountains."[67] The more Ridgway succeeded, the more pronounced MacArthur's November failure became.

Emotionally wounded and progressively more intent on saving face on a variety of fronts, MacArthur acted as if he feared peace could break out before he had had a chance at redemption. Indeed, a peace without victory became Truman's primary purpose once Ridgway stabilized the battle line. By mid-March, Truman began to hint that he would accept a final settlement of the Korean border near the current battle line (or roughly the original North-South border). MacArthur panicked. Pushing the limits of Truman's "gag order," he issued a statement on March 23, which reiterated his complaint about the "inhibitions," which restricted the "activity of the United Nations forces," but gave China "corresponding military advantages." Nevertheless, despite these constraints, "we have now substantially cleared South Korea of Communist forces." Chinese designs had been thwarted. More ominously, MacArthur warned that "the United Nations" might "depart from its tolerant effort to contain the war to the area of Korea" and expand "our military operations to [China's] coastal areas and interior bases" unless China came to negotiate a diplomatic solution, which MacArthur stood ready to personally lead.[68]

Many in the press understood that MacArthur's statement had no teeth to it. Rather, it signaled a breakdown in foreign policymaking. Soon after his statement went public, the State Department responded that, "The political issues which General MacArthur has stated are beyond his responsibilities . . . and are being dealt with in the United Nations."[69] Within the White House, Truman and his foreign policy team were furious. But Truman's advisers did not want to give the appearance of dissension within the ranks. Truman settled for a communiqué from the Joint Chiefs of Staff to MacArthur simply reminding him of the gag order.[70]

Unbeknownst to the administration, three days earlier MacArthur had written a letter to Congressman Joseph W. Martin, Jr., a Republican from Massachusetts, in which he reiterated his support for using a Chinese Nationalist army to invade mainland China. More to the point, he felt that the Asian theater deserved more attention than Europe, and finally that "there is no substitute for victory."[71] Once Martin received the letter, he decided to read it from the floor of the House. For Truman, it was the last straw.

On April 11, 1951, President Truman "fired" MacArthur. "I deeply regret," he wrote, "that it becomes my duty as President and Commander-in-Chief of the United States military forces to replace you as Supreme Commander, Allied Powers; Commander-in-Chief, United Nations Command; Commander-in-Chief, Far East; and Commanding General, U.S.

Army, Far East." Truman then named Ridgway as MacArthur's successor. "You will turn over your commands, effective at once, to Lt. Gen. Matthew B. Ridgway." Truman then added, "It is fundamental, however, that military commanders must be governed by the policies and directives issued to them in the manner provided by our laws and Constitution. In time of crisis, this consideration is particularly compelling."[72] In one stroke Ridgway became not only the man to bring the Korean War to a conclusion, but also (and most important for Dodge) the new SCAP.

As MacArthur feuded with Truman, SCAP officials had begun feuding with the State Department for a different set of reasons. The advent of the Korean War signaled to the State Department how critical Japanese loyalty had become in the Cold War, making a peace treaty increasingly paramount, regardless of the economic concerns raised by Dodge. State drafted a secret report that echoed Dodge's critics in the Japanese press, suggesting that stabilization had created significant hardships without much economic success. It concluded that political opposition against "the 'Dodge Line' . . . had general popular support" and predicted a total collapse of the occupation unless Dodge relented in his budgetary vigilance. Better to let the Japanese run their own economy as they wished, it concluded.[73]

When he learned of the report, Dodge responded with fury. "This is, without doubt, one of the most vicious attempts I have ever seen to portray a depreciation in the United States political position in Japan," he wrote Marquat.[74] SCAP's Economic Division wrote a terse letter of protest to Dean Rusk, the man in charge of the report, to share their "extreme concern" over a "substantial portion of the information presented in the report" that stood "in distinct contradiction to information available in the files of the Department of the Army."[75] After a series of sharp memos and phone calls, the controversy quieted. But it did not change State's sense of the situation.

When Ridgway became military governor, he had essentially no experience with Japan and, given the urgent fighting in Korea, minimal interest. When asked by the Japanese to deliver a speech on the anniversary of the new Japanese Constitution, he accepted but entirely deferred the construction of the speech to his political advisers from State. They drafted a speech that included a wordy and technical announcement stating: "The Japanese government has been authorized to review existing . . . directives from this headquarters, for the purpose of evolving . . . such modifications as . . . the present situation renders necessary and desirable." Despite the stilted prose,

Japanese officials understood exactly what the statement meant. They could begin to undo any SCAP directives if they felt it "necessary or desirable" to do so. Behind the scenes, State officials told the officials specifically to "review . . . the economic stabilization directive."[76]

Ridgway did not understand how he had been used. But Marquat did. He immediately wrote Dodge to vent his anger. "The complete lack of loyalty . . . must be apparent," he complained. "The Japanese have jumped on the bandwagon." They had organized a "high level committee," which would recommend rescinding those directives "considered inimical to the best interests of Japan in compliance with the SCAP's invitation."[77] Stabilization seemed ready to come undone.

Dodge agreed with Marquat. "I believe there is every possibility that the Japanese will break out into a rash of inflationary action," he complained. In particular, "the vested interests that have been established in [the] inflation" could now take charge again. It infuriated him that "over-extended . . . business and industry" would use inflation to bail "them out of debts" and might use the inflationary environment "to buy businesses and pay off the acquisition costs or loans with cheaper yen." It all heralded an attempt to "re-establish some form, even if modified, of the traditional monopoly capitalism of Japan."[78]

Marquat did his best to reverse what State had done, with some success. But the bigger issue lay in whether the Japanese had fully embraced the principles of transparent budgeting and the balanced budget. "The budget is under fairly serious attack through efforts to reduce . . . tax rates," a SCAP memo from spring 1951 noted. "While I think we will win out in the present instance I am quite sure that this is the last budget in which we will be able to maintain our position." The future depended on finding a "politically stable group capable of carrying through with a sound financial program." The voters had to keep Japanese officials in check. The various ministers could "recognize the problem and the measures best suited to its solution," but they nearly always chose "specific action . . . dictated by an immediate political expedience rather than by the long run good of the country."[79] Marquat wrote Dodge: "I am convinced that the Japanese are in the insipient stages of a planned inflation which can and will develop rapidly unless checked."[80]

Once again, Marquat asked Dodge to return to Japan. Once again, Dodge agreed. But by this time, the Japanese had signed a treaty with the United States. The occupation would come to an end soon. Dodge had become nothing more than the symbol of the political economy that military government stood for. He decided to appeal to the Japanese people and warn them to keep a close eye on their government. "Everyone should clearly understand the fundamental problem of Japan." Japan needed access to raw materials, which the United States could not guarantee once the Peace Treaty of San Francisco (officially ending the war) went into effect. Japan would have to compete with the rest of the world for American goods, and its "ability to compete in export markets, which is a matter of price and quality and not the mere ability to increase production," would largely determine Japan's future standard of living. He warned that Japan might "price itself out of its export markets with a domestic inflation." Summing up, Dodge argued that "Japan cannot afford to be misled by the honeyed promises of the Pied Pipers of inflation," who represented "the speculators, the hoarders of goods, and the unworthy and extended borrowers." Indeed, these special interests continued the plot "to milk the value from the workers' wages and the people's income and savings in the future as they have done in times past." Japan's future really boiled down to a simple question: "Whether Japan will gain its political independence and remain economically a dependent nation or whether it will do what is necessary to create and establish its economic self-sufficiency and [true] independence." If the Japanese could continue in the stabilization and rationalization program, "there should be little need for Japan to be dependent on others." If, however, they choose the path of inflation, "there can be little *justification* for assistance from others."[81]

With these words Joseph Dodge took leave of Japan.

In retrospect, Dodge profoundly underestimated his impact. True, once the occupation ended, Yoshida, Ikeda, and other Japanese officials resurrected the Reconstruction Finance Bank and used it along with other state institutions, such as the Ministry of International Trade and Industry, to funnel public funds into the private economy to spur economic growth.[82] Yet, contrary to Dodge's pessimistic assessment, they had almost totally embraced his policy regime. Japanese officials referred to it generally as the "balanced budget rule," and (as the name suggests) it meant that the federal government should not spend more than it received in taxes. But in addition to maintaining a balance between revenue and expenditures, in planning for the future the Ministry of Finance consistently underestimated future tax revenue. Indeed, Japanese officials adhered to the balanced budget rule so strictly that the federal government did not issue a single new bond that would add to the national debt until 1965.[83] As a result, by the 1960s Japan's federal government spent less (as a percentage of GDP) than any other industrialized country.[84]

As it turned out, in one respect Japan's economic policies through the 1950s ended up paralleling those in the United States. In both countries, state institutions existed that could have been used along Keynesian lines; they could have facilitated deficit spending to spur growth in the name of full employment. Yet both countries adopted policy regimes that eschewed government debt in the name of low inflation. How the United States came to follow Japan in this sense is the subject of the next chapters.

Chapter 11

Truman and Eisenhower

How Harry S. Truman (the "S" never stood for anything) learned he had become president remains one of the most revealing stories in American political history. Just before five o'clock, on April 12, 1945, Truman had gone to House Speaker Sam Rayburn's office for bourbon prior to a game of poker. When he arrived, Rayburn told him the White House had called. Truman reached Stephen Early, Franklin Roosevelt's press secretary, who told him to come to the White House right away.

When Truman arrived, the staff rushed him to Eleanor Roosevelt's study. She greeted him, as did her daughter (then serving as FDR's personal secretary) and son-in-law, Colonel John Boettiger. Truman knew "at once that something unusual had taken place." Eleanor put an arm gently on Truman's shoulder.

"Harry," she said, "the President is dead."

Truman flushed. He did not know what to say. He struggled to fight off tears. Finally, he turned to Eleanor. "Is there anything I can do for you?" he asked consolingly.

"Is there anything *we* can do for *you*?" she replied. "For you are the one in trouble now."

And there it was. With a brief turn of phrase, Harry Truman realized he had just become president of the United States. "The lightning had struck," he said later of that moment, "and events beyond anyone's control had taken command. America had lost a great leader, and I was faced with a terrible responsibility." For some moments he stood speechless. Eleanor, her daughter, and son-in-law remained silent as well, waiting for Truman to speak. After a few moments, a knock interrupted the quiet. Edward Stettinius, the secretary of state, entered the room with tears in his eyes.[1]

Historians cannot resist retelling this story because it does more than convey the poignant passing of Roosevelt. At a symbolic level, it also captures the uncertain future the country faced with Truman now in charge. Truman did not know Roosevelt's postwar plans for Germany, Japan, or the Soviet Union. He had no knowledge of the Manhattan Project and the development of the atomic bomb. He had some sense of Roosevelt's domestic priorities, but little awareness of the growing Keynesian framework buttressing those plans. He had little sense of the plans to convert the economy from wartime to peacetime. Worse, he inherited a federal bureaucracy that contained over-lapping responsibilities functioned more on relationships than expertise. Roosevelt flourished in this atmosphere. But Truman struggled. It is, there-fore, no surprise that many of the important pieces of legislation just after the war involved executive reorganization.[2] It is also no surprise that Truman made missteps and struggled to bring order to the organizational confusion— with one result being the greater freedom enjoyed by military government.[3] That Truman did not possess Roosevelt's charisma compounded the sense within the press that things were not working as they should. "In a huge government machine . . . it is always easy to point out confusions," wrote the journalist Arthur Krock in September 1945. "But just now the Federal organization of this country appears to contain a much greater number of clashing cogs and idling turbines than are justified."[4]

When Eisenhower returned to the United States in December of 1945 (to become army chief of staff), he landed in the midst of massive labor unrest. The year following Japan's surrender the country saw more strikes than any comparable time in American history. In January, one hundred and seventy-four thousand electrical workers struck, followed by another ninety-three thousand meatpackers, and then three-quarters of a million steel workers. Additional strikes seemed to follow each week.[5] To capture the mood in Washington, Eisenhower shared a joke with his son John, who still served abroad. The joke "probably gives you a better idea of what we are going through than could a volume of description." To wit:

> A Sergeant who had just recently returned from duty in Germany came to a recruiting office and wanted to re-enlist for overseas ser-vice. The recruiting officer inquired as to his reasons for wanting to go right back, stating that everything in Europe was in chaos. The Sergeant replied, "Yes, I know, but over there the chaos is better organized.[6]

The joke captured the nostalgia Eisenhower felt for a clarity that had evaporated after the war. He could not "conceive of any day being bigger in its meaning and significance for me than May 8, 1945," the day Germany surrendered. Having accomplished all he wanted, he hoped to go back to a "normal" civilian life as soon as possible.[7] Instead, he found a never-ending series of problems. "I have been back from Europe exactly a year," he wrote in his journal. "It has been a most difficult period for me, with far more frustrations than progress."[8] To his journal he expressed the feelings of many Americans just after the war. The conclusion of hostilities had not brought a confidence in lasting peace. Domestically, the transition out of war brought inflation, shortages, and waves of labor conflict. The government's response to these problems often seemed confused and disorganized. "I am suspicious of anyone who believes he could take over the presidency successfully in these days and times," he concluded.[9]

But his own celebrity told him he might not escape this very fate. Everyone seemed to turn to him to solve the next "great problem." The broadcast journalist Edward R. Murrow considered him the "only man" to make the United Nations work. The labor leader Sidney Hillman saw him as the only person to safely guide Germany into democracy.[10] Truman broached the idea of the presidency even before the war had fully ended.[11] In nearly every case and whatever the task, Eisenhower's name simply floated to the top of the short list. When Truman appointed Eisenhower as army chief of staff, the *New York Times* spoke for many in arguing that, "The one regret of most Americans will be that General Eisenhower is not twins so that he might take this post and still remain our military representative in Germany during the difficult days ahead."[12]

Of course, other generals also seemed poised for greater political responsibility. As Arthur Krock wrote in the fall of 1946, within Washington's inner circles and for "some time . . . there is serious and unfrightened discussion of such military men as Dwight D. Eisenhower, George C. Marshall and Douglas MacArthur" as presidential candidates.[13] The *Chicago Tribune* concurred: "Americans have been traditionally suspicious of the military arm in time of peace," yet "Americans have a weakness for war heroes and have often rewarded them with the highest office in the land" out of a "sense of gratitude."[14] It seemed plausible, even likely, that the next decade would see an army hero ascend to the White House. The question, however, was which one?

Marshall eliminated himself from consideration fairly quickly, continually downplaying his interest until, at the time he took the position of secretary of state in January 1947, he announced, "I will never become involved in political matters, and therefore I cannot be considered a candidate for political office." Just to make sure people got the message, he added "I cannot be *drafted* for any political office."[15] Marshall was out. That left MacArthur and Eisenhower, the two most prominent figures to emerge from the war: the "two outstanding military men who are today most frequently mentioned as potential or possible candidates for President."[16] Over the next years the two played a game of cat and mouse over their intentions and desire to be president.

Whether to prepare himself for the presidency or simply to clarify his own thoughts, Eisenhower began to work out policy solutions within the confines of his journal. "These must be studied," he wrote, "closed-shop . . . industry-wide unions, responsible, corporate organization of trade unions (one side). Effective antitrust laws, lockouts, control of raw materials, sound financing—private and government—limiting bureaucratic rule (other side)."[17] For the next several years, he did precisely this, studying the Truman administration's every move and resolving his own mind on these issues.

On economic matters, however, he found himself at a loss. He had missed the shift in economic thinking inspired by John Maynard Keynes because he had left for the Philippines just as Keynes' *General Theory* went to press. Between the release of the book and his return to the United States, Eisenhower had thought relatively little about American political economy (for obvious reasons). In the meantime, Keynes' approach had, in the American context, taken hold of a young generation of economists who had come of age in the late 1930s and 1940s. Having witnessed the way their seniors had struggled helplessly against the Great Depression, this new generation embraced Keynesianism with the zeal of new converts.[18]

The young generation of American Keynesians, taking positions in government and academia during the war, largely agreed that economic downturns (as well as upturns) could be explained by looking at investment spending. Whenever investors stopped investing, the whole economy declined. Keynes famously saw investor behavior as irrational—as possessed by "animal spirits." By the 1940s, American Keynesians, influenced by the Harvard professor Alvin Hansen (who became Keynes' greatest articulator), expressed more equanimity toward investors. True, investors might at times act irrationally, but sometimes there really wasn't anything worth investing in. Keynes had explained how an economy could stay in depression for endogenous reasons. The Americans decided to look at exogenous reasons for economic decline as well. Indeed, in Hansen's mind, economies could experience long-term, "secular" drops in investment due to broad shifts in population, war, or waning technological advances.[19]

As a result, by the time Harry Truman became president, economists within his administration argued that "investment opportunities are much too small" for Western economies, "thus piling up idle funds for which there is no outlet and resulting in a downward spiral of income and production." To combat this "liquidity trap," the country needed: "(1) an easy-money policy (reduced interest rates), . . . (2) high taxes on large incomes to reduce saving, (3) large governmental expenditures of all types, and (4) huge public works programs financed by public borrowing." These policies were meant to "put the . . . idle money to work."[20]

Ultimately, these prescriptions found expression in the Employment Act of 1946, which made economic growth and high employment into national goals in an oft-cited preamble. As for institutional changes, the primary innovation came in the creation of the Council of Economic Advisers (CEA), a three-person committee with direct access to the president and a mandate to provide economic expertise as well as assistance in the creation of policy.[21]

As it turned out, when the war ended, and for the next several years, the economy did not lack for investment opportunities, nor did it go into depression or deflation. Instead, it exhibited strong inflationary tendencies, shortages, and high levels of employment. The legislation's sponsors continued to speak of depression and deflation, even as unemployment stayed low and prices took off.[22]

If a simple reading of Keynes suggested that the cure for an economic depression lay in government spending and a growing money supply, then Keynes' cure for inflation should lie in opposite measures like cutting government spending and shrinking the money supply. Not so, concluded the Keynesians. Inflation and depression came from different economic phenomena, and therefore called for different cures. "The crude notion that any increase in the money supply will produce a price inflation is wholly untenable," argued Hansen in 1946 (in direct contradiction to what Dodge was concluding at that moment in Germany). "In the immediate future, inflationary pressures can be controlled by a budgetary surplus and by price and other direct controls," stated Hansen, downplaying concerns about rising prices. The real (and, frankly, only) problem remained depression. "For the longer run, the danger is much more that we shall be confronted with inadequate aggregate demand in view of our vast productive potential."

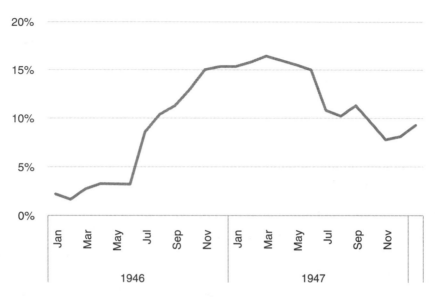

Figure 13. U.S. prices, 1946–1947 (increase over same month of previous year). Source: Bureau of Labor Statistics, Table 24: Historical Consumer Price Index (CPI-U).

Yes, he argued, driving down the money supply and reining in spending could stop an inflation. However, "if aggregate demand were reduced by monetary, fiscal, and other over-all measures [sufficiently] . . . we should have to produce a gigantic deflation and reduce employment to a level perhaps as low as that of 1933 or even lower."[23] Depression remained the real danger, and it remained perilously close at all times.[24]

But this left no really good solution for inflation. In a much read report, Lord William Beveridge, an early admirer of Keynes, recognized this problem and decided the only solution lay in political rather than economic measures. "So long as freedom of collective bargaining is maintained, the primary responsibility of preventing a full employment policy from coming to grief in a vicious spiral of wages and prices will rest on those who conduct the bargaining on behalf of labour." Beveridge had faith that labor would indeed restrain its demands for better wages because during the war "organized Labour in Britain has sufficiently demonstrated its sense of citizenship and responsibility to justify the expectation that it will evolve, in its own manner, the machinery by which a better coordinated wage policy can be carried through."[25]

Truman's administration followed Beveridge's hopes that patriotism could trump inflation. In November 1945, Truman called together a "Labor-Management" conference to address the problem of postwar inflation, where he suggested that the only solution lay in both groups' devotion to their country. "The time has come for labor and management to handle their own affairs in the traditional, American, democratic way." They should show restraint in their wage and price demands. Indeed, "the whole system of private enterprise and individual opportunity" depended upon it.[26]

Labor and management could not, however, stop the progress of inflation after the war. Truman found himself forced to continue wage and price controls throughout 1946, controls that seemed increasingly intrusive to many Americans. As had happened in Germany and Japan, the United States sprouted a black market for basic goods (particularly meat). In November 1946, Truman finally conceded he had lost the battle to maintain price controls.[27] Yet he continued to exhort business and labor to show restraint. Indeed, the inaugural report from the newly created Council of Economic Advisers concluded that, "the outlook for production and jobs in 1947 lies primarily in whether the responsible persons in [labor and management] groups will show a willingness to face the issues and demands of a free enterprise system."[28]

Unfortunately for Truman, in following his advisers his position became increasingly untenable as he proposed one day to cure the short-term danger of inflation only to propose a new measure to prevent the long-term danger of depression. His schizophrenic approach ultimately made its way into popular satire: in the movie *The Senator Was Indiscreet* (1947), the fictional Senator Melvin G. Ashton (played by William Powell) announces, while running for president, that he wanted "not inflation, not deflation, but good old American *flation*."[29] As *Time* magazine noted, "Government bigwigs got a laugh out of the senator's [statement]." Unfortunately, "nobody was laughing over the Administration's meandering in the no man's land of *flation*."[30]

Recognizing the tough spot, Truman decided to parody his own parody. At a subsequent press conference, a reporter tried to get him to finally decide which "-flation" he thought best characterized the economy. Is "the [inflationary] spiral going down?" he asked.

"Not necessarily," the president replied.

"Is it going up?" the reporter asked. Truman paused.

"It's going both ways," he said with a smile. The press corps burst into laughter.[31]

Through his first term, though, Truman never managed to articulate a coherent answer to the problem of prices because his economists struggled to find a Keynesian framework that made sense of the postwar experience.[32]

As Truman struggled, Eisenhower observed from the wings. "International [problems] are bad enough," he wrote in his journal near the end of 1946, "but they are insignificant compared to domestic issues." When it came to inflation, he reverted to his work on industrial conversion. Like Truman, he believed that patriotic appeals should keep prices in line. "Although everyone believes in cooperation (the single key) as a principle, no one is ready to abandon immediate advantage or position . . . Moral regeneration, revival of patriotism," he continued, "[and] clear realization that progress in any great segment is not possible without progress for the whole, all these are necessary."[33]

Still, Eisenhower kept his views to himself, because he felt the army chief had no role in domestic politics. If asked, he supported the president. Late in 1946, in back-to-back speeches before the Congress of Industrial Organizations and then before 2,200 business executives, he pleaded for cooperation, "because cooperation will make this country great. . . . All of the things in which I am concerned," he added, "the security against external threat, the safety of this nation, depend absolutely upon a solid nation behind it."[34]

Much as the press wanted to get Truman to take a stand on domestic economics, so too it wanted to hear Eisenhower's real thoughts. About a year after the speeches, Eisenhower attended a dinner hosted by a number of businessmen who also invited Senator Robert Taft, "Mr. Republican," at this point an aspiring presidential candidate. Taft saw Eisenhower (correctly, as it turned out years later) as his chief rival for the presidency, and saw the dinner as a chance to get Eisenhower's politics on the record. When the topic of the domestic economy came up at the dinner, Taft pressed Eisenhower for specifics: what, exactly, did he mean when he talked about "sacrifice" and "cooperation?"

Eisenhower elaborated. If some leading industrialist, Eisenhower speculated, maybe even "the president of United States Steel," announced that "his company, regardless of profit or loss, would not raise prices for one year," it might change the inflationary psychology within the country. Perhaps the men in the room might lead the way? Such a willingness to sacrifice profits out of patriotic duty could break the price/wage spiral.

Taft made sure the story quickly leaked, and radio personality Fulton Lewis, Jr., made it the subject of a broadcast at the end of 1947, embellishing in the process. Eisenhower, he said, had "called on top industrial leaders to reduce all prices," and "if the industrialists balked, the government should level a confiscatory tax on all corporate profits."[35]

Eisenhower was deeply embarrassed. As he wrote to Arthur Krock, who had also attended the dinner, "I normally succeed in keeping my mouth closed about matters concerning which soldiers are not expected to have opinions." Still, "something suddenly touched upon one of my deep-seated convictions and I was guilty of very warm advocacy of a particular idea." This did not mean Eisenhower had misspoken: "I still believe that some really big man in the industrial world has an opportunity . . . by sincere, even dramatic action, to help halt the inflationary spiral." But in the future, if he ever spoke like this again, he hoped that Krock would "make no mention of my name."[36]

By 1948, however, Eisenhower's views began to change. While he never stated the moment it happened, in his speeches, in his journal, and in his private correspondence, he abandoned the view that inflation could be cured by selfless patriotism. In fact, he embraced more and more the reports from Lucius Clay coming out of Germany. Moreover, Eisenhower appears to have made a cognitive leap that seemed to elude many in Washington: he realized that the inflation in Germany and the inflation in the United States did not represent distinct phenomena stemming from distinct political cultures. Rather, both had the same source—the combination of government spending and credit expansion that had come from the war.

An important step in this direction came in the form of a report from Lewis Brown, the head of the Johns-Mannville Corporation, who had gone to Germany as an informal adviser to Clay in mid-1947.[37] Clay asked Brown to convey the situation in Germany to Americans in hopes that it might build support for the long-delayed currency reform. Along with his chief economist, Brown spent several months summarizing the insights first forged by Dodge in 1946, and compiling them into an easily understood report to be publicized back in the United States.[38] The report included the central insight military government had acquired from the Germans: "There are only two ways of making people work. One way is to drive them with a club. That requires a strong fist, the iron fist of the police-state. . . . The other way to get people to work is to offer rewards in the form of high living standards, in other words, through an ample supply of consumer goods and services." To accomplish this, the economy needed "strong money . . . that can be depended on in the present and in the future to buy the things that people need and want. For such money they will work hard."[39] Unfortunately, Germany remained locked in a "system of price control, wage control, profit control, exchange control, foreign trade control, rationing, quotas, priorities, allocations, special licenses . . . red tape, and paper work."[40]

Brown sent copies and summaries of the report to Clay, Eisenhower, and other members of the military establishment at the end of 1947, as well as to members of the press.[41] Eisenhower called the report "illuminating" in a letter of thanks.[42] Soon the two men struck up a correspondence in which Brown forwarded additional analysis and suggestions to Eisenhower.

Specifically, Brown linked the situation in Germany to the Keynesian trend he saw within the Truman administration. Americans were "living under a Keynsian [sic] state, whether we wish to or not. Keynes had replaced Adam Smith" in guiding policy, and this meant that Americans "no longer favored opportunity over security." In particular, "those who run Big Government rather than those who run Big Business or Finance" would run the economy, and inflation would continue. The "middle class people or upper-income people with savings" would see "that Keynsianism [sic] will permanently devalue" their savings and other investments. A "Police State," he argued, "may not be so many steps further."[43]

Eisenhower read the memos and, in a note of thanks, explained, "I was particularly interested in [the] theory of the Keynsian [sic] state." As a follow-up, he wanted to understand the implications of Keynesian economics for international trade. "What will be the effect of the changing situation in foreign markets on success in maintaining the Keynsian [sic] state?" he asked.[44] He concluded that, "[These] economic presentations continue to make much sense to me."[45]

Even as Eisenhower became increasingly concerned with Keynesianism, Truman began to embrace it. Put more accurately, Truman moved toward a particular brand of Keynesianism that rejected the initial fears expressed by Alvin Hansen that the country faced a secular decline due to lack of investment opportunities. That is, if economists in the early 1940s viewed Keynes as a kind of antibiotic that could cure the disease of depression, by the later 1940s, Keynes seemed more like a steroid, capable of boosting the economy's performance well beyond its traditional limits.

No one embodied the latter view more than Leon Keyserling, a profoundly confident economic adviser who had circulated around Democratic circles in the 1930s (both in the Roosevelt administration and in Congress) until landing in the Truman administration as an original member of the Council of Economic Advisers (CEA). For all the Keynesians around him, Truman had hardly embraced deficit spending in his first years as president, taking pride in balancing the budget and (in particular) keeping defense spending in check.[46] But his election in 1948 brought him close to Keyserling, who stood unflinchingly by Truman even as many fellow Democrats abandoned the president as a lost cause during his difficult 1948 campaign. Truman rewarded Keyserling for that loyalty, giving him a growing role in policymaking and, in 1949, appointing him chairman of the CEA. Keyserling became the most influential economic adviser within the White House and, through that influence, helped move Truman increasingly toward a full-throated embrace of Keynesianism as economic steroids.[47] If "the federal budget is brought into balance under the Truman administration," he explained early in 1950, "it will be strictly accidental."[48]

Keyserling openly rejected Hansen's fear of "secular stagnation" even while he rejected concerns over inflation. America could avoid both problems through expanded production driven by growing demand. Indeed, he felt that "nothing, to my mind, could be a greater illusion from the viewpoint of sheer economics than the idea . . . [that] the American economy has reached the point where it cannot consume what it can produce—or even *nearly* what it can produce." In short, he took seriously the idea that demand creates its own supply.[49]

More than anyone else (as he would later claim), Keyserling invented "growth" economics—what historians have subsequently called "growthmanship" or "growth liberalism."[50] The distinction between Keynesian countercyclical economics and Keynesian growth economics is easy to miss (as is, therefore, the contrast between Hansen and Keyserling). At root, though, the distinction lay in the question of whether Keynesian spending would return the economy to its normal limits, or whether it could transcend those limits. As Keyserling argued for the latter view, he suggested that nearly all government spending had a positive economic effect.[51] As one of his fellow economists in the administration complained, Keyserling "says the basic question is whether a given expenditure is desirable *per se*, that is, calculated to conserve or expand productivity. . . . Keyserling seems to think that no matter how wide you open the throttle 'selective controls' will prevent unfavorable consequences."[52] Yet Keyserling solved this problem in the same way he solved all others. "My basic position," he explained, "is that you have got to measure your federal budget against your national budget." So long as the economy expanded faster than the carrying charges of the debt, the debt "is easily absorbable."[53]

Inflation, then, remained at most a short-term problem that resulted from structural difficulties within the economy. Industry must have planned poorly and ordered too little of one thing or too much of something else. The cure, therefore, was better information about industrial needs and a clear commitment from the federal government to keep production high. Keyserling solved the informational problem by providing industry, labor, and farmers with a "prosperity" budget that would outline "for a few years ahead the maximum output that our resources and skills can achieve," (which the Council of Economic Advisers provided in its annual economic report under Keyserling's chairmanship). He believed that "objective analysis of the relationships among profits, wages and other incomes" might then "distinguish the long-run welfare of all from the short-run gains of contending groups, and thus provide a surer foundation for the mutual adjustment of industry, agriculture and labor through voluntary action." It might also allow Congress to better utilize "farm price supports, taxation, minimum wage legislation and public works, all of which promote adjustment or aggravate maladjustment depending upon how well they are attuned to the whole situation."[54]

For his stout defense of Truman and his unflinching support of deficit spending, he eventually became a target of Senator Joseph McCarthy's, who called Keyserling a Communist in February of 1952. "This story is utter nonsense," responded Keyserling. McCarthy had simply "repeated second hand, with some variations, an entirely false story about me."[55] McCarthy, never one to back down, then went after Keyserling's wife: the "former Mary Dublin," he charged, had at one time "been a member of the Communist party," and therefore also "belonged to an unlimited number of Communist fronts."[56] Because she held a job in the Commerce Department, she took a leave of absence pending an investigation. She was fully reinstated three months later.[57]

*　*　*

Keyserling's thinking found its way into all areas of Truman's policy, most famously in NSC 68, the influential Cold War study produced by Truman's

Policy Planning Staff in early 1950.[58] NSC 68 assumed that since the Soviets had mastered the atomic bomb (they detonated their first in 1949), they would waste little time in amassing a stockpile and preparing a surprise attack on the United States. The point of greatest danger, the report estimated, would occur in the mid-1950s, when Soviet nuclear power would be enough to launch a devastating strike.[59] NSC 68 argued that only a massive expansion of arms could counter this vulnerability. While the report did not provide a specific price tag for the expansion, even a casual reading showed that it would more than double the 1948 and 1949 budgets.[60]

To justify the hefty charge on the budget, the Policy Planning Staff borrowed from Keyserling's approach.[61] The "United States could achieve a substantial absolute increase in output and could thereby increase the allocation of resources to a build-up of the economic and military strength of itself and its allies without suffering a decline in its real standard of living." Crucially, the report justified all its economic claims by setting World War II as the baseline of American productive potential. "In March 1950 there were approximately 4,750,000 unemployed," it explained, "as compared to 1,070,000 in 1943 and 670,000 in 1944."[62] Indeed, "One of the most significant lessons of our World War II experience was that the American economy, when it operates at a level approaching full efficiency, can provide enormous resources for purposes other than civilian consumption while simultaneously providing a high standard of living." After all, personal consumption "rose by about one-fifth between 1939 and 1944, even though the economy had in the meantime increased the amount of resources going into Government use by $65 billion (in 1939 prices)."[63]

More to the point, NSC 68 prophesied that overall economic growth "might itself be aided by . . . a buildup of the economic and military strength of the United States and the free world. . . . [The] necessary buildup could be accomplished without a decrease in the national standard of living."[64] Given its robust growthmanship framework, NSC 68 implied that anything short of a massive expansion of the military wasted American economic potential and left the country needlessly at risk. "These then are our potential capabilities," the report summarized. "Between them and our capabilities currently being utilized is a wide gap of unactualized power."[65] Still, when he first saw the report, Truman hesitated. He remained wary of the price tag. But the advent of the Korean War in June 1950 made it appear prophetic, and Truman ultimately embraced its recommendations.[66]

The outbreak of war and new spending, however, revised a controversy that had simmered since the end of World War II. As early as 1940, Marriner Eccles, chairman of the Federal Reserve, had urged Franklin Roosevelt as soon as he saw war coming to take "action now to assure adequate supplies of materials and thereby to keep prices within bounds . . . [in order to] prevent the necessity later on for direct price fixing and restrictive credit policies." His concern came from the high volume of federal debt that the Federal Reserve and commercial banks had started to absorb as soon as the country began producing for war. Eccles circulated a report that suggested ways to ward off the pending inflation.[67] However, the report found little interest among the New Dealers. Eccles' worries seemed too much, as one critic said, like "a typical banker's ploy to get higher interest rates."[68] By agreement, the Treasury mandated that the Federal Reserve buy government bonds at a low, fixed rate (2.5 percent for long-term bonds). In practice, this meant that whenever the Treasury could not find private buyers for its bonds, the Fed stepped in. It also meant, any time banks could buy at a better rate from private citizens, they would turn around and sell to the Fed for an immediate profit.[69]

After the war, Eccles' fears became a reality. "I have frequently sought to emphasize in the past," he explained in January of 1946, that "the primary source of the inflation . . . is the vast accumulation of currency and bank deposits. . . . Too much of the cost of the war was financed through the creation of commercial bank credit and not enough was financed out of taxes and the savings of the public."[70] To a smaller degree than Germany, but in the same way, the United States had paid for the war by creating money. "In retrospect," he explained, "we can see that we could have, and probably should have, taxed more and borrowed more from nonbank investors, and less from the banking system."[71]

Still, in June 1950, when the Korean War erupted, the Treasury assumed that the Reserve System would guarantee its issue of long-term debt at no more than 2.5 percent. But by this time many of the Federal Reserve Board of Governors had come to believe Eccles' explanation for American inflation. Indeed, a new round of inflation had already broken out, which Congress and the administration had tried to quell with a new round of price controls and rations. Eccles vowed not to make the same mistake again. While no longer chairman of the Federal Reserve, he remained on the board, where he could defend his views. Yet Truman remained committed

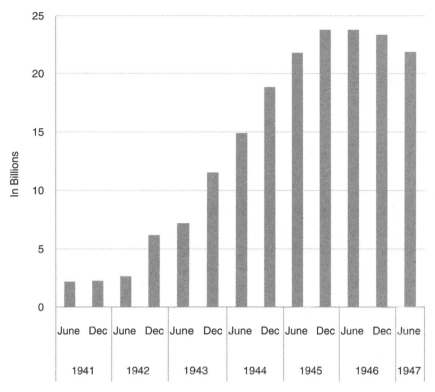

Figure 14. U.S. Federal Reserve holding of federal debt, 1941–1947 (volume of monetized debt). Source: *Federal Reserve Bulletin, 1941–1947.*

to the old agreement, telling the Federal Reserve's board members that their patriotic duty demanded that they support the war effort.[72] The conflict between the Federal Reserve and the Treasury grew to a head when China intervened in the Korean War.

More immediately, though, the Allied reversals on the battlefield in Korea sounded alarms for military leaders in Washington who feared that China's entry into the Korean War presaged a similar attack in Europe. Thus, at the end of 1950, the need for a strong Western alliance seemed urgent. Truman helped solidify a European alliance on December 16, 1950, when he named Eisenhower as the first supreme allied commander of the newly formed North Atlantic Treaty Organization (NATO). On New Year's Day, 1951, Eisenhower left on a whirlwind tour of European capitals. He

Figure 15. U.S. prices, 1950–1954 (increase over prior year). Source: Bureau of Labor Statistics, Table 24: Historical Consumer Price Index (CPI-U).

did his best to rally Europeans to rebuild their defenses at a time when few had the resources to do so. More important, after the crippling experience in World War II, few Europeans wanted to contemplate even more armed conflict.

As Eisenhower tried to rally Western Europe, the dispute between Truman and the Fed became a public controversy.[73] To clear the air, both sides decided to meet late in the afternoon of January 31, 1951.[74] They had to meet late because on that same day Eisenhower returned to Washington to give his initial report to Truman and share his first impressions of NATO. Truman met Eisenhower at noon on the tarmac of Washington's National Airport; however, as they traveled together in the president's limousine, Truman spent little time talking to Eisenhower. Instead, he spent the ride preparing for his meeting with the Fed later that afternoon. Eisenhower could not help but listen in and wonder what kept the Federal Reserve under the thumb of the Treasury. How did this affect the economy?

Later than night he raised the issue with his friend, Chief Justice Fred Vinson (former secretary of the treasury). Vinson shared a few thoughts and then said, "If you want to know about that, why don't you ask Bob Anderson?" Vinson considered Anderson, a Texas banker, to have a good understanding of monetary issues, and Eisenhower decided to invite him for drinks and discussion.[75] Anderson arrived to find "General Eisenhower,

Milton Eisenhower, Chief Justice Vinson of the Supreme Court, and General Gruenther, and their wives." Eisenhower turned to Anderson and said, "President Truman [says] the Federal Reserve Board was trying to undermine the bond market . . . I would like to know something about it." Trying not to be overawed by his distinguished listeners, Anderson explained "as best I could the pros and the cons . . . what the thoughts were on both sides, and what I was trying to accomplish." The conversation lasted about two hours, after which Eisenhower said, "I need to have somebody with whom I can keep in touch from time to time, to give more thoughts and consideration to economic problems . . . may I keep in touch with you?" Anderson was flattered and the two became friends.[76] While Anderson tried to remain unbiased, his views were well known. "When Government bond prices were 'pegged,' [during the war]," he explained, the "Federal Reserve had to buy securities offered at a fixed price—and thus make credit easier to get."[77] This made the Fed into nothing more than the Treasury's surrogate, which supplied it with "artificially easy credit in a way that [led] to ruinous inflation."[78]

At precisely the same moment that Anderson shared his views with Eisenhower, Truman lectured the Federal Reserve Board members on their obligation to support his administration. In dire terms, Truman warned that "the present emergency is the greatest this country has ever faced, including the two World Wars and all the preceding wars." The Fed *had* to support the 2.5 percent rate; if it refused, the country could lose the Cold War. "If the people lose confidence in government securities," he explained, "all we hope to gain from our military mobilization . . . might be jeopardized."[79] He had thrown down the gauntlet. If the financial system failed, the Fed would be responsible.

Surprisingly, though, he left the meeting having only stated his own demands; he never asked the men around him for a commitment of support. Unaware of the oversight, Truman announced the next morning that the Fed had agreed to continue buying bonds at 2.5 percent (which it had not). In response, Marriner Eccles leaked the minutes of the meeting to show that Truman had never asked, nor received, such an agreement. Truman was furious and embarrassed. Relations between the Truman administration and the Fed deteriorated further until, by the end of February, the Fed announced that it would no longer support the 2.5 percent policy. Unsure what to do, Truman decided the next month to send William McChesney Martin, then undersecretary at Treasury, to talk with the

Federal Reserve Board of Governors to see if some kind of arrangement could be made. McChesney Martin managed to strike an "accord" with the Fed involving a complicated agreement on bond purchases over the short term. Over the long term, however, the Fed escaped any obligations to the Treasury. The fight cost Thomas McCabe his job as head of the Fed (to be replaced by McChesney Martin). It also cost Truman political capital at a time he could ill afford it.[80]

Eisenhower returned to Europe shortly thereafter, more suspicious of Truman than ever. He asked several friends to keep him abreast of the developments in Truman's fight with the Fed. The entire affair "was very badly handled," wrote one friend."[81] Another explained that, "Purely for the purposes of saving interest on the public debt, the Administration wanted to dictate the policy of the Federal Reserve System." This violated the purpose of the Fed. "As you well know, [it] is supposed to be an independent body." Worse, letting the Treasury dictate Fed policy disrupted the dynamics of the market. Because the Fed guaranteed a minimum price, the banks could always "sell Government bonds at a premium," essentially guaranteeing them a profit. Bankers "were almost completely united in their desire to see higher interest rates used as one of the various measures which are needed to combat the inflationary trend." Indeed, the bankers— not the administration—held the moral high ground in this fight. "Despite the fact that the banking system as a whole will suffer a sizable loss in their portfolios," Eisenhower's friend concluded, "they are happy to suffer these portfolio losses in the interest of sound banking."[82]

By this point, Eisenhower had finally connected the conventional wisdom of the occupations with the American postwar experience. Indeed, the prewar German experience became a warning for America of the 1950s. "Because some stock a man owns may gain a few points," he wrote a friend, summarizing his thoughts, "or because he may be able to sell real estate for more dollars than he paid for it, he cannot be certain that he is prospering. He may be nothing but the victim of inflation." In fact, "these things were true of Germany in the late 1920s and we know what happened; utter and complete collapse!"[83]

* * *

In the days leading to MacArthur's dismissal, in April 1951, Truman made sure to build a consensus within his foreign policy team before taking action. He held a series of meetings with his principal advisers: George

Marshall, serving in 1951 as Truman's secretary of defense; Dean Acheson, the man who followed Marshall as secretary of state; Averell Harriman, serving as the chief administrator of the Marshall Plan; and Omar Bradley, the former commander of the U.S. First Army under Eisenhower in Normandy and now the first chairman of the Joint Chiefs of Staff. Truman waited until they all came to agreement before deciding to relieve MacArthur.[84]

Truman wisely understood the need for consensus in the public fight he knew would follow. "General MacArthur's spokesman said the General did not have the faintest idea of why he has been relieved," said a reporter to Truman in the days following the announcement. "Would you care to comment on it?"

"Everybody else knows why!" blurted out Truman. The press corps burst into laughter.[85]

But it turned out Truman was almost entirely wrong on this point. Many people in the country did not understand why Truman had relieved MacArthur, nor did they agree with him. "In telephone calls, telegrams, and conversations with their fellow citizens and reporters," wrote the *Chicago Tribune*, the people "demanded the restoration of Gen. MacArthur." A quick "sampling of opinion on Chicago streets by *Tribune* reporters disclosed citizens were about four to one opposed to the removal of Gen. MacArthur."[86] Subsequent polling showed that Chicagoans were not alone. Gallup polls demonstrated that in the weeks afterward, 62 percent of Americans opposed Truman's discharge of MacArthur, with only 29 percent supporting it.[87]

The polling numbers revealed, in a crude way, the simplest manner in which to view Truman's conflict with MacArthur. On the surface it came across as a school-yard fight between alpha males, a question about whether Truman or MacArthur would lead the American team. The Gallup polls in the spring of 1951 spoke to that, and it proved no contest in the eyes of the majority. In terms of personality, charisma, and leadership, strong majorities of Americans favored MacArthur over Truman.

For intellectuals and scholars (then and now), the fight had another dimension. They tended to frame the personality dispute within a larger constitutional context, where Truman's dismissal of MacArthur confirmed the Constitution's assertion of civilian authority prevailing over the military.[88] A resolution signed by political scientists in the University of California shortly after MacArthur's dismissal read: "It is Gen. MacArthur, not

President Truman, whose actions have imperiled the basis of our constitutional system. . . . The Constitution of the United States . . . declares with unmistakable clarity that the President is commander in chief."[89]

But in the middle term, a different question emerged, namely: which wing of the American military would prevail within the American state. The middle term became clearer as the drama moved to Capitol Hill and the Senate's investigation into the matter. MacArthur asserted, in a speech before a joint session of Congress a little more than a week after his relief, that his "views have been fully shared in the past by practically every military leader concerned with the Korean campaign, including our own Joint Chiefs of Staff."[90] In reality, the literal opposite was true.[91] "Frankly," Omar Bradley famously confessed to Senate investigators several weeks later, "in the opinion of the Joint Chiefs of Staff, [MacArthur's] strategy would involve us in the wrong war, at the wrong place, at the wrong time, and with the wrong enemy."[92]

While, again, on the surface this looked like a victory for Truman in his fight with MacArthur, more astute observers recognized something else. "How can it have happened that we have sunk to the point," asked the journalist Walter Lippmann, "where the two parties are rallying around opposing generals, and where no civilian in the government or the Legislature is regarded as having any authority?" Lippmann noted the fact that in the years since the end of World War II, "the rise, not by usurpation but by . . . default, of the generals to a place which they should not, which they cannot, which the best of them do not wish to hold in the government of the republic."[93]

Lippmann was right that World War II had elevated the military within American policy circles. He was also right that the conflict surrounding MacArthur pitted generals against each other as much as it pitted generals against civilians. But he misunderstood which generals were actually in conflict and what they stood for. On many levels, the Senate's hearings really established which of the two proconsuls emerging from the external state found favor within the military and, therefore, which would most likely come to dominate future policymaking. Bradley's testimony before the Senate signaled that the military had, essentially, sided with Eisenhower and his European experience over MacArthur and his Asian focus.

In fact, other columnists recognized much of this point by returning to the same Gallup polls that showed MacArthur dominating Truman. These polls also showed the "extraordinary fact," wrote the columnist Richard

Strout, "that a majority of voters in both political parties favor one man—General Eisenhower—for the presidency." In other words, in the battle between Truman and MacArthur, a second "great personal drama now begins" between Eisenhower and MacArthur, centering on the 1952 election.[94]

For his part, Eisenhower had grown exhausted with MacArthur. When reporters informed him in Paris that MacArthur had just been fired, "I naturally refused to comment and shall continue to do so," he wrote in his journal.[95] Indeed, it was all he would say.

*   *   *

William Draper managed to avoid much of the fight over MacArthur. On February 28, 1949, just after Joseph Dodge began his mission in Japan, just after Harry Truman began his second term, and two years before Truman got into his fight with Eccles and then MacArthur, Draper resigned as undersecretary of the army. He had wanted to retire for some time so he could return to Dillon, Read, & Co., the investment bank he had left in 1940. Germany finally experienced its currency conversion. Japan, in Dodge's hands, had a chance to recover. So Draper decided to quit. He offered Truman his "sincere appreciation for the support and assistance," and added, "as a Republican in a Democratic administration . . . I have never been asked to influence a decision or make an appointment . . . on a political basis." Truman accepted his resignation "with real regret," but thanked him for his "genuine patriotic service to the United States."[96] Draper could leave government service and resume his private life, which he embraced by remarrying (his first wife had passed away years earlier). Eunice Barzynski, who held the rank of captain in the Women's Army Corps, had served as Draper's assistant during the occupations. Her father, like Draper, held the rank of general, and the Chicago wedding included a who's who of military brass ready to celebrate the "May-December" wedding (Draper was 52, his bride 33).

The happy couple made their way to New York, where Draper resumed his duties at Dillon, Read, & Co. But his time in the private sector proved short-lived. The Long Island Rail Road, one of the original rail lines in the country, had recently declared bankruptcy. Worse, no sooner had the courts begun to review the bankruptcy, than the line suffered a series of

brutal wrecks, killing more than one hundred passengers in separate incidents during 1950.[97] New York Governor Thomas Dewey, in search of
someone to revive the line and make it safe, took advantage of Draper's
availability and worked with the bankruptcy judge to make him the railroad's trustee.[98] The task proved daunting. Draper managed to raise fares
and move the line closer to breaking even. More important, he found investors to finance the upgrades necessary to make commuting safe again. But
in the end, he could not reconcile the public demand for low-cost commuting with the basic costs of operation. He recommended that the New York
Transit Authority assume ownership (so the state could subsidize fares)
while a private vendor be subcontracted for the day-to-day operations.[99]

No sooner had Draper finished his work on the railroad than Truman
came calling again, asking him to serve as a special "ambassador" to NATO.
By the end of 1951, NATO had come to a crossroads. Eisenhower had
worked for the prior year trying to cobble together a coherent defense of
Western Europe, but nearly all of his success came from the "cement" of
his personality rather than the "bricks" of a functioning bureaucracy.[100]
Administratively speaking, the organization was a mess. The basic problem
lay in the relationship between its civilian and military wings. Among many
problems, the civilian/policymaking wing of NATO resided in England,
while the military wing resided in France. Worse, the civilian wing had
overlapping jurisdictions, which did not necessarily match up with the
many American efforts in Europe (such as the Marshall Plan). "NATO has
for a long time been sprouting legs and arms," wrote the *Economist*, "in a
vain attempt to make up for the fact that it had no effective head."[101] In
essence, Truman called upon Draper to be a part of NATO's "head."
NATO's "Council was moving from London to Paris and being upgraded,"
Truman explained to Draper, and he hoped Draper could represent his
interests in the revised and expanded organization.[102] Just as Eisenhower
served as "the top military man in NATO," Draper was "to be the top
civilian on the U.S. side on the NATO Council."[103]

Draper consented to the new assignment provisionally. He "asked for
the opportunity to visit Europe briefly and talk with General Eisenhower"
to be sure that the two could work "in close harmony."[104] Of course, the
two men had known each other for years, but this would be the first time
Draper would (at least nominally) function as Eisenhower's civilian
supervisor—a role reversal that largely mirrored his similar reversal with
Clay several years earlier. Thus, it was no surprise that when the two men

met at Eisenhower's headquarters in France a week before Christmas, 1951, they mostly talked about Clay.[105]

They also discussed Draper's work as trustee for the Long Island Railroad at length, which Eisenhower found so fascinating he asked Draper for more information. So he sent Eisenhower his informal report on the railroad's future, a report that elicited a long response from Eisenhower. "I cannot tell you how interested I am in the kind of problem that you . . . are called upon to solve," he wrote. "Here in Europe we see so much experimentation with 'governmental ownership' that I was interested to read your statement . . . with respect to the Long Island Railway."[106] Eisenhower encouraged Draper to accept the position with NATO.

Throughout 1951, Eisenhower had concluded that European defense required an economic as much as military strategy. In a long letter to Averell Harriman, Eisenhower expressed his fear of "the bad consequences that would follow upon a financial and economic breakdown in European countries as a result of unjustifiable emphasis on their defense programs." The push for military preparedness had real risks. Much as had been true in the Philippines, economic realities created military limits. Moreover, he could not see how to build an effective defense unless "the masses of Western Europe have complete conviction that the free governments of Western Europe will provide for them a better life than they can attain under Communist dictatorships." Eisenhower wanted Truman to understand that defense included "butter" as much as "guns," that "European economic health and morale are both essential ingredients to the security of the region." Western Europeans must see an improving "economic lot of the people through efficient and effective tax laws, liberalising [sic] trade restrictions and proper distribution of taxes." In particular, Washington needed to recognize "the great need for striking a proper balance between runaway inflation and economic collapse on the one hand and dawdling and indifferent performance on the other."[107]

This last point animated Eisenhower's thoughts because inflation had become again, in 1951, probably the single most pressing economic issue in Western Europe. The advent of the Korean War saw a global bump in prices. The French, suffering the greatest inflation, struggled to find a politically palatable solution. Premier René Pleven staked his political career on halting inflation over the last months of 1951 by cutting the deficits in a number of government accounts (particularly social security). He was rewarded by a no-confidence vote that resulted in the collapse of his government.[108]

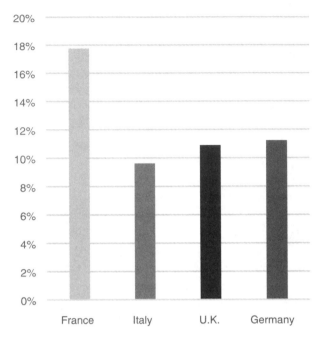

Figure 16. Annual inflation rate in France, Italy, U.K., and Germany (December 1950–December 1951). Source: OEEC, "Europe: The Way Ahead" (Paris: Organization for European Economic Co-operation, December 1952), 86.

Looking for help in solving Europe's economic problems, Eisenhower immediately wrote Draper. "I have not yet heard whether you are taking the European job," he explained. "This morning, with the French Government just fallen, I should like more than ever to have you here. I think I need a shot in the arm."[109] As Draper understood, this was as close as Eisenhower got to begging. He agreed to join Eisenhower and NATO, which Truman announced on January 14, 1952, signaling that NATO would be reorganized along the lines Eisenhower had called for over the previous months (focusing as much on economic integration as military preparedness).[110]

The French, not surprisingly, objected to Draper's appointment because they remembered his work in Germany. "Working sometimes against official directive," wrote *Le Monde*, "he became the ardent defender of a policy of refloating Germany." The French paper feared that Draper's interest in

German revival stemmed from his "private interests" as a partner in Dillon, Read, & Co. In short, the French feared that he cared more about money than European justice.[111]

By contrast, Eisenhower was delighted to have Draper for exactly the same reason the French feared him. "[We] welcome Mr. Draper . . . over here, a man who possesses the greatest possible experience in this region," he told the European press on January 23. "You will recall he served as General Clay's deputy. . . . He is a great personal friend, a man for whom I not only have the highest admiration but from whom I am expecting great service." Together, Eisenhower hoped to make NATO an effective force in uniting Western Europe politically, economically, and militarily. "As I go around to many government officials in Europe," he explained, "I have yet to run into one of them who didn't believe economic and political union was necessary. Not one has ever quarreled with the theory."[112] Now Eisenhower had an effective counterpart to help make the theory a reality. As he welcomed Draper to Europe, Eisenhower decided to distance himself from Truman. He had a newspaper friend get the word out that "merely because I have responded to a simple call to military duty" as the head of NATO, he had not "embraced without reservation almost all of the foreign, domestic, and political policies of the Administration." In reality, he "violently opposed [many] of the policies of the current Administration." He hoped no one would interpret his "readiness to respond to military orders" as tacit support for Truman's domestic policies.[113]

While Eisenhower had remained outside the circle that drafted NSC 68, once it moved from a policy paper to budgeting, he became aware of both. "This morning's paper states that the president's budget, just submitted to Congress, amounts to something over $85 billion with a contemplated deficit for the year of $14 billion," he noted in his journal. He felt betrayed. "Only two or three years ago the president told me very solemnly that an aggregate national budget of more than $42 billion would quickly spell unconscionable inflation in the United States."[114]

Eisenhower vented to his journal. Since the end of the war he had argued that "the purpose of [military defense] is to defend a way of life rather than merely to defend property, territory, homes, or lives." Because of this, "everything done to develop a defense against external threat . . . must be weighed and gauged in the light of probable long-term, internal, effect." In short, he feared that "we will be so committed to a possibly unwise military program that either we will begin to go far more rapidly down the inflation road or we will again have to accomplish a sudden and expensive contraction in that program." Sitting in France, surveying the entire Western European political and military scene as the head of NATO, he could not help observing the parallels: "I am well acquainted with some of the countries in which the size of national budgets has stifled initiative and caused great difficulties otherwise."[115]

This all led in a single, important direction. After the end of World War II, every conceivable public leader had broached with him the idea of running for president. Again and again he had refused. Still, he had grown increasingly fearful he might *have* to run. In part, he feared that the Republicans would nominate the isolationist Robert Taft, who might allow MacArthur into his administration, further shifting the focus from NATO to Asia.[116] He also feared another four years of Truman-like domestic policies. Still, he could always find a reason not to run despite the frequent entreaties.

But the pressure mounted, particularly in the fall of 1951, when Clay joined with Thomas Dewey and other liberal Republicans in a cabal to get Eisenhower into the 1952 presidential race. Clay pressured Eisenhower personally, while Dewey used his political contacts to create a groundswell of support back in the United States for Eisenhower's candidacy.[117] Until this point, Eisenhower had always managed to say to those who wanted him to run, "I have no bounded duty to become the Republican candidate."[118] By early in 1952, as he contemplated the implications of NSC 68, he admitted that "there appears to me to be such compelling reasons to enter the political field," that if he refused, he would later feel he had "failed to do my duty."[119] Now, "if the Republicans decide to place a political mandate upon me, I would not attempt to evade it."[120]

Chapter 12

"The Great Equation"

In 1950, Robert Taft had every reason to believe he would become the Republican nominee for president in 1952. After years of patiently leading the resistance to Roosevelt and then Truman, he had become "Mr. Republican" and should have had the nomination sewn up. He worried, though, about the generals. Either MacArthur or Eisenhower could jump into the primaries and upset his plans; so he tried to sound out both men's intentions.

He learned of MacArthur's plans through a friend who reported exactly what Taft wanted to hear: "Nothing in the world . . . could induce me to again become a candidate for President," MacArthur said. Even better, if Eisenhower became a candidate, MacArthur would throw his support to Taft. Eisenhower had no "basic knowledge of the principles of government," MacArthur explained. In what became a standard criticism in the future, MacArthur assumed Eisenhower "is likely to accept the advice of those who happen to be intimate with him at the moment, whether they have backed him with money . . . or have backed him with political support."[1] Taft was delighted.

As for Eisenhower, Taft had a chance to discover his intentions at a secret meeting just before Eisenhower left for Europe to become NATO's commander in chief, late in December 1950. Eisenhower initiated the meeting to commit Taft in the ongoing "Great Debate" occupying Congress over a permanent garrison of American troops in NATO.[2] Eisenhower knew "that troops could be maintained in Europe only as Congress provided money for their maintenance." He therefore tried to lobby Taft to support appropriations for a permanent troop deployment as part of NATO. Taft agreed to talk, but decided to come quietly to the Pentagon. Before the meeting, Eisenhower asked his staff to write a statement he planned to "issue that evening, on the assumption that Senator Taft would agree that collective security should be adopted as a definite feature of our foreign policy." He dropped it in his pocket and waited for Taft. The two men had a long talk in which Eisenhower posed a single question: "Would you, and your associates in the Congress, agree that collective security is necessary for us in Western Europe—and will you support this idea as a bi-partisan policy?" If Taft could answer "yes," then Eisenhower would "spend my next years attempting to fulfill the great responsibility given me. But if this was going to be a matter of deep and serious division within the Congress, between the Congress and the President, then NATO would be set back, and," he explained, hoping that Taft would read between the lines, "I would probably be back in the United States."

Taft was wary. "I do not know whether I shall vote for four divisions or six divisions or two divisions," he explained. Taft may have thought the meeting was a trap. In any event, he refused to commit, and after several hours, he left Eisenhower's office without making any promises to Eisenhower.

Once Taft left, Eisenhower called back his aides and pulled the statement from his pocket. It read: "Having been called back to military duty, I want to announce that my name may not be used by anyone as a candidate for President—and if they do I will repudiate such efforts." He tore the statement to pieces. "I had lost the chance to settle the political question once and for all."[3]

For most Americans, Eisenhower's work in NATO took a backseat to the unfolding drama in Korea and the climactic confrontation that ended when Truman fired MacArthur. Throughout the controversy, Taft stood behind MacArthur, perhaps because MacArthur became a vociferous critic of Truman. "I have received thirty-five hundred telegrams and twelve thousand letters from all over the country, of which 99 per cent attack the President for removing MacArthur, and about 70 per cent demand impeachment," Taft informed a Truman supporter. "As for unity with the President, this is desirable if possible, but there is a fundamental difference in foreign policy, and I am quite certain the Russians would prefer unity with the wrong policy instead of the division in this country which is not likely to be of any assistance to them."[4]

Congress had promoted MacArthur to "General of the Army" in 1944, which made him a general for life.[5] Even after being "fired," he continued to wear his uniform while he went on a speaking tour, where he relitigated his dismissal in Korea.[6] The increasingly strident speeches eventually included criticism of Truman's domestic as well as foreign policy, all of which delighted Taft. "I have received the most enthusiastic and complimentary reports on your Cleveland visit and on the meeting itself," he wrote MacArthur after one speech. "No one could leave behind a more favorable and enthusiastic impression than you did in that city."[7] In flattering MacArthur, Taft followed the counsel of his political advisers, who felt that a united Taft-MacArthur front might counter Eisenhower's presumed strengths as a war hero. Indeed, in an effort to consummate the relationship, Taft eventually traveled to MacArthur's suite at the Waldorf in New York in December 1951. He found a willing partner. MacArthur explained that Taft had his "fullest support for the Republican nomination."[8]

As MacArthur barnstormed the country, Lucius Clay found himself at a crossroads. In May of 1949, he had been "welcomed . . . as a returning hero" to the United States, with a speech before both houses of Congress and a ticker-tape parade in New York.[9] Thereafter, he left the military and became chairman of the Continental Can Company in April, 1950. When the Korean War broke out he again returned to Washington to join the Defense Production Agency. But his Korean War experience paled in comparison to his service under Franklin Roosevelt during the Great Depression and World War II. While Clay personally admired President Truman, he concluded that the Democratic Party had overstayed its time.[10] In particular, the controversy over MacArthur's "firing" left him frustrated. While Clay refrained from any public comment, privately he could not believe the Administration had not foreseen the problems that came along with letting MacArthur remain a sovereign in Japan in perpetuity. Instead of relieving him "on the grounds of his age or the time he'd been away from the United States" before the Korean War got going, Truman had instead "allowed [the situation] to get to [a] controversial stage."[11]

Around this time Clay decided to "do my utmost to get General Eisenhower to run for the Republican nomination."[12] Eisenhower, he concluded, had the best chance to resolve the war and redirect the focus of the nation. Indeed, he felt so strongly about Eisenhower that Clay broke with family tradition and decided to become a Republican, something he did because he thought it would help in the effort to "draft" Eisenhower as a presidential candidate.[13]

Still, Eisenhower vacillated about running. Observing from Europe through the end of 1951 and into 1952, he resisted Clay's entreaties to enter the race. Finally, on April 2, 1952, Eisenhower agreed to run and asked Truman to be relieved as NATO's supreme commander. Remaining true to his criticism of seeking office while on active duty, he also told Truman he intended to resign his commission. The country now knew he had become a candidate for the Republican nomination.[14] MacArthur came out swinging. Speaking before a joint session of the Michigan state legislature, he attacked Eisenhower's candidacy without ever mentioning his name. "Nothing is more conducive to arbitrary rule than the military junta. It would be a tragic development indeed if this generation was forced to look to the rigidity of military dominance and discipline to redeem it from the tragic failure of civilian administration," he explained without irony.[15]

"I think your Michigan speech was the most effective political speech, in the best sense of the word, that you have made," wrote Taft the next day. "We are trying to build our publicity around your thesis that the Democrats and New Dealers are trying to take over the Republican Party [through Eisenhower]. It is absolutely true."[16]

As the convention approached, Taft's campaign continued to solicit MacArthur.[17] Indeed, by the time of the convention, Taft heard from his staff that MacArthur would agree to become his running mate. Either way, though, MacArthur made clear that "Win or lose, I am with you."[18] Yet, it was not enough. When the time came, the early counting showed Eisenhower just nine votes short of victory, at which point former governor Harold Stassen switched Minnesota's delegates to Eisenhower.[19]

In a painful postmortem, Taft felt that the press had done him in. He reflected on what he might have done differently. Perhaps he could not have beaten Eisenhower personally, but if he had thrown his support behind "some other candidate holding my general views," (that is, MacArthur) once "it became clear that I could not be nominated," perhaps that candidate "would have been stronger on the second ballot than I."[20] Either way, Taft's loss meant that his particular brand of conservatism had been blocked; MacArthur, too, would no longer play a strong role in politics.

*   *   *

In the presidential election of 1952, nearly all Americans wanted their next president to end the Korean War; they also feared communism, especially communist "subversion" within government; and they worried that Washington had seen too many scandals.[21] But they also worried about the economy, and Eisenhower advanced an argument largely honed by the lessons he and the military establishment had learned abroad. "I propose to show you," he told the American people, "that whatever economic gains have been made since 1932 have been due, not to administration ingenuity, but to war or threat of war." Here, Eisenhower made a subtle but important distinction: whereas Keynesians concluded that massive *spending* on armaments had initiated recovery, Eisenhower argued World War II had changed the *incentive* structure of the economy. "Our country's danger quickly mobilized the incentives of all the American people—something the administration program had never been able to do." American economic output rose dramatically because of the "patriotism of our people," not fiscal stimulus. Indeed, continued fiscal stimulus in times of peace tended to reverse that same incentive structure. Eisenhower noted that "1939 standards of living" had only achieved "the same level as 1929." Similarly, "1952 standards of living" stood "slightly below the level of 1945." In between came "the gains borne out of World War II." Thus, he concluded, "War, not the New Deal, brought about the end to unemployment. The legacy of war, not the Fair Deal [Truman's policies], helped to sustain a high level of economic activity."[22]

Eisenhower also pressed on what he saw as a basic inconsistency at the heart of Keynesian economics. "With one hand the Administration has been turning up the water pressure at the hydrant, while with the other hand it has been trying to check the water's flow." As a result, "the Administration's controls over prices are nothing but weak stop-gaps." He referenced the lessons that came out of the German experience, "The really effective controls—those over money and credit—were ignored by the Administration." The reason? "Resort to those controls would have paralyzed their scheme to use 'cheap money' for their own ends."[23] In short, Eisenhower attributed to Roosevelt and Truman an intentional effort to deceive the public—in a sense, a version of "silent financing" found in Germany—and this deception slowly corrupted the body politic because it disguised economic reality with a politically motivated illusion. Inflation had "put more and more dollars" in the American people's pockets, and "handling more money tends to make you feel more prosperous."[24] But this approach aimed "to fool the people with a deceptive prosperity . . . to give more people more money that is worth less."[25] Reversing his views of 1930, he now criticized price controls and rationing, explaining in a televised press conference that he had "far more faith in the interplay of . . . supply and demand" than in price controls, and he preferred "the normal action of the Government in extending and reducing credits, and discount rates, and so on" for controlling inflation.[26]

Watching Eisenhower's press conference at home, Bernard Baruch felt betrayed. As Eisenhower's longtime mentor, Baruch had always taken the position, first articulated when he supervised the War Industries Board, that in times of crisis, direct controls provided the only real solution to inflation. He immediately called Eisenhower's campaign and complained that Eisenhower's words were "most disturbing." Echoing his conversations with Eisenhower two decades earlier, he said, "You cannot mobilize to the extent security requires without priorities over production." Moreover, "you cannot have priorities without price and other controls." To Baruch, "no other single problem save peace itself is more basic than this." He felt Eisenhower needed to give the matter "more judicious thinking through" because America could not "have peace without the controls necessary to mobilize the strength that is all that keeps the world free."[27]

The break from his mentor had been coming for some time. Eisenhower, ever the diplomat, soft-pedaled their disagreement. "I have sat at your feet for many years and listened to your ideas," he wrote in a letter, "and as you know I have, in the main, thoroughly agreed with them." He had learned a great deal, however, in the ensuing years. While he still felt that "in emergencies political controls must be established," he had raised the bar of what counted as an emergency, and he did not feel that the Cold War—or even the Korean conflict–qualified. Worse, the controls on the economy remained piecemeal. As a result, they tended to "unbalance our price structure."[28]

On the campaign trail, Eisenhower tried to explain the lessons of the occupations. "I have spent a number of years in Western Europe," he concluded, "trying to help our friends there set their houses in order and in strength. I have seen these war-shaken countries grapple with terrible problems of shortages and prices." There he learned the only solution to the many problems facing the world. "You must strengthen your currencies, beat back inflation, set your economic affairs straight—or you will lose the battle with Communism without a gun being fired." American problems were neither unique nor isolated. "Ours is an age of interdependence . . . all the problems we face—economic or political, domestic or internal—are intimately related."[29] Even when speaking of Korea, communism, or corruption, he often returned to political economy as the way to link them together in a broad critique of Democratic policy over the prior decades.

In November, Eisenhower swept to victory, getting 55 percent of the vote and carrying 39 states including Texas and Virginia, traditional Democratic strongholds. His coattails also brought Republican majorities in both the House and Senate. For the first time since the 1920s, the GOP controlled the executive and legislative branches. Taft took some solace that he would be the Senate majority leader.

* * *

Even before the election, Eisenhower sought the right personnel to execute his policies, if he were to win. In reality, that meant he turned to Clay to help him find the right people. "Clay was so close to Eisenhower," observed Eisenhower's campaign manager, Herbert Brownell, "that people felt he could always get Eisenhower's concurrence to any program that he recommended."[30] He trusted Clay as someone who shared his policy ideas but also as someone who knew the right people for translating ideas into reality. During the campaign, Clay and Brownell (along with Thomas Dewey, the governor of New York) worked as a team to vet prospective candidates for the administration. The selection of Richard Nixon as a running-mate proved typical. At the convention, Eisenhower sat down for dinner with Brownell, who asked Eisenhower his suggestions for vice president. Eisenhower looked surprised. "I thought the convention had to do that," he said. "I didn't realize that was for me to decide."

Put on the spot and thinking out loud, Eisenhower began naming men he liked and respected, mostly from his business contacts. Brownell interrupted him. "These are all fine men," he said, "but we really need a name that would be recognizable to the average delegate on the floor, someone they can relate to." Clay, Brownell, and Dewey had someone in mind: Richard Nixon. Brownell explained that Nixon's youth and the fact he came from California helped with voters. Moreover, he had a record that would appeal to the more "conservative" wing of the Republican Party.

Eisenhower thought for a minute and said, "Fine"—that he "would be guided" by Clay, Brownell, and Dewey's advice. The next day, the three men crowded into a small office and made the call to Nixon, each holding a receiver to hear Nixon's response. Nixon (of course) jumped at the chance.[31]

After the convention, Brownell had his choice of positions in the new administration and decided on attorney general. Dewey and Clay wanted no part of the new administration—Dewey because of age, and Clay because he did not want the cabinet to appear top-heavy with military men. Moreover, Clay told Eisenhower, he could "be of more service to you if I'm not in your administration." He thought Eisenhower might "need somebody [he could] call on to do things," someone not working directly for him.[32] The men then turned to the position of director of the Budget Bureau because Eisenhower wanted to work immediately on getting the budget back into balance. Clay knew exactly whom to suggest. He told Eisenhower to ask Joseph Dodge to take the position. The trick would be getting him to accept. Eisenhower had to make it difficult for him to say no, and Clay concocted a plan.

Clay invited Dodge to come to Eisenhower's campaign headquarters at the Commodore Hotel in New York for election night. Almost immediately after Adlai Stevenson conceded the election, with emotions still running high, Clay pulled Dodge into a separate room where Eisenhower waited. Standing to either side, they told Dodge that the country needed his service one more time. On this momentous night, as his first act as president-elect, Eisenhower called upon Dodge to save his country's economy. Would he accept the appointment?

Dodge, confronted by his friend Clay and the newly elected president, "was as moved by the occasion as anyone." He answered "in a choked voice [that] he would be glad to help the General out on any immediate problem."[33] Eisenhower made clear that Dodge would have an expanded role in the government with a voice in all aspects of policy formation—especially foreign policy and defense. He wanted Dodge to attend all important meetings, including the National Security Council.

After budget director, perhaps the most important domestic position went to George Humphrey as treasury secretary. Like Dodge, Clay knew Humphrey from Germany (Humphrey had participated in one of many fact-finding missions).[34] As for secretary of state, Clay and Eisenhower favored John McCloy, another important figure with deep experience in the postwar occupations and Clay's successor in Germany. Here, Brownell and Dewey disagreed. They felt that nearly all the Republican establishment assumed the post would go to John Foster Dulles. Eisenhower and Clay ultimately conceded.

Eisenhower tried to bring Draper into his inner circle. But by the end of 1952, Draper had decided to finish his government service. He wanted more time with his wife and a chance to make money. "As was customary,

I gave the incoming President my resignation," Draper explained. Eisenhower wanted Draper to reconsider. But Draper insisted. Including "the war years, I had been about ten years in Government service, or more." Eisenhower finally accepted Draper's resignation, but asked Draper to postpone it as long as possible. They agreed that Draper would go back to the private sector "about the middle of '53," but only after Draper had spent ample time with Eisenhower's new cabinet, getting the new administration up to speed on European political economy.[35]

For the remaining positions, Eisenhower did not provide Clay with specific instructions. "I think he had enough confidence in our judgment to know that we were going to try to find men of high caliber," Clay explained. "After all, he didn't give us the power of decision: ours was the power of recommendation." Still, while Eisenhower always "made the final decision," he gave broad deference to Clay's views.[36]

Because Harry Truman had felt so unprepared when Franklin Roosevelt died, he went out of his way to ensure that Eisenhower transitioned smoothly into the White House. No sooner did Eisenhower win, than Truman invited the president-elect to his briefings. Eisenhower chose to send liaisons in his place, though, dispatching Dodge to all budget briefings.[37] Truman "might try to put over the idea that the new administration was agreeing to certain . . . measures," he warned Dodge. "Leave no doubt on this point in the mind of [Truman's] Director of the Budget . . . that in the work you are doing you are not prepared either to concur or to disapprove any specific item in the budget."[38] Dodge agreed.

In the meantime, Eisenhower prepared to go to Korea. He had promised, on October 1953, just weeks before Election Day, to do so. Before a national television audience he said, "Where will a new Administration begin? It will begin with its President taking a simple, firm resolution," namely, "to forgo the diversions of politics and to concentrate on the job of ending the Korean War." For emphasis he explained, "That job requires a personal trip to Korea." Then, in a dramatic flourish, "I shall make that trip . . . I shall go to Korea. . . . Only in that way," he declared, "could I learn how best to serve the American people in the cause of peace."[39] An Associated Press writer at the speech noted, "For all practical purposes, the contest ended that night."[40]

It was "a grandstand play to get votes," argued the chairman of the Democratic National Committee.[41] Adlai Stevenson called it a "last desperate bid" for support.[42] And Democrats were largely correct. When

Eisenhower finally went to Korea in December, he learned nothing particularly new and the trip did little to end the war.[43] In reality, he had planned to make the trip all along. It fit a pattern he established during World War II, where he felt frequent visits to the front boosted morale and showed a connection between the soldiers doing the fighting and the leaders giving the orders.

The real impact of the trip came on the return leg, aboard the *USS Helena* (a navy cruiser), which Eisenhower boarded for the trip home. He asked Dodge, Clay (not a member of the cabinet, but always included in important meetings), Dulles, Humphrey, Douglas McKay (interior secretary designee), and Charles Wilson (defense secretary designee) to join him. Each concocted a cover story and secretly boarded the *Helena* in Guam. The few days it took to sail to Hawaii allowed the men time to outline a plan for implementing Eisenhower's broad policy goals. They aimed to solve what came to be called the "Great Equation": namely, "how to equate needed military strength with maximum economic strength."[44]

Clay provided the common link among the men on the *Helena*. They spent the first day "visiting around and getting acquainted and finding out where we separately stood."[45] At first they called each other Mr. Dodge and Mr. Dulles. Eventually it became "Herb and Foster and George and Joe and Doug." The next day, they turned to business. Dodge, by virtue of his time observing the Truman budget, directed the discussion. Eisenhower spoke first to express his policy goals, essentially the lessons gained abroad: balance the budget, revise the tax code and reign in defense spending, expand some social welfare, and maintain the strength of the dollar as the global reserve currency. Dodge then explained what he had learned from his time in the Truman White House. Truman projected a $10 billion deficit for 1954. Roughly 70 percent of the budget went to the military (which included atomic energy, foreign aid, and foreign military bases). Of the remaining 30 percent of the budget, a large part (roughly 18 percent) went to programs that could not be cut (such as veterans' payments, interest on the debt, and grants to state and local governments). This left roughly 12 percent devoted to operational expenses. "So," explained Dodge, "the only place where we could hope to make headway fast is in that last, cramped sector—the running expenses of the government—and here we have left a sum which itself [is] about equal to the estimated deficit."[46] Since firing the entire executive branch seemed rash, this meant that military spending had to provide the savings necessary to reach a balanced budget.

Table 2. Truman budgets (actual and projected), FY 1951–FY 1957 (billions of U.S. dollars).

	FY51	FY52	FY53	FY54*	FY55*	FY56*	FY57*
Gov. Receipts	51.6	66.1	69.6	68	70	71	72
Gov. Expenses	45.5	67.6	76.1	77.9	85	83	83
GDP	320.6	348.6	372.9				
Difference	6.102	−1.519	−6.493	−9.9	−15	−12	−11

Source: Extrapolations from estimates in "Notes on the Fiscal Problem and Tax Problem," May 20, 1953, Budget Bureau, Box: 17, The Budget, JMD as well as interviews in Charles J. V. Murphy, "The Eisenhower Shift," *Fortune,* January, 1956; also, *Budget of the U.S. Government: Fiscal Year 2012*, Historical Tables (Washington, DC: Government Printing Office), tables 1.1 and 1.2.
*Denotes Joseph Dodge's estimates.

But here, too, the way Congress went about authorizing and spending created a problem. Typically, the government authorized and signed contracts for military hardware with the promise to pay upon delivery. These authorizations did not appear as budget items until years later, even though the government carried a legal obligation to meet the contract. Dodge called these "COD's" and "licenses to spend" and noted that Congress had ordered up almost $81 billion of unfunded authorizations since 1950. The bulk of these claims would arrive in FY 1954 and FY 1955 (the year of "maximum danger" according to NSC 68). Indeed, from what Dodge observed, no one in the Truman administration anticipated a balanced budget before 1960 (if ever).[47] In the meantime, canceling these projects midstream meant wasting work that was already half finished. So, even here, the new administration's options seemed limited. As a result, Dodge could see no way to balance the budget for at least several years. If the new administration could renew some Korean War taxes and revise some contracts, the next year might get the new administration closer to balance. But a fully balanced budget would likely not come until 1955.

Dodge's report proved sobering. Many of the assembled had assumed that Truman's deficits resulted from waste, corruption, and handouts; they had hoped to balance the budget by "trimming the fat." Dodge disabused them of this fantasy, pointing out that reducing government spending required more than simple thrift. It required policy change. Eisenhower realized the heart of the problem and compared the situation to "a heavy truck racing down an icy hill." In such a situation, "the brakes must be lightly and expertly applied to avoid losing control."[48]

With the parameters of the "Great Equation," the men on the *Helena* began work on a policy solution that took seriously the security threat outlined in NSC 68, without relying on the deficit spending meant to meet it. In these early discussions they conceived in embryo what would later be called a "New Look" approach to national defense and a doctrine of "massive retaliation." As they crossed the Pacific, Eisenhower's principal advisers reasoned through the irony that the weapons necessary to end civilization proved cheaper to produce and sustain than the cost of the garrisons necessary to win smaller wars like Korea. In short, to keep America from becoming a garrison state, they decided to increase the risk of human annihilation, making a nuclear arsenal delivered by a modern air force the solution to the Great Equation.[49]

When Eisenhower became president in January 1953, the Great Equation moved to the background because the immediate economic question had to do with the price controls included in the Defense Production Act of 1950, which gave the president discretion to set and administer price, rent, and wage ceilings. In early 1952, Congress amended the original act by adding an expiration date on these powers: April 30, 1953. Before the inauguration, Truman administration officials worked diligently behind the scenes to commit the new administration to controls as the best way to limit inflation. Michael DiSalle, the head of Truman's Office of Price Administration, called Sherman Adams, Eisenhower's designee as chief of staff, and lectured him on the irresponsibility of decontrol. In no uncertain terms he warned Adams, "It would be a catastrophe to remove [controls] too soon." He provided a "memorandum full of calculations which showed an inflation effect of many billions of dollars." He insisted that Adams "advise the President-elect not to lift controls rapidly but to do it gradually" over a period of months, if not a year.[50]

As it turned out, Eisenhower had already made up his mind. Price controls had come up on the *Helena,* where Clay spoke forcefully for ending all controls immediately (echoing his experience in Germany). Humphrey seconded.[51] Thus, despite DiSalle's warnings, Eisenhower planned to end the controls in dramatic and immediate fashion.[52] In his first State of the Union, just two weeks after taking office, he announced he did "not intend to ask for a renewal of the present wage and price controls" in any form.

He asserted that "direct controls, except those on credit, deal not with the real causes of inflation but only with its symptoms." In short, "we should combat wide fluctuations in our price structure by relying largely on the effective use of sound fiscal and monetary policy, and upon the natural workings of economic law." Then, sounding very much like Ludwig Erhard, Eisenhower linked market freedom with political freedom: "A maximum of freedom in market prices as well as in collective bargaining is characteristic of a truly free people"; indeed, "the great economic strength of our democracy has developed in an atmosphere of freedom." Summing up, Eisenhower suggested that if America hoped to remain politically free, it must encourage "competitive enterprise and individual initiative precisely because we know them to be our Nation's abiding sources of strength."[53]

The *Los Angeles Times* noted the "drastic change of policy" from Truman. "Aside from any . . . philosophical" disagreement, the paper wrote, "there is plenty of reason for discontinuing the wage and price controls," which had become "an expensive nuisance [that did] nobody any good, except perhaps the several thousand individuals working in the control offices."[54] The *New York Times* agreed. "Well, rising and falling prices have been a feature of the American economy since [its] founding." Indeed, "we do not like to contemplate . . . where . . . we would be as a nation if this hadn't been the case."[55] The *Wall Street Journal* felt that "the new Administration has correctly appraised the country's internal economic condition."[56] The influential Committee for Economic Development embraced not only the end of controls, but also the economic thinking behind it, endorsing the use of monetary policy and a balanced budget to stabilize the price level.[57]

By contrast, a large group of congressmen called for the creation of a committee to "counterbalance producer lobbies and help protect the housewife now that controls were being lifted." Specific union bosses worried that the "decontrol program" would lead to a "sharp increase in living costs" (as Anthony Valente, the president of the United Textile Workers, argued).[58] Senator Paul Douglas (D-IL), the former University of Chicago economics professor, saw "danger signals" of coming inflation.[59] For his part, Michael DiSalle decided to take his warnings public, telling the press that "indirect controls" would not stop inflation. He advocated the creation of a new agency to regulate prices and wages.[60]

Still, Eisenhower stuck with his approach and the economy largely responded as he hoped. Between April and December, 1953, the consumer price index barely moved, rising just over 1 percent. "I have been gratified to see that there has been little discernible evidence that anyone is trying to . . . take advantage of the situation," Eisenhower told the press. "There has been a moderation and a restraint [in prices] that I think have been noticeable and admirable."[61]

*   *   *

On April 30, 1953, Eisenhower invited Robert Taft and other Republican congressional leaders to the White House to meet with Dodge, Humphrey, and other cabinet heads. All together, about thirty officials from Congress and the administration circled around to listen to Eisenhower explain the "extent of the changes that would be recommended by the administration in the Truman budget," and devise a legislative strategy to accomplish those changes.[62] Emphasizing the "dual threat facing the United States"—that is, "the external threat of Communism and the internal threat of a weakened economy"—he made clear he "would no longer ignore the internal threat" that resulted from deficit spending, as Truman had done. The last Truman budget, "could cause an aggregate budget deficit over the next five years of $44 billion. The new policy," he explained, will "seek . . . to avoid weakening the economy even while providing adequate security."

This all sounded like standard conservative rhetoric, as congressional Republicans recognized. Yet from this point forward, Eisenhower diverged from the party line because of what Dodge clarified aboard the *Helena*. "[A] balanced budget [cannot] be obtained immediately," he explained, because "too arbitrary or too precipitate action in reducing Federal expenditures could produce dangerous and undesirable domestic and international repercussions." Over time, there might be "further reductions," but in the short term national security and domestic considerations required a great deal of spending.

Humphrey and Dodge then confirmed the president's position with specific numbers. In particular, they warned that the Republican Congress would probably have to *extend* several taxes initially enacted to pay for the Korean War. Humphrey thought it possible to get "a deficit of only $1.3 billion—provided the scheduled tax reductions now on the books [do not] take effect." To have any chance of reducing the deficit, Congress had to extend those tax hikes as one of its first acts. Dodge agreed, and reiterated to the group what he had explained aboard the *Helena*. "Mr. Truman foresaw a deficit of $15 billion," he explained. But "67 percent of the budget is devoted to security programs, another $16 billion is for interest and other untouchables, [leaving] only about $10 billion left to work on—out of which some people want to eliminate the [whole] deficit. The great increase in the budget since 1950 has been in national security matters."

As the meeting wore on, Taft grew increasingly frustrated. Eisenhower really wanted to *raise* taxes? Even then, the budget would be unbalanced for years? He could contain himself no more and interjected. Assuming "this meeting had been called to secure the comments of the Leaders," he felt an obligation to unburden himself. Specifically, he wanted to "express . . . his disappointment at the program the Administration presented today. The net result of it," he went on, "would be to spend as much as Mr. Truman spent. Either there would be a large deficit or Congress would have to levy new taxes." Both would be a disaster. If either happened, it would "be impossible to elect a Republican Congress in 1954." Eisenhower seemed to have no idea how important deficit reduction was to the Republican Congress. "Two-thirds of Republican Congressmen would vote for further reductions and be at odds with the Administration," he threatened.

But that was not all. Taft called the reductions Eisenhower proposed, "puny." Acknowledging that the budget "was essentially a military problem," he noted that, "with all due respect for the NSC, [I don't] believe the members [know] anything more than [I do] about these problems." He ridiculed Eisenhower's friend and successor as army chief of staff, Omar Bradley, who "had said in 1950 that $13–1/2 billion was fine but now [he says] $50 billion wasn't enough. . . . [I have] no confidence in the people who . . . recommended this program."

Two things were true of Eisenhower since he was a child. First, he had a temper. Second, he wore it on his face. As his friends around the table saw what was coming, they feared that a full break between the new president and the Senate majority leader was imminent. But Taft continued: The current situation required "a complete reconsideration of our entire military program against Russia. The NSC has relied on the same JCS people who have been here [in Washington] and they can't change their positions"—a barb at Eisenhower's judgment in his prior work within the Truman administration. "[I] could not defend this program" in public, he warned. "There ought to be a complete resurvey by the best military people available who are not already committed," implicitly suggesting that the men in the room around him obviously did not represent the "best military people available." Taft concluded by echoing MacArthur while taking a swipe at Eisenhower's work with NATO: Is it "sound to base the [entire defense] program on the concept of a land war in Europe?" Unless Eisenhower took a new approach, he felt the administration "would fall," taking down the Republican Congress with it.

Eisenhower was furious. But before he could launch into a counter-attack, Humphrey broke in intentionally, keeping Eisenhower from talking until he had cooled down.[63] "[I agree] with much of what Senator Taft . . . said." But, he continued, Taft needed to remember that the new administration only had "a three-month start on the problem, and that the Administration would be keeping on for the next fifteen months."

"A whole new study [is] needed," Taft reiterated.

"[That's] impossible in the three months available," said Humphrey.

Could "the Administration . . . at least say it would make the new study?" asked Taft.

Of course. It "was implicit that the Administration would keep on studying the problem."

Taft was unsatisfied. "Republicans [haven't] moved an inch from the Truman program," he complained, "and Democrats would waste no time exploiting the situation."

"$41 billion of the '54 budget had been spent by Mr. Truman before Republicans took over," replied Humphrey. There wasn't much "situation" left to exploit.

But, interrupted Taft, Republicans had campaigned on getting "the budget below $70 billion." When would that happen? The "Administration is not going to save anything except as related to Mr. Truman's desire to spend a lot more [in the future]," he finally blurted out. And in a sentence, he essentially got it.

Taft realized, much to his discomfort, that Eisenhower did not want to roll back the state so much as prevent it from heading further in the direction Truman had pointed it. Eisenhower wanted to refocus federal spending, given his expectation of a long, protracted Cold War of attrition rather than the apocalyptic showdown at a particular point in the near future (implicit in NSC 68, but also implicit in the foreign policy of Douglas MacArthur). If this meant a rejection of Leon Keyserling's total faith in a world without economic trade-offs, it also meant a rejection of reducing expenditures "regardless" of the domestic or international consequences.[64]

As he settled into this realization, Taft shifted tactics to talk specifics. He may not get all of what he wanted, but he could at least negotiate closer to what he wanted. "[On] a ten year basis," he began, "no more than $35 billion per year on the average should be needed [for defense], as compared with $50 billion now."

Humphrey agreed, still doing the talking as Eisenhower cooled. He "was just as disappointed as was Senator Taft that this year's budget had to be so large." But, he pointed out, "the change could not be done too quickly." He tried to give Taft perspective. "[No] one could merely fire a stenographer and claim to have reorganized the business. Thus far," he went on, "we have fired the stenographer, but now we've got to reorganize the business."

Finally calm, Eisenhower decided to speak quietly as he reviewed "the essentials": everyone "agreed that Europe must not be allowed to fall to Russia . . . [but] there was no desire on the part of the United States to take over political control of Europe, and . . . our policy must therefore be founded upon making the free countries of Europe stronger both physically and in spirit." Eisenhower then recalled the "careful process by which the budget had been developed": the "logic" used "could not be refuted. . . . What was important," he concluded, "was to take hold of the upward trend of expenditures and bend it down."

Before Taft could respond, Dodge jumped in. He felt that some "non-security aspects of the Budget" might generate more savings. He could not "pinpoint where" exactly they would come from, but he remained confident more savings were on the way.

Taft paused. Maybe if "the Administration would not now make any commitments as to the size of the FY '55 budget [due the next year] . . . it would leave some room for hope."

"[There] is hope for further reduction but it [is] still too soon to make any promises," Eisenhower replied. "As for the major issue here," he went on, "[I know] no other way to approach it than as an honest struggle and in an effort to accomplish a meeting of the minds."

At this point, Taft's congressional colleagues began to jump in. They raised questions about how the administration would go about rolling out its budget. They agreed on the need to work together. Perhaps sensing that he might have lost the room, or feeling sheepish at lashing out so directly at the president, Taft began to go along as well.

"All [I] wanted," he finally explained, was "that *if* Republicans had to defend a $50 billion military program and *if* taxes had to be increased, then something more than what had yet been done ought to be done."

"[The] problem was one of lead-time," Eisenhower replied. "As for the coming year . . . much of the money has already been contracted, and the Administration can't make a good showing, except as it shows that policies have been changed."

Eventually, the conversation began to wear down, at which point Vice President Richard Nixon, who had remained silent, finally chose to speak. He was "the only one . . . from the legislative side who also had attended all the National Security Council meetings." There, he had seen "the dedicated work of the members of the Council, who held exactly the same objectives as those in this meeting."

"[I] had no intention of reflecting on the members of the Council," Taft apologized. "[In] the last analysis there must be reliance on the military planners" he admitted.

After the meeting, cabinet members found an excuse to come by the West Wing and talk to Eisenhower. Collectively, they tried to look on the bright side. The exchange had at least "cleared the air." Eisenhower also realized how Humphrey and Dodge had intentionally jumped in to calm the situation. In his journal, he confided he was happy he "did not add any fuel to the flames, even though it is possible that I might have done so except for the quick intervention of my devoted friends." But, of course, he remained wary of Taft's support moving forward.[65]

In retrospect, though, the meeting did more than "clear the air." Most of all, it established the basic positions of the key players and their views of political economy. Everyone in that room had rejected the position taken by NSC 68 that the economy had, essentially, no limits. Yet a deep disagreement remained between the president and Taft as to whether the state should remain roughly where it stood before Truman embraced NSC 68 or whether it needed rolling back. Beneath this argument lay the question of exactly what commitments the state needed to maintain in the postwar, global environment. Eisenhower's investment in the global defense against communism, with Europe as the first line, stood in contrast to Taft's desire to leave Europe and shrink the American state closer to its 1920s incarnation. Ultimately, the president prevailed on both issues. He reduced defense spending, but never got close to the $35 billion level that Taft hoped for. Moreover, the country remained committed to NATO and Europe.

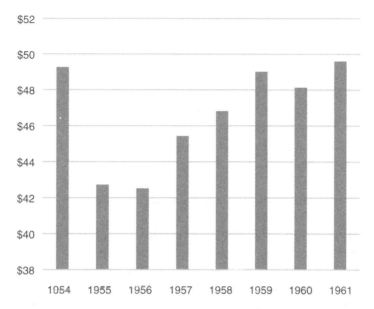

Figure 17. U.S. defense spending, 1954–1961 (billions of U.S. dollars). Source: *Budget of the U.S. Government: Fiscal Year 2012*, Historical Tables (Washington, DC: Government Printing Office), table 3.1.

At the same time, Taft correctly predicted that Republicans would lose the Congress, but probably not because of this issue.[66] Yet, despite their differences, and despite the heat of their exchange, Eisenhower came to eat his words about Taft's leadership. After their blowup, Taft decided working with Eisenhower got him more of his agenda than otherwise. Soon, Eisenhower could say that "Senator Taft and I early reached an amicable and definite understanding . . . and, indeed, he never once failed to carry forward vigorously any mission that I asked him to undertake in the Senate." Tragically, given their growing friendship, Taft developed pancreatic cancer just weeks after this meeting. He died on July 31, 1953.

∗   ∗   ∗

With the congressional leadership on board, Eisenhower turned his attention to the group most affected by his political economy: the American military. "Since December [1952] when I first began assembling . . . my principal advisers," Eisenhower wrote his brother Milton, "it has been our general intention to use 1953 largely as a period of study and formulation of programs." Once the "study" came to conclusion, the "'Administration Bible' would be brought out for publication in the delivery of the 1954 Message to the Congress."[67] The basic contours of the "Bible" emerged aboard the *Helena,* yet the military establishment had to have a chance to express its views on the nation's security needs. Throughout the year, Eisenhower, Dodge, Humphrey, and Dulles deliberated with the NSC about the best way to reduce military expenditures without placing the nation at risk. At times, the conversation became testy. At one point Dodge heatedly complained that, contrary to military assertions, he "was innocent of any charge that the Bureau of the Budget was attempting to establish foreign and military policy by means of budget restrictions."[68] Yet, in reality he was doing precisely this, and the military knew it.

Military brass tried to get around Dodge's "penny pinching" by swaying public opinion. The well-known columnist Drew Pearson proved a willing accomplice. "Eisenhower," he wrote, had to decide whether to "A. Let the budget stay out of balance; B. Increase taxes; C. Or Sacrifice the safety of the nation."[69] Echoing Pearson, Defense Secretary Charlie Wilson declared in the autumn of 1953, that "there is nothing we can do" to get the defense budget low enough to balance the overall budget. Besides, balancing the budget was "someone else's worry."[70] His focus lay in protecting the nation, not in counting pennies.

"I not only was appalled but completely discouraged to read in this morning's paper the alleged statement of Secretary Wilson," Dodge complained in a private note to Eisenhower. Wilson's statement simply increased the "difficulties in resolving the budget problems with the Services, the Congress, and the public." Eisenhower handwrote a reply: "Joe, I know exactly what you mean. I'll see what I can do! . . . P.S. Charlie Wilson says he was misquoted."[71]

As fall turned to winter, however, the military leaders wore down. Whenever the discussion came to a loggerhead, Eisenhower would lean on the military a little harder. "I am afraid," he told them in October 1953, "that the Joint Chiefs of Staff are just going to have to work their heads off. . . . I'd like to see . . . a complete and thorough reexamination by the Joint Chiefs of Staff of this whole problem, in which they would really take a corporate view, and see how far they could get."[72] Under pressure, military leaders agreed by December to cut about $4 billion from their previous budget. In the process, the entire emphasis of defense changed. The "New

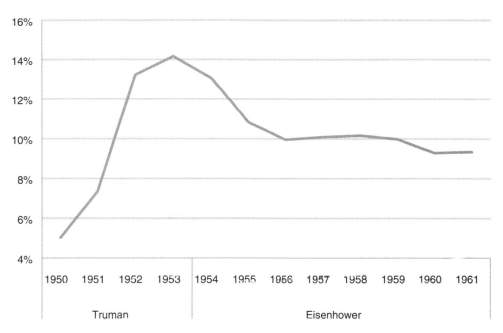

Figure 18. U.S. defense spending, 1950–1961 (as a percentage of GDP). Source: *Budget of the U.S. Government: Fiscal Year 2012*, Historical Tables (Washington, DC: Government Printing Office), table 3.1.

Look" made clear that American defense would balance the trade-off between military strength and economic cost. As Dulles explained in January 1954, the new defense posture anticipated, "for ourselves and for others a maximum deterrent at bearable cost." Of course, conventional garrisons (what Dulles called "local defense") remained important in the new scheme; "but there is no local defense which alone will contain the mighty land power of the Communist world." As a result, "local defense must be reinforced by the further deterrent of massive [i.e. nuclear] retaliatory power."[73] Henceforward, the United States would depend on airpower and nuclear weapons as the major deterrent to Soviet aggression, a strategy that saved money even if it threatened the end of civilization. By 1955, defense spending leveled off at roughly 10 percent of GDP. This allowed Eisenhower to reverse the spending trend implicit in NSC 68 and begin to balance the budget.

With the armistice of July 27, 1953, the Korean War came to an end. Unfortunately for the administration, this political triumph was followed

by an economic slowdown. As troops returned and the economy transitioned from war spending, production became sluggish. By January 1954,
there were clear signs of recession. Automobile officials in Detroit did not
"want to be quoted," wrote the business columnist J. A. Livingston, but "a
large majority [share the] opinion that . . . [the Administration] . . . may
be bringing on a depression."[74]

Eisenhower took a calculated risk. He would take no dramatic action
to cure the economy unless a full-blown depression emerged. The stakes
could not have been higher. During the 1952 campaign, Truman had
barnstormed on behalf of Adlai Stevenson, arguing that a vote for Eisenhower meant a vote for the "policies [that] led us into the darkest depression that this rich country has ever seen."[75] As soon as the signs of an
economic downturn appeared toward the end of 1953, many Democrats
felt vindicated. Stevenson argued that under Eisenhower "four fears" had
replaced Roosevelt's "four freedoms," first among them, the fear of
depression.[76] The well-known British economist Colin Clark predicted
a deep depression with "6 or 7 million unemployed, unless the federal
government cut back taxes on a massive scale."[77] By early 1954, Truman
again entered the political fray to warn that the longer the Eisenhower
administration waited to pursue fiscal stimulus, "the more danger we run
of a real depression."[78]

The administration became increasingly concerned through the spring
of 1954. At a March cabinet meeting, Eisenhower asked his head of the
Council of Economic Advisers, Arthur Burns, to discuss the economy with
the cabinet and help them develop a plan in case of depression. The lengthy
list of recommendations called for massive public works, pressure on the
Federal Reserve to ease credit restrictions, tax cuts, and other fiscal stimuli.
But Eisenhower held off putting any of the suggested plans into effect. It
became, in effect, his contingency plan in case of emergency. Meanwhile,
more calls came for federal action. With the Depression still a clear memory, David McDonald, head of the United Steel Workers, demanded that
Eisenhower initiate massive spending and a tax cut ($5 billion in housing
and slum clearing; $5 billion for public works; $4 billion in income tax
reduction; and $3 billion in additional unemployment benefits). Similar
calls came from other quarters of the country. Walter Reuther, President of
the Congress of Industrial Organizations (CIO), convened a national full-
employment conference. Truman attended where he accused Eisenhower
of "creeping McKinleyism." But Eisenhower refused to budge.[79]

By June 1954, Burns again reported to the cabinet meeting, this time with "the heartening news of a lengthening workweek and signs that the unemployment increase was coming to a stop." Within a few months the economy started a boom that lasted three years. For Eisenhower, it was a personal victory that refuted his critics and vindicated his judgment. He could favorably compare his management of the adjustment from a war economy in 1954 to the transition under Truman in 1946. As he explained later, "In this transition we saw demonstrated the fact that if the government acts wisely and early, and resists panic, it can do much to stave off serious difficulties later."[80]

* * *

In the summer of 1953, a friend wrote Eisenhower to hurry up with tax relief. If "Republicans do not make a real cut in taxes next year they are going to have very, very tough going," he warned.

"Thank you very much for your note," Eisenhower replied. "I have always maintained one thing—that the federal deficit must be eliminated in order that tax reduction can begin. Reverse this order and you will never have tax reduction."[81] The year 1953 had largely gone toward solving the Great Equation and included more, not fewer taxes. But it ended with the promise that budgets would be balanced soon. Thus, by early 1954 Eisenhower felt ready to reform the tax code.

He first hinted of his intentions in his Economic Report from January 1954, where he asked for "tax laws [designed] to increase incentives and to remove certain impediments to enterprise, especially of small business."[82] In reality, while most Republicans talked about tax *reduction*, Eisenhower really aimed for tax *reform*. The reforms ultimately involved some reductions, largely to the highly regressive excise taxes on consumer goods. But the majority of what became the Internal Revenue Act of 1954 (the first comprehensive revision of the tax code since its origin in 1913) included targeted incentives that advanced Eisenhower's ambitions to increase productivity without lowering overall tax rates.

In general, the reforms broke down into four broad categories:

• First, the reforms subsidized private welfare. Eisenhower made personal medical expenses deductible. Of lasting consequence, he created a tax deduction for employer contributions to employee medical insurance. This move allowed the IRS to recognize an increasingly common bargaining chip in labor-management negotiations since World War II.[83] Most important, by codifying this benefit into the tax code, Eisenhower largely guaranteed that health care for Americans would be tied to jobs (thus linking a welfare benefit inextricably to productive labor).[84]

- Second, the legislation included tax relief for "good behaviors," such as charitable donations (to hospitals, schools, or churches), raising and educating children, and childcare (provided the childcare allowed the parent to go to work).

- Third, the new law directly subsidized individual investment by reducing the taxes and the regulations for pension and profit-sharing plans for employees, cutting taxes on annuities, and (most controversially) reducing the taxation on dividend income. Stock owners could deduct the first $50 of dividend income and 4 percent of all dividend income after that. By creating the deduction in this way, the reform encouraged people of lower income brackets to get into the market. In 1956, studies showed that roughly 10 percent of Americans owned stock, but the number grew by another third every four years. By the end of the decade, women stockholders had come to outnumber men 51.6 percent to 48.4 percent because the deduction worked per individual (meaning husband and wife could both claim the benefit). The median income of the average stockholder dropped from $7,100 to $6,200, and most new stockholders came from the burgeoning suburbs.[85] The stock market reflected the influx of new investors as the Dow Jones almost doubled between the passage of the Internal Revenue Act and the end of Eisenhower's presidency.

- Finally, the reforms aimed to encourage businesses to invest by liberalizing the depreciation rules for existing plants, deducting research and development costs from corporate income, and reducing the burden of an "excess profits tax." The act also encouraged foreign direct investment by reducing the tax liability on corporate income from a foreign source.[86]

Opponents felt the tax cut on dividends would "exhume the 'trickle-down' theory of taxation of Alexander Hamilton and, more recently, Andrew Mellon." Rather than providing broad relief, opponents argued that "ninety-two percent of American families own no stock whatever" and "six-tenths of 1 percent own 80 percent of all publicly held stock." In short, Eisenhower hoped to reduce "the taxes of only 8 percent of American families, and primarily for the benefit of only six-tenths of 1 percent."[87] In addition, Democrats in Congress feared that Eisenhower had entirely ignored the lessons of the Great Depression.

Senator Paul Douglas sent a letter to Eisenhower early in 1954, disagreeing that "stimulants to business and investors" could create more production or employment. "Under such a premise, who will buy the goods?" Echoing Keynes, Douglas agreed that "in normal times, savings are converted to investments." However, "in times such as these, while savings may flow into banks they do not flow out to the same degree in the form of actual Investments." Articulating in simple terms the Keynesian fear of a liquidity trap, he suggested that at present, "With the large supply of idle industrial equipment on hand, business in general does not want to borrow to add to it. The savings therefore tend to be in large part sterilized and do not expand production and employment as they would in normal times."[88] Watching from the sidelines, Leon Keyserling agreed. A "more favorable tax [reform]," he explained, "would be stimulated by . . . surrender of tax revenues to expand the buying of consumers."[89]

But the real goal of the dividend reforms had to do with Eisenhower's hope to tie investment to the growing safety net. Nearly all retirement plans (pensions, annuities, insurance) pooled the earnings of workers and invested them in the economy. The tax reforms simply amplified his feeling that welfare and economic growth amounted to the same thing. During hearings on the legislation, this approach became clear.

"Of course," Senator Douglas lectured George Humphrey, "the overwhelming proportion of dividends are received by those in the upper income group."

"I do not believe I will agree to that," replied Humphrey. "It is the great mass of the American people that are getting the great ownership in American industry today, and it is coming through pension funds and through insurance funds and things of that kind."

"Is it the poor people who receive the dividends?" Douglas asked.

"Oh, yes; indeed . . . they get dividends through their pension funds and through their insurance."

Douglas remained unconvinced. "I have no further questions," he explained, "but in order that the statistics may partially catch up with the statements, I should like to put into the record two pages from a study by

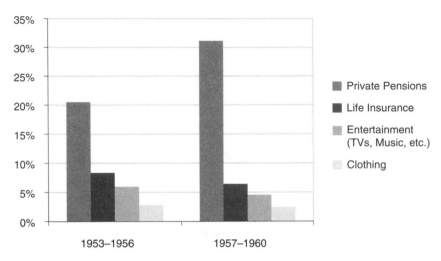

Figure 19. U.S. average annual increase in spending by product type (1953–1956 vs. 1957–1960) (percentage). Source: *Historical Statistics of the United States, Colonial Times to 1970*, Bicentennial Edition, Part 1 (Washington, DC: Department of Commerce), F 144–185.

the Brookings Institute." The study indicated that "only 4.2 percent of the population" owned stock and "that the percentage of stock ownership is, as one would believe, infinitely higher in the larger income groups than in the lower income groups."

"No. I think I told you," Humphrey replied, "the thing that that list, of course, does not show, the thing that I spoke about, is the participation in corporate profits that accrue to people through their insurance and pension plans." Specifically, these "investments will be favorably affected by the dividend, depreciation, and other tax proposals improving the climate for risk-taking and investment."[90]

Savers seemed to agree with Humphrey. The combination of a balanced budget, low inflation, and tax incentives produced a boom for pensions and life insurance. By nearly all measures, most families placed far more of their wages into pensions and life insurance than they spent on the more popular consumer items of the decade (such as entertainment and clothing). If 1950s American domesticity included a home in the suburbs and a kitchen full of the latest appliances, it also included life insurance, a pension, and some common stock. As Humphrey explained to Douglas early in Eisenhower's tenure, that had been the plan all along.

Chapter 13

Protecting the Global Economy

The heated exchange between Eisenhower and Taft in 1953 illustrated the way Eisenhower's political economy differed from conservative orthodoxy. The less heated exchanges between the administration and Senator Paul Douglas illustrated Eisenhower's disagreements with the growing Keynesian orthodoxy. The fight over the Interstate Highway Act, however, demonstrated how Eisenhower's approach fit no ideological categories.

In April 1954, Eisenhower announced to his staff that he wanted a "dramatic plan to get 50 billion dollars' worth of self-liquidating highways under construction."[1] Nearly everyone agreed that the nation's highway system needed significant upgrading. The growth of car ownership and spread of the suburbs led to a tragic jump in vehicle fatalities in the first years of the decade. Most Americans wanted something done to make the roads safer and less congested. Yet, typical of his background, Eisenhower brought an additional sensibility to the modernization of America's highways. His experience in Germany taught him that the autobahn had not only made German travel safer, it had made the country militarily stronger *and* economically more efficient. As Gabriel Hauge, one of Eisenhower's economic advisers, explained, the program's "motivation was economic development . . . what the program could contribute to economic growth of industry and of agriculture and of our communities." The problem, however, lay in the fact that the benefits of growth would remain hidden until far in the future. It "was such a long range program" that the administration felt obligated to talk of it in terms of national defense and safety to get it through Congress.[2]

Richard Nixon unveiled Eisenhower's goals while speaking to the forty-sixth Conference of Governors. Unfortunately, things went poorly from the start. "We want to continue to build our own roads unimpeded by a Federal system," complained John S. Fine, the Republican governor of Pennsylvania. More worrisome, the governors feared federal road construction would become the justification for making the "temporary" federal tax on gasoline a permanent part of federal revenue. "We want the Federal Government to get out of the gas tax and fuel oil fields once and for all," Fine explained, "and now is the time to do it before we embark on any new Federal aid program."[3] Compounding his problems, the announcement came before his own administration could agree on the best way to implement the program. "I originally preferred a system of self-financing toll highways," Eisenhower said.[4] Yet financing through tolls created a kind of financial chicken-and-egg dilemma: tolls could not be charged until the roads were built, but the roads could not be built until money came in from the tolls. Where, exactly, would the start-up capital come from?

Eisenhower decided to solve these concerns by creating two separate committees to tackle different aspects of the program: one within the administration to hammer out policy details; another a blue-ribbon commission of nongovernment officials to craft the legislation and build public support. Eisenhower formed the first by executive order. But when he told his chief of staff, Sherman Adams, about the second, Adams asked who might head this private committee. "Call General Clay," Eisenhower said. So Adams asked Clay.

"Yes," said Clay, "If the president wants me to." Thus, the second committee had a name: the Clay Commission.[5]

Clay brought his German experience to bear on the problem. He understood that the program aimed at long-term economic expansion, not a means to counter a recession. "Later on [with different Administrations] it became that, but not at that time." He knew the plan went back to Germany. Eisenhower "realized what a very important contribution [good highways] had made to the national defense and security of Germany—the *Autobahns* were very impressive."[6] The whole effort got a boost when, in the summer of 1954, a group of state highway officials devised a program that solved the chicken-and-egg financing dilemma. It asked the federal government to sell bonds as a way to generate the start-up capital for road construction and then used an expanded federal gas tax as a dedicated source of revenue for paying off the bonds. Governors might be placated by giving them a greater say in the placement and pace of road construction. Finally, it suggested the creation of a new entity within the federal government—a "road authority"—overseeing both finance and construction.[7]

While this approach seemed promising, Eisenhower had insisted from the beginning that the program not add to the national debt. Many in the administration liked the idea of using bonds, but bonds were a form of debt. With most other concerns resolved, by the fall of 1954, the question boiled down to this: how to issue billions in new *government* debt without adding to the *national* debt.

On January 18, 1954, just as the highway program got underway, Joseph Dodge decided to finally go back to his bank. "Beginning in 1942," he explained, "I repeatedly have been drafted to meet various Government emergencies, at home and abroad." He had "accepted [the Budget Bureau] assignment on a short-term basis and principally to help meet the emergency connected [to] . . . the 1954 Truman Budget." He had promised he would return after "a period of not more than one year." The year had passed. It was time to resign. "While I am not at all satisfied with what I have been able to do for the President," he wrote, "I hope it can be fairly said that I helped accomplish some of the things he wanted done. . . . I have been included in more responsibilities and have been engaged in more diversified activities than former Directors." At least, "the trend of the Budget and of mounting deficits have been reversed and a new pattern of action and direction established." He could take confidence that "someone else should be able to continue the work to the President's complete satisfaction."[8]

Initially, Eisenhower refused to let Dodge go. But as Dodge persisted, Eisenhower eventually relented. "Dear Joe," he wrote in March, "I must, of course, respect your wish to leave governmental service." Still, "I assure you that it is only with the greatest reluctance that I accept your resignation." On a personal note, "I shall sorely miss your advice, counsel and your friendly helpfulness."[9] Dodge officially left his Washington office on April 15: Tax Day.[10] The man who through devotion and tenacity had become "the most feared and inaccessible official in Washington" could finally go back to Detroit.[11]

If Dodge had stayed in Washington another year, he might have helped rethink a scheme for highway finance that ultimately proved a little too-clever-by-half. In his absence, the Bureau proposed the creation of a National Road Authority constituted as a quasi-independent corporation. The heads of the new corporation would come from the obvious federal departments (Treasury and Commerce, for example), but it would issue bonds in its own name—not the federal government's. While the gas tax would ultimately provide funds to pay the bonds, it would be clear—by statute if necessary—that the bonds did *not* have the full faith and credit of the government backing them. In its institutional form, it represented an innovative way to expand federal capacities while limiting the fiscal impact. Most important, technically speaking the Bureau managed the impossible task of issuing new quasi-governmental debt without adding to the official national debt.[12]

With the financing scheme settled (at least within the administration), Clay shored up support among governors quickly by promising to increase federal aid for new roads. He also generated support from industry and businesses associated with travel by promising no new taxes on their industries, only on gas. But most of all, he moved quickly. Eisenhower feared that without a plan coming from Clay soon, Congress (which would be in Democrats' hands starting in 1955) might seize the initiative where it might become a "jobs" bill along the lines of the New Deal or Fair Deal.[13] Clay submitted his report in January 1955, just six months after he began, but still after the Democrats had taken control of Congress.

The initial response to the legislation followed predictable lines. From the right, Clarence Manion, the former dean of the Notre Dame Law School and also the former chair of Eisenhower's own Commission of Inter-Governmental Relations, complained that this "new federal octopus would be patterned after the Tennessee Valley authority whose brand of 'creeping socialism' would henceforth be given an endless ride over all the country's highways."[14] From the left, the National Farmers Union complained that the legislation did not do enough to guarantee full employment. "We can only maintain full employment and have an expanded economy if we have courage enough to [not only] build highways [but also] schoolhouses and raise minimum wages [and] reduce taxes on low-income consumers."[15]

But the criticism that hurt most went at the financing, and it struck home. Senator Harry Byrd (D-VA), who by virtue of the 1954 election had become chair of the Senate Committee on Finance, feared that Clay's proposal "establishes a government corporation without income or assets and authorizes the corporation to borrow $21 billion . . . and by legerdemain excludes the debt from the debt limitation fixed by Congress." Byrd then used bits of Eisenhower's rhetoric against him. "In these days when we are continuously piling up debt," he went on, "the least we can do is to keep the books honest and make full disclosure of the obligations we are incurring."[16] Adding insult to injury, one of Eisenhower's appointees publicly came out against it: "It is our opinion," explained Joseph Campbell, the man Eisenhower had named comptroller of the United States just months earlier, "that the Government should not enter into financing arrangements which might have the effect of obscuring the financial facts of the Government's debt position."[17] In their rush to get a report done and keep it from expanding the debt, Clay and Eisenhower appeared to be playing with the books. They had overthought the plan and now the legislation was in real trouble. The critics piled on. In the spring of 1955, the Senate Public Works Committee voted down the administration's bill, eight to four, and substituted its own bill that would pay for everything out of annual appropriations, implicitly breaking open the budget. Fortunately for Eisenhower, the House did not follow along, and at the end of 1955, highway legislation appeared dead.[18]

While Eisenhower, even toward the end of his life, liked the institutional innovation represented by the National Road Authority, by late 1955 he realized it could not get past Congress.[19] Privately to congressional members, he made clear he did not feel bound by the Clay Commission: so long as a plan met his basic criteria of self-liquidation without adding to the national debt, he could support a new measure with sounder financial "machinery." He would even lend quiet technical support from his staff. Early in 1956, the dead legislation showed faint signs of life.

Fortunately, Congressman George H. Fallon, a Democrat from Baltimore and the chair of the House Subcommittee on Roads, saw an opportunity for a legacy. "If highway people ever had a friend in Congress," explained a leader of the American Road Builders Association, "it is George H. Fallon, and I believe the 'H' stands for 'highways.' "[20] With both the administration's bill and the Senate bill stalled, Fallon began working on a new piece of legislation that would accomplish what everyone hoped for. Officially, the new legislation had to come from Fallon because Eisenhower could not publicly repudiate his previous effort. Yet privately his administration developed many of the plan's details. Most important, it would not include the quasi-independent government corporation Clay imagined.[21]

Fallon's bill ultimately included two innovations that made it palatable to Eisenhower as well as to senators like Harry Byrd. First, it raised taxes on gasoline, trucks, and other road-related products to generate the needed start-up capital. In other words, no bonds. Fallon then dedicated these revenues to a highway "trust fund" patterned after the already existing system of social security (where a dedicated tax went into "trust" that paid out benefits). While Fallon's approach meant that construction would begin in smaller increments, it remained budget-neutral—it would not add to the debt. Plus, it looked a lot like a known institutional structure. As a result, Fallon's bill raced through Congress. By the end of June 1956, it had become law.

In his memoirs, Eisenhower summarized the entire fight over financing this way: "Though I originally preferred a system of self-financing toll highways, and though I endorsed General Clay's recommendation, I grew restless with the quibbling over methods of financing. I wanted the job done."[22] The way it turned out probably fit Eisenhower's philosophy best; hence, he could dismiss the grueling infight as "quibbling over methods of financing." In reality, the "quibbles" over financing made all the difference. Indeed, the final product accomplished roughly what he wanted better than he had originally conceived it. Yet, in another example of how the political economy of the occupations often cut across the typical party and ideological lines of American politics, it took a Democrat from Maryland to provide the final impetus for a program originally conceived in postwar Germany.

*   *   *

On August 1, 1953, Eisenhower sent a message to Congress explaining that, "Retirement systems . . . have become an essential part of our economic and social life." Because they involved contributions during working years to provide for later years, they reflected "the American heritage of sturdy self-reliance." The most obvious form of retirement came from social security, which "furnishes, on a national scale, the opportunity for our citizens, through that same self-reliance, to build the foundation for their security." In 1953, about eleven million Americans had no access to the program. "We are resolved to extend that opportunity to millions of our citizens who heretofore have been unable to avail themselves of it."[23]

The announcement, coming from a Republican, surprised some. Yet during the campaign, Eisenhower had told Americans he wanted to expand social security. "[We] accept certain specific goals for all our people," he explained, including "adequate security for old age and insurance for our workers against unemployment, accident and ill-health."[24] Democrats remained skeptical. Senator John Sparkman (D-AL), Adlai Stevenson's running mate in 1952, warned against Eisenhower's "seductive promises," suggesting once in power, the Republican leadership would "wreck the social security system."[25]

In reality, though, Eisenhower sincerely intended to expand the program, which, since its inception, had remained piecemeal. Despite efforts to expand its coverage, seasonal workers (especially on farms) remained uncovered. This group included many of the poorest Americans and particularly African Americans. If successful, Eisenhower would correct for the racial disparity that had characterized the program from its inception.[26] Yet, as was often true of Eisenhower, social security connected to other aspects of his political economy. He helped make these connections clear to Richard Nixon in a letter written shortly after Nixon agreed to join the ticket. It outlined Eisenhower's legislative agenda and reiterated his plan to expand social security, but added, "Inflation has already eaten up so much of the real value of the [social security] allowances of people who are wholly dependent upon old age or other pensions. . . . [We] must make such necessary adjustments as will give these allowances pre-war purchasing power." In short, "I have constantly stressed that the only sound way to maintain the value of . . . 'social security law and appropriations' is to restore the sound dollar."[27]

The link between welfare, inflation, and budgetary restraint fit Eisenhower's holistic approach to government. Later in life, he elaborated his thinking. "If a man's active life is 30 years, and the median of his dollar value [occurs] . . . 15 years earlier, then for every dollar he puts in, well, he will be getting 85 cent or 80 cent dollars." In short, inflation undermined the basic promise of a defined retirement benefit. While the payout could be adjusted for inflation, the inflated benefit just added to the overall inflation. "Finally," he concluded, "we're going to have the kind of inflation that ruined Japan, Greece, Italy, Brazil, Germany, and caused great upheavals, not only political but social as well. As a matter of fact, this kind of thing brought about Hitler. We certainly don't want to do anything like that."[28]

Eisenhower wanted the extended benefit to come along with an increase in the contributory tax. The old guard of the Republican Party felt little enthusiasm for an extension of a program they associated with the New Deal and even less support for increasing taxes. As a result, despite Eisenhower's enthusiasm, the social security amendments languished in Congress through 1953. Frustrated, Eisenhower took his case to the American people. In January 1954, he took advantage of television to explain that "the fear of poverty in old age—in fact, any real injustice in the business of living—penalizes us all."[29] Ten days later he sent Congress a special message on social security that echoed his message to the nation: "One . . . problem that faces every individual is the provision of economic security for his old age."[30]

With the president's clear support, Congress began to take action. The House Ways and Means Committee conducted hearings through early April and eventually reported a bill to the full House that largely embodied Eisenhower's recommendations. It passed the House on June 1 by almost 350 votes. The Senate made a few modifications and passed its bill on August 13. After a short conference, Congress sent a completed bill to Eisenhower who signed the extensions into law on September 1, 1954.[31]

The debate in Congress tended to echo the concerns that led Eisenhower to support the measure in the first place. "History shows that as a nation becomes predominantly industrial," Senator Eugene Millikin (R-CO) explained, "security must be found . . . in the ability of the worker to buy his security from that which is in his pay envelope." Thus, the program's "cost is met by the production of the worker and his employer through the payroll."[32] Indeed, paying for extended and increased benefits remained a critical part of the legislation. Eisenhower insisted, and the Republican Congress agreed, that "the old-age and survivors insurance program should be on a completely self-supporting basis from contributions of covered individuals and employers, with employers and employees sharing equally."[33] To meet the demands of the revised program, Congress raised the payroll tax by 1.5 percent, which led actuaries to believe the program could survive without revision until roughly 1995.[34]

In reality, the congressional debate lacked drama. Everyone seemed to acknowledge that Eisenhower would get his way, the central question being whether he really deserved the credit for expanding the program. "I should like to point out that the credit for originally suggesting these improvements may properly be claimed by this side of the aisle," explained Senator Herbert Henry Lehman (D-NY). "I introduced a bill . . . on behalf of myself and 10 other Senators, which contained almost all the provisions now contained in the [Eisenhower] bill."[35] Regardless of who deserved credit, most observers supported the measure. The New York Times called it one "of the outstanding achievements of the last session of Congress," agreeing with Eisenhower that, unlike other welfare measures, nothing "in this [legislation] is contradictory with free enterprise; nothing . . . weakens a rational individual's incentive to work and save."[36]

As he concluded his first term in office, Eisenhower could look back and take some pride: he ended price controls and balanced the budget, and enjoyed several important legislative triumphs: the Internal Revenue Act of 1954, the Social Security amendments of 1954, and the Interstate Highway Act of 1956. Collectively, they demonstrated Eisenhower's personal success as a chief executive. But they also caused confusion within the ideological categories of the time. Social security and highway construction seemed to extend the New Deal's interest in a welfare net and public works. On the other hand, the tax reforms and fiscal restraint worked against the growing Keynesian framework often used to justify a policy of welfare and public works.

On a macroeconomic level, it is easier to see the distinctions between Eisenhower's political economy and Franklin Roosevelt's political economy. For example, at no point during his presidency did the federal government spend less (as a percentage of GDP) than at the highest point of the New Deal (roughly 1933 to 1940, after which war spending dominated

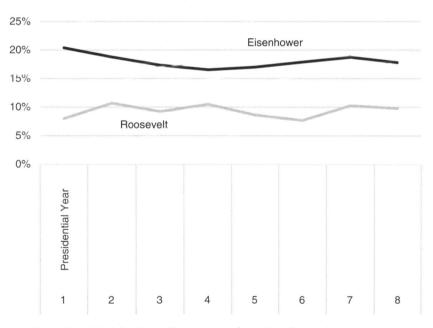

Figure 20. U.S. federal spending, Roosevelt vs. Eisenhower (as a percentage of GDP). Source: *Budget of the U.S. Government: Fiscal Year 2012*, Historical Tables (Washington, DC: Government Printing Office), table 1.2.

federal spending). That is, Roosevelt never spent *more* during the Depression than was spent at any point during Eisenhower's relatively prosperous years. Indeed, in most years, Roosevelt never came close.

Eisenhower differed dramatically, however, in the way he generated the revenue for his much larger federal budget. Roosevelt funded the New Deal largely through a combination of borrowing and excise taxes (taxes on specific items such as cigarettes, gasoline, and electricity). Despite the regressive nature of this approach, these two sources of revenue accounted, on average, for about 55 percent of the fedeal revenue during the Depression years. By contrast, and despite often outspending the New Deal two-to-one, Eisenhower generated almost no revenue through debt and very little through excise taxes. Instead, the vast majority of federal income during the 1950s arrived in the form of individual and corporate taxes. These provided about two-thirds of federal income. New debt amounted to less than 3 percent.

Because he never chose a label, nor found a good way to negotiate the labels he inherited, the coherence of Eisenhower's economic approach remained elusive. For American observers then and afterwards, Eisenhower's approach seemed to "normalize" the New Deal, or alternatively, reveal his "instinctive" conservatism.[37] In reality, he did both and neither because he never really engaged in the fight between American liberals and conservatives. His political economy fit a global context where he never lost his focus. In practical terms, he harmonized American policy with a political economy he and the military helped establish in West Germany and Japan. In each nation, the state played a more active role in advancing economic growth and providing welfare, but never risked price stability in advancing those aims. "German currency is now one of the hardest in the world," explained Ludwig Erhard shortly after Eisenhower won reelection in 1956. Indeed, "this programme of material reconstruction was crowned by a social development of the highest order, the great insurance reform, which guaranteed the whole German people not merely a steady increase in prosperity but also higher social security."[38] Similarly, the constitution of the Liberal Democratic Party (the dominant party in Japan from the 1950s until the 2000s) called "stabilized currency value and balanced international payments the prerequisites" to economic independence. At the same time, the Party also linked price stability to "present programs for the social security covering the medical treatment, old age pension [and] relief of the poor."[39] In all three nations—the United States, Germany, and Japan—a

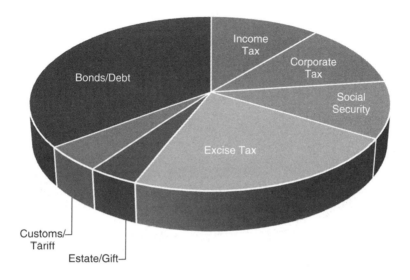

Figure 21. U.S., sources of average annual federal revenue, 1933–1941.
Source: *Budget of the U.S. Government: Fiscal Year 2012*, Historical Tables
(Washington, DC: Government Printing Office), table 2.2.

muscular state continued to play a growing role in economic and welfare
matters, but not in a way that upset the underlying mechanism of a free
market economy, namely, the autonomous movement of prices.

In one area, though, America remained the exception. The world used
dollars in global trade, not yen, marks, francs, pounds, or any other currency. And dollars were backed (as a legacy of the Bretton Woods agreements) by gold at the rate of $35 an ounce. In April 1955, Treasury Secretary
George Humphrey informed Eisenhower that more dollars now circulated
than the country could cover in gold at that rate. From then on, the United
States served not only as the world's bank, but as a fractional bank at that,
meaning that if the "depositors" (that is, other nations) panicked, they
could conceivably make a "run" on the U.S. gold supply, and at some point
the country would exhaust its gold reserves. "Frankly," Eisenhower replied,
"it appears from your memorandum that a lot of bad things would have to

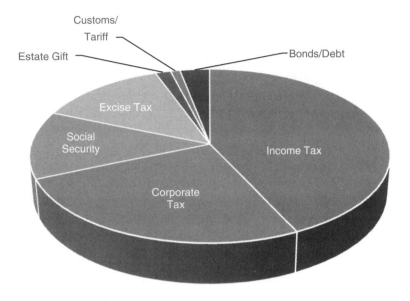

Figure 22. U.S., sources of average annual federal revenue, 1953–1961.
Source: *Budget of the U.S. Government: Fiscal Year 2012*, Historical Tables
(Washington, DC: Government Printing Office), table 2.2.

happen in a hurry for us to get into real trouble." He asked Humphrey to
"watch the whole situation," but felt no immediate concern.[40]

As much as any other officials involved in foreign policy, veterans of
the occupation believed in the Bretton Woods agreements. Having seen
the consequences of war, they trusted the institutions designed to prevent
it—especially the economic framework for linking global currencies.
Eisenhower, in particular, took seriously the role played by the United
States as the "world banker."[41] "International cooperation is the key to
peace," he told economists from the World Bank and the International
Monetary Fund. "There are men in this audience who were my associates
in [the war]. We early found one thing: without the heart, without the
enthusiasm for the cause in which we were working, no cooperation was
possible. With that enthusiasm, subordinating all else to the advancement

of the cause, cooperation was easy." In the end, "As confidence grows, in turn based upon mutual understanding, and based upon meetings such as these, we are bound to have a general rise in the living standards of the world."[42]

The currency agreements made at Bretton Woods waited to go into effect because most countries after the war did not have enough dollars to participate in global trade. Programs such as the Marshall Plan aimed to counteract this problem. Yet most countries needed almost a decade to achieve full convertability.[43] As global commerce revived, dollars continued to make their way overseas—hence Humphrey's letter to Eisenhower about gold reserves in 1955.

In 1958, the Bretton Woods system became fully functional. Countries removed the last controls on currency exchange. Yet, no sooner had this happened than foreign governments began to convert their dollars into gold at an alarming rate. The explanation, as expressed to Robert Anderson (who succeeded Humphrey as treasury secretary in July 1957), came during an October meeting with finance ministers from around the globe held in New Delhi and sponsored by the International Monetary Fund. Collectively, the minsters expressed fear that Eisenhower might embark on a Keynesian program of deficit spending and the country would become "trapped in an inflationary spiral."[44] This would essentially reduce the value of dollars held by foreign countries; thus, as a kind of speculative hedge, they began to trade in their dollars for gold, making the kind of "run" on American gold Humphrey had feared.

They were not entirely wrong. In the second half of 1957, the American economy went into a brief but severe recession, leading to a significant budget shortfall ($12 billion) as tax revenue slackened. Worse, the Soviets launched *Sputnik* at exactly that moment, an event that confirmed fears already expressed in a secret report on American missile preparedness that had been widely leaked.[45] While Eisenhower (thanks to secret U-2 flights) knew the United States had little to fear from Soviet missiles, Senator John F. Kennedy summed up the feeling of many observers in late 1957: America was "losing out in the satellite-missile field to Russia because of . . . complacent miscalculations, penny-pinching, budget cutbacks, incredibly confused mismanagement and wasteful rivalries and jealousies."[46]

As the slump continued into the first months of 1958, a debate emerged within the administration about whether to use tax cuts to stimulate the

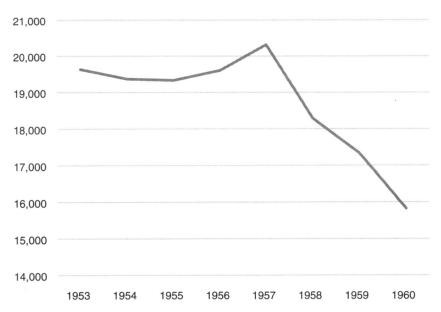

Figure 23. U.S. gold reserves (in metric tons). Source: World Gold Council, "Central Bank Gold Reserves, An Historical Perspective Since 1845 (November 1999)."

economy. Already looking forward to running for president in 1960, Richard Nixon advocated strongly for this approach. Others, such as Anderson, thought the administration should "bide its time." By the time Congress acted, it seemed any recovery measures would probably arrive *after* the recession had ended.[47]

At a press conference in the spring of 1958, Eisenhower indicated which way he leaned. "Mr. President," asked Edwin L. Dale of the *New York Times,* "the additional measures . . . to halt the recession would involve a very large increase in the budget deficit, easily as much as 10 billion or even more. Do you believe this is a legitimate price to pay, if necessary, to halt the slump?"

"Well," said Eisenhower, "I will tell you . . . when you get very large deficits then you have to go into deficit financing, then the money supply gets much more plentiful, and the prices of everything . . . begin to go up." Then, in a nod to his German experience, he explained, "I was interested when I had . . . my last German friend, the finance Officer, [Ludwig]

Erhard—he came to my office and he said this: 'It is a strange thing . . . [Y]ou people, as a people, are always worried about a recession, even a minor recession, going into a big depression. But . . . in our country, with our experience, there is only one thing we are concerned about, and that is inflation. . . . So we have the worries exactly on the opposite side of this balance that you people do.' "[48]

Thus, Eisenhower opposed efforts to spend the economy into health. He paid the political price, though: the 1958 midterm elections turned into a Democratic rout. "Democrats achieved major gains in the Nov. 4 election contests for Senators, Representatives and Governors as a record number of Americans went to the polls," noted *Congressional Quarterly*. Democrats picked up thirteen Senate seats and forty-seven seats in the House, bringing their totals to the highest since the middle of the New Deal.[49] It was a resounding defeat, and the next day, members of the press waited for Eisenhower to "eat crow."

"Mr. President," asked a United Press reporter, "during the . . . campaign, you told the public repeatedly that the Democrats were left-wing extremists . . . apostles of . . . reckless spending, phony doctrines, committed to demagogic excess. . . . [What] do you think caused the Democratic landslide, and particularly how do you propose . . . to fight these Democrats who now are in commanding control of the House and Senate?"

"Well," replied Eisenhower, "I am sure you will never find any place . . . [where] I talked about the Democratic Party as a whole." Yet, "I did talk about the spender-wing [of the Party], and apparently that didn't make any great impression, for obviously we didn't get enough Republican votes." That is, the country "obviously voted for people that I would class among the spenders."[50]

The press prodded him to admit mistakes or repudiate his earlier policies, particularly on spending. "Mr. President," concluded an Associated Press reporter, "does the sort of thing that happened yesterday, the widespread Democratic victories, discourage you in your earlier views for molding the Republican Party along lines of what you called 'Modern Republicanism?' "

The question went to the heart of Eisenhower's basic political economy. He had applied in the American context what he and others serving in the occupations had learned abroad and, for lack of a better term, had come to call it "modern republicanism." Now, six years into his presidency, the political economy from the occupations appeared repudiated.

"I don't believe that anyone who has such strong convictions as I do . . . can afford to be discouraged," he replied. "I had a very tough counterattack once in Kasserine, and another in 'The [Battle of the] Bulge.' Well, if you'd got discouraged and [felt] nothing but defeat and pessimism and didn't have the strength, really, to look upon them as opportunities of some kind, then, indeed, you would be rather futile. So I don't for one minute expect to be discouraged by [the election results]." And, as it turned out, he wasn't.[51] Privately, he "determined to wage the most intensive campaign within my physical powers to hold the line against the prodigals."[52] To his cabinet, he explained he wanted a "budget of Spartan austerity, and [to] say [to Congress] 'This is what we think we should do for the good of our country.' "[53]

As foreign countries watched the deficit balloon in 1958 and anticipated more spending for economic recovery and defense, they reacted by exchanging dollars for gold. Their anxiety only grew with reports that banks had taken to financing large portions of the debt. As the *Wall Street Journal* observed that October: "61 per cent of [treasury] notes and 17 per cent of [treasury] bills were [purchased] by the commercial banks." The "complicated chemistry of the Federal Reserve System [then] converts [these purchases] into new money as surely as if the bills were run off the printing press."[54]

As soon as the new Congress convened in 1959, Eisenhower set the battle lines. At a meeting with legislative leaders in January, he said, "Every sort of foolish proposal will be advanced in the name of national security and the 'poor' fellow. . . . We've got to convince Americans that thrift is not a bad word." Attention turned to Eisenhower's proposed FY 1960 budget (which would need approval during the summer of 1959). He wanted a balanced budget at $77 billion. He then let congressional leaders know that anything that "materially added to the budget, I would respond with a veto, and that if the veto were overridden I would propose a tax increase to cover the increase in spending, and if necessary call a special session for the purpose."[55] As a basic legislative tactic, Eisenhower asked the Budget Bureau to make cost estimates on any serious proposal in Congress. He then asked his surrogates to talk about the price tag for every proposal. It proved a powerful rhetorical weapon.[56]

As Eisenhower took the lead in fighting congressional spending proposals, Anderson monitored the gold situation. He also articulated the reason for defending the Bretton Woods system, and particularly the $35/ounce gold backing. It was theoretically possible to raise the price of gold so that, at some point, the ration of gold reserves to dollars would once again be one-to-one. But raising the price of gold (that is, devaluing the dollar) caused distinct Cold War problems. It "would be a boon to the Russians," explained Anderson, because the Soviet Union held some of the largest gold mines in the world, and that gold would become relatively more valuable in global markets, boosting the Soviet economy. More immediately, it would "seriously shake the world's confidence in the U.S. dollar," and thereby threaten the Western alliance.[57]

It seemed especially disconcerting to revalue gold at exactly the moment that the world finally implemented the Bretton Woods agreements. The burden rested on Washington to prove that the American-led agreement could work.[58] "It is still touch and go whether the President will get from this Congress exactly the budget he has asked for," wrote the journalist Walter Lippmann in May 1959. "Nevertheless, the news from the money markets gives little support to the idea that the battle against inflation is being won." Investors and speculators were betting against Eisenhower.[59]

Democrats drew their battle lines as well. Two well-known Keynesian economists, Walter Heller (who later served as the chair of John F. Kennedy's Council of Economic Advisers) and Paul Samuelson (who later became the first American to win the Nobel Prize in economics) both argued that Eisenhower's fears of inflation were misplaced. Samuelson's "own tentative advice would be to put the major emphasis on growth of real income . . . not letting concern over price inflation dominate our decisions." Heller, by contrast, was more direct. An "obsession with Federal expenditure cutbacks and early budget balance as a prerequisite to price stability is unfounded." Indeed, the "costs of a restrictive budgetary policy to promote price stability are great." They included the "loss of production by slowing the pace of recovery [and] lower investment in public education and other public services that strengthen our long-run economic and military potential." Summing up, Heller warned that Eisenhower's insistence on "price stability and balanced budgets . . . represent[s] as great a risk, calculated or otherwise, as this country has ever incurred in peacetime economic policy."[60]

In large part, these men were laying the groundwork for the "New Economics," an approach to Keynesianism that became the focus of the Kennedy administration and built on Keyserling's "growth economics." The key insight came from a New Zealand economist, A. W. H. Phillips, who noted that since the 1850s, unemployment and inflation seemed to move inversely within the United Kingdom. That is, in times of inflation, unemployment dropped; in times of rising unemployment, inflation subsided, oscillating dependably between one and the other with neither rising to particularly high levels.[61]

Samuelson concluded two things from Phillips' study. In a much-cited paper, he argued, first, that "It may be that creeping inflation leads only to creeping inflation." Contrary to the insights of the occupation, Samuelson (along with his coauthor Robert Solow) suggested that inflation had not become a vicious spiral of growing prices and government intervention leading to a dictatorship. On the contrary, Phillips showed that it went up and down somewhat regularly. Samuelson then added some Keynesianism to the mix, suggesting that government could, through fiscal policies, target a particular level of employment and obtain it by deliberately causing the right amount of inflation. For example, in order "to achieve the nonperfectionist's goal of high enough output to give us no more than 3 per cent unemployment, the price index might have to rise by as much as 4 to 5 per cent per year."[62]

Despite the opposition from these high-powered economists, Eisenhower persisted in opposing any spending not covered by revenue, and as the summer wore on, he started to win. *Time* magazine explained how. Eisenhower "wrote personal letters to political, business and civic leaders around the nation, urged his cause in press conferences and on radio and television, worked closely with Republican Congressional leaders, and used his veto and the threat of his veto against lollygagging money bills."[63] In fact, he vetoed ten separate spending bills. Most important for Eisenhower, the more he fought, the more the public supported him. His approval rating grew from a low in early 1957 of about 57 percent to a high of 71 percent by the end of 1959. Despite the lopsided numbers in Congress, Democrats struggled to override his vetoes or dent his message. With his popularity rising and the Democrats unable to coalesce around a specific stimulus package, congressional leaders decided to "hold down spending in this session," with an eye to the upcoming presidential election in 1960.[64]

In fact, 1960 loomed as a significant problem for Eisenhower. He could not run again, and none of the others involved in the occupation were in a position to run either. Draper, Dodge, and Clay had all become too old. His two treasury secretaries, George Humphrey and Robert Anderson, also did not want to run. Humphrey was also too old, and Anderson (whom Eisenhower tried to convince) was not interested.[65] That left Richard Nixon as front-runner for the nomination. In an effort to ensure consistency between his administration and a potential Nixon administration, Eisenhower created a Cabinet Committee on Price Stability for Economic Growth and made Nixon the chairman in January 1959. Six months later Nixon released the committee's first report and largely towed the Eisenhower line, arguing that Congress should prioritize "reasonable price stability."[66] By the end of 1959, however, Nixon's campaign interests began to crowd out Eisenhower's views. The committee began issuing reports focused on growth and opportunity, "higher levels of education and rising levels of living" and accepting a "relatively small change in the level of prices."[67]

In marked contrast, John F. Kennedy and the Democrats announced intentions to spend generously on defense as well as on domestic projects. The "Communists [held] a dangerous lead in intercontinental missiles," read the 1960 party platform. Worse, "conventional military forces, on which we depend for defense in any non-nuclear war, have been dangerously slashed for reasons of 'economy.'" Along with more spending on defense and domestic programs, the Democrats promised an "end to the present high-interest, tight-money policy," opening up credit to government and business alike. With the encouragement of Leon Keyserling, the platform also promised that, "Democrats believe that our economy can and must grow at an average rate of 5 percent annually, almost twice as fast as our average annual rate since 1953."[68] (As it turns out, 5 percent annual growth was also more than twice that achieved by the country, on average, since 1880.[69])

Still, despite the Democrats bravado, Eisenhower had some reasons for optimism. He had just beaten back the "spenders" in Congress, balanced the budget against significant odds, and won *Time* magazine's Man of the Year for the effort. In January 1960, he delivered his last budget, which projected a *surplus* of $4.2 billion (which he hoped could help retire some of the national debt).[70] Gold continued to leave the country, but the flow slowed to half the rate of 1958. Finally, Nixon seemed largely to embrace his political economy and held a good chance of winning.

But then Nixon lost. Eisenhower took it in stride. "Your hard-fought courageous campaign to carry forward the principle of sound government will have my lasting respect," he wrote Nixon. "It has been a matter of deep personal satisfaction to have served closely with you these past eight years and I shall always cherish your friendship."[71] Nixon, however, ultimately blamed Eisenhower's effort in 1959 to balance the budget for his loss. He felt it caused a small slowdown in the economy in 1960, lending credence to Kennedy's attacks on the administration's economic policies.[72]

Not long after the election Eisenhower convened a press conference—"not a press conference as such," he explained, really an announcement of a policy directive "that is of such importance that I thought it was worthwhile to come down and tell you something of my own feelings about it."[73] He worried about the growing gap between what the country spent abroad compared to what it sold abroad—that this would slowly erode the value of the U.S. dollar. "Financial circles and financial pages have been watching it," he explained; "moreover, foreign financial institutions also have been very much concerned about it." In the end, though, "our national security as well as our own soundness of our economy are affected by a healthy situation in this balance of payment." Indeed, the link between the economy and security tied together NATO as much as the Bretton Woods system.[74] While the press reported what Eisenhower said, it did not make a public splash. A new president had been elected, and press's attention began to turn increasingly toward him.

Thus, Eisenhower decided to focus his final speech, his farewell address, on the question of political economy. He had decided on a farewell address well before he knew what he planned to say. As early as May of 1959, he met with speechwriters at his brother Milton's home to consider possible topics. "I have, as yet, no fixed idea that I should deliver a so-called 'farewell' talk to the Congress," he explained in a follow-up letter to Milton. In general, he wanted all his addresses to combine economic and foreign policy considerations: "I have the feeling that the subject of the American economy, like that of foreign affairs, should flavor every single talk that is delivered formally or informally by one in my position." But how that fit into a farewell address remained, at that point, unclear. "I think the purpose [of a farewell address] would be to emphasize a few homely truths that apply to the responsibilities and duties of government . . . [and] of course, merely to say 'goodbye.' "[75]

The focus of the speech became clearer as 1960 passed and, particularly, after Kennedy's victory. The speech is best remembered today for coining the term "military-industrial complex" and the enjoinder to fear its "unwarranted influence" in the "councils of government."[76] In this respect it has become arguably, "with the possible exception of George Washington's departing speech, the best-known presidential farewell address in U.S.

history."⁷⁷ "We must never let the weight of this combination endanger our liberties or democratic processes," Eisenhower warned. "Only an alert and knowledgeable citizenry can compel the proper meshing of the huge industrial and military machinery of defense with our peaceful methods and goals, so that security and liberty may prosper together." For many Americans, and particularly the political Left, Eisenhower seemed to provide an explanation for the intractable Cold War and the country's growing involvement in Vietnam.

Really, though, the speech summarized the political economy that began decades earlier as the American military began to make policy for foreign people. It is important to remember that Eisenhower never questioned whether the United States needed a military-industrial complex. He had, after all, helped create one. Rather, the issue centered on how the complex should function and with what limits. Of course, the same thing proved true of the growing American welfare state: Eisenhower never sought its abolition. He was, in this sense, not particularly conservative. He simply reiterated its limits and most of all sought its sustainability. In important ways, the issue of limits had preoccupied him since the fight that began with MacArthur in 1936. "Crises there will continue to be," he explained in his farewell. "In meeting them, whether foreign or domestic, great or small, there is a recurring temptation to feel that some spectacular and costly action could become the miraculous solution to all current difficulties." That had been the mistake he tried to keep MacArthur from making in 1936. NSC 68 made essentially the same mistake. It had been the mistake of German and Japanese militarists that led them into World War II. The "New Economics," embraced by Kennedy, provided only an academic veneer to the same impulse that seemed coming under the new administration, to solve once and for all the trade-off between "guns and butter." The lessons learned during the occupation provided evidence of the eventual consequences—economic, political, even spiritual—that followed from an overemphasis on the present emergency.

By contrast, Eisenhower felt every government proposal "must be weighed in the light of a broader consideration: the need to maintain balance in and among national programs—balance between the private and the public economy, balance between cost and hoped for advantage—balance between the clearly necessary and the comfortably desirable; balance between our essential requirements as a nation and the duties imposed by the nation upon the individual; balance between actions of the moment and the national welfare of the future."

"As we peer into society's future," Eisenhower explained, "we—you and I, and our government—must avoid the impulse to live only for today, plundering, for our own ease and convenience, the precious resources of tomorrow. We cannot mortgage the material assets of our grandchildren without risking the loss also of their political and spiritual heritage." Linking, again, the political with the economic, he concluded that, "We want democracy to survive for all generations to come, not to become the insolvent phantom of tomorrow."[78]

In this light, Eisenhower's Farewell Address indeed offered a prophecy—not so much of the Vietnam War but of the stagflation of the 1970s. The hope for permanent low unemployment promised by the New Economics refused, again and again, to materialize. The promise, articulated by Keyserling, that eventually production would expand enough to wipe away price rises never fully arrived. Instead, Joseph Dodge's observation of Japan in its postwar years seemed to fit the American economy of the 1970s: each attempt at recovery ended up as a fiction. The overextension of American power and resources in the 1960s eventually led to unbalanced budgets, growing inflation, and a drain of American gold as foreign countries lost confidence in the nation's willingness to prudently act as "the world's bank." In January 1971, President Richard Nixon announced that "I am now a Keynesian in economics," distancing himself from his record as Eisenhower's vice president and announcing a budget that would remain in deficit for the next few years. "It will not be an inflationary budget," he argued (sounding much like Tanzan Ishibashi), "because it will not exceed the full-employment surplus."[79] Except it was. Prices continued to climb even as unemployment failed to improve. Nixon finally acted exactly how occupation officials might have predicted. In August of 1971, he ordered a "freeze on all prices and wages throughout the United States" and at the same moment suspended "the convertibility of the dollar into gold or other reserve assets."[80] In short, he killed the Bretton Woods framework of managed currency exchange in the interest of domestic stimulus.

For more than a decade Eisenhower, Clay, Dodge, Draper, and other veterans of the occupations had always privileged price stability over stimulus. They thought price stability would preserve cooperation at the global level and protect against government overreach at the domestic level. They saw extraordinary success in setting Japan and Germany on pathways to economic recovery and democratic consolidation. They helped build a durable western alliance built upon overlapping security, political, and economic ties. But in the end, they could not guarantee that their insights would last beyond their time. Indeed, the last and cruelest cut came from one of their own, Richard Nixon, Eisenhower's vice president.

Epilogue

Henry Stimson retired from government service for the last time on his 78th birthday, September 21, 1945. While officially out of government after that, he remained active and curious about the occupations. He asked Eisenhower to come see him in July 1950, to discuss some things he had just learned from John McCloy, at that point American high commissioner for occupied Germany.[1] It was their last time spent together; Stimson passed on October 20th of that year.

After 1952, Douglas MacArthur played a smaller role on the public stage. He became chairman of Remington Rand and spent most of his time in New York until July 1961, when he made a sentimental return to the Philippines. It was his only trip abroad after returning to the United States in 1951. In an interview shortly before his death, he concluded, "Eisenhower should not have taken the presidency . . . had he not taken the presidency, he would be taken today for a great soldier."[2] MacArthur passed away on April 6, 1964. "Virtually every military honor was bestowed upon him," eulogized the *New York Times,* "yet his active career ended in bitterness and recrimination."[3]

Joseph Dodge thought he could return to his bank in 1954. But Eisenhower had more for him to do. Recognizing that economic development would be critical for the newly independent countries of Asia and Africa, Eisenhower asked Dodge to write a report on coordinating America's economic assistance to these emerging countries. His report met with "general agreement" within the administration and, as officials discussed who "might be considered as best qualified to carry out this new important assignment [all] were of the opinion that the obvious choice was Mr. Dodge himself."[4] Later in 1954 he once again agreed to serve, this time as chairman of the Council on Foreign Economic Policy. He continued to resign and get reappointed through the last years of Eisenhower's administration until, in 1961, he finally finished government service. He passed on December 2, 1964. "In the death of Joseph Dodge," Eisenhower said in a statement, "I lost a dear friend to whom I was both devoted and obligated."[5]

Dodge's counterpart in Japan, Hayato Ikeda, held government responsibilities through the 1950s, in particular serving in 1955 as president of the Liberal Democratic Party. He became prime minister in 1960, and as such, he tried to resolve lingering social divisions by appealing to the national goal of "doubling income" for all individuals by the end of the decade.[6] Whatever bad feelings might have existed between Dodge and Ikeda in 1949, these had disappeared by 1962, when Ikeda invited Dodge to Tokyo and awarded him "The Grand Cordon of the First Class Order of the Rising Sun."[7] In 1964, two important events symbolized Japan's return to global respectability. In September, it welcomed a general meeting of the International Monetary Fund, and in October, the Olympic Games came to Tokyo. Ikeda acted as official host at both events, yet these would be some of his last public functions. He had throat cancer and died the next year.[8]

Dwight Eisenhower lived nearly to the end of the 1960s. An unwilling politician, he felt that his particular views belonged "above politics." He spent his last years writing his memoirs and painting—a hobby he took up later in life. He managed a rapprochement with Harry Truman and remained close to the many friends he had acquired through the years. He passed away on March 28, 1969, as one of the most popular men ever to have occupied the presidency.

Ludwig Erhard remained active in West German government through the 1950s. Like Ikeda, he also reached the pinnacle of politics by becoming chancellor in 1963. He remained devoted to market economics and fearful of inflation throughout his public career; but his ability to guide the economy shone less when he was chancellor than when he served in his many economic offices. In October 1966, in the midst of a recession, he proposed tax increases to keep the budget in balance. His coalition partners, the Free Democrats, walked out on his government, and Erhard resigned, leaving public life thereafter.[9] He passed away in May 1977.

Lucius Clay survived them all. After his service in Germany, he retired to the private sector as chairman of Continental Can. At the center of so many critical points after World War II, Clay became a magnet for historians and political scientists who, throughout the 1960s and 1970s, had just discovered oral history and made their way to interview him. He would, in each interview, profess that his memory had faded, only to retell critical events with astonishing clarity and consistency. He remained close to Eisenhower until Eisenhower died. John F. Kennedy asked him to travel to Berlin and advise him during the Berlin Wall crisis in 1961. Several years later he joined Kennedy in Berlin during Kennedy's famous *Ich bin ein Berliner* speech. Indeed, Kennedy began the speech by remarking, "I am proud to come to this city . . . in the company of my fellow American, General Clay, who has been in this city during its great moments of crisis and will come again if ever needed."[10] He passed away in 1978.

In 1992, the National Bureau of Economic Research (NBER) held a retrospective symposium on the Bretton Woods system. The economist Michael Bordo began by noting the "incontrovertible conclusion" that the system in both "nominal and real variables exhibited the most stable behavior in the past century," all of which "raises questions about why Bretton Woods was statistically so stable and why it was so short-lived."[11] The answer, at least in part, lies in the preceding pages. It worked because a small group of people, in and around the American military, managed to influence governments at key places around the world to accept the policies necessary to make that system work. But the strange confluence of events that allowed the military to dominate policy in so many different places also guaranteed that its influence would remain short-lived. Eventually, economic policymaking would come from professional economists who functioned according to a different set of institutional parameters and incentives. With the accoutrements of Keynesian expertise, the economists of the 1960s had an additional advantage: they could claim, at least for a while, that they had the cure for all economic ills, even small recessions, through "fine tuning" of the economy.[12]

In retrospect, it seems overwrought to think that creeping inflation would inevitably lead to dictatorship along the lines of Nazism. But at mid-century, the world had no ready example of a low-level inflation remaining just that; to the contrary, the occupations confronted overwhelming evidence of inflation starting at a crawl and ending in a gallop. As a result, they could not imagine the Keynesian experiment ending any way other than it did—in the profound inflations that followed World War II. Today, there is more reason to believe that central banks can "target" inflation to keep it at a crawl. But getting to this point has taken time, and in the American context required the dismal experience of 1970s stagflation before the Federal Reserve finally agreed with Dodge to choose stability ahead of recovery—which in practical terms meant markets would take seriously the ability of central bankers to do as Erhard told Eisenhower—to tolerate a great deal more unemployment than inflation.[13]

In the wake of the Great Recession, many governments (although not Germany) have once again run up large debts. Concerns about "rigged" exchange rates have led to calls for a "new" Bretton Woods agreement. And through it all the American military continues to play a role in nation-building—that is, in functioning as an "external state" governing foreign peoples. It remains an open question whether the wisdom of soldier sovereigns, so hard won after World War II, has really been learned. Or if the world will call upon them again in the future.

Notes

Introduction

1. The first account of this lunch appears in Clay's memoir from his time in Germany: Lucius D. Clay, *Decision in Germany* (London: William Heinemann Ltd, 1950) 54. He elaborated on the story in subsequent oral history interviews, particularly: Interview with General Lucius D. Clay by Colonel R. Joe Rogers, January 24, 1973, New York, Box: 19, Folder: "1972 May 3–1973 Mar 15," Lucius Clay Collection, GML, 5.

2. U.S. Army Joint Chiefs of Staff Order (hereafter JCS) 1067/8, April 26, 1945, *FRUS 1945*, vol. 3: European Advisory Commission, 493.

3. The Clay quotes come from Interview #16 with General Lucius Clay by Jean Smith, February 5, 1971, New York, DDEPL, 529; the last quote is from Dwight D. Eisenhower, *Crusade in Europe* (Garden City, NY: Doubleday, 1948) 442.

4. Clay, *Decision in Germany*, 54.

5. Henry L. Stimson and McGeorge Bundy, *On Active Service in Peace and War* (New York: Harper and Brothers, 1947) 139–150.

6. Interview with General Lucius D. Clay by Colonel R. Joe Rogers, GML, 5.

7. Clay, *Decision in Germany*, 54.

8. Interview #7 with General Lucius Clay by Jean Smith, November 30, 1970, New York, DDEPL, 534.

9. It is true that military government ruled for a time between 1867–1877 in the former confederacy after the Civil War (see Gregory P. Downs, *After Appomattox: Military Occupation and the Ends of War* [Cambridge, MA: Harvard University Press, 2015]). Jeremi Suri shows how military government has played a role in state building not only during the Reconstruction Era but beginning at the founding of the country (see Jeremi Suri, *Liberty's Surest Guardian: American Nation-Building from the Founders to Obama* [New York: The Free Press, 2011], especially chapters one and two). I begin my study with the Spanish-American War because that is, roughly speaking, the point after which the military has increasingly been asked to govern territory never considered for (re)incorporation into the constitutional order as a (new) state.

10. Historians have not created a significant historiography on military government. There is a growing interest in nation-building generally, spurred by the military experience in Iraq and Afghanistan among other places around the globe. See, among many, James Dobbins, *America's Role in Nation-Building: From Germany to Iraq* (Santa Monica, CA: RAND, 2003); James Dobbins, Seth G. Jones, Keith Crane, and Beth Cole DeGrasse, *The Beginner's Guide to Nation-Building* (Santa Monica, CA: RAND, 2007); Francis Fukuyama, ed., *Nation-Building Beyond Afghanistan and Iraq* (Baltimore, MD: Johns Hopkins University Press, 2006);

Roland Paris and Timothy D. Sisk., eds., *The Dilemmas of Statebuilding: Confronting the Contradictions of Postwar Peace Operations* (New York: Routledge, 2009); and Richard Caplan, ed., *Exit Strategies and State Building* (New York: Oxford University Press, 2012). Still, within history, Jeremi Suri's observation remains true: "No one has done for the global history of American nation-building what countless writers have done for the global history of American business expansion or cultural penetration of foreign societies" (Suri, *Liberty's Surest Guardian,* 45).

11. Headquarters, Department of the Army, *Army Doctrine Reference Publication Adrp 3–07 Stability Change 31 August 2012* (Washington, DC: US Army, 2013) 1–1.

12. George Bookman Papers, Box: 1, Folder: "Chapter 14," DDEPL; and Irwin F. Gellman, *The President and the Apprentice: Eisenhower and Nixon, 1952–1960* (New Haven, CT: Yale University Press, 2015) 346.

13. C. Wright Mills, *The Power Elite* (New York: Oxford University Press, 1956).

14. See, among many, Wyatt C. Wells, *Antitrust and the Formation of the Postwar World* (New York: Columbia University Press, 2002).

15. This claim is, of course, a twist on John Gerard Ruggie, who saw Keynesian domestic policy as compatible with the Bretton Woods system. See Ruggie, "International Regimes, Transactions, and Change: Embedded Liberalism in the Postwar Economic Order," in *International Regimes*, ed. Stephen D. Krasner (Ithaca, NY: Cornell University Press, 1983) 195–231. In a sense, occupation officials stumbled on what has subsequently been called a "trilemma." "At the most general level, policymakers in open economies face a macroeconomic trilemma. Typically they are confronted with three . . . desirable, yet contradictory, objectives: 1. to stabilize the exchange rate; 2. to enjoy free international capital mobility; 3. to engage in a monetary policy oriented toward domestic goals. Because only two out of the three objectives can be mutually consistent, policymakers must decide which one to give up. This is the trilemma." Maurice Obstfeld, Jay C. Shambaugh, and Alan M. Taylor, "The Trilemma in History: Tradeoffs among Exchange Rates, Monetary Policies, and Capital Mobility," National Bureau of Economic Research Working Paper 10396 (Cambridge, MA: NBER, March 2004) 1. The Bretton Woods system hoped to encourage stable exchange rates and capital mobility. The framers of that system (including Keynes) also hoped that it would make domestic economic policymaking more flexible than it had been under the gold standard. Keynes' aim in this regard did not come to fruition. J. Marcus Fleming and the Nobel Prize winner Robert A. Mundell first elaborated how the Bretton Woods system could not accommodate all three policy goals in their path breaking research in the early 1960s (not coincidentally, in my view, *after* Eisenhower left the presidency and the consequences of Keynesian domestic policies began to be felt). See J. Marcus Fleming, "Domestic Financial Policies under Fixed and Floating Exchange Rates," *IMF Staff Papers* 9 (1962): 369–379; and Robert A. Mundell "Capital Mobility and Stabilization Policy under Fixed and Flexible Exchange Rates," *Canadian Journal of Economics and Political Science* 29, no. 4 (1963): 475–485. Keynes appears to have understood this problem, although he ultimately proved unable to resolve the trilemma during the negotiations of the system: "Capital controls, Keynes argued, would also have to be made 'a permanent feature of the post-war system, at least so far as we [the British] are concerned.' His conceptual logic was that 'the whole management of the domestic economy depends upon being free to have the appropriate rate of interest without reference to the rates prevailing elsewhere in the world. Capital control is a corollary to this.' This

thinking has today become orthodox Keynesianism, advocated by globalization critics such as Joseph Stiglitz and opposed by global currency union advocates such as Robert Mundell." Benn Steil, *The Battle of Bretton Woods: John Maynard Keynes, Harry Dexter White, and the Making of a New World Order* (Princeton, NJ: Princeton University Press, 2013) 145–146.

16. "348: To Benjamin Franklin Caffey, Jr., July 27, 1953," *PDDE* 14:429.

17. The literature in this regard is massive. Several works relevant here include: Brian Balogh, "Reorganizing the Organizational Synthesis: Federal-Professional Relations in Modern America," *Studies in American Political Development* 5, no. 1 (March 1991): 119–172; Alan Brinkley, *The End of Reform: New Deal Liberalism in Recession and War* (New York: Vintage Books, 1996); Robert M. Collins, *More: The Politics of Economic Growth in Postwar America* (New York: Oxford University Press, 2002); Meg Jacobs, *Pocketbook Politics: Economic Citizenship in Twentieth Century America* (Princeton, NJ: Princeton University Press, 2006).

18. For a recent reiteration of this debate (albeit in slightly different terms) see William J. Novak, "The Myth of the 'Weak' American State," *American Historical Review* 113, no. 3 (2008): 752–772; along with the *AHR* Roundtable: "[Introduction]," *American Historical Review* 115, no. 3 (2010): 766–767; John Fabian Witt, "Law and War in American History," *American Historical Review* 115, no. 3 (2010): 768–778; Gary Gerstle, "A State Both Strong and Weak," *American Historical Review* 115, no. 3 (2010): 779–785; Julia Adams, "The Puzzle of the American State . . . and Its Historians," *American Historical Review* 115, no. 3 (2010): 786–791; and William J. Novak, "Long Live the Myth of the Weak State? A Response to Adams, Gerstle, and Witt," *American Historical Review* 115, no. 3 (2010): 792–800. See also Ira Katznelson and Bruce Pietrykowski, "Rebuilding the American State: Evidence from the 1940s," *Studies in American Political Development* 5, no. 2 (Fall 1991): 307.

19. See, in this regard, Jeremi Suri: "During the 1960s one factor was preeminent in igniting the flames of revolution. Leaders promised their citizens more 'progress' than ever before. . . . A number of societies—particularly in North America and Western Europe—were remarkably successful in creating affluence during the second half of the twentieth century. They failed, however, to meet the rising popular expectations that they inspired. The rhetoric of both capitalism and communism became harmfully exaggerated in the context of Cold War competition. A perception of 'false promises' among young and ambitious citizens pervaded the language of dissent and contributed directly to protest activities in nearly every state." *Power and Protest: Global Revolution and the Rise of Détente* (Cambridge, MA: Harvard University Press, 2003) 165.

20. These claims should all be familiar to students of American Political Development. In many ways I am building on a founding text in that tradition. Stephen Skowronek saw the army as a critical component of the modernizing American state, although subsequent scholars have not given it as much attention (see Skowronek, *Building a New American State* [New York: Cambridge University Press, 1982]); for other foundational works, see Peter B. Evans, Dietrich Rueschemeyer, and Theda Skocpol, eds., *Bringing the State Back In* (Cambridge, UK: Cambridge University Press, 1985); Theda Skocpol, *Protecting Soldiers and Mothers: The Political Origins of Social Policy in the United States* (Cambridge, MA: Harvard University Press, 1992); Christopher Howard, *The Hidden Welfare State: Tax Expenditures and Social Policy in the United States* (Princeton, NJ: Princeton University Press, 1997); Julian Zelizer, *Taxing America: Wilbur D. Mills, Congress, and the State, 1945–1975* (Cambridge, UK: Cambridge University Press, 2000); Ira Katznelson and Martin Shefter, eds., *Shaped by War and Trade:*

International Influences on American Political Development (Princeton, NJ: Princeton University Press, 2002); James T. Sparrow, William J. Novak, and Stephen W. Sawyer, eds., *Boundaries of the State in US History* (Chicago: University of Chicago Press, 2015).

21. The literature on policy history often overlaps with American Political Development. For some introductory articles on policy history specifically, see: Robert Kelley, "The Idea of Policy History," *Public Historian* 10, no. 1 (Winter 1988): 35–39; Hugh Davis Graham, "The Stunted Career of Policy History: A Critique and an Agenda," *Public Historian* 15, no. 2 (Spring 1993): 15–37; Donald T. Critchlow, "A Prognosis of Policy History: Stunted: Or Deceivingly Vital? A Brief Reply to Hugh Davis Graham," *Public Historian* 15, no. 4 (Autumn 1993): 50–61; Peter N. Stearns and Joel A. Tarr, "Straightening the Policy History Tree," *Public Historian* 15, no. 4 (Autumn 1993): 63–67; Julian Zelizer, "Clio's Lost Tribe: Public Policy History Since 1978," *Journal of Policy History* 12 (2000): 369–394, and "Introduction: New Directions in Policy History," *Journal of Policy History* 17, no. 1 (2005): 1–11; Robert McMahon, "Diplomatic History and Policy History: Finding Common Ground," *Journal of Policy History* 17 (2005): 93–109; Barry Eichengreen, "Economic History and Economic Policy," *Journal of Economic History* 72, no. 2 (June 2012): 289–307.

22. This phrase appears in Karen Orren and Stephen Skowronek, *The Search for American Political Development* (New York: Cambridge University Press, 2005) 16. Scholars have used the rubric to describe urban policy in Karen Mossberger and Gerry Stoker, "The Evolution of Urban Regime Theory: The Challenge of Conceptualization," *Urban Affairs Review* 36, no. 6 (2001): 810–835; and Clarence N. Stone, *Regime Politics: Governing Atlanta, 1946–1988* (Lawrence: Kansas University Press, 1989). They have used the rubric to compare national policy, such as Gosta Esping-Anderson, *The Three Worlds of Welfare Capitalism* (Princeton, NJ: Princeton University Press, 1990) as well as Howard P. Kitschelt, "Structure or Process Driven Explanations of Political Regime Change?" *American Political Science Review* 87, no. 4 (1992): 1028–1034. The rubric has also appeared as a way of describing stable global relations in Stephen D. Krasner, *International Regimes* (Ithaca, NY: Cornell University Press, 1983); Friedrich Kratowhil and John Gerald Ruggie, "International Organization: A State of the Art on an Art of the State," *International Organization* 40, no. 4 (1986): 753–775; Lisa L. Martin and Beth A. Simmons, "Theories and Empirical Studies of International Institutions," *International Organization* 52, no. 4 (1998): 729–757.

23. Thomas J. Sargent, "The Ends of Four Big Inflations," in *Rational Expectations and Inflation* (New York: Harper and Row, 1986) 24. The literature on "empire" is vast and growing. Of the many possible works, some definitions that proved helpful to me include: Michael W. Doyle, *Empires* (Ithaca, NY: Cornell University Press, 1986) 30–45; Herfried Münkler, *Empires: The Logic of World Domination from Ancient Rome to the United States* (Cambridge, UK: Polity Press, 2007) 1–40; Geir Lundestad, *The Rise and Decline of the American "Empire"* (New York: Oxford University Press, 2012) 92–98.

25. Elihu Root purportedly uttered the sentence, "The Constitution follows the flag, but it does not catch up with it," to explain the Supreme Court's ruling in *Downes v. Bidwell,* 182 U.S. 244 (1901) (as quoted in Arthur Wallace Dunn, *From Harrison to Harding* [New York: G. P. Putnam's Sons, 1922] 256–257). In *Downes* the Court famously declared of Puerto Rico: "Whilst in an international sense Porto Rico was not a foreign country, since it was subject to the sovereignty of and was owned by the United States, it was foreign to the United States in a domestic sense." See also Bartholomew H. Sparrow, *The Insular Cases and the Emergence of American Empire* (Lawrence: Kansas University Press, 2006).

26. Robert Latham, *The Liberal Moment: Modernity, Security, and the Making of Postwar International Order* (New York: Columbia University Press, 1997) 67.

27. Interview #17 with General Lucius Clay by Jean Smith, February 9, 1971, New York, DDEPL, 579.

28. "In general, the positing of an external state permits us to move beyond the portrayal of U.S. hegemony as simply an outward projection of U.S. power, bureaucracy, and interests. . . . This formulation fails to distinguish between organs at the center that are oriented externally and organs that are actually deployed externally. . . . A third advantage to the external state construct is its specificity regarding the scope of its actions. What constitutes an external state—in contrast to the mere posting of representatives or sending of troops abroad—is the deployment of organs that administer a range of relations in the external realm. Such relations can bear on states, societies, or multilateral institutions. In this capacity, external state organs move across state boundaries and territories. They are transterritorial." Latham, *The Liberal Moment,* 68–69.

29. Melvyn P. Leffler, *A Preponderance of Power: National Security, the Truman Administration, and the Cold War* (Stanford, CA: Stanford University Press, 1992) 104.

30. Adam Sheingate, "Institutional Dynamics and American Political Development," *Annual Review of Political Science* 17, no. 1 (2014): 462. See also William I. Hitchcock: "France's postwar revival was due, this study shows, to the surprising tenacity with which leading French planners, technocrats, and policymakers pursued a national strategy of recovery. . . . The institutional weaknesses of the Republic as it was reconstructed after the war offered *opportunities for maneuver and innovation in policymaking.* Thus, the lack of an effective governing structure, the absence of coherent argumentation in much of French political life, and the apparently insurmountable divisions among ideologically charged sectors of the population led innovative planners to champion technocratic, ostensibly apolitical solutions to the host of difficult problems facing the nation" (emphasis added). *France Restored: Cold War Diplomacy and the Quest for Leadership in Europe, 1944–1954* (Chapel Hill: University of North Carolina Press, 1998) 2.

31. This list could take up pages. For a "traditional" account of the Cold War's origins, see Arthur Schlesinger, Jr., "Origins of the Cold War," *Foreign Affairs* 46, no. 1 (October 1967): 22–52; the quotation comes from Joyce Kolko and Gabriel Kolko, *The Limits of Power: The World and United States Foreign Policy, 1945–1954* (New York: Harper and Row, 1972) 2; for national security approaches, see Daniel Yergin, *Shattered Peace: The Origins of the Cold War and the National Security State* (Boston: Houghton Mifflin Co., 1977); and Leffler, *A Preponderance of Power.* For corporate reconstruction, see Michael J. Hogan, *The Marshall Plan: America, Britain, and the Reconstruction of Western Europe, 1947–1952* (New York: Cambridge University Press, 1987). On the question of the New Deal for the world, see Theodore Cohen, *Remaking Japan: The American Occupation as New Deal,* ed. Herbert Passin, Studies of the East Asian Institute (New York: Free Press, 1987); and Elizabeth Borgwardt, *New Deal for the World: America's Vision for Human Rights* (Cambridge, MA: Harvard University Press, 2005). For "Americanization," see Volker Berghahn, *The Americanisation of West German Industry 1945–1973* (Leamington Spa, UK: Berg, 1985); and Victoria de Grazia, *Irresistible Empire: America's Advance Through Twentieth-Century Europe* (Cambridge, MA: Harvard University Press, 2005), among many.

32. For this argument in the German context, see (among many) James Martin, *All Honorable Men* (Boston: Little Brown, 1950); Carolyn Eisenberg, *Drawing the Line: The American Decision to Divide Germany* (New York: Cambridge University Press, 1996); as well as

Rebecca L. Boehling, *A Question of Priorities* (Providence, RI: Berghahn Books, 1996). For similar accounts of Japan, see William S. Borden, *The Pacific Alliance: United States Foreign Policy and Japanese Trade Recovery, 1947–1955* (Madison: University of Wisconsin Press, 1984); Michael Schaller, *The American Occupation of Japan: The Origins of the Cold War in Asia* (New York: Oxford University Press, 1985); and Howard B. Schonberger, *Aftermath of War: Americans and the Remaking of Japan, 1945–1952* (Kent, OH: Kent State University Press, 1989).

33. See, for example, Edward N. Peterson, *The American Occupation of Germany: Retreat to Victory* (Detroit, MI: Wayne State University Press, 1977); and John W. Dower, *Embracing Defeat: Japan in the Wake of World War II* (New York: W. W. Norton and Company, 1999). This approach is particularly pronounced among German economic historians, who see the occupation as having little impact on the "economic miracle" that followed the 1948 currency conversion. Here, again, the literature is quite large. The argument began when Werner Abelshauser showed that the war had caused surprisingly less damage to Germany's industrial capital than first thought: *Wirtschaft in Westdeutschland 1945–1948: Rekonstruktion und Wachstumsbedingungen in der amerikanischen und britischen Zone* (Stuttgart, Germany: Deutsche 1975); and *Wirtschaftsgeschichte der Bundesrepublik Deutschland 1945–1980* (Frankfurt: Suhrkamp, Verlags-Astalt, 1983). Abelshauser went on to argue that much of the "economic miracle" could be traced back to this fact, suggesting that the economic miracle really amounted to a rapid return to the trendline in German economic growth. In response, a number of other German economic historians took issue with the accuracy of his baseline statistics (see Albrecht Ritschl, "Die Wahrungsreform von 1948 und der Wiederaufstieg der westdeutschen Industrie: zu den Thesen von Mathias Manz und Werner Abelshauser über die Produktionswirkungen der Wahrungsreform," *Viertel-jahrshefte fur Zeitgeschichte* 33 [1985]; others noted that prior to the currency reform, most firms stockpiled raw materials and semi-finished goods (Christoph Buchheim, "The Currency Reform in West Germany in 1948," *German Yearbook on Business History, 1989–92* [Munich: K. G. Saur, 1993] 85–120). Thus, in the absence of the occupation-imposed reform, little recovery could have occurred (see Chapter 4 below for more discussion). Other German scholars have criticized Abelshauser for ignoring the "social market" ideology that provided the political framework for recovery (see Rainer Klump, *Wirtschaftsgeschichte der Bundesrepublik Deutschland: Zur Kritik neuerer wirtschaftshistorischer Interpretationen aus ordnungspolitischer Sicht* [Wiesbaden, Germany: In Kommission bei F. Steiner, 1985]). Today, "There seems to be a broad consensus that the sound potential for reconstruction rightly diagnosed by Abelshauser, contrary to earlier opinions, was an important factor in the sustained postwar boom. Even so, it could not become properly effective until after the currency reform because, without it, the threat of loss of real assets, high costs, and the impossibility of calculating profits realistically made production and market sales unattractive to most private businesses." Christoph Buchheim, "From Enlightened Hegemony to Partnership: The United States and West Germany in the World Economy, 1945–1948," in *The United States and Germany in the Era of the Cold War, 1945–1968*, ed., Detlef Junker, et al. (Cambridge, UK: Cambridge University Press, 2004) 1:270.

34. The quote is from Nicole Phelps, "Agency and Nation in Williams's Tragedy," *Passport* 40, no. 2 (September 2009): 26. In this regard, see also Ira Katznelson: "The large and growing body of work by scholars of international relations . . . has broken with the model of the state as a unitary rational actor" ("Rewriting the Epic of America," in *Shaped by War and*

Trade: International Influences on American Political Development, 3). Diplomatic historians, in particular, have agonized over the proliferation of terms, attempting to define their standing after the international turn among American historians. For a broad but sometimes maddening discussion, see "re: terminology" H-Diplo discussion, http://h-net.msu.edu/cgi-bin/ logbrowse.pl?trx = vx&list = H-Diplo&month = 0903&week = c&msg = RWOhObKQ1Y16Vm Jxi%2BOMXg, which ran through the spring of 2009.

35. See, for example, Sanjeev Khagram, James V. Riker, and Kathryn Sikkink, eds., *Restructuring World Politics: Transnational Social Movements, Networks and Norms* (Minneapolis: University of Minnesota Press, 2002); Ann M. Florini, ed., *The Third Force: The Rise of Transnational Civil Society* (Washington, DC: Carnegie Endowment for International Peace, 2000).

36. Mary Nolan, *The Transatlantic Century: Europe and America, 1890–2010* (New York: Cambridge University Press, 2014) 6.

Chapter 1

1. Skowronek, *Building a New American State*, 86.

2. Ibid., 86–87.

3. Ibid., 88–91, 212–213.

4. James I. Robertson, Jr., *Soldiers Blue and Gray* (New York: Warner Books, 1988) 122; he writes "Civil War troops were the worst soldiers and the best fighters that America has ever produced."

5. Skowronek, *Building a New American State*, 86–87.

6. "It is Admiral Dewey Now: A Modest Despatch [sic] from Manilla Confirms the Report" [sic] *New York Observer and Chronicle*, May 12, 1898: 76.

7. "Dewey's Great Victory," *Independent*, May 12, 1898: 12.

8. Ivan Musicant, *Empire by Default: The Spanish-American War and the Dawn of the American Century* (New York: Henry Hold and Company, 1998) chap. 16.

9. Ibid., 565–585.

10. Ibid.

11. Ibid., 583.

12. Ibid., 586–626.

13. Ibid., 589–595.

14. As quoted in Anna Leah Fidelis Castaneda, "Spanish Structure, American Theory: The Legal Foundations of a Tropical New Deal in the Philippine Islands, 1898–1935," in *Colonial Crucible: Empire in the Making of the Modern American State*, ed. Alfred W. McCoy and Francisco A. Scarano (Madison: University of Wisconsin Press, 2009) 366.

15. Ibid.

16. "President McKinley on the Philippines," *Outlook*, September 9, 1899: 63.

17. Ibid., 461.

18. Brian McAllister Linn, "The Impact of the Philippine Wars (1898–1913) on the U.S. Army," in McCoy and Scarano, *Colonial Crucible*, 461ff.

19. Kenneth Ray Young, *The General's General: The Life and Times of Arthur MacArthur* (Boulder, CO: Westview Press, 1992) chap. 13.

20. For a discussion of the Taft-MacArthur feud, see (in addition to Young's, *The General's General*) Rowland T. Berthoff, "Taft and MacArthur, 1900–1901: A Study in Civil-Military Relations," *World Politics* 5, no. 2 (January 1953): 196–213.

21. Estimates of the cost of pacification vary widely, from more than one million to several hundred thousand casualties and dollar estimates adjusted in various ways for inflation. I have followed the Historian for the U.S. State Department; see Department of State Office of the Historian, "The Philippine-American War, 1899–1902," https://history.state.gov/milestones/1899-1913/war. For a broader discussion of the costs of the war, see Leon Wolf, *Little Brown Brother: How the United States Purchased and Pacified the Philippine Islands at the Century's Turn* (New York: History Book Club, [1961] 2006).

22. In reality, MacArthur also had a fair amount of legal experience. He belonged to the Wisconsin bar and spent nine years in the Adjutant General's office. See Young, *The General's General*, 269.

23. Ibid., chap. 13.

24. U.S. Congress, An Act to Provide for the Administration of the Affairs of Civil Government in the Philippine Islands, and for Other Purposes, Public Law 295 (1902).

25. *Downes v. Bidwell*, 182 U.S. 244 (1901) 341–342.

26. Sparrow, *The Insular Cases*.

27. Daniel Rodgers, *Atlantic Crossings: Social Politics in a Progressive Age* (Cambridge, MA: Harvard University, Belknap Press, 1998). This institutional distinction is often important for those who want to distinguish American colonial possessions from European "empire."

28. As quoted in Richard Hofstadter, "The Paranoid Style in American Politics," in *The Paranoid Style in American Politics and Other Essays* (New York: Vintage Books, 2008) 166

29. As quoted in Philip C. Jessup, *Elihu Root* (Hamden, CT: Archon Books, 1938) 384.

30. Linn, "The Impact of the Philippine Wars," in *Colonial Crucible*; see also D. Clayton James, *The Years of MacArthur, 1880–1941* (Boston: Houghton Mifflin, 1970) 1:73.

31. John A. Gable, "Credit a 'Splendid Little War' to John Hay," *New York Times* (hereafter *NYT*) July 9, 1991: A18.

32. Brigadier General William H. Carter, "A General Staff for the Army," *North American Review* (October 1902): 558.

33. As quoted in Matthew M. Oyos, "Theodore Roosevelt, Congress, and the Military: U.S. Civil-Military Relations in the Early Twentieth Century," *Presidential Studies Quarterly* 30, no. 2 (June 2000): 317.

34. As quoted in Peter Karsten, "Armed Progressives: The Military Reorganizes for the American Century," in *The Military in America: From the Colonial Era to the Present,* ed. Peter Karsten (New York: Free Press, 1980) 251.

35. Russell F. Weigley, *History of the United States Army* (New York: Macmillan, 1967) 325. See also Richard M. Abrams, "The U.S. Military and Higher Education: A Brief History," *Annals of the American Academy of Political and Social Science* 502 (March 1989): 15–28. Ultimately, these efforts resulted in the Army Reserve Officers' Training Corps (ROTC) Program by 1916.

36. James, *The Years of MacArthur,* 1:77.

37. As quoted in Jean Edward Smith, *Lucius D. Clay: An American Life* (New York: Holt, 1990) 40.

38. Stephen Ambrose, *Eisenhower: Soldier and President* (New York: Touchstone, 1990) 25.

39. Jörg Muth, *Command Culture: Officer Education in the U.S. Army and the German Armed Force, 1901–1940, and the Consequences for World War II* (Denton, TX: University of North Texas Press, 2011) 43.

40. Ibid.

41. As quoted in William A. Ganoe, *MacArthur Close-Up: Much Then and Some Now* (New York: Vantage Press, 1962) 97.

42. Dwight D. Eisenhower, *At Ease: Stories I tell to Friends* (Fort Washington, PA: Eastern National, [1967] 2000) 19–20.

43. Douglas MacArthur, *Reminiscences: General of the Army Douglas MacArthur* (New York: McGraw-Hill Book Company, 1964) 29.

44. Ibid., 88. See also, James, *The Years of MacArthur*, 1:88–94.

45. As quoted in James, *The Years of MacArthur*, 1:109.

46. For a retelling of this episode, see Weigley, *History of the United States Army*, 326–334. As it turned out, the downsizing did affect MacArthur in the sense that, in order to keep MacArthur and comply with Congress, Wood had to use an accounting trick and list MacArthur as a member of his "personal staff" until April 1913 (see James, *The Years of MacArthur*, 1:112).

47. James, *The Years of MacArthur*, 1:112–113.

48. Frederick Palmer, *Bliss, Peacemaker: The Life and Letters of General Tasker Howard Bliss* (New York: Dodd, Mead and Company, 1934) 106–107.

49. Edward M. Coffman, "The American Military and Strategic Policy in World War I," in *War Aims and Strategic Policy in the Great War*, ed. Barry Hunt and Adrian Preston (Totowa, NJ: Rowman and Littlefield, 1977) 68.

50. Robert A. Doughty, *Pyrrhic Victory* (Cambridge, MA: Harvard University Press, 2008).

51. Timothy K. Nenninger, "American Military Effectiveness in the First World War," in *Military Effectiveness*, ed. Allan R. Millet and Williamson Murray, vol. 1, *The First World War* (Boston: Allen and Unwin, 1988) 119.

52. Ibid., 122.

53. Jean Edward Smith, *Eisenhower: in War and Peace* (New York: Random House, 2012) 37–38.

54. Ibid., 38–48.

55. Smith, *Lucius D. Clay*, 42–45.

56. James, *The Years of MacArthur*, 1:134–135.

57. Ibid., 1:139–246.

Chapter 2

1. The literature of World War I and Woodrow Wilson is vast. The works that seemed particularly helpful to me include Frank A. Ninkovich, *The Wilsonian Century: U.S. Foreign Policy Since 1900* (Chicago: University of Chicago Press, 1999); Margaret Macmillan, *Paris 1919: Six Months That Changed the World* (New York: Random House, 2001); Tony Smith, *America's Mission: The United States and the Worldwide Struggle for Democracy in the Twentieth Century* (Princeton, NJ: Princeton University Press, 1994); Adam Tooze, *The Deluge: The Great War and the Remaking of Global Order, 1916–1931* (London: Penguin Books, 2014). For

a good overview of the historiography on Wilson, see Justus D. Doenecke, "Neutrality Policy," in *A Companion to Woodrow Wilson*, ed. Ross A. Kennedy (New York: Wiley-Blackwell, 2013) 243–269.

2. Woodrow Wilson, "Address to the Senate of the United States: 'A World League for Peace,'" January 22, 1917, APP, http://www.presidency.ucsb.edu/ws/index.php?pid=65396& st=peace+without+victory&st1.

3. Woodrow Wilson, "Address to a Joint Session of Congress on the Conditions of Peace," January 8, 1918, APP, http://www.presidency.ucsb.edu/ws/index.php?pid=65405& st=&st1.

4. Woodrow Wilson, "Address to Congress on International Order," February 11, 1918, APP, http://www.presidency.ucsb.edu/ws/index.php?pid=110448&st=may+now+be+ dominated+and+governed+only+by+their+own+consent&st1.

5. Ibid.

6. In particular, see Lloyd E. Ambrosius, *Wilsonian Statecraft: Theory and Practice of Liberal Internationalism During World War I* (Washington, DC: Scholarly Reviews, 1991); and Kennedy, *The Will to Believe*.

7. Woodrow Wilson, "Remarks at the University of Paris," December 21, 1918, APP, http://www.presidency.ucsb.edu/ws/index.php?pid=117738&st=history&st1.

8. Woodrow Wilson, "Address to the Senate on the Versailles Peace Treaty," July 10, 1919, APP, http://www.presidency.ucsb.edu/ws/index.php?pid=110490&st=league+of+na tions&st1.

9. Lloyd E. Ambrosius, *Wilsonianism: Woodrow Wilson and His Legacy in American Foreign Relations* (New York: Palgrave Macmillan, 2002), particularly chap. 1.

10. Ibid., 26–28.

11. Tooze, *The Deluge*, 497–507.

12. Ibid., 488–489.

13. This analysis follows closely on Tooze, *The Deluge*, especially chap. 26.

14. "Colonel E. M. House to President Wilson, London, 30 July 1919," *FRUS* 1919, vol. 11: The Paris Peace Conference: 623.

15. Liaquat Ahamed, *Lords of Finance: The Bankers Who Broke the World* (New York: Penguin, 2009) 130–144.

16. There are different ways of measuring relative costs over time. One way is to simply multiply the cost by the change in the consumer price index. This measure, however, does not capture the relative burden, particularly on very large public undertakings. I have chosen to measure the cost of reparations as a percentage of gross domestic product. In other words, how much of the total economy would $33 billion in reparations represent in 2015? See "Measuring Worth," https://www.measuringworth.com/uscompare/ for an explanation of methodology. The website also provided the calculator for my estimate.

17. "Germany—Reparation—Exchange and Bourse—Trade And Employment—Prices," *The Economist*, February 12, 1921: 279. For his part, John Maynard Keynes famously articulated this problem in John Maynard Keynes, *The Economic Consequences of the Peace* (New York: Harcourt, Brace, and Howe, 1920).

18. Ross A. Kennedy, *The Will to Believe: Woodrow Wilson, World War I, and America's Strategy for Peace and Security* (Kent, OH: Kent State University Press, 2009); David W. Noble,

"*The New Republic* and the Idea of Progress, 1914–1920," *Mississippi Valley Historical Review* 38 (1951): 388–400.

19. In general, see Ajay K. Mehrotra, *Making the Modern American Fiscal State: Law, Politics, and the Rise of Progressive Taxation, 1877–1929* (New York: Cambridge University Press, 2013).

20. "Commentators have not fully appreciated, however, the gap between the rhetoric and reality of the WIB experiment. . . . The enthusiastic, even congratulatory, tone of so much of the contemporary literature . . . points to . . . how successful the WIB was in maintaining the symbol and myth of an integrated system which in reality lay beyond its grasp." Robert D. Cuff, *The War Industries Board: Business-Government Relations During World War I* (Baltimore: Johns Hopkins University Press, 1973) 265. For a good historiographic discussion in this regard, see Mark Wilson, "Economic Mobilization," in *A Companion to Woodrow Wilson*, 289–306.

21. Ross A. Kennedy, "Preparedness," in *A Companion to Woodrow Wilson*, 270–285. See also Millett, "Over Where?" in *Against All Enemies: Interpretations of American Military History from Colonial Times to the Present*, ed. Kenneth J. Hagen and William R. Roberts (Westport, CT: Greenwood Press, 1986) 236: "In 1915 Assistant Chief of Staff Tasker H. Bliss calculated that equipment and munitions shortages alone would require nearly two years to correct in order to place an expeditionary force of just five hundred thousand men in the field—unless American industry could rapidly increase its production of military supplies. With the Allies already drawing heavily upon American manufacturers, the degree of industrial expansion became a critical unknown."

22. James Grant, *Bernard M. Baruch: The Adventures of a Wall Street Legend* (New York: John Wiley and Sons, 1997) 164.

23. Nenninger, "American Military Effectiveness," 121–122.

24. Weigley, *History of the United States Army*, 362–369.

25. Nenninger, "American Military Effectiveness," 137–138.

26. Up to that point, Pershing (with Wilson's encouragement) had insisted that American troops fight only under American leadership. See Millett, "Over Where?" in *Against All Enemies*, 241.

27. Grant, *Bernard M. Baruch*, 146–147. See also Ajay K. Mehrotra, "Lawyers, Guns, and Public Moneys: The U.S. Treasury, World War I, and the Administration of the Modern Fiscal State," *Law and History Review* 28 (2010): 173–225.

28. Nenninger, "American Military Effectiveness," 119.

29. Grant, *Bernard M. Baruch*, 163.

30. Bernard M. Baruch, *Baruch: My Own Story* (New York: Henry Holt and Company, 1957), especially chap. 1–4 and 8. See also Grant, *Bernard M. Baruch*, chap. 2–7.

31. Eisenhower, *At Ease*, 155.

32. MacArthur, *Reminiscences*, 72.

33. This culminated in the conclusion that the "armaments industry" had tricked the country into fighting. Gerald P. Nye, a Republican from North Dakota, summarized this view: "To save [the] skins of American bankers who had bet too boldly on the outcome of the war and had two billions of dollars of loans to the Allies in jeopardy" (as quoted in Doenecke, "Neutrality Policy," in *A Companion to Woodrow Wilson*, 244). See also, Helmut Carol Engelbrecht and Frank Cleary Hanighen, *Merchants of Death: A Study of the International Armament Industry* (New York: Dodd, Mead and Company, 1934).

34. "Plan to Cut Guard Stirs Washington," *The Sun* (Baltimore), September 7, 1922: 8.

35. Smith, *Eisenhower in War and Peace*, 60; Weigley, *History of the United States Army*, 399–404.

36. Smith, *Lucius D. Clay*, 94–95.

37. Kerry E. Irish, "Apt Pupil: Dwight Eisenhower and the 1930 Industrial Mobilization Plan," *Journal of Military History* 70, no. 1 (January 2006): 34.

38. Smith, *Lucius D. Clay*, 95–96.

39. Eisenhower, *At Ease*, 169.

40. Dwight D. Eisenhower, "A Tank Discussion," *Infantry Journal* 27 (1920): 453–458.

41. This feeling remained throughout the decade, long after it became clear that the United States had fallen far behind other nations in exploring the usefulness of tanks in battle. Recognizing the problem in the early 1930s, then general of the army Douglas MacArthur allowed the cavalry to develop its own tanks, but only after reclassifying them as "combat cars" to get around the 1920 act. See Weigley, *History of the United States Army*, 410; Matthew F. Holland, *Eisenhower Between the Wars: The Making of a General and Statesman* (Westport, CT: Praeger, 2001) 82.

42. Holland, *Eisenhower Between the Wars*, 72, 173.

43. Karl-Heinz Frieser, *The Blitzkrieg Legend: The 1940 Campaign in the West*, ed. John T. Ringwood (Annapolis, MD: Naval Institute Press, 2005).

44. Eisenhower, *Crusade in Europe*, 19.

45. "Allied Armistice Terms," November 11, 1918, http://www.firstworldwar.com/source/armisticeterms.htm.

46. Ibid., 51.

47. Ibid., 80–81.

48. Ibid., 170.

49. Ibid.

50. Ibid., 77.

51. Ibid., 128–129.

52. Ibid., 107–144.

53. MacArthur, *Reminiscences*, 72.

54. Conversation with Lucius Clay by Professor George K. Romoser and Mr. Robert Wolfe, New York, July 19, 1977, Box 20: Speeches by Lucius D. Clay 1950–1959, Folder: Articles, Interviews & Statement. January 6, 1977–March 3, 1978, Lucius Clay Collection, GML, 3.

55. George Malcolm, "The Status of the Philippines," *Michigan Law Review* 14, no. 7 (May 1916): 529, 543. Italics in original.

56. The national legislature could override the veto, but only in the sense that the legislation then went to the U.S. president for final arbitration. See Maximo M. Kalaw, *The Present Government of the Philippines* (Manila: McCullough Print Co., 1921) 10, and chap. 1 and 2, generally.

57. "Conditions Not as Bad as Painted: Wood-Forbes Commission Believes Philippines Have Done Fairly Well," *Los Angeles Times*, May 13, 1921. See also, Henry L. Stimson, "Future Philippine Policy Under the Jones Act," *Foreign Affairs* 5, no. 3 (April 1927): 463.

58. "The Future of the Philippines," *New Republic*, May 1, 1929: 294; Vicente G. Bunuan, "History of Independence Movements in Philippines," *Congressional Digest* 3 (April 1924): 228.

59. James, *The Years of Macarthur*, 1:301–302.

60. Harry N. Howard, *Military Government in the Panama Canal Zone* (Norman: University of Oklahoma Press, 1931) 18–19.

61. Ibid., 23–24.

62. Ibid., 24–25.

63. Edward L. Cox, *Grey Eminence: Fox Conner and the Art of Mentorship* (Stillwater, OK: New Forums Press, Inc., 2011).

64. Holland, *Eisenhower Between the Wars*, 100.

65. Eisenhower, *Crusade in Europe*, 18.

66. Eisenhower, *At Ease*, 186.

67. Smith, *Lucius D. Clay*, 54.

68. Interview with General Lucius Clay by Colonel R. Joe Rogers, Lucius Clay Collection, GML, 17.

69. Stimson and Bundy, *On Active Service*, 117–118.

70. Stimson, "Future Philippine Policy," 459.

71. Ibid., 460.

72. MacArthur, *Reminiscences*, 89.

73. Smith, *Eisenhower in War and Peace*, 78–79.

74. Dwight D. Eisenhower, Course at the Army War College 1927–1928: War Plans—Industrial Mobilization, 1928, Dwight D. Eisenhower Pre-Presidential Papers (Miscellaneous), DDEPL, 1.

75. Ibid., 16.

76. Eisenhower, *At Ease*, 211.

77. Ibid.

78. As Eisenhower explained, writing the Mobilization Plan "was a long, irksome job. Many people in the War Department were flatly opposed to Br. Baruch's ideas" (Ibid.).

79. Dwight D. Eisenhower, Plan for Industrial Mobilization, 1930, Dwight D. Eisenhower Pre-Presidential Papers (Miscellaneous), DDEPL; Dwight D. Eisenhower, "War Policies (November, 1931)," in *Eisenhower: The Prewar Diaries and Selected Papers, 1905–1941*, ed. Daniel D. Holt, et al. (Baltimore: Johns Hopkins University Press, 1998).

80. Ibid., 6, 26. Here, Eisenhower largely restated his views from his earlier paper for the Army War College: "Mr. Gormley, in his lecture on railroads, pointed out that much better service can be expected from transportation systems in time of war provided they are allowed to function as closely as possible along lines they use at present. This idea . . . should be applied to all facilities, installations, and organizations," Dwight D. Eisenhower, Course at the Army War College 1927–1928: War Plans—Industrial Mobilization, Pre-Presidential Papers (Miscellaneous), DDEPL, 1.

81. Eisenhower, Plan for Industrial Mobilization, 1930, Pre-Presidential Papers (Miscellaneous), DDEPL, 25.

82. Eisenhower, "War Policies (November, 1931)," in *The Prewar Diaries*, 196.

83. Eisenhower, Plan for Industrial Mobilization, 1930, Pre-Presidential Papers (Miscellaneous), DDEPL, 26.

84. Ibid.

85. Ibid., 197.

Chapter 3

1. Smith, *Lucius D. Clay*, 56.

2. Ben S. Bernanke, "The Macroeconomics of the Great Depression: A Comparative Approach," *Journal of Money, Credit and Banking* 27, no. 1 (February 1995): 2. I follow (in very brief terms) his "nonmonetary/financial hypothesis" along with Barry Eichengreen's analysis of the gold standard. See Ben S. Bernanke, "Nonmonetary Effects of the Financial Crisis in the Propagation of the Great Depression," *American Economic Review* 73, no. 3 (1983): 257–276; Ben S. Bernanke and Harold James, "The Gold Standard, Deflation, and Financial Crisis in the Great Depression: An International Comparison," in *Financial Markets and Financial Crises*, ed. R. Glenn Hubbard (Chicago: University of Chicago Press, 1991); Barry Eichengreen, *Golden Fetters: The Gold Standard and the Great Depression, 1919–1939* (New York: Oxford University Press, 1992); also Tooze, *The Deluge*; Ahamed, *Lords of Finance*.

3. Ahamed, *Lords of Finance*, 283.

4. Edward W. Bennett, *Germany and the Diplomacy of the Financial Crisis* (Cambridge, MA: Harvard University Press, 1962) 7–8.

5. As quoted in John Gerard Ruggie, "Taking Embedded Liberalism Global: The Corporate Connection," in *Taming Globalization: Frontiers of Governance*, ed. David Held and Mathias Koenig-Archibugi (Cambridge, UK: Polity Press, 2003) 207.

6. Barry Eichengreen, *Hall of Mirrors: The Great Depression, the Great Recession, and the Uses—-and Misuses—of History* (New York: Oxford University Press, 2015) 254.

7. Tooze, *The Deluge*, 487–488.

8. Because of an undervalued franc, France did not suffer deflation. Yet it chose to "sterilize" its gold—that is, the French refused to turn portions of their growing gold reserve into money—so that it experienced net gold inflows without any inflationary effect. See Eichengreen, *Hall of Mirrors*, 60–61.

9. Ibid.

10. The other factor affecting the flow of gold into Europe was the passage of the Smoot-Hawley Act, which raised tariffs on foreign goods, effectively ruining the possibility of Europe regaining gold through exports to the United States. See ibid., 120–122.

11. "Schacht Sees War Barriers Reducing Trade of World," *Chicago Daily Tribune*, November 20, 1930: 17.

12. "Schacht, Here, Sees Warning in Fascism," *NYT*, October 3, 1930: 12.

13. Ahamed, *Lords of Finance*, 409–421.

14. S. Palmer Harman, "Britain's Great Struggle: Epic of the Pound," *NYT*, September 27, 1931: 21.

15. John Steele, "Europe Passes Buck on Debts to Uncle Sam," *Chicago Daily Tribune*, July 13, 1932: 1.

16. Stimson and Bundy, *On Active Service*, 212–213.

17. Walter Lippmann, "The Second Reconstruction," *American Magazine* 166 (September 1933): 16–17.

18. MacArthur, *Reminiscences*, 99.

19. Franklin D. Roosevelt, "Inaugural Address," March 4, 1933, APP, http://www.presidency.ucsb.edu/ws/index.php?pid=14473&st=democracy&st1.

20. Rexford G. Tugwell, "Design for Government," address delivered at the Eighth Annual Meeting of the Federation of Bar Associations of Western New York, June 24, 1933, in *The Battle for Democracy* (New York: Columbia University Press, 1935) 14.

21. Smith, *Lucius D. Clay*, 57.

22. Eisenhower, "March 10, 1933," in *The Prewar Diaries*, 249. It's worth noting that Eisenhower supported Roosevelt's austerity measures even though it meant that "my own salary will be cut some more if these things come to pass. I cannot afford it. . . . Nevertheless he *should* do it—and if he doesn't I will be disappointed in him" (emphasis in original).

23. Eisenhower, "June 15, 1932," in *The Prewar Diaries*, 229. Eisenhower clearly misdated this entry since the NRA did not exist in 1932. See ibid., 231, n.1.

24. Brinkley, *The End of Reform*, 35–37; Ellis Wayne Hawley, *The New Deal and the Problem of Monopoly: A Study in Economic Ambivalence* (Princeton, NJ: Princeton University Press, 1966) 23–25; Arthur M. Schlesinger, *The Age of Roosevelt: The Coming of the New Deal* (Boston: Houghton Mifflin, 1957) 2:176.

25. Eisenhower, "October 29, 1933," in *The Prewar Diaries*, 253–254 (emphasis in original).

26. J. Fred Essary, "$144,000,000 Cut Ordered in Army Budget," *Sun* (Baltimore) April 18, 1933: 1; "$468,407,608 Slash in Offices Budget," *NYT*, April 21, 1933: 1.

27. MacArthur, *Reminiscences*, 101.

28. Smith, *Lucius D. Clay*, 62–63.

29. Holland, *Eisenhower Between the Wars*, 169–170.

30. Smith, *Lucius D. Clay*, 64.

31. MacArthur, *Reminiscences*, 101.

32. Philippine Independence Act of 1934, 73rd Cong., 2nd sess., *United States Statutes at Large* (Washington, DC: United States Government Printing Office, 1934) 456–458.

33. Nicholas Roosevelt, "Laying Down the White Man's Burden," *Foreign Affairs* 13, no. 4 (July 1935): 684.

34. Eisenhower, "November 1935," in *The Prewar Diaries*, 287–288.

35. Eisenhower, *At Ease,* 219.

36. For the size of the American army, see Robert Harvey, *American Shogun: General MacArthur, Emperor Hirohito and the Drama of Modern Japan* (New York: The Overlook Press, 2006) 216; for MacArthur's salary, see "Philippine Service," in Eisenhower, *The Prewar Diaries*, 283.

37. Eisenhower, "January 20," in *The Prewar Diaries*, 304.

38. Eisenhower, "February 6," in *The Prewar Diaries*, 305.

39. Eisenhower, "May 29," in *The Prewar Diaries*, 311.

40. Harvey, *American Shogun*, 219.

41. Smith, *Lucius D. Clay*, 76–77.

42. Clay, being modest, believed that the only reason for this mention was that the writer happened to be a neighbor (Interview with General Lucius D. Clay by Colonel R. Joe Rogers, Lucius Clay Collection, GML, 27–28).

43. Eisenhower, "June 21" and "June 28," in *The Prewar Diaries*, 335, 338.

44. Eisenhower, "October 8," in *The Prewar Diaries*, 360–363.

45. Ibid.

46. Smith, *Lucius D. Clay*, 78.

47. Interview with General Lucius D. Clay by Colonel R. Joe Rogers, Lucius Clay Collection, GML, 29.

48. Smith, *Lucius D. Clay*, 78–79.

49. Eisenhower, *At Ease*, 228.

50. Interview with General Lucius D. Clay by Colonel R. Joe Rogers, Lucius Clay Collection, GML, 29–30.

51. Eisenhower, "November 10," in *The Prewar Diaries*, 411.

52. Eisenhower, *At Ease*, 231.

53. Interview with General Lucius D. Clay by Colonel R. Joe Rogers, Lucius Clay Collection, GML, 30.

54. Smith, *Lucius D. Clay*, 81.

55. Among many, see John J. Mearsheimer, *Liddle Hart and the Weight of History* (Ithaca, NY: Cornell University Press, 2010).

56. Carl von Clausewitz, *On War*, chap. 1, §24. Translators often use the alternative, "War is the continuation of policy by other means." This is true of the standard translation: *On War*, trans. Michael Howard and Peter Paret (Princeton, NJ: Princeton University Press, [1976], 1984). For purposes of this analogy, I have preferred the term "politics." Eisenhower had become deeply familiar with Clausewitz while in Panama and under the instruction of Fox Conner, who gave him military treatises and then held long discussions on their meaning. See Cox, *Grey Eminence*, 89.

57. Dayna L. Barnes, *Architects of Occupation: American Experts and the Planning for Postwar Japan* (Ithaca, NY: Cornell University Press, 2017) 17.

58. Rudolf V. A. Janssens, *"What Future for Japan?": U.S. Wartime Planning for the Postwar Era, 1942–1945* (Atlanta: Rodopi, 1995) 47–48.

59. J. Fred Essary, "Cabinet Shifts Aimed to Meet People's Wish," *Sun* (Baltimore), June 21, 1940: 1.

60. Dr. George Gallup, "The Gallup Poll: Naming Of Knox, Stimson to Cabinet Approved by Large Vote in Survey," *Sun* (Baltimore) July 5, 1940: 11.

Chapter 4

1. The literature on Keynes is enormous. Useful for this study are Roger E. Backhouse, "The Keynesian Revolution," in *The Cambridge Companion to Keynes*, ed. Roger Backhouse, et al. (New York: Cambridge University Press, 2006); and David E. W. Laidler, *Fabricating the Keynesian Revolution: Studies of the Inter-War Literature on Money, the Cycle, and Unemployment* (Cambridge, UK: Cambridge University Press, 1999).

2. Adam Smith, *An Inquiry into the Nature and Causes of the Wealth of Nations* (Chicago: University of Chicago Press, 1976) 358–359.

3. Thus, he characterized savings only in relation to consumption and not as spending that makes its way back into the economy—as "the excess of income over what is spent on consumption": John Maynard Keynes, *The General Theory of Employment, Interest, and Money* (London: Macmillan, 1936) 74.

4. Ibid., 150–151.

5. Ibid., 154.

6. Ibid., 27 (emphasis added).

7. Ibid., 28.

8. Alan Brinkley, "The New Deal and the Idea of the State," in *The Rise and Fall of the New Deal Order, 1930–1980*, ed. Steve Fraser and Gary Gerstle (Princeton, NJ: Princeton University Press, 1989) 99; see also Brinkley, *The End of Reform*.

9. Franklin D. Roosevelt, "Address at Madison Square Garden, New York City, October 31, 1936," APP, http://www.presidency.ucsb.edu/ws/?pid = 15219.

10. "At one time, in the early bloom of the Keynesian Revolution, it was common to attribute Keynes's triumph simply to his superior policy proposals. Orthodox economists offered no remedies for the depression except a balanced budget and an all-round deflation to force down real wages; only Keynes advocated a deliberately unbalanced budget and compensatory spending on public works. More recent historical research has thoroughly undermined this mythical picture of Keynes as a 'voice crying in the wilderness.' Much of the mythology that still surrounds popular accounts of the Keynesian Revolution relies on disguising the radical difference in the state of pre-Keynesian economics in the USA and Britain. There were some outstanding economists in the USA who favoured monetary over fiscal measures in dealing with the Depression, but the majority of US economists strongly supported a public works programme financed by borrowing, and went out of their way to attack the concept of an annually balanced government budget as an old-fashioned dogma." Mark Blaug, *John Maynard Keynes: Life, Ideas, Legacy* (New York: St. Martin's Press, 1990) 27.

11. Robert Dallek, *Franklin D. Roosevelt and American Foreign Policy, 1932–1945* (New York: Oxford University Press, 1995) 122–130.

12. Harley Notter and the Department of State, Office of Public Affairs, *Postwar Foreign Policy Preparation, 1939–1945* (Washington, DC: U.S. Government Printing Office, 1949) 7–9. See also Hugh Borton, "First Session Discussion," in *Americans as Proconsuls: United States Military Government in Germany and Japan, 1944–1952*, ed. Robert Wolfe (Carbondale: Southern Illinois University Press, 1984) 6.

13. Notter and Department of State, *Postwar Foreign Policy Preparation*, 23.

14. Steil, *The Battle of Bretton Woods*, 120–121.

15. Cordell Hull, "Reciprocal Trade Agreements," *Vital Speeches of the Day*, May 1, 1943, 9:433–435. This is central also to Leffler, *A Preponderance of Power*.

16. Franklin D. Roosevelt, "Fireside Chat," April 14, 1938, APP, http://www.presidency .ucsb.edu/ws/?pid = 15628.

17. Council on Foreign Relations, *Studies of American Interests in the War and Peace*, vol. E-C 15 (New York: Council on Foreign Relations, 1944). Contrast this with Borgwardt, *New Deal for the World*, and human rights scholars generally.

18. Cordell Hull, "Reciprocal Trade Agreements," in *Vital Speeches of the Day*, 433.

19. House Special Committee on Post-War Economic Policy and Planning, *Post-War Economic Policy and Planning: Hearings Before the Special Committee on Post-War Economic Policy and Planning* (Washington, DC: U.S. Government Printing Office, 1944) 1082. This passage is frequently cited among revisionist historians as evidence that American economic aims dominated its political aims for the postwar world. My point is that the two were not so easily separated.

20. As quoted in Steil, *The Battle of Bretton Woods*, 24.

21. Oral History Interview with J. Burke Knapp by Richard D. McKinzie, Bethesda, MD, July 24, 1975, HSTPL.

22. Memorandum from H. D. White to Secretary Morgenthau, May 8, 1942, *Diaries of Henry Morgenthau, Jr.* (April 27, 1933–July 27, 1945), Franklin D. Roosevelt Presidential Library, 526:111.

23. Steil, *The Battle of Bretton Woods*, 130–161.

24. John Maynard Keynes, "The Keynes Plan," in *The International Monetary Fund, 1945–1965: Twenty Years of International Monetary Cooperation*, ed. J. Keith Jorsefield, vol. 3, *Documents* (Washington, DC: International Monetary Fund, 1969) 4.

25. Steil, *The Battle of Bretton Woods*, 97.

26. "Morgenthau Monetary Conclave Text," *Boston Globe*, July 2, 1944: D4.

27. F. Blumenfeld, "Gold and the Dollar," *Congressional Quarterly Press Editorial Research Reports* (1960), http://library.cqpress.com/cqresearcher/cqresrre1960121500.

28. Scholars have for years seen Bretton Woods as evidence of a broad Keynesian consensus, which is true but only in the sense that experts would be called upon to manage both the national and international economies.

29. There is a fairly significant literature on development of postwar policy for Germany. Among many, see Diane Shaver Clemens, *Yalta* (New York: Oxford University Press, 1970); Bruce Kuklick, *American Policy and the Division of Germany: The Clash with Russia over Reparations* (Ithaca, NY: Cornell University Press, 1972); Robert Dallek, *Franklin D. Roosevelt and American Foreign Policy, 1932–1945: With a New Afterword* (New York: Oxford University Press, [1979] 1995) 406–538; Eisenberg, *Drawing the Line*, 14–120.

30. Notter and Department of State, *Postwar Foreign Policy Preparation*, 558–559.

31. Eisenberg, *Drawing the Line*, 32–36.

32. As reported by Drew Pearson in "Merry-Go-Round," *Washington Post*, September 21, 1944: 9. Apparently, the story came from Morgenthau.

33. George M. Elsey, *An Unplanned Life: A Memoir* (Columbia: University of Missouri Press, 2005) 67.

34. John Morton Blum, *From the Morgenthau Diaries: Years of War, 1941–1945* (Boston: Houghton Mifflin, Co., 1967) 127.

35. See, among many, ibid., particularly chap. 12; Anthony J. Nicholls, "American Views of Germany's Future During World War II," in *Das "andere Deutschland" in Zweiten Weltkrieg: Emigration und Widerstand in interationalie Perspektive*, ed. Lothar Kettenacker (Stuttgart: Klett, 1977) 77–87; Warren Kimball, *Swords or Ploughshares? The Morgenthau Plan for Defeated Nazi Germany, 1943–1946* (Philadelphia: Lippincott, 1976); Eisenberg, *Drawing the Line*, particularly chap. 1; Wilfried Mausbach, *Zwischen Morgenthau und Marshall: Das wirtschaftspolitische Deutschlandkonzept der USA 1944–1947* (Düsseldorf: Droste, 1996). For an account that places this debate within the broader American political culture, see Michaela Hönicke Moore, *Know Your Enemy: The American Debate on Nazism, 1933–1945* (Cambridge, UK: Cambridge University Press, 2014).

36. Richard Breitman and Allan J. Lichtman, *FDR and the Jews* (Cambridge, MA: Belknap Press of Harvard University Press, 2014) 215–237.

37. "Memorandum by the Secretary of the Treasury (Morgenthau) to President Roosevelt, January 10, 1945," *FRUS* 1945, vol. 3: European Advisory Commission, Austria, Germany: 376.

38. For a succinct discussion of the Temporary National Economic Committee, see Brinkley, *The End of Reform*, 123–136. The quotation about international cartels comes from the Senate Committee on Military Affairs, Cartels and National Security, *Report from the Subcommittee on War Mobilization to the Committee on Military Affairs*, ed. Harley Martin Kilgore (Washington, DC: U.S. Government Printing Office, 1944) 5.

39. Ibid., 2.

40. Ibid., 3.

41. Stimson and Bundy, *On Active Service*, 579.

42. Ibid.

43. "Annex 2: Memorandum by the Committee on Post-War Programs," *FRUS* 1944, vol. 1: General: 307.

44. U.S. Congress, Senate Committee on the Judiciary, Subcommittee to Investigate the Administration of the Internal Security Act and Other Internal Security Laws, *Morgenthau Diary (Germany)*, vol. 2, 90th Cong., 1st sess. (Washington, DC: U.S. Government Printing Office, 1967) 1117.

45. For a particularly good rendering of their exchange, see Michael Beschloss, *The Conquerors: Roosevelt, Truman, and the Destruction of Hitler's Germany, 1941–1945* (New York: Simon and Schuster, 2002) 67–74.

46. Eisenhower, *Crusade in Europe*, 287.

47. U.S. Congress, Senate Committee on the Judiciary, Subcommittee to Investigate the Administration of the Internal Security Act and Other Internal Security Laws, *Morgenthau Diary (Germany)*, vol. 1, 90th Cong., 1st sess. (Washington, DC: U.S. Government Printing Office, 1967) 414. Morgenthau did not note in his diary something Eisenhower included in his memoir in 1947. On the specific question of deindustrialization, Eisenhower claims to have told Morgenthau, "The Germans should be permitted and required to make their own living, and should not be supported by America. Therefore choking off natural resources would be folly" (Eisenhower, *Crusade in Europe*, 287).

48. "Before I left Washington I understood from the President and the War Department that it was desired to make the organization of military government in Germany civilian in character at earliest possible date. I reported this to General Eisenhower on my arrival and found him in full agreement with this policy. We have proceeded to increase the civilian personnel in [U.S.] Group [Control] Council rapidly and to place some civilians in Head-[83] quarters, United States Forces European Theater [USFET]." Lucius Clay, "37. Transfer of Military Government to Civilian Authority, 18 September 1945, From Clay for War Department," in *The Papers of General Lucius D. Clay,* ed. Jean Edward Smith, vol. 1, *Germany 1945–1949* (Bloomington: Indiana University Press, 1974) 82–83.

49. U.S. Congress, *Morgenthau Diary (Germany)*, vol. 1: 589.

50. Smith, *Lucius D. Clay*, 211–212.

51. U.S. Congress, *Morgenthau Diary (Germany)*, vol. 2: 1108.

52. Ibid., 1122.

53. U.S. Congress, Senate Committee on Banking and Currency, *Bretton Woods Agreements Act, Hearings Before the Committee on Banking and Currency*, 79th Cong., 1st sess., on *H.R. 3314* (Washington, DC: U.S. Government Printing Office, 1945) 17–18.

54. Interview #16 with Lucius Clay by Jean Smith, 516–517.

55. Ibid., 517.

Chapter 5

1. Interview with General Lucius D. Clay by Colonel R. Joe Rogers, Lucius Clay Collection, GML, 6–7.

2. Eisenhower, *Crusade in Europe*, 136.

3. Ibid., 218.

4. This is a central point in the first chapters of John Gimbel's *The Origins of the Marshall Plan* (Stanford, CA: Stanford University Press, 1976).

5. Kenneth O. McCreedy, *Planning the Peace: Operation Eclipse and the Occupation of Germany* (Fort Leavenworth, KS: School of Advanced Military Studies, 1995) 717–718.

6. Interview #16 with General Lucius Clay by Jean Smith, DDEPL, 533.

7. Ibid., 458–459; Clay, *Decision in Germany*, 46.

8. Eisenhower, *Crusade in Europe*, 469.

9. Clay, *Decision in Germany*, 354.

10. "Secretary of State to the Secretary of the Treasury (Morgenthau), Currency Arrangements During Invasion and Occupation of Enemy-Occupied Territories by United Nations Armed Forces," July 31, 1942, *FRUS* 1943, vol. 1: General: 1029.

11. Oral History Interview with Bernard Bernstein by Richard D. McKinzie, New York, July 23, 1975, HSTPL, 53.

12. "Memorandum Regarding Invasion and Occupation Currencies," March 30, 1943, *FRUS* 1943, vol. 1: General, 1034–1036.

13. U.S. Congress, Senate Committee on Appropriations, Banking and Currency, *Occupation Currency Transactions: Hearings Before the Committees on Appropriations, Armed Services, and Banking and Currency,* 80th Cong., 1st sess. (Washington, DC: Government Printing Office, 1947) 184–185.

14. U.S. Congress, *Occupation Currency Transactions*, 16.

15. Ibid., 274.

16. Ibid., 328.

17. Ibid., 343.

18. Joseph M. Dodge October 21, 1945, Box: 2, Correspondence, Folder: Reports from Germany, German Assignment, JDP.

19. "Four Million Dollars Sent Home by 33,000 Berlin Yanks in July," *Stars and Stripes*, August 1, 1945.

20. Robert Murphy, *Diplomat Among Warriors* (Garden City, NY: Doubleday, 1964) 288–289.

21. "230. To Walter Bedell Smith," August 2, 1945, *PDDE 6:* 244–245. See also U.S. Congress, *Occupation Currency Transactions*, 366.

22. U.S. Congress, *Occupation Currency Transactions,* 376.

23. Ibid., 51.

24. Ibid., 400.

25. Ibid., 637.

26. Ibid., 269–270. For the basis of the inflation-adjusted figure, see U.S. Department of Labor, Bureau of Labor Statistics, "Consumer Price Index," http://www.bls.gov/data/inflation_calculator.htm.

27. Interview #21 with General Lucius Clay by Jean Smith, New York, March 3, 1971, DDEPL, 700.

28. "City of Death," *Time*, July 16, 1945.

29. "Germany Faces the Winter," *Economist*, September 14, 1946: 406.

30. Lucius D. Clay, "Conditions in Germany, May 7, 1945" in *The Papers of General Lucius D. Clay*, 1:12.

31. "Awesome & Frightful," *Time*, November 5, 1945.

32. Tom Buchanan, *Europe's Troubled Peace, 1945–2000* (Malden, MA: Blackwell, 2009) 29.

33. John Keegan, *The Second World War* (New York: Penguin Books, 2005) 592–594.

34. Buchanan, *Europe's Troubled Peace*, 30.

35. Eisenhower, *Crusade in Europe*, 442–443; Interview #16 with General Lucius Clay, DDEPL, 21; see also Smith, *Lucius D. Clay*, 338: "[Clay's assistant William] Whipple complicates Clay's often-stated rationale that his primary interest in German recovery was to reduce the drain on the American taxpayer. 'But I do not believe that was his primary reason. . . . He simply didn't like to see the Germans starving.'" The revisionist literature on the early Cold War usually follows Morgenthau's logic when it comes to Germany. It usually downplays the suffering of the Germans and dismisses the possibility that military government might have found this suffering intolerable. Instead, revisionists argue that military government aimed all along to revive German industry as part of an ideologically driven interest that precipitated the Cold War (see Eisenberg, *Drawing the Line*). By contrast, (and more recently), some human rights theorists have argued that the Allied failure to better feed the Germans amounts to war crimes (see Richard Dominic Wiggers, "The United States and the Refusal to Feed German Civilians After World War II," in *Ethnic Cleansing in Twentieth-Century Europe*, ed. Steven Béla Várdy, et al. [New York: Social Science Monographs, 2003]). Given the longer lens of this study, it seems unlikely Clay or Eisenhower had any strong ideological leanings at war's conclusion. If anything, they leaned toward the New Deal and not a nascent "conservatism"—whatever that meant at the time. More than anything, they seem motivated by a pragmatic moralism.

36. "3. Conditions in Germany, April 20, 1945, From Clay for Byrnes (Letter)," in *Papers of General Lucius D. Clay*, 1:6.

37. Interview #16 with General Lucius Clay, DDEPL, 529. Before war's end, some military planners in Washington had anticipated this problem and questioned the effectiveness of rigorous denazification. In September 1944, Assistant Secretary of War John J. McCloy explained that, "We can't undertake to eliminate immediately every member of the Nazi Party." "Why not?" asked Morgenthau. "Because there are too many of them," answered McCloy. "There are all sorts of grades but one way or another they are all affiliated with the Nazi Party," he continued. Getting to his point, he explained, "We have a real manpower job. . . . We are going to run an entire nation and we haven't the officers to do it, nor have we immediately the means of finding out who the other [qualified non-Nazis] are. You have a practical problem to deal with." "You don't mind if I don't agree with you?" demurred Morgenthau (U.S. Congress, *Morgenthau Diary [Germany]*, vol. 1: 559–560).

38. JCS 1067/8, April 26, 1945, *FRUS* 1945, vol. 3: European Advisory Commission: 484–503.

39. JCS 1067/8, 487, 493, 494 (emphasis added).

40. Henry Morgenthau, *Germany Is Our Problem* (New York: Harper and Brothers, 1945) 37: "For the most part, cartel agreements are illegal in the United States. In Germany they are not only legal, but since 1933, compulsory in many instances. They have been rigidly controlled and supervised, as was all business, by the Ministry of Economic Affairs, so the government really directs their policies. Between the world wars, some two or three thousand cartels were organized in Germany."

41. JCS 1067/8, 497.

42. Lewis Douglas served as budget director from Franklin Roosevelt's inauguration until late summer, 1934. See also Smith, *Lucius D. Clay*, 232.

43. Oral History Interview with General William H. Draper Jr. by Jerry N. Hess, Washington, D.C., January 11, 1972, HSTPL. See also Murphy, *Diplomat Among Warriors,* 250.

44. Murphy, *Diplomat Among Warriors,* 26.

45. Ibid., 251.

46. Conversation with Lucius Clay by Professor George K. Romoser and Mr. Robert Wolfe, Lucius Clay Collection, GML, 3.

47. Staff Meeting for U.S. Group Control Council (hereafter USGCC), May 26, 1945, Record Group 260, Microcopy M1075, Roll 1, NA, 123.

48. Staff Meeting USGCC, June 9, 1945, Record Group 260, Microcopy M1075, Roll 1, NA, 145.

49. Ulrich Kluge, "Agriculture and European Recovery Program," in *American Policy and the Reconstruction of West Germany, 1945–1955,* ed. Jeffry M. Diefendorf, et al. (Cambridge, UK: Cambridge University Press, 1993) 157.

50. Barbara Marshall, "German Attitudes to British Military Government 1945–47," *Journal of Contemporary History* 15, no. 4 (1980).

51. *Papers of General Lucius D. Clay,* 1:47.

52. Oral History Interview with Bernard Bernstein by Richard D. McKinzie, HSTPL, 1–50.

53. Ibid., 52–53.

54. Ibid., 59.

55. *Diaries of Henry Morganthau, Jr.* (December 19–22, 1944), Franklin D. Roosevelt Presidential Library, 864: 13.

56. U.S. Congress, *Morgenthau Diary (Germany),* vol. 1: 21.

57. Oral History Interview with Bernard Bernstein by Richard D. McKinzie, HSTPL, 111.

58. Mark Trachtenberg, *A Constructed Peace: The Making of the European Settlement, 1945–1963* (Princeton, NJ: Princeton University Press, 1999) 46–47; Melvyn P. Leffler, *The Struggle for Germany and the Origins of the Cold War* (Washington, DC: German Historical Institute, 1996) 20; Gimbel, *The Origins of the Marshall Plan.*

59. Gimbel, *The Origins of the Marshall Plan,* 25–26.

60. Clay, *Decision in Germany,* 53–54.

61. Interview with General Lucius D. Clay by Colonel R. Joe Rogers, GML, 5.

62. Stimson and Bundy, "Memo for the President, July 22, 1945," in *On Active Service,* 594.

63. "Officials in Washington could not sort out priorities among their foreign policy goals and could not choose between domestic and international objectives. The president failed to organize his administration effectively: his advisers bickered among themselves, antagonized influential legislators, and forfeited leadership to powerful proconsuls abroad. . . . Decision making responsibility, therefore, lodged itself in the field, where MacArthur in Japan, Clay in Germany, Hodge in Korea, and Marshall in China played critical roles." Leffler, *A Preponderance of Power,* 104–105.

64. Oral History Interview with J. Burke Knapp by Richard D. McKinzie, Bethesda, Maryland, July 24, 1975, HSTPL, 61–62.

65. Staff Meeting USGCC, June 9, 1945, Record Group 260, Microcopy M1075, Roll 1, NA, 145.

66. Smith, *Lucius D. Clay,* 232.

67. Special Meeting USGCC, August 1, 1945, Record Group 260, Microcopy M1075, Roll 1, NA, 216.

68. Staff Meeting USGCC, August 4, 1945, Record Group 260, Microcopy M1075, Roll 1, NA, 222.

69. Special Meeting USGCC, August 1, 1945, Record Group 260, Microcopy M1075, Roll 1, NA, 216.

70. "17. Conditions in Germany, Letter From Clay for McCloy (June 29, 1945)," in *Papers of General Lucius D. Clay*, 1:41.

71. U.S. Congress, *Morgenthau Diary (Germany)*, vol. 2: 1610.

72. Oral History Interview with General William H. Draper Jr. by Jerry N. Hess, HSTPL, 40–41.

73. Interview #17 with General Lucius Clay by Jean Smith, DDEPL, 579. In short, McCloy advised Clay to take advantage of the flexibility McCloy himself had worked to include in the directive.

74. "The Honorable Joseph M. Dodge: Resume," and, "Dynamic Detroiter," Box: 1, Folder: 1, Biography, JDP.

75. "Obituaries: Joseph M. Dodge, Banker, 74, Dead," *NYT*, December 3, 1964.

76. Lucius D. Clay, Letter to Joseph M. Dodge, May 10, 1945, Box: 1, Correspondence, Folder: Gen. Lucius Clay, German Assignment, JDP.

77. Joseph M. Dodge, August 31, 1945, Box: 2, Correspondence, Folder: Reports from Germany, German Assignment, JDP; also Staff Meeting USGCC, September 1, 1945, Record Group 260, Microcopy M1075, Roll 1, NA.

78. Joseph M. Dodge, September 1, 1945, Box: 2, Correspondence, Folder: Reports from Germany, German Assignment, JDP, 4.

79. General Orders No. 52, September 12, 1945, Box: 5, Memorandum, Folder: German Assignment Memos 1945, German Assignment, JDP.

80. Eisenberg, *Drawing the Line*, 37.

81. Joseph M. Dodge, September 1, 1945, Box: 2, Correspondence, Folder: Reports from Germany, German Assignment, JDP.

82. Letter to General Lucius D. Clay from Joseph M. Dodge, May 3, 1945, Box: 1, Correspondence, Folder: Gen. Lucius Clay, German Assignment, JDP.

83. Joseph M. Dodge, November 3, 1945, Box: 2, Correspondence, Folder: Reports from Germany, German Assignment, JDP.

84. Carolyn Eisenberg, "U.S. Policy in Post-War Germany: The Conservative Restoration," *Science and Society* 46, no. 1 (Spring 1982): 28: Eisenberg writes, "During the early fall of 1945 a staff of more than one hundred lawyers and economists was recruited [and] . . . placed in the Finance Division of the Office of U.S. Military Government (OMGUS). . . . Since the Treasury was sympathetic to the decartelization program, it had packed the Finance Division with like-minded people."

85. U.S. Congress, Senate Committee on Military Affairs, *Cartels and National Security: Report from the Subcommittee on War Mobilization to the Committee on Military Affairs, Part 1: Findings and Recommendations,* 78th Cong., 2d sess. (Washington, DC: Government Printing Office, 1944) 7. See also Morgenthau, *Germany Is Our Problem*, 33–38.

86. U.S. Congress, Senate Committee on Military Affairs, Subcommittee on War Mobilization, *Elimination of German Resources for War,* part 8, 79th Cong., 1st sess. (Washington, DC: Government Printing Office, 1946) 1064.

87. Christoph Buchheim, "The Establishment of the Bank Deutscher Länder and the West German Currency Reform," in *Fifty Years of the Deutsche Mark: Central Bank and the Currency in Germany Since 1948*, ed. Ernst Baltensperger, et al. (Oxford, UK: Clarendon Press, 1998) 63.

88. Lucius D. Clay, Letter to Joseph M. Dodge, May 10, 1945, Box: 1, Correspondence, Folder: Gen. Lucius Clay, German Assignment, JDP.

Chapter 6

1. "681. To Douglas MacArthur (January 28, 1946)," *PDDE*, 7:799.

2. "The United States Political Adviser for Germany (Robert Murphy) for the Acting Secretary of State, January 13, 1946," *FRUS* 1946, vol. 5: The British of Commonwealth, Western and Central Europe: 485.

3. House Subcommittee on War Department Appropriations, *Military Establishment Appropriation Bill for 1947*, May 8, 1946, (Washington, DC: U.S. Government Printing Office, 1946) 45.

4. Oral History Interview with General William H. Draper Jr. by Jerry N. Hess, HSTPL, 30–31.

5. Kluge, "Agriculture and European Recovery Program," in *American Policy and the Reconstruction of West Germany*, 158.

6. Marshall, "German Attitudes."

7. J. Bradford De Long and Barry Eichengreen, "The Marshall Plan: History's Most Successful Structural Adjustment Program," National Bureau of Economic Research Working Paper 3899 (Cambridge, MA: NBER, 1991) 43–44.

8. Leffler, *The Struggle for Germany*, 58; Buchheim, "From Enlightened Hegemony to Partnership," in *United States and Germany*, 1:259.

9. Interview #21 with General Lucius Clay by Jean Smith, DDEPL, 682.

10. Oral History Interview with Charles P. Kindleberger by Richard D. McKinzie, Cambridge, MA, July 16, 1973, HSTPL, 51.

11. Joseph M. Dodge, November 13, 1945, German Assignment, Box: 2, Correspondence, Folder: Reports from Germany, JDP.

12. Adam Tooze, *The Wages of Destruction: the Making and Breaking of the Nazi Economy* (New York: Penguin, 2006) 43–44.

13. Ibid., 108–112.

14. What follows is military government's understanding of Nazi finance (see Edward Tennenbaum, "The German Mark" [unpublished], Edward A. Tennenbaum Papers, Box: 2, Folder: The German Mark, HSTPL. See also Tooze, *The Wages of Destruction*.

15. For a discussion of "silent financing," see also Harold James, *The Nazi Dictatorship and the Deutsche Bank* (Cambridge, UK: Cambridge University Press, 2004) 16; also Tooze, *The Wages of Destruction*, 353–358.

16. Appendix A: Basic Economic Facts, Appendixes to a Plan for the Liquidation of War Finance and the Financial Rehabilitation of Germany, Record Group 260 (Finance Division), Box: 909, Folder: Appendixes to Colm-Goldsmith Plan, NA, A-1.

17. See, in this regard, Tooze, *The Wages of Destruction*, 285–357.

18. Harold James, "The Reichsbank, 1876–1945," in *Fifty Years of the Deutsche Mark*, ed. Ernst Baltensperger, et al. (Oxford, UK: Clarendon Press, 1998) 41–42.

19. Edward A. Tennenbaum Papers, Box: 3, Folder: The German Mark (4) HSTPL 22–29. Also Wilfried Mausbach, "Restructuring and Support: Beginnings of American Economic Policy in Occupied Germany," in *The United States and Germany*, 1:286.

20. Gerhard Colm, Joseph Dodge, and Raymond W. Goldsmith, "A Plan for the Liquidation of War Finance and the Financial Rehabilitation of Germany," *Zeitschrift für die gesamte Staatswissenschaft* 111 (May 20, 1946): 207.

21. On this point, see, in particular, Tooze, *The Wages of Destruction*, 285–357.

22. Joseph M. Dodge, Letter to Russell Nixon, November 8, 1945, Box: 1, Correspondence, Folder: N, German Assignment, JDP. On this point, I depart most clearly from revisionist accounts of the German occupation. See Eisenberg, *Drawing the Line*, 146–147: reformist "expectations were shattered in early September, when General Clay decided to remove Bernard Bernstein as acting director of Finance, and to replace him with Detroit banker, Joseph P. Dodge [*sic*]. Bernstein's replacement was a long-anticipated, but nonetheless momentous change. For months, he had used his berth to lobby passionately for denazification, industrial disarmament, and economic decentralization." On my account, Eisenberg, et al., see in Dodge a "conservative restoration" largely because they ignore the importance of finance to economic concentration. See especially, Kolko and Kolko, *The Limits of Power*, 142: "Essentially, Dodge, like Clay's top advisers, expected to work within the framework of Germany's prewar banking and industrial system."

23. Joseph M. Dodge, "November 13," "November 22," and "November 27, 1945," Box: 2, Correspondence, Folder: Reports from Germany, German Assignment, JDP.

24. Buchheim, "The Establishment of the Bank deutscher Länder and the West German Currency Reform," 67–68.

25. Joseph M. Dodge, "November 2, 1945," Box: 2, Correspondence, Folder: Reports from Germany, German Assignment, JDP.

26. Letter to General Lucius D. Clay from Joseph M. Dodge, January 20, 1947, Box: 1, Correspondence, Folder: Gen. Lucius Clay, German Assignment, JDP.

27. Buchheim, "The Establishment of the Bank deutscher Länder and the West German Currency Reform," 75.

28. Ibid., 73–75; Regina Ursula Gramer, "From Decartelization to Reconcentration: The Mixed Legacy of American-Led Corporate Reconstruction in Germany," in *The United States and Germany* 1:290.

29. Buchheim, "The Establishment of the Bank deutscher Länder and the West German Currency Reform," 70–80.

30. Joseph M. Dodge, "September 17, 1945," Box: 2, Correspondence, Folder: Reports from Germany, German Assignment, JDP.

31. Eckhard Wandel, "Historical Developments Prior to the German Currency Reform of 1948," *Zeitschrift für die gesamte Staatswissenschaft* 135, no. 3 (1979): 323.

32. Wolfram Hoppenstedt, *Gerhard Colm: Leben und Werk (1897–1968)* (Wiesbaden, Germany: Franz Steiner Verlag, 1997) 194.

33. Joseph M. Dodge, "November 11, 1945," Box: 2, Correspondence, Folder: Reports from Germany, German Assignment, JDP.

34. Charles P. Kindleberger and F. Taylor Ostrander, "The 1948 Monetary Reform in Western Germany," in *International Financial History in the Twentieth Century: System and Anarchy*, ed. Marc Flandreau, et al. (New York: Cambridge University Press, 2003) 176.

35. Ibid.

36. Special Directors Meeting USGCC, January 22, 1946, Record Group 260, Microcopy M1075 Roll 1, NA, 412.

37. Lucius D. Clay, Cable, Mission on Anti-Inflation, January 25, 1946, Box: 1, Correspondence, Folder: Gen. Lucius Clay, German Assignment, JDP.

38. "Administration of the U.S. Zone, January 27, 1946, From Clay Personal for Hilldring," in *Papers of General Lucius D. Clay*, 1:151.

39. Lucius D. Clay, Cable, Mission on Anti-Inflation, JDP.

40. Oral History Interview with Raymond W. Goldsmith by Richard D. McKinzie, New Haven, CT, June 25, 1973, HSTPL, 20.

41. Hoppenstedt, *Gerhard Colm*, 197 (author's translation).

42. Oral History Interview with Raymond W. Goldsmith by Richard D. McKinzie, HSTPL, 18.

43. Joseph M. Dodge, April 25, 1946, Box: 2, Correspondence, Folder: Reports from Germany, German Assignment, JDP.

44. Oral History Interview with Raymond W. Goldsmith by Richard D. McKinzie, HSTPL, 20.

45. Appendix Q: A Survey of Various German Proposals for Monetary and Financial Reform, Appendixes to a Plan for the Liquidation of War Finance and the Financial Rehabilitation of Germany, Record Group 260 (Finance Division), Box: 909, Folder: Appendixes to Colm-Goldsmith Plan, NA, Q-1.

46. Ibid., Q-2, Q-5.

47. Letter to General Lucius D. Clay from Joseph M. Dodge, October 17, 1946, Box: 1, Correspondence, Folder: Gen. Lucius Clay, German Assignment, JDP.

48. Ibid.

49. Colm, Dodge, and Goldsmith, "Liquidation of War Finance," *Zeitschrift* 111:216. In many ways, Morgenthau accepted this same way of thinking: the destruction of Germany's real property suggested to him the destruction of its wealth. But as technology developed, this notion of wealth made less sense. Indeed, Galbraith took Dodge's side in this dispute while critiquing Morgenthau's plan. "If tomorrow German industry were brought down to the level prescribed in the agreements and the occupation armies withdrawn, very little in the way of security would have been achieved," he explained. "Capital equipment . . . is readily reproducible. Left to themselves the Germans could restore their capital plant in a very few years and the new plant would be considerably more modern and potentially more dangerous than the present plant" (John Kenneth Galbraith, *Planning Pamphlets*, vol. 53, *Recovery in Europe: An International Committee Report* [Washington, DC: National Planning Association, 1946], 24).

50. Colm, Dodge, and Goldsmith, "Liquidation of War Finance," *Zeitschrift* 111: 222: "The ratio of liquid funds in 1935 to national income in that year was approximately .60. If this ratio, which was a normal one for most pre-war years, were to be re-established in 1946, it would be necessary to reduce the sum of currency and deposits to about 20 billion DM. This represents a reduction of more than 90 percent in the present total of currency and deposits; it is an important reason for the recommendation in the present report that new currency be exchanged for old, in the ratio of 10 RM = = 1 DM."

51. Colm, Dodge, and Goldsmith, "Liquidation of War," *Zeitschrift* 111: 211–212.

52. Ibid., 213–214.

53. "Fiscal Reform (From Clay Personal for Echols)," in *Papers of General Lucius D. Clay*, 1:245.

54. Ibid., 246.

55. Kindleberger and Ostrander, "The 1948 Monetary Reform in Western Germany," in *International Financial History*, 178.

56. Letter to William H. Draper, Jr., from Joseph M. Dodge, July 29, 1946, Box: 1, Correspondence, Folder: Wm H. Draper, Jr., German Assignment, JDP.

57. Appendix O: Recent Foreign Experiences with Monetary and Financial Reform, Appendixes to a Plan for the Liquidation of War Finance and the Financial Rehabilitation of Germany, Record Group 260 (Finance Division), Box: 909, Folder: Appendixes to Colm-Goldsmith Plan, NA, O-1.

58. Ibid., O-4 (emphasis added).

59. Letter to W. Randolph Burgess from Joseph M. Dodge, September 16, 1946, Box: 1, Correspondence, Folder: B, German Assignment, JDP.

60. Letter to William H. Draper, Jr., from Joseph M. Dodge, July 29, 1946, Box: 1, Correspondence, Folder: Wm H. Draper, Jr., German Assignment, JDP.

61. Letter to Joseph M. Dodge from Dr. Gerhard Colm, June 26, 1946, Box: 1, Correspondence, Folder: Dr. Gerhard Colm, German Assignment, JDP.

62. Letter from John C. de Wilde to Joseph M. Dodge, September 3, 1946, Box: 1, Correspondence, German Assignment, JDP: "You may have heard that thanks to a herculean effort of Ken Galbraith who got the acting Secretary to intervene with the Secretary of War, the War Department finally agreed to instruct Clay to go ahead with the CDG plan without alteration. Clay accordingly introduced the plan at the 73rd meeting of the Coordinating Committee on August 29, and it was referred to the Finance Directorate." Dodge and Galbraith worked together through the summer on the currency plan (see also Joseph M. Dodge, Letter to Dr. Gerhard Colm, July 1, 1946, and Letter to General Lucius D. Clay, July 15, 1946, Box: 1, Correspondence, Folder: Dr. Gerhard Colm and Folder: Gen. Lucius Clay). It appears that Galbraith used much of what he learned from this experience in drafting his paper, "Recovery in Europe," in *Planning Pamphlets*.

63. Letter to General Lucius D. Clay from Joseph M. Dodge, July 16, 1946, Box: 1, Correspondence, Folder: Gen Lucius Clay, German Assignment, JDP.

64. Wilfried Mausbach, "Restructuring and Support: Beginnings of American Economic Policy in Occupied Germany," in *The United States and Germany* 1:284–285.

65. Letter to Joseph M. Dodge from Lucius D. Clay, December 23, 1946, Box 1: Correspondence, Folder: Gen. Lucius Clay, German Assignment, JDP.

66. Hitchcock, *France Restored*, 34.

67. Oral History Interview with Charles P. Kindleberger by Richard D. McKinzie, HSTPL, 17.

68. Pope Pius XII, "The Gravity of the Present Hour: Lack of Moral Principles Leads to Unrest," Vatican City, December 24, 1946, *Vital Speeches of the Day*, January 1, 1947, 13:163.

Chapter 7

1. Department of State, ed., United Nations Monetary and Financial Conference: Bretton Woods, Final Act and Related Documents, New Hampshire, July 1 to July 22, 1944 (Washington, DC: U.S. Government Printing Office, 1944) 4, 121.

2. Gimbel, *The Origins of the Marshall Plan*, 54.

3. Borden, *The Pacific Alliance*, 23.

4. "Initially, Americans did not realize or confess the full extent of support they would have to provide. Only after two years of false starts did they face up to the problem of Europe's dollar gap in its full magnitude." (Charles S. Maier, "The Politics of Productivity: Foundations of American International Economic Policy After World War II," in *Between Power and Plenty*, ed. Peter J. Katzenstein [Madison: University of Wisconsin Press, 1978] 39.)

5. The Marshall Plan literature is enormous. See, in particular, Gimbel, *The Origins of the Marshall Plan*; Hogan, *The Marshall Plan*; and De Long and Eichengreen, "The Marshall Plan."

6. Interview with General Lucius Clay by Forrest C. Pogue, GML, 8.

7. "The Americans had foreseen that the inclusion of West Germany in the Marshall Plan would be essential to its success, and this was precisely why the United States had made German inclusion the second central condition for the granting of aid. Germany had been the principal supplier of capital goods to many European countries before the war." (Buchheim, "From Enlightened Hegemony to Partnership," in *The United States and Germany*, 1:265.)

8. On this point see, in particular, De Long and Eichengreen, "The Marshall Plan."

9. Joseph M. Dodge, "Broadcast over Columbia Broadcasting System Network, Monday, October 13, 1947, at 11:15 p.m., from Station WJR in Detroit," Box: 1, Folder: 43. Speeches European Aid and The Marshall Plan 13, 1947, Additional Papers, Speeches, JDP.

10. "German Economic Recovery (from Clay for Marshall [letter]), (May 2, 1947)," in *Papers of General Lucius D. Clay*, 1:348. See also Leffler, *A Preponderance of Power*, 158: "U.S. officials wanted European countries to boost their productivity and efficiency, compete effectively in international markets, and find sources of supply outside the Western Hemisphere. If these countries succeeded, they would cut their deficits, overcome the dollar gap, free themselves of U.S. subsidies, and be able to adopt multilateral trade arrangements. [Dean] Acheson, [William] Clayton, and their associates knew that it would take several years to achieve these goals. In the interval, European governments would need to hold down wages, curb inflation, constrain domestic consumption, cap welfare programs, balance budgets, and stabilize currencies." In short, Marshall, Acheson, et al., observed for Europe what Clay, Dodge, et al., had observed in Germany in the first months after surrender.

11. Here I echo Eichengreen and De Long's understanding of the Marshall Plan and, its genesis in the occupation. See De Long and Eichengreen, "The Marshall Plan," 46–51.

12. Joseph M. Dodge, "Broadcast over Columbia Broadcasting System Network, Monday, October 13, 1947, at 11:15 p.m., from Station WJR in Detroit," JDP. See also Charles S. Maier, "The Politics of Productivity," 39: "Only after two years of false starts did they face up to the problem of Europe's dollar gap in its full magnitude. But the issue of expanding foreign aid beset their postulates with new difficulties. Originally an apolitical aid was thought to secure the broad range of American objectives. Once, however, the Soviet Union was acknowledged as a threat, the liberals' image of a healthy political economy became strained." Also Leffler, *A Preponderance of Power*, 158; Mausbach, "Restructuring and Support: Beginnings of American Economic Policy in Occupied Germany," in *The United States and Germany*, 1:280.

13. Clay, "182. Currency Reform (From Clay Personal for Noce)" in *Papers of General Lucius D. Clay*, 1:303.

14. "The German Mark," Edward A. Tennenbaum Papers, Box: 2, Folder: 3, HSTPL, 206.

15. Lucius D. Clay, Letter to Joseph M. Dodge, February 25, 1947, Box: 1, Correspondence, Folder: Gen. Lucius Clay, German Assignment, JDP.

16. "The German Mark," Edward A. Tennenbaum Papers, Box: 2, Folder: 3, HSTPL, 3:205.

17. Kindleberger and Ostrander, "The 1948 Monetary Reform in Western Germany," in *International Financial History*, 183.

18. Clay, "246. Currency Reform (From Clay personal for Petersen) August 8, 1947," in *Papers of General Lucius D. Clay*, 1:398.

19. Clay, *Decision in Germany*, 211.

20. Kindleberger and Ostrander, "The 1948 Monetary Reform in Western Germany," in *International Financial History*, 183.

21. Murphy, *Diplomat Among Warriors*, 312. See also "Memorandum of Conversation, by the Political Adviser for Germany (Murphy) December 18, 1947," *FRUS* 1947, vol. 2: Council of Foreign Ministers; Germany and Austria: 827–830.

22. Buchheim, "The Establishment of the Bank deutscher Länder and the West German Currency Reform," in *Fifty Years of the Deutsche Mark*, 89.

23. Alfred C. Mierzejewski, *Ludwig Erhard: A Biography* (Chapel Hill and London. University of North Carolina Press, 2004) 55; see also Werner Plumpe, "Opting for the Structural Break: The West German Currency Reform and Its Consequences," in *The United States and Germany*, 1:265.

24. "Obituaries: Ludwig Erhard: Guided W. Germany's Recovery," *Boston Globe*, May 5, 1977: 39.

25. James C. Van Hook, *Rebuilding Germany: The Creation of the Social Market Economy, 1945–1957* (Cambridge, UK: Cambridge University Press, 2004) 128–129.

26. Ibid., 165–166.

27. Buchheim, "The Establishment of the Bank deutscher Länder and the West German Currency Reform," in *Fifty Years of the Deutsche Mark*, 61.

28. Mierzejewski, *Ludwig Erhard: A Biography*, 66.

29. Van Hook, *Rebuilding Germany*, 163. See also Clay, *Decision in Germany*, 201: "Dr. Agartz was then replaced by Dr. Ludwig Erhard, although as a result the Social Democratic party refused to participate further in the executive work of the administration. Thus the political struggle for control of the economic machine between the CDU, which while not supporting full free enterprise wants only limited controls, and the SPD, which desires a fully controlled economy, broke into the open. It continues to be the main issue in German political life. The selection Dr. Erhard to head the Economic Administration was to be of special significance after currency reform."

30. Mierzejewski, *Ludwig Erhard: A Biography*, 67.

31. Smith, *Lucius D. Clay*, 485–486.

32. Ludwig Erhard, "The Road to the Future (Speech at the 14th plenary session of the Economic Council in Frankfurt-am-Main on April 21, 1948)" in *The Economics of Success*, trans. J. A. Arengo-Jones and D. J. S. Thomson (Princeton, NJ: Van Nostrand, 1963) 22–44.

33. Mierzejewski, *Ludwig Erhard: A Biography*, 68.

34. Ibid., 69.

35. Ludwig Erhard, "The New Rate, (Broadcast, June 21, 1948)" in *Economics of Success*, 50–51.

36. Ibid., 486.

37. Jack Bennett, Letter to Sir Eric Coates, Box: 93 (Financial Reform), Folder: Colm-Dodge-Goldsmith Plan, Record Group 260 (Finance Division), NA, 1–2.

38. "Effects of the 'Sonderstelle' Proposals," Box: 102, Folder: Pre-Currency Reform No. 2, Record Group 260 (Finance Division), NA, 2.

39. Jack Bennett, "Financial Stabilization after Currency Conversion," Box: 102, Folder: Pre-Currency Reform No. 2, Record Group 260 (Finance Division), NA, 1.

40. Ibid.

41. Ibid., 4.

42. Ibid., 8.

43. "Conditions in Germany, September 18, 1948," in *Papers of General Lucius D. Clay*, ed. Jean Edward Smith (Bloomington IN: Indiana University Press, 1974) 2: 858–859.

44. Herbert Giersch et al., *The Fading Miracle: Four Decades of Market Economy in Germany* (Cambridge, UK: Cambridge University Press, 1994) 42.

45. Mierzejewski, *Ludwig Erhard: A Biography*, 73, and Giersch et al., *The Fading Miracle*, 42.

46. Clay, *Decision in Germany*, 219–220.

47. Giersch et al., *The Fading Miracle*, 41.

48. "Proclamation to the German People on the Western Currency Reform by Marshal Sokolovsky, June 19, 1948," in *Documents on Berlin*, ed. Wolfgang Heidelmeyer and Guenter Hindrichs (Munich: R. Oldenbourg Verlag, 1963) 59.

49. Roger G. Miller, *To Save a City: The Berlin Airlift, 1948–1949* (College Station: Texas A&M University Press, 2000).

50. See generally, Eisenberg, *Drawing the Line.*

51. "The German Mark," Edward A. Tennenbaum Papers, Box: 2, Folder: 1, The German Mark, HSTPL, 1–10.

52. "Clay's Service," *Washington Post*, May 5, 1949: 14.

53. Anne O'Hare McCormick, "Change-Over from Military to Civilian Rule in Germany," *NYT*, May 7, 1949: 12.

54. Clay, *Decision in Germany*, 281.

55. Walter Lippmann, "Draper, Clay, and Acheson," *Hartford Courant*, February 22, 1949: 10.

Chapter 8

1. Arthur Alexander, *The Arc of Japan's Economic Development* (New York: Routledge, 2008) 17–18.

2. "Letters from President Fillmore — Asia for Educators," StudyLib, http://studylib.net/doc/8236569/letters-from-president-fillmore---asia-for-educators.

3. Jason Ananda Josephson, *The Invention of Religion in Japan* (Chicago: University of Chicago Press, 2012) 1.

4. Alexander, *Arc of Japan's Economic Development*, 24–25.

5. As quoted in Bruce Cumings, *Parallax Visions: Making Sense of American–East Asian Relations* (Durham, NC: Duke University Press, 2002) 17.

6. Harvey, *American Shogun*, 138.

7. Ibid., 163–164.

8. Masao Maruyama, "Theory and Psychology of Ultra-Nationalism," in *Thought and Behavior in Modern Japanese Politics*, ed. Ivan Morris (Tokyo: Oxford University Press, 1979) 16.

9. Ibid., 87–88.

10. Barnes, *Architects of Occupation*, 30–32.

11. Cohen and Passin, *Remaking Japan*, 29–30.

12. Borton, "First Session Discussion," in *Americans as Proconsuls*, 69.

13. Marlene J. Mayo, "American Wartime Planning," in *Americans as Proconsuls*, 8–9; Eleanor M. Hadley, "From Deconcentration to Reverse Course in Japan," in *Americans as Proconsuls*, 139.

14. See, among many, Hadley, "From Deconcentration to Reverse Course in Japan," 139; Mayo, "American Wartime Planning," 34–35 in ibid. Eiji Takemae, *Inside GHQ: The Allied Occupation of Japan and Its Legacy*, trans. Robert Ricketts and Sebastian Swann (New York: Continuum, 2002) 203–205; and Wyatt C. Wells, *Antitrust and the Formation of the Postwar World* (New York: Columbia University Press, 2002) 146–147.

15. Alexander, *Arc of Japan's Economic Development*, 52–53.

16. United States Mission on Japanese Combines and Corwin D. Edwards, *Report of Mission on Japanese Combines*, ed. Department of State and the War Department (Washington, DC: U.S. Government Printing Office, 1946) 8.

17. Cohen and Passin, *Remaking Japan*, 13.

18. The Potsdam Declaration is available from many sources. I've chosen, Supreme Commander for the Allied Powers, "Government Section," *Political Reorientation of Japan, September 1945 to September 1948: A Report* (Washington, DC: U.S. Government Printing Office, 1949) 2:413.

19. Both quotes come from Michael D. Pearlman, *Truman and MacArthur: Policy, Politics, and the Hunger for Honor and Renown* (Bloomington: Indiana University Press, 2008) 13.

20. Typed Note of President Harry S. Truman, June 17, 1945, Truman Papers, President's Secretary's Files, HSTPL, https://www.trumanlibrary.org/whistlestop/study_collections/tru manpapers/psf/longhand/index.php?documentVersion = both&documentid = hst-psf_naid 735225-02&pagenumber = 2.

21. Harvey, *American Shogun*, 324.

22. Lincoln Gould, "Army Ban on Politics May Aim at M'Arthur," *Boston Globe*, April 7, 1943: 1.

23. "Stimson Says Politics Ban Not Meant for MacArthur," *Christian Science Monitor*, April 8, 1943: 7.

24. As quoted in James, *The Years of MacArthur*, 2:406.

25. Ibid., 408.

26. As quoted in ibid., 438.

27. "To Fredric E. Schluter, February 5, 1944," in *The Papers of Robert A. Taft*, vol. 2, *1939–1944*, ed. Clarence E. Wunderlin, Jr. (Kent, OH: Kent State University Press, 2001) 526.

28. "To Julius Klein, September 5, 1945," in *The Papers of Robert A. Taft*, in *The Papers of Robert A. Taft*, vol. 3, *1945–1948*, ed. Clarence E. Wunderlin, Jr. (Kent, OH: Kent State University Press, 2003) 73.

29. James, *The Years of MacArthur*, 2:408–409.

30. Ibid., 3:197.

31. James, *The Years of MacArthur*, 1:48–50.

32. MacArthur, *Reminiscences*, 282.

33. Ibid., 282–283.

34. "Appendix A-13: JCS 1380/15, Basic Initial Post-Surrender Directive to Supreme Commander for the Allied Powers for the Occupation and Control of Japan," in *Political Reorientation of Japan*, 2:429–434.

35. See Cohen and Passin, *Remaking Japan*, in particular, on this point.

36. T. J. Pempel called the arrangement "functional feudalism." T. J. Pempel, "The Tar Baby Target: 'Reform' of the Japanese Bureaucracy," in *Democratizing Japan: The Allied Occupation*, ed. Robert Edward Ward and Yoshikazu Sakamoto (Honolulu: University of Hawaii Press, 1987).

37. Schaller, *The American Occupation of Japan*, 28.

38. Ibid.

39. Dower, *Embracing Defeat*, chap. 12 and 13; Hideo, "The Conflict Between Two Legal Traditions in Making the Constitution of Japan," in *Democratizing Japan*.

40. As quoted in Dower, *Embracing Defeat*, 373.

41. "Report by Dr. George E. Blakeslee on the Far Eastern Commission's Trip to Japan, December 26, 1945–February 13, 1946," *FRUS 1946*, vol. 8: The Far East: 164, 167.

42. Mark Gayn, *Japan Diary* (New York: W. Sloane Associates, 1948) 1.

43. These statistics are available from a variety of sources. See Takafusa Nakamura and Jacqueline Kaminski, trans., *The Postwar Japanese Economy: Its Development and Structure* (Tokyo: University of Tokyo Press, 1981) 9–22; Shigeto Tsuru, *Japan's Capitalism: Creative Defeat and Beyond* (New York: Cambridge University Press, 1993) 8–11.

44. Nakamura and Kaminski, *The Postwar Japanese Economy*, 22.

45. As quoted in Toshio Nishi, *Unconditional Democracy: Education and Politics in Occupied Japan, 1945–1952* (Stanford, CA: Hoover Institution Press, Stanford University, 1982) 62.

46. Department of State, "The Acting Political Adviser in Japan (Atcheson) to President Truman, January 4, 1946," *FRUS 1946*, vol. 8: The Far East: 89.

47. As quoted in Nishi, *Unconditional Democracy*, 62.

48. Nina Serafino, Curt Tarnoff, and Dick K. Nanto, "U.S. Occupation Assistance: Iraq, Germany and Japan Compared," *Congressional Research Service Report for Congress* (March 23, 2006): CRS-5.

49. "SWNCC [State-War-Navy Coordinating Committee] 162/2, Reorientation of the Japanese," *FRUS 1946*, vol. 8: The Far East: 108.

50. "The Political Adviser in Japan (Atcheson) to President Truman, January 5, 1947," *FRUS 1947*, vol. 6: The Far East: 159.

51. "Appendix A-13: JCS 1380/15," in *Political Reorientation of Japan*, 2:433.

52. Nihon Keizai Kenkyū Sentā, *Basic Problems for Postwar Reconstruction of Japanese Economy: Translation of a Report of Ministry of Foreign Affairs' Special Survey Committee, September 1946*, ed. Saburo Okita (Tokyo: Japan Economic Research Center, 1977) 56. See also Laura Hein, *Reasonable Men, Powerful Words: Political Culture and Expertise in Twentieth-Century Japan* (Washington, DC: Woodrow Wilson Center Press, 2004).

53. Sentā, *Reconstruction of Japanese Economy*, 2.

54. Bai Gao, "Arisawa Hiromi and His Theory for a Managed Economy," *Journal of Japanese Studies* 20, no. 1 (1994): 135–138.

55. As quoted in Yutaka Kōsai, *The Era of High-Speed Growth: Notes on the Postwar Japanese Economy*, trans. Jacqueline Kaminski (Tokyo: University of Tokyo Press, 1986) 43. See also Takemae, *Inside GHQ*, 310.

56. William M. Tsutsui, *Banking Policy in Japan: American Efforts at Reform During the Occupation* (New York: Routledge, 1988) 34.

57. Hiroshi Shinjo, *History of the Yen: 100 Years of Japanese Money-Economy* (Kobe, Japan: Research Institute for Economics and Business Administration, 1962) 154–155.

58. Ibid., 150; Tsutsui, *Banking Policy in Japan*, 27–28.

59. Shinjo, *History of the Yen*, 154–155. The freezing of personal and corporate accounts had the single benefit of helping commercial banks rebalance their books since, as the reforms played out, the banks largely confiscated these savings. See Tsutsui, *Banking Policy in Japan*, 28.

60. The "Basic Initial Post-Surrender Directive" had included instructions that MacArthur see "that all practicable economic and police measures are taken to achieve the maximum utilization of essential Japanese resources in order that imports into Japan may be strictly limited. Such measures will include production and price controls, rationing, control of black markets, fiscal and financial controls and other measures directed toward full employment of resources, facilities and means available in Japan." "Government Section," in *Political Reorientation of Japan*, 2:436.

61. As quoted in Kōsai, *The Era of High-Speed Growth*, 43.

62. Sharon H. Nolte, *Liberalism in Modern Japan: Ishibashi Tanzan and His Teachers, 1905–1960* (Berkeley: University of California Press, 1987) 307–308.

63. "General of the Army Douglas MacArthur to the Japanese Prime Minister (Yoshida)," March 22, 1947, *FRUS 1947*, vol. 6: The Far East: 191.

64. For a nice rendering of SCAP's failed effort to censor reports on inflationary problems in the United States, see Gayn, *Japan Diary*, 477.

65. Orville J. McDiarmid, "Comments," in *The Occupation of Japan: Economic Policy and Reform (the Proceedings of a Symposium Sponsored by the MacArthur Memorial, April 13–15, 1978)*, ed. Lawrence H. Redford and MacArthur Memorial (Norfolk, VA: The Memorial, 1980) 64.

66. "Appendix F: 38: Second Anniversary of Surrender," in *Political Reorientation of Japan*, 2:775.

67. Oral History Interview with General William H. Draper Jr. by Jerry N. Hess, HSTPL, 49–52.

68. Felix Belair, Jr., "Truman Names Six as Defense Chiefs," *NYT*, August 30, 1947 as well as Harry S. Truman: "The President's News Conference," June 5, 1947, APP, http://www.presidency.ucsb.edu/ws/?pid = 12660 and "The President's News Conference," August 21, 1947, APP, http://www.presidency.ucsb.edu/ws/?pid = 12743. These reappointments occurred just one month after Truman signed the National Security Act, which created the new Department of Defense and fit within a broader reshuffling of assignments.

69. Oral History Interview with General William H. Draper, Jr., by Jerry N. Hess, HSTPL, 53.

70. Lindesay Parrott, "Assurances Given Japan on Defense," *NYT*, September 28, 1947. See also Cohen and Passin, *Remaking Japan*, 401.

71. Oral History Interview with General William H. Draper Jr. by Jerry N. Hess, HSTPL, 54.

72. "Proposed Statement by General McCoy to the Far Eastern Commission on the Role of Japan's Economic Recovery in Far Eastern Economic Reconstruction (November 12, 1947)," *FRUS*, 1947, vol. 6: The Far East: 315.

73. "Memorandum by the Assistant Secretary of State for Occupied Areas (Saltzman), to the Under Secretary of the Army (Draper)," *FRUS*, 1947, vol. 6: The Far East: 313–314.

74. "SWNCC 384: Statement to Be Made to Far Eastern Commission by United States Member and Transmitted to SCAP for Information and Released for Publication," *FRUS*, 1948, vol. 6: The Far East and Australasia: 654–655.

75. Oral History Interview with General William H. Draper Jr. by Jerry N. Hess, HSTPL, 55.

76. "Memorandum of Conversation on the Subject 'Economic Aspects of the Japanese Occupation,' 27 July 1948," in *Economic Reform*, Doc #: 6–301–19, OJMS, 2.

77. See, among many, Takemae, *Inside GHQ*, 461; Schonberger, *Aftermath of War*, 203.

78. Cohen and Passin, *Remaking Japan*, 408–409. A curious inconsistency in Cohen's memoir involves Draper. Cohen deplores the "old Japan hands" for being too close to the Japanese and applauds New Dealers (like himself) who had little background in the Far East and only their liberal universalism to guide them. Cohen then turns around and criticizes the next generation of Washington planners on precisely the grounds the old Japan hands had criticized him: "Nothing [Draper] or the Washington economists did ever betrayed a sense of Japan as a different country. His was a curiously denationalized application of a universal international aid formula" (ibid). See, for a contrast, Wells, *Antitrust*, 183: "William Draper was the villain—he had used the Review Board 'to change policy, while apparently not changing policy.' In truth, the division had only itself to blame."

79. McDiarmid, "Comments," in *The Occupation of Japan: Economic Policy and Reform*, 66.

80. "Memorandum by the Assistant Secretary of State for Occupied Areas (Saltzman), to the Director of the Office of Far Eastern Affairs (Butterworth)," *FRUS*, 1948, vol. 6: The Far East and Australasia: 732.

81. Leffler, *A Preponderance of Power*, 298; Yoshikazu Sakamoto, "The International Context of the Occupation of Japan," in *Democratizing Japan*, 61.

82. "Conversation Between General of the Army MacArthur and Mr. George F. Kennan, March 5, 1948," *FRUS*, 1948, vol. 6: The Far East and Australasia: 699–700.

83. The international dimension of the Cold War has dominated the literature on this point. Because I focus largely on the lessons of political economy *learned* in the occupations, this part of the story remains important but in the background. For a classic statement of the traditional approach, see Borden, *The Pacific Alliance*, 120: "American economic and strategic policy in Asia can be reduced to a simple equation: Japan's dependence on trade would force her into accommodation with China unless she achieved a large stable trade with Southeast Asia. American officials, from Fearey and Kennan through Dulles, argued that Japan lacked the capitalistic and individualistic heritage of Europe, and could thus quickly adapt to socialistic organization and policies." See also Bruce Cumings "Japan's Position in the World System," in *Postwar Japan as History*, ed. Andrew Gordon (Berkeley: University of California

Press, 1993); Robert Edward Ward, "Conclusion," in *Democratizing Japan*; Sakamoto, "The International Context of the Occupation of Japan," in *Democratizing Japan*.

84. Oral History Interview with General William H. Draper Jr. by Jerry N. Hess, HSTPL, 53.

85. "Conversation Between General of the Army MacArthur and Mr. George F. Kennan, March 5, 1948," *FRUS*, 1948, vol. 6: The Far East and Australasia: 703.

86. "Appendix F 30: Interview with Press Correspondents, Primarily Concerning Plan for United Nations Administration of Japan," in *Political Reorientation of Japan*, 2:776.

87. Historians have also adopted the term, although they have argued over the exact causes of the reverse course (whether driven by the Cold War, the reassertion of business cliques in Japan, or a conservative resurgence in American foreign policy) and the timing of the shift. See, in general, John W. Dower, *Embracing Defeat* and *Empire and Aftermath: Yoshida Shigeru and the Japanese Experience, 1878–1954* (Cambridge, MA: Harvard University Press, 1979); Borden, *The Pacific Alliance*; Schonberger, *Aftermath of War*; Chalmers A. Johnson, *MITI and the Japanese Miracle: The Growth of Industrial Policy, 1925–1975* (Stanford, CA: Standford University Press, 1982); Takemae, *Inside GHQ*; Mark Caprio and Yoneyuki Sugita, "Introduction: The U.S. Occupation of Japan—Innovation, Continuity, and Compromise"; and Bruce Cumings, "Japan's Position in the World System." Takeshi Matsuda has expanded the reach of the "reverse course" thesis to include a Soviet reverse course as well: see Takeshi Matsuda, *Soft Power and Its Perils: U.S. Cultural Policy in Early Postwar Japan and Permanent Dependency* (Stanford, CA: Stanford University Press, 2007). Of those who agree that policy took on a new emphasis but did not amount to a "reversal," see Ward, "Conclusion," in *Democratizing Japan*; Janssens, "What Future for Japan?" For a general overview, see Hiroshi Kitamura, "The Occupation of Japan: A History of Its Histories," in *A Companion to Harry S. Truman*, ed. D. S. Margolies (Oxford, UK: Wiley-Blackwell, 2012).

88. As quoted in James, *The Years of MacArthur* 3:199.

89. As quoted in ibid., 204.

90. Interview with Dwight D. Eisenhower by D. Clayton James, August 29, 1967, Gettysburg, PA, DDEPL, 4.

91. "1998: To Leonard Finder, January 22, 1948," *PDDE*, 9:2192–2193.

92. As quoted in William B. Pickett, *Eisenhower Decides to Run: Presidential Politics and Cold War Strategy* (Chicago: Ivan R. Dee, 2000) 44.

93. "Would Meet 'Duty,'" *NYT*, March 9, 1948: 1.

94. Arthur Evans, "Contrast of Rule of MacArthur with Germany," *Chicago Tribune*, January 31, 1948: 9.

95. "Ike Declares Soviet Seeks No War Now," *Christian Science Monitor*, February 6, 1948: 13.

96. Interview with Senator Watkins, Box: 3, Folder: ACW Diary December 1954 (5), Presidential Papers of Dwight D. Eisenhower, Ann Whitman Diary Series, November, DDEPL.

97. Clayton Knowles, "Wisconsin Votes in Primary Today with MacArthur Heavily Favored," *NYT*, April 6, 1948: 16.

98. Arthur Krock, "In the Nation: The Large Casualty List of Wisconsin," *NYT*, April 8, 1948: 24.

99. James, *The Years of MacArthur*, 3:214.

Chapter 9

1. "NSC 13/2: Report by the National Security Council on Recommendation with Respect to United States Policy Toward Japan, Oct 7, 1948," *FRUS*, 1948, vol. 6: The Far East and Australasia: 860.

2. Ibid., 5:861.

3. Cable to Joseph M. Dodge from George C. Marshall, Secretary of State, April 29, 1947, Box: 1 (Correspondence 1947), Folder: May–Aug 1947, Austria, JDP.

4. "Mr. Dodge," *Fortune*, June 1948: 120.

5. Ibid.

6. Oral History Interview with General William H. Draper Jr. by Jerry N. Hess, HSTPL, 56.

7. Yoneyuki Sugita and Marie Annette Thorsten Morimoto, *Beyond the Line: Joseph Dodge and the Geometry of Power in US-Japan Relations, 1949–1952* (Okayama-shi, Japan: University Education Press, 1999) 22.

8. Memorandum to Cleveland Thurber from Joseph M. Dodge, December 13, 1948, Box: 1, Folder: Appointment, Japan 1949, JDP, 3.

9. Oral History Interview with General William H. Draper Jr. by Jerry N. Hess, HSTPL, 56.

10. Memorandum to Cleveland Thurber from Joseph M. Dodge, December 13, 1948, Box: 1, Folder: Appointment, Japan 1949, JDP, 1.

11. Oral History Interview with General William H. Draper Jr. by Jerry N. Hess, HSTPL, 57.

12. Memorandum to Cleveland Thurber from Joseph M. Dodge, December 13, 1948, Box: 1, Folder: Appointment, Japan 1949, JDP, 1.

13. Ibid., 2.

14. Ibid., 2–3. Also, Oral History Interview with General William H. Draper Jr., by Jerry N. Hess, HSTPL, 57.

15. Letter to Joseph Dodge from President Harry S. Truman, January 17, 1949, Box: 1, Folder: Appointment, Japan 1949, JDP.

16. Personal, to MacArthur from Royall, December 11, 1948, Box: 1, Folder: Appointment Correspondence, Japan 1949, JDP.

17. Cohen and Passin, *Remaking Japan*, 428.

18. "Austerity for Japan," *Economist*, April 16, 1949: 709.

19. "Press Conference of Mr. Joseph M. Dodge, (Q & A Session)," in *Economic Reform, 1945–1953*, Doc #:4–102–13, OJMS.

20. "Summary of Meeting with Finance Minister Ikeda on the Japanese Government Budget held 9 March from 1430 to 1600," Box: 1, Folder: Ikeda Interviews (listed as Ikeda "Industries" on folder), Japan 1949, JDP, 4.

21. Dower, *Embracing Defeat*, 535.

22. "Official Corruption," *Oriental Economist*, October 16, 1948: 862.

23. "Memorandum by the Chief of the Division of Northeast Asian Affairs (Bishop) to the Director of the Office of Far Eastern Affairs (Butterworth)," February 18, 1949, *FRUS* 1949, vol. 7: The Far East and Australasia (in two parts): 2:660–663.

24. Joseph M. Dodge, "Journal entries/Letter to Julia Dodge covering February 21–February 26," February 22, 1949, Box: 7, Folder: General Notes, Comments, Japan 1949, JDP, 2.

25. Herbert M. Bratter, "Letter to Hugh Morrow [of the] *Saturday Evening Post*," Box: 1, Folder: 1, Biography, JDP.

26. "Japanese Budget," February 9, 1949, Box: 2, Folder: Budget Policy Memos, Japan 1949, JDP, 3.

27. This is, in many ways, the essence of Dower's *Embracing Defeat*.

28. "Proposed Recommendations, February 18, 1949," "Attachment, February 8, 1949," both documents in Box: 9, Folder: Program Materials Official Memos, Japan 1949, JDP 1, 1–2 (emphasis added).

29. This fact helps explain some of the animosity against him in the historical literature. Some of the most critical historical appraisals of his time come from SCAP bureaucrats (such as Cohen).

30. Herbert M. Bratter, "Letter to Hugh Morrow [of the] *Saturday Evening Post*," Box: 1, Folder: 1, Biography, JDP.

31. Cohen and Passin, *Remaking Japan*, 432: "Dodge's modus operandi, like the cultivation of the lawns of England, was fundamentally simple but not easy. It was painstaking accounting followed by painful surgery. He questioned every expenditure without revenue to match and brought every subsidy, no matter how indirect and well-hidden, to light. Day after day, Japanese Finance Ministry officials trooped to his Forestry Building office carrying masses of documents, only to go back, invariably, for more data. In a matter of two months, Dodge personally knew more about the details of each ministry's budget than the ministers and of every special account more than the specialists. More important, he understood the impact of each entry on the economy, as he demonstrated in two lucid discourses to an awed press corps. He maintained independent lines of communication to Washington, radioing reports of his findings, accomplishments, and recommendations every two or three days on the average. It was an awesome and strange job. Commissioners had been dispatched by imperialist nations to backward countries in the nineteenth century to safeguard the tax collections that secured foreign loans. But here was a foreign Lord High Imperial Accountant sitting in the capital of a large industrial power, tirelessly auditing every phase of its financial operations 'for its own good.' Dodge was demonstrating that control of the budget from one small office was more powerful than the 150,000-man Occupation army commanded by General MacArthur."

32. "Personal to Acting Secretary Draper from Dodge, Serial Number 2," February 11, 1949, C-67802, *Economic Reform*, 1945–1953, Doc #: 4–101–164, OJMS, 1.

33. "Monetary Situation in Japan with Special Reference to Expansion of Credit and Credit Controls," January 28, 1949, Box: 1, Folder: Banking - Credit Expansion Control, Japan 1949, JDP, 4.

34. Anil Kashyap, Takeo Hoshi, and Gary Loveman, "Financial System Reform in Poland: Lessons from Japan's Main Bank System," in *The Japanese Main Bank System: Its Relevance for Developing and Transforming Economies*, ed. Masahiko Aoki and Hugh T. Patrick (Oxford, UK: Oxford University Press, 1994) 602–603. See also Norio Tamaki, *Japanese Banking: A History, 1859–1959* (Cambridge, UK: Cambridge University Press, 1995) 188.

35. Lawrence H. Redford et al., *The Occupation of Japan: Economic Policy and Reform*, 237.

36. Tsuru, *Japan's Capitalism*, 44.

37. SCAP records showed that "94.5% of all [RFB] loans were in A category; 5% were in B category, and .5% in C category." Memorandum, "Monetary Situation in Japan with Special

Reference to Expansion of Credit and Credit Controls," January 28, 1949, Box: 1, Folder: Banking—Credit Expansion Control, Japan 1949, JDP, 4.

38. Tsutsui, *Banking Policy in Japan*, 25–26; Hein, *Reasonable Men, Powerful Words*, 93.

39. "History of Reconstruction Finance Bank Traced — Tokyo Shimbun — 26 Sep 48," *Economic Reform*, 1945–1953, Doc #: 4–133–01, OJMS.

40. Tsutsui, *Banking Policy in Japan*, 34–35, 93.

41. "History of Reconstruction Finance Bank Traced — Tokyo Shimbun — 26 Sep 48," *Economic Reform,* Doc #: 4–133–01, OJMS.

42. Tamaki, *Japanese Banking*, 196.

43. Memorandum to General Marquat, "Government Financing of Private Industry Deficits," March 6, 1948, *Economic Reform*, 1945–1953, Doc #: 4–133–03, OJMS, 1.

44. Joseph M. Dodge, "Journal entries/Letter to Julia Dodge covering February 21– February 26," February 21, 1949, Box: 7, Folder: General Notes, Comments, Japan 1949, JDP, 1.

45. "Personal to Draper from Dodge. Serial Number 4, Message in Six Parts," February 21, 1949, C-68012, *Economic Reform*, 1945–1953, Doc #: 4–101–151, OJMS, 1.

46. "Personal to Draper from Dodge, Serial Number 8, Message in Three Parts," February 26, 1949, C-68120, *Economic Reform, 1945–1953*, Doc #: 4–101–155, OJMS, 1.

47. "Personal to Voorhees from Dodge, Serial Number 9, Message in Two Parts," March 4, 1949, C-68241, *Economic Reform, 1945–1953*, Doc #: 4–101–156, OJMS, 3.

48. "Personal to Draper from Dodge, Serial Number 8, Message in Three Parts," February 26, 1949, C-68120, *Economic Reform, 1945–1953*, Doc #: 4–101–155, OJMS, 1.

49. Joseph M. Dodge, "Journal entries/Letter to Julia Dodge covering February 21– February 26," February 26, 1949, Box: 7, Folder: General Notes, Comments, Japan 1949, JDP, 6.

50. "Personal to Draper from Dodge, Serial Number 8, Message in Three Parts," February 26, 1949, C-68120, *Economic Reform, 1945–1953*, Doc #: 4–101–155, OJMS, 1.

51. Harry S. Truman, "Radio Report to the American People on the Status of the Reconversion Program," January 3, 1946, APP, http://www.presidency.ucsb.edu/ws/?pid = 12489.

52. As quoted in Bai Gao, *Economic Ideology and Japanese Industrial Policy: Developmentalism from 1931 to 1965* (Cambridge, UK: Cambridge University Press, 2002) 161–164. I draw extensively on Gao as well as Kōsai, *The Era of High-Speed Growth*, 56–58, in the discussion of Arisawa and his debate with Kimura in the following paragraphs.

53. As quoted in Kōsai, *The Era of High-Speed Growth*, 57.

54. In fairness, Arisawa did not follow Keynes and differed from Ishibashi on whether effective demand alone could drive production. Within Yoshida's broad program, however, both elements remained central (see Gao, *Economic Ideology*, 164).

55. Kōsai, *The Era of High-Speed Growth*, 56. See also Hein, *Reasonable Men, Powerful Words*.

56. Gao, *Economic Ideology*, 162.

57. The irony makes a little more sense if a bit on intellectual genealogy is added. Many Japanese Marxists had studied in Germany in the years after World War I. They encountered Marx at a time when Europe experienced steep inflation and the economic disruptions that followed the war. In some cases, the same groups of professors who taught the Japanese Marxists in the 1920s later taught Dodge about inflation when he helped craft the German

currency conversion in 1946. Thus, while Dodge had almost nothing else in common with Japan's Marxists, they nevertheless shared intellectual influences. See also Hein, *Reasonable Men, Powerful Words.*

58. "Summary of Meeting with Finance Minister Ikeda on Japanese Government Budget held 3 March 1949 from 1400 hours to 1645," Box: 1, Folder: Ikeda Interviews (listed as Ikeda "Industries" on folder), Japan 1949, JDP, 1.

59. "Summary of Meeting with Finance Minister Ikeda on the Japanese Government Budget held 9 March from 1430 to 1600, Box: 1, Folder: Ikeda Interviews (listed as Ikeda "Industries" on folder), Japan 1949, JDP, 1–4.

60. "Personal Dodge to Voorhees, Serial No. 14, This Radio in Two Parts," March 14, 1949, C-68539, *Economic Reform, 1945–1953,* Doc #: 4–101–161, OJMS.

61. "Appendix A-13: JCS 1380/15," in *Political Reorientation of Japan,* 2:429.

62. "Personal Dodge to Voorhees, Serial No. 15, Subject: Counterpart Fund, Reported Part One," March 22, 1949, C-68699, *Economic Reform, 1945–1953,* Doc #:4–101–162, OJMS.

63. Lawrence H. Redford, et. al., *The Occupation of Japan: Economic Policy and Reform,* 65.

64. "Memorandum: Radio W 846348, 30 March, Subject: Foreign Exchange Rate," April 1, 1949, Box: 9, Folder: Program Materials Official Memos, Japan 1949, JDP, 2. Dodge had considered a lower rate but found himself overruled by the National Advisory Council (NAC) back in Washington. The NAC had learned that the British planned to devalue the pound and decided to factor that into the rate for the yen. See Schonberger, *Aftermath of War,* 211.

65. "Personal from Dodge to Voorhees, Serial No. 16," March 23, 1949, C-68539, *Economic Reform, 1945–1953,* Doc #: 4–101–161, OJMS.

66. "Personal to Voorhees from Dodge, Serial No. 10, This Message in Five Parts," March 9, 1949, C-68397, *Economic Reform, 1945–1953,* Doc #: 4–101–157, OJMS.

67. "Personal to Voorhees from Dodge, Serial No. 14, This Radio in Two Parts," March 14, 1949, C-68539, *Economic Reform, 1945–1953,* Doc #: 4–101–161, OJMS.

68. "Minutes of Budget Meeting, March 14, 1949," Box: 2, Folder: Budget Policy Memos, Japan 1949, JDP, 5.

69. "Personal to Voorhees from Dodge, Serial No. 14, This Radio in Two Parts," March 14, 1949, C-68539, *Economic Reform, 1945–1953,* Doc #: 4–101–161, OJMS.

70. "Minutes of Budget Meeting, March 14, 1949," Box: 2, Folder: Budget Policy Memos, Japan 1949, JDP, 1.

Chapter 10

1. "Summary of Meeting with Finance Minister Ikeda from 1045 to 1200, March 25, 1949," Box: 1, Folder: Ikeda Interviews (listed as Ikeda "Industries" on folder), Japan 1949, JDP (emphasis added).

2. "Review of the Week," *Oriental Economist,* May 21, 1949: 476.

3. "Despatch No. 237 dated April 19, 1949 from United States Political Adviser to Japan, Tokyo, on the subject "transmitting Statement on Japanese Budget by Minister Joseph M. Dodge and Editorial Comment Thereon,'" *Economic Reform, 1945–1953,* Doc #: 6–301–45, OJMS.

4. Ibid.

5. Ibid.

6. Ibid.

7. Ibid.

8. Ibid.

9. "Review of the Week," *Oriental Economist*, April 30, 1949: 401–402.

10. "Austerity for Japan," *Economist*, April 16, 1949: 709.

11. "From SCAP Tokyo to Dept of Army" Z-48663, May 2, 1949, Box: 1, Folder: Appointment, Japan 1949, JDP.

12. Sugita and Thorsten Morimoto, *Beyond the Line*, 31.

13. Takemae, *Inside GHQ*, 472–473.

14. Cohen and Passin, *Remaking Japan*, 452.

15. Takemae, *Inside GHQ*, 472.

16. "Unmistakable Signs Seen of Economic Crisis Here," *Oriental Economist*, July 19, 1949.

17. "Public Relations Aspects of the Economic Stabilization Program in Japan," enclosed with Robert W. Barnett's July 15, 1949 message, *Economic Reform, 1945–1953*, Doc #: 6–402–05, OJMS, 1.

18. Memorandum, "Economic Stabilization Program Analysis," July 25, 1949, *Economic Reform, 1945–1953*, Doc #: 4–104–29, OJMS, 3.

19. "Memorandum to General William F. Marquat: Summary Analysis of Current Economic Situation," August 1, 1949, Box: 3, Folder: Devaluation, Japan 1949, JDP, 2.

20. Cohen and Passin, *Remaking Japan*, 437.

21. "Letter to Hayato Ikeda from Joseph M. Dodge," August 8, 1949, Box: 2, Folder: Correspondence—Marquat, Japan 1949, JDP.

22. "Letter to Minister Ikeda from Joseph M. Dodge," August 9, 1949, Box: 3, Folder: Official Correspondence, Japan 1949, JDP.

23. "To DA Wash DC for West from SCAP Tokyo Japan from Shoup," Z-15877, July 7, 1949, Box: 9, Folder: Taxation 49–50, Japan 1949, JDP.

24. "Letter to Joseph M. Dodge from Ralph W. E. Reid," August 8, 1949, Box: 9, Folder: Shoup Recommendations, Japan 1949, JDP, 1. For a broader discussion of the relationship between the Shoup Mission and Dodge, see, W. Elliot Brownlee, "Shoup vs. Dodge: Conflict over Tax Reform in Japan, 1947–1951," *Keio Economic Studies* 47 (2011): 91–122.

25. For a discussion of the Shoup Mission somewhat critical of Dodge, see Brownlee, "Shoup vs. Dodge," 91–122.

26. "Letter to Joseph M. Dodge from Jerome B. Cohen," September 20, 1949, Japan 1949, Box: 9, Folder: Shoup Recommendations, JDP.

27. Ibid.

28. "Letter to Joseph M. Dodge from William B. Marquat," September 16, 1949, Box: 2, Folder: Correspondence—Marquat, Japan 1949, JDP, emphasis in original.

29. "Letter to Orville McDiarmid from Joseph M. Dodge," October 14, 1949, Box: 3, Folder: Official Correspondence, Japan 1949, JDP, 2.

30. "Letter to David Ginsburg from Joseph M. Dodge," December 1, 1949, Box: 2, Folder: Correspondence (1 of 4), Japan 1949, JDP.

31. "Summary/Analysis of Current Economic Situation," February 15, 1950, *Economic Reform, 1945–1953*, Doc #: 4–102–110, OJMS, 1.

32. "Letter to Joseph M. Dodge from Douglas MacArthur," May 22, 1950, Japan 1950, Box: 4, Folder: Correspondence—Marquat, Japan 1950, JDP.

33. "Japan's Economy in 1950," *Oriental Economist*, January 7, 1950: 5.

34. "Dodge-Ikeda Talk Urged Necessary: Gov't Facing Economic Blind Alley, Seeking Revision of 'Line,'" *Nippon Times*, March 19, 1950, Box: 3, Folder: Correspondence—Gov. U.S., JDP.

35. "Letter to Hayato Ikeda from Joseph M. Dodge," August 8, 1949, Box: 2, Folder: Correspondence—Marquat, Japan 1949, JDP.

36. "Shocks for the Japanese Communists," *Economist*, March 25, 1950: 660; Matsuda, *Soft Power and Its Perils*, 46–48. Before 1950, the Soviets had largely accepted the wisdom of Japan's Communist leader Sanzo Nosaka, who believed that the Japanese needed to learn "democracy before they will be ready for Communism." His gradualism led to consistent gains for the Communists in the Diet after the war. The stabilization effort, however, seemed to unnerve the Soviets, and the Cominform repudiated Sanzo's approach. By March 1950, Moscow had Sanzo sacked.

37. For a perspective on the break between SCAP and Japanese labor as told from labor's perspective, see Cohen and Passin, *Remaking Japan*, 443–454; Takemae, *Inside GHQ*, 473–485.

38. "Views of Social Democratic Party and Economic Stabilization Board with Regard to Economic Stabilization, Tokyo Despatch, No. 767," November 4, 1949, *Economic Reform, 1945–1953*, Doc #: 6–402–09, OJMS.

39. "Memorandum to General Marquat: Summary Analysis of Current Economic Situation," August 1, 1949, Box: 3, Folder: Devaluation, Japan 1949, JDP, 2.

40. "Letter to Joseph M. Dodge from William F. Marquat," August 24, 1949, Box: 2, Folder: Correspondence—Marquat, Japan 1949, JDP.

41. "Letter to Joseph M. Dodge from Jerome B. Cohen," September 20, 1949, Box: 9, Folder: Shoup Recommendations, Japan 1949, JDP.

42. "Recovery in the Year of the Tiger," *Economist*, February 25, 1950: 435.

43. U.S. Congress, Senate Committee on Foreign Relations, Subcommittee on Armed Services, *Military Situation in the Far East, Part 3*, 81st Cong., 1st sess. (Washington, DC: Government Printing Office, 1951) 1715.

44. D. Clayton James, *The Years of Douglas MacArthur*, vol. 3, *1945–1964* (Boston: Houghton Mifflin Co., 1985), chap. 14. The literature on the Korean War is vast and follows the pattern of nearly all historiography in diplomatic history. The initial take largely followed the Truman administration in viewing the war as directed by Stalin from Moscow: see Harry S. Truman, *Memoirs*, vol. 2, *Years of Trial and Hope* (Garden City, NY: Doubleday, 1956). A subsequent revision took place, largely emphasizing that the Korean War was in fact a civil war in which the United States defended the more authoritarian side: see Bruce Cumings, *The Origins of the Korean War*, vol. 1, *Liberation and the Emergence of Separate Regimes, 1945–1947* (Princeton, NJ: Princeton University Press, 1981), *The Origins of the Korean War*, vol. 2, *The Roaring of the Cataract, 1947–1950* (Princeton, NJ: Princeton University Press, 1990). Most recently, and with the help of more archival sources from the former Soviet Union and China, scholars have placed the Korean conflict in an international context: see Allan R. Millett, "Introduction," in *The Korean War* (Lincoln, NE: University of Nebraska Press, Korean Institute of Military History, 2001) 3.

45. Takemae, *Inside GHQ*, 485.

46. See, in particular, Schaller, *The American Occupation of Japan*.

47. "The World Overseas: War Boom in Japan," *Economist*, November 18, 1950.

48. "Letter to Joseph M. Dodge from Ralph W. E. Reid," August 9, 1950, Box: 1, Folder: Appointment, Japan 1950, JDP.

49. "Bulletin: Mr. Dodge Leaves for Japan," Box: 1, Folder: Appointment, Japan 1950, JDP.

50. Letter to Joseph M. Dodge from William F. Marquat, August 12, 1950, Box: 1, Folder: Appointment, Japan 1950, JDP.

51. Statement by Joseph M. Dodge—Yokohama, Japan, October 7, 1950, Box: 1, Folder: Memoranda incident to 1950 Mission to Japan October-November-December, Japan 1950, JDP (emphasis added).

52. "Conference: Mr. Dodge–Mr. Ikeda," October 25, 1950, Box: 1, Folder: Memoranda incident to 1950 Mission to Japan October-November-December, Japan 1950, JDP (italics in original).

53. For a contrary view of Inch'on's importance, see Cumings, *Origins of the Korean War*, vol. 2, *The Roaring of the Cataract, 1947–1950*; Pearlman, *Truman and MacArthur*, chap. 4.

54. "The Acting Secretary of State to the United States Mission at the United Nations," September 26, 1950, *FRUS*, 1950, vol. 7: Korea: 781.

55. Alonzo Hamby, *Man of the People: A Life of Harry S. Truman* (New York: Oxford University Press, 1995) 542.

56. Pearlman, *Truman and MacArthur,* 115.

57. Barbara Barnouin and Changgeng Yu, *Zhou Enlai: A Political Life* (Hong Kong: Chinese University Press, 2006) 147–148. Mao's reason for entering the war remains a bit controversial among scholars. Some argue that Mao acted largely out of security concerns, fearing that if North Korea fell, a large contingent of Western forces would rest on his border. See Allen S. Whiting, *China Crosses the Yalu: The Decision to Enter the Korean War* (Stanford, CA: Stanford University Press, 1970); Russell Spurr, *Enter the Dragon: China's Undeclared War Against the U.S. in Korea, 1950–1951* (New York: Newmarket Press, 1988); and Yufan Hao and Zhai Zhihai, "China's Decision to Enter the Korean War: History Revisited," *China Quarterly* 121 (March 1990): 94–115. More recently, and with access to more Chinese documents, scholars have considered the way Mao hoped to repay North Korea for help in the Chinese Civil War, sought to reestablish China as a great power, and was himself prodded into action by Stalin. See Chen Jian, *China's Road to the Korean War: The Making of the Sino-American Confrontation* (New York: Columbia University Press, 1994); Michael M. Sheng, *Battling Western Imperialism: Mao, Stalin, and the United States* (Princeton, NJ: Princeton University Press, 1997); Shu Guang Zhang, *Mao's Military Romanticism: China and the Korean War, 1950–53* (Lawrence: Kansas University Press, 1995); Mark F. Wilson, ed., *The Korean War at Fifty: International Perspectives* (Lexington: Virginia Military Institute, 2004).

58. Billy C. Mossman, *The United States Army in the Korean War: Ebb and Flow, November 1950–July 1951* (Washington, DC: Center of Military History U.S. Army, 1990) 158–162.

59. Hamby, *Man of the People,* 553–555.

60. "General Critical: He Says Orders Barring Attacks on Manchuria Aid Chinese Invaders," *NYT*, December 2, 1950: 1, 4.

61. "Harry S. Truman to Omar Bradley, December 6, 1950," MacArthur Douglas-general, General File, PSF, HSTPL.

62. Hamby, *Man of the People*, 553–555.

63. Pearlman, *Truman and MacArthur*, 175.

64. Ibid., 5.

65. Barton J. Bernstein, "New Light on the Korean War," *International History Review* 3, no. 2 (April 1981): 256–277; Conrad Crane, "To Avert Impending Disaster: American Military Plans to Use Atomic Weapons During the Korean War," *Journal of Strategic Studies* 23, no. 2 (June 2000): 72–78; Sean L. Malloy, "A 'Paper Tiger?': Nuclear Weapons, Atomic Diplomacy and the Korean War," *New England Journal of History* 60, no. 1–3 (Fall 2003–Spring 2004): 227–252.

66. William T. Bowers, *Battles and Campaigns: The Line: Combat in Korea, January–February 1951* (Lexington: University Press of Kentucky, 2008).

67. Joseph C. Harsch, "UN Air Blows Stagger Foe; MacArthur Authority Sags Along with 'Invincibility,'" *Christian Science Monitor*, January 20, 1951: 1.

68. "Text of MacArthur's Korea Statement," *NYT*, March 24, 1951: 2.

69. "MacArthur's Move Stirs New Controversy," *NYT*, March 25, 1951: 119.

70. Hamby, *Man of the People*, 555.

71. "MacArthur Backs Chiang Troop Use: Proposal Logical One, General Writes GOP Leader in House," *Los Angeles Times*, April 6, 1951: 4.

72. Harry S. Truman, "Statement and Order by the President on Relieving General MacArthur of His Commands," April 11, 1951, APP, http://www.presidency.ucsb.edu/ws/?pid =14058.

73. Memorandum for the record, "OIR Report No. 5247," July 12, 1950, Box: 4, Folder: Correspondence—U.S. Gov., Japan 1950, JDP, 6.

74. "Letter to Major General William F. Marquat from Joseph M. Dodge," July 17, 1950, Box: 4, Folder: Correspondence—Marquat, Japan 1950, JDP, 2.

75. "Letter to Honorable Dean Rusk from Carter B. McGruder," July 12, 1950, Box: 4, Folder: Correspondence—U.S. Gov., Japan 1950, JDP.

76. "Letter to Joseph M. Dodge from William F. Marquat," May 21, 1951, Box: 3, Folder: Correspondence—Marquat, Japan 1951, JDP, 3.

77. Ibid.

78. "Letter to Marquat," May 29, 1951, Japan 1951, Box: 3, Folder: Correspondence—Marquat, Japan 1951, JDP.

79. "Letter to Joseph M. Dodge from E. M. Reid," March 20, 1951, *Economic Reform, 1945–1953*, Doc #: 4–125–01, OJMS.

80. "Letter to Joseph M. Dodge from William F. Marquat," March 22, 1951, Box: 3, Folder: Correspondence—Marquat, Japan 1951, JDP.

81. "Statement by Joseph M. Dodge," November 27, 1951, *Economic Reform, 1945–1953*, Doc #: 4–102–51, OJMS.

82. Chalmers Johnson, *MITI and the Japanese Miracle*.

83. Hiromitsu Ishi, *Making Fiscal Policy in Japan: Economic Effects and Institutional Settings* (Oxford, UK: Oxford University Press, 2000) 126–130.

84. Gardner Ackley and Hiomitsu Ishi, "Fiscal, Monetary, and Related Policies," *Asia's New Giant: How the Japanese Economy Works*, ed. Hugh Patrick and Henry Rosovsky (Washington: Brookings Institution, 1976) 213.

Chapter 11

1. This account is repeated a number of times, largely based on Truman's own account. See Truman, *Memoirs* (Garden City, NY: Doubleday, 1955) 1:1–5; also Hamby, *Man of the People*, 290; David McCullough, *Truman* (New York: Simon and Schuster, 1992) 342.

2. See, for example, Michael J. Hogan's discussion of the National Security Act in *A Cross of Iron: Harry S. Truman and the Origins of the National Security State, 1945–1954* (Cambridge, UK: Cambridge University Press, 1998), chaps. 1–3, as well as the discussion of the Employment Act and the Creation of the Council of Economic Advisers below. See also Joanna Grisinger, *The Unwieldy American State: Administrative Politics Since the New Deal* (Cambridge, UK: Cambridge, 2012).

3. Hamby, *Man of the People,* chap. 18.

4. Arthur Krock, "In the Nation: Laborings of the Federal Machinery," *NYT,* September 20, 1945: 22.

5. George Lipsitz, *Rainbow at Midnight: Labor and Culture in the 1940s* (Urbana: University of Illinois Press, 1994) chap. 4–6.

6. "To John Sheldon Doud Eisenhower (1 July 1946)," *PDDE,* 7:1165.

7. Ed Edwin, Interview with Eisenhower, July 20, 1967, DDEPL, 49.

8. Dwight D. Eisenhower, "November 12, 1946," in *The Eisenhower Diaries,* ed. Robert H. Ferrell (New York: Norton, 1981) 137.

9. Ibid.

10. Ambrose, *Eisenhower: Soldier and President*, 204–208.

11. Eisenhower, *Crusade in Europe*, 444.

12. "The Top Command," *NYT*, November 21, 1945: 20.

13. Arthur Krock, "Taboo Against Soldiers May Die in the '48 Race," *NYT,* September 29, 1946: 95.

14. "Revive Issue: War Hero as a President?" *Chicago Daily Tribune*, December 7, 1947: 46.

15. Neal Stanford, "Marshall Takes Oath of Office, Will Bar Draft to Political Post: General's Refusal Includes Presidency 'Once and for All,'" *Christian Science Monitor,* January 21, 1947: 1 (emphasis added).

16. Kyle Palmer, "Only Sherman Slammed the Door," *Los Angeles Times,* October 5, 1947: A4.

17. Eisenhower, "November 12, 1946," in *The Eisenhower Diaries*, 138.

18. "Within the space of about a decade, 1936–46, the vast majority of economists throughout the Western world were converted to the Keynesian way of thinking. Many of those early converts felt themselves impelled to repudiate virtually the entire corpus of received economic doctrine, taking up the Keynesian system with an ardor that is more commonly associated with religious conversions. Moreover, it was the younger generation who proved most susceptible to the Keynesian infection; criticism of Keynes came almost solely from the older members of the profession." Blaug, *John Maynard Keynes*, 25.

19. For the way Hansen blended Keynesian thinking with his own sense of "secular stagnation," see Theodore Rosenof, *Economics in the Long Run: New Deal Theorists and Their Legacies, 1933–1993* (Chapel Hill: University of North Carolina Press, 2009), particularly chap. 4 and 5. Also Blaug, *John Maynard Keynes*, 35–36. For a more recent version of this thesis,

see Robert Gordon, *The Rise and Fall of American Growth: The U.S. Standard of Living Since the Civil War* (Princeton, NJ: Princeton University Press, 2016).

20. "Background: The Keynes and Beveridge Plans," *Congressional Digest,* October 1, 1945, 229. The tendency to "over save" ultimately led to the "paradox of thrift": see Paul Anthony Samuelson, *Economics* (New York: McGraw-Hill Book Co., 1948) 284.

21. For the best blow-by-blow account of the legislation, see Stephen Kemp Bailey, *Congress Makes a Law: The Story Behind the Employment Act of 1946* (New York: Columbia University Press, 1950). See also Roger B. Porter, "Presidents and Economists: The Council of Economic Advisers," *American Economic Review* 87, no. 2 (May 1997); Martin Feldstein, "The Council of Economic Advisers: From Stabilization to Resource Allocation," *American Economic Review* 87, no. 2 (May 1997).

22. For a discussion of the way economic events undermined the purposes of the act, see Bailey, *Congress Makes a Law.*

23. Alvin H. Hansen, "Inflation," *Yale Review* 35, no. 4 (1946): 692–711.

24. Keynes, *The General Theory of Employment,* 162.

25. William Henry Beveridge, *Full Employment in a Free Society: A Report* (London: G. Allen, 1944) 200, 202.

26. Truman, "Address at the Gilmore Stadium in Los Angeles," September 23, 1948. APP: http://www.presidency.ucsb.cdu/ws/?pid = 13012,

27. See, among many, Meg Jacobs, *Pocketbook Politics,* 225.

28. As quoted in Edwin G. Nourse, *Economics in the Public Service: Administrative Aspects of the Employment Act* (New York: Harcourt, 1953) 127.

29. George S. Kaufman et al., *The Senator Was Indiscreet* (Hollywood, CA: Universal Pictures, 1947).

30. "The Economy: Flation," *Time,* August 23, 1948.

31. Truman, "The President's News Conference," March 3, 1949. APP: http://www.presidency.ucsb.edu/ws/?pid = 13396.

32. For his part, Keynes realized soon after he published the *General Theory* that war financing could apply his insights too aggressively and, as a result, unleash inflationary trends that worked at cross-purposes to social justice. "A rising cost of living puts an equal proportionate burden on every one," he wrote, "irrespective of his level of income . . . and is a cause, therefore, of great social injustice" (John Maynard Keynes, "Paying for the War, I: The Control of Consumption, A Problem of Social Justice," *Times,* November 14, 1939). His American interpreters remained slower to think through the problem, however—something Keynes did not fail to observe. Even before the United States entered World War II, he "tried to persuade . . . [his American counterparts in the Roosevelt Administration] that they should be more cautious," he wrote a friend in mid-1941. "I am afraid I have only partially succeeded, though I expect the results of the argument will sink in [once the inflation begins]." To Professor J. M. Clark, July 26, 1941, Papers of Walter S. Salant, Box: 1, HSTPL.

33. Eisenhower, "November 12, 1946," in *The Eisenhower Diaries,* 138.

34. "Snyder Urges Cut in Debt, Not Taxes," *NYT,* November 21, 1946: 35.

35. "To Arthur Krock," in PDDE 9:2133, n. 1.

36. Ibid., 9:2132–2133.

37. Brown later helped found the American Enterprise Association, which became the American Enterprise Institute, a libertarian think tank in Washington. As it turned out, Clay

felt Brown acted too boldly, creating a backlash against (instead of support for) Clay's efforts. As Clay mentioned to William Draper in August of 1948, "Lewis Brown damn near ruined us politically in Germany." *Papers of General Lucius D. Clay*, 2:756–775.

38. Lewis H. Brown, *A Report on Germany: How to Get Germany Eventually Off the Backs of the American Taxpayers* (New York: Farrar, Straus, 1947).

39. Brown, *A Report on Germany*, 128, 41.

40. Ibid., 48–49.

41. Eisenhower, PDDE, 9:993. See also "Lewis Brown Reports on Germany; Asks Marshall Plan Support; Says War, Communism Alternative," *Wall Street Journal*, October 23, 1947: 2.

42. Eisenhower, PDDE, 9:1878, n. 3.

43. Ibid., 10:441, n. 3.

44. Ibid., 440.

45. Ibid., 477.

46. Hogan, *A Cross of Iron*, 38.

47. Hamby, *Man of the People*, 500–501; Hogan, *A Cross of Iron*, 93, 277; Collins, *More*, chap. 1; see more generally, Donald K. Pickens, *Leon H. Keyserling: A Progressive Economist* (New York: Lexington Books, 2007); W. Robert Brazelton, *Designing U.S. Economic Policy: An Analytic Biography of Leon H. Keyserling* (New York: Palgrave, 2001).

48. Thomas Furlon, "Keyserling Frank: He's for Spending," *Chicago Tribune*, May 18, 1950: D9.

49. Leon Keyserling, "Wage-Price-Profit Relationships in Economic Growth," Washington, DC, March 14, 1950, Department of State, Foreign Service Institute, Leon H. Keyserling Papers: Speech and Article File, Box: 29, HSTPL.

50. Collins, *More*, especially chap. 2. See also Bertram M. Gross and Jeffrey D. Straussman, "'Full' Employment Growthmanship and the Expansion of Labor Supply," *The Annals of the American Academy of Political and Social Science* 418 (March 1975): 1–12; W. Robert Brazelton, *Designing US Economic Policy*.

51. For a brief analysis of Keyserling's economic theory, see W. Robert Brazelton, "Retrospectives: The Economics of Leon Hirsch Keyserling," *Journal of Economic Perspectives* 11, no. 4 (Fall 1997): 189–197.

52. Edwin G. Nourse, Memorandum, August 9, 1949, Student File: Economic Growth, Box: 1 HSTPL, 4.

53. Leon H. Keyserling, "Wage-Price-Profit Relationships in Economic Growth."

54. Leon H. Keyserling, "For 'a National Prosperity Budget,'" *NYT*, January 9, 1949: SM7.

55. "Keyserling Brands McCarthy's Remarks 'Utter Nonsense,'" *Boston Globe*, February 11, 1952: 18.

56. "Mrs. Keyserling A Former Red, M'Carthy Says," *Atlanta Constitution*, April 2, 1952: 14.

57. Pickens, *Leon H. Keyserling*, 108–109.

58. "NSC 68: United States Objectives and Programs for National Security," *FRUS*, 1950, vol. 1: National Security Affairs; Foreign Economic Policy, 234–292. Also Leffler, *A Preponderance of Power*, 356.

59. Leffler, *A Preponderance of Power*, chap. 8.

60. Eisenhower, "February 19, 1949," in *The Eisenhower Diaries*, 157; Hogan, *A Cross of Iron*, 301.

61. Hogan, *A Cross of Iron*, 299.

62. "NSC 68: United States Objectives and Programs for National Security," *FRUS*, 1950, 1:258.

63. Ibid., 286.

64. Ibid., 258.

65. Ibid., 254. As it would turn out, the language of "gaps" and economic "potentials" would animate a generation of economists in and around Democratic politics for the following decades. See in particular Herbert Stein, *The Fiscal Revolution in America* (Chicago: University of Chicago Press, 1969).

66. For a good discussion of the economics of NSC 68, see Curt Caldwell, *NSC 68 and the Political Economy of the Early Cold War* (New York: Cambridge University Press, 2011); see also Hogan, *A Cross of Iron*, chap. 7.

67. Among other things, the report suggested that the Fed free itself of the Treasury's demand that it finance government spending at a fixed interest rate and that Roosevelt give up the powers Congress gave him early in his first term to devalue gold, issue greenbacks, and utilize silver seigniorage. See Sidney Hyman, *Marriner S. Eccles, Private Entrepreneur and Public Servant* (Palo Alto, CA: Stanford University, 1976) 274–275.

68. Ibid., 275.

69. Ibid., 274–275.

70. Statement for the Press by Chairman Marriner Eccles, January 17, 1946, Papers of Gerhard Colm, Student File: Economic Growth, folder 7, HSTPL.

71. United States Joint Committee on the Economic Report, *Anti-Inflation Program as Recommended in the President's Message of November 17, 1947* (Washington, DC: Government Printing Office, 1948) 135.

72. Robert L. Hetzel and Ralph F. Leach, "The Treasury-Fed Accord: A New Narrative Account," Federal Reserve Bank of Richmond, *Economic Quarterly* 87, no. 1 (Winter 2001): 39–40.

73. See, among many, "Gambling with Inflation," *NYT*, January 26, 1951; "Defense Financed by Taxes Is Urged," *NYT*, January 23, 1951; Paul Heffernan, "New Debate Looms over Money Rate; Treasury and Reserve System Renew Row over Effect of Low Fixed Interest, Eccles Again Attacks, Sees Bank By-Passed by Fiscal Agency, Despite its Duty to Fix Monetary Policy," *NYT*, January 28, 1951; Paul Heffernan, "Rebuke Discerned in U.S. Money Move: Snyder's Financing Program at Odds with Top Opinion in the Banking World," *NYT*, January 21, 1951: 109; John D. Morris, "Eccles for Curb on Pay, Not Prices," *NYT*, January 26, 1951: 12.

74. Hetzel and Leach, "The Treasury-Fed Accord"; also Allan H. Meltzer, *A History of the Federal Reserve, volume 1, 1913–1951* (Chicago: University of Chicago Press, 2003) 691–712.

75. William Bragg Ewald, *Eisenhower the President: Crucial Days, 1951–1960* (Englewood Cliffs, NJ: Prentice Hall, 1981) 192.

76. Herbert Parmet, Interview with Robert B. Anderson, March 11, 1970, DDEPL, 10–11.

77. Robert B. Anderson, "The Money and Credit System of the United States and How It Works," September 19, 1957, Administration Series, Box: 2, Anderson (4), DDEPL, 2, 6.

78. "Remarks by Robert B. Anderson (Secretary of the Treasury) at Dinner of the Republican Finance Committee," Detroit, MI, Thursday, October 31, 1957, Administration Series, Box: 2, Anderson (4), DDEPL, 2, 6.

79. As quoted in Hetzel and Leach, "The Treasury-Fed Accord," 45.

80. Hamby, *Man of the People*, 583.

81. George Whitney, Letter to Eisenhower, March 20, 1951, Pre-Presidential Papers Box: 123, DDEPL.

82. Clifford Roberts, Letter to Eisenhower, March 13, 1951, Pre-Presidential Papers Box: 98, Clifford Roberts (6), DDEPL.

83. Eisenhower, "To Martin Withington Clement, December 4, 1951," *PDDE*, 12:754.

84. Hamby, *Man of the People*, 555–556.

85. Harry S. Truman, "The President's News Conference," April 26, 1951, APP, http://www.presidency.ucsb.edu/ws/index.php?pid = 14073&st = april + 26&st1.

86. "Chicago Public Blasts Actions of President: With Few Exceptions Rallies to MacArthur," *Chicago Tribune*, April 12, 1951: 12.

87. "Gallup Poll and the Letter Count," *Los Angeles Times*, April 19, 1951: A4.

88. Richard Rovere and Arthur M. Schlesinger, Jr., *The General and the President and the Future of American Foreign Policy* (New York: Straus and Giroux, 1951).

89. James Reston, "Historians Support Truman on Dismissal," *Atlanta Constitution*, April 28, 1951: 4.

90. "MacArthur's Complete Speech Before Joint Meeting of Congress," *Atlanta Constitution*, April 20, 1951: 8.

91. On this point, see Pearlman, *Truman and MacArthur*, 209–212.

92. Senate Committee on Armed Services and Foreign Relations, *Military Situation in the Far East, Part 2*, 82nd Cong., 1st sess. (Washington, DC: Government Printing Office, 1951) 732.

93. Walter Lippmann, "Truman Lacks Civilians, So Turns to Generals," *Los Angeles Times*, May 23, 1951.

94. Richard L. Strout, "General Mac and General Ike: An Intimate Message from Washington," *Christian Science Monitor*, April 20, 1951: 22.

95. Eisenhower, "April 17, 1951," in *The Eisenhower Diaries*, 191.

96. "Draper Quits Post: Truman Hails Him," *NYT*, February 20, 1949: 23.

97. The crash took place at Rockville Centre (February 1950; 31 dead) and Richmond Hill (November 1950; 71 dead). See Edgar A. Haine, *Railroad Wrecks* (New York: Cornwall Books, 1994).

98. "Draper is Named to Run LI Road: Kennedy Signs Order at End of Public Hearing—Choice to Be Ratified by I.C.C.," *NYT*, December 9, 1950: 17.

99. "Draper Supports State Transit Unit," *NYT*, February 7, 1951: 31; and "Draper Stresses Need for L.I. Rise," *NYT*, March 7, 1951: 35.

100. Volney D. Hurd, "Numerous Limitations Shaken Off by NATO, Permanent Council Draper Welcomed," *Christian Science Monitor*, January 16, 1952: 3.

101. "Notes of the Week," *Economist*, January 19, 1952: 128.

102. Oral History Interview with General William H. Draper, Jr., by Jerry N. Hess, HSTPL, 5.

103. Ibid.

104. Ibid.

105. "To Lucius DuBignon Clay, 19 December 1951," *PDDE*, 12:798.

106. "To William Henry Draper, Jr., 9 January 1952," *PDDE*, 12:863.

107. Eisenhower, Letter to Averell Harriman, June 30, 1951, Pre-Presidential Papers, from Harriman May 1951– July 1951, DDEPL.

108. Lansing Warren, "Pleven's Cabinet Falls in France: Long Crisis Likely," *NYT*, January 8, 1952: 1.

109. "To William Henry Draper, Jr., January 9, 1952," *PDDE*, 12:864.

110. Raymond Daniel, "West Pact Make-Up to Be Reorganized," *NYT*, January 15, 1952: 5.

111. Volney D. Hurd, "French See Draper Weak Prop for 'Ike,'" *Christian Science Monitor*, January 30, 1952: 7.

112. "Excerpts from Eisenhower's New Conference on European Unity," *NYT*, January 23, 1952: 4.

113. "To William E. Robinson, March 6, 1951," PDDE, 13:1–2.

114. Eisenhower, "January 22, 1952," in *The Eisenhower Diaries*, 209.

115. Ibid., 209–210, 214.

116. For a broader discussion of Eisenhower's decision to run for president, see Pickett, *Eisenhower Decides to Run*.

117. See, generally, Pickett, *Eisenhower Decides to Run*. See also Smith, *Eisenhower in War and Peace*, 498–514. For a fascinating description of how public relations firms helped in the effort to "draft" Eisenhower, see David Haven Blake, *Liking Ike: Eisenhower, Advertising, and the Rise of Celebrity Politics* (Oxford: Oxford University Press, 2016) chap. 3.

118. Eisenhower, "November 3, 1949," in *The Eisenhower Diaries*, 165.

119. Ibid.

120. Eisenhower, "January 22, 1952," in *The Eisenhower Diaries*, 212.

Chapter 12

1. Robert A. Taft, "Letter to Robert S. Beightler, November 24, 1950," in *Papers of Robert A. Taft*, 3:217–218.

2. Hogan, *A Cross of Iron*, 325; Hamby, *Man of the People*, 559.

3. Eisenhower, *At Ease*, 372–374.

4. Robert A. Taft, "Ulysses S. Schwartz, April 30, 1951," in *Papers of Robert A. Taft*, 3:281–282.

5. Congress did the same for Dwight D. Eisenhower, George Marshall, and Omar Bradley. See "U.S. Army Five-Star Generals," http://www.history.army.mil/html/faq/5star.html.

6. James, *The Years of MacArthur*, 3:642.

7. Robert A. Taft, "To Douglas MacArthur, September 12, 1951," in *Papers of Robert A. Taft*, 3:318.

8. As quoted in James, *The Years of MacArthur*, 3:648.

9. Leo Egan, "250,000 Cheer Clay as City Gives Him a Hero's Welcome," *NYT*, May 20, 1949: 1.

10. Smith, *Lucius D. Clay*, 576–579.

11. Interview #26 with General Lucius Clay by Jean Smith, April 1, 1971, New York, DDEPL, 864.

12. Ibid., 866.

13. Ibid.

14. "784: To Harry S. Truman, April 2, 1952," *PDDE*, 13:1154–1156.

15. "Text of Address by Gen. MacArthur," *Los Angeles Times*, May 16, 1952: 22.

16. Robert A. Taft, "To Douglas MacArthur, May 16, 1952," in *Papers of Robert A. Taft*, 3:376.

17. James T. Patterson, *Mr. Republican: A Biography of Robert A. Taft* (Boston: Houghton Mifflin, 1972) 549.

18. As quoted in James, *The Years of MacArthur*, 3:651.

19. Jim Newton, *Eisenhower: The White House Years* (New York: Anchor Books, 2012) 64.

20. As quoted in Patterson, *Mr. Republican*, 571.

21. This is the "K1C2" or sometimes "3 C's" Republican strategy (Korea, communism, and corruption). See Robert North Roberts, *Presidential Campaigns, Slogans, Issues and Platforms*, vol. 3, *Presidential Campaigns, 1912 to 2008* (Santa Barbara, CA: Greenwood, 2012) 255.

22. Address by Dwight D. Eisenhower, Republican Nominee for President, delivered at Peoria, IL, October 2, 1952, Box: 2, Folder: Sept. 26, 1952 to Oct. 13, 1952, Papers as President Speech Series, DDEPL.

23. Text of Dwight D. Eisenhower's Speech in Portland's Civil Auditorium, October 7, 1952, Box 2, Folder: Sept. 26, 1952 to Oct. 13, 1952, Papers as President Speech Series, DDEPL.

24. Address by Dwight D. Eisenhower, delivered at Peoria, IL, October 2, 1952, DDEPL.

25. Text of Dwight D. Eisenhower's Address on Inflation, September 23, 1952, Box: 1, Folder: Sept. 15, 1952 to Sept. 25, 1952, Papers as President Speech Series, DDEPL.

26. "Transcript of General Eisenhower's First Press Conference, Giving His Political Views," *NYT*, June 6, 1952: 10.

27. Bernard M. Baruch, Telephone Message for General Eisenhower (Bob Schulz), June 25, 1952, Box: 5, Folder: Bernard M. Baruch (6), Papers as President, DDEPL.

28. Eisenhower, "To Bernard Mannes Baruch, June 31, 1952," *PDDE*, 12:1263.

29. Text of Dwight D. Eisenhower's Address on Inflation, September 23, 1952, DDEPL.

30. Dwight D. Eisenhower, "The Washington Mess," *Vital Speeches of the Day*, October 15 1952, 19: 3.

31. Oral History Interview with Herbert Brownell by Jean Smith, 1971, Columbia Oral History Project. See also Gellman, *The President and the Apprentice*, 15–28.

32. Smith, *Lucius D. Clay*, 608.

33. Duncan Norton-Taylor, "The Banker in the Budget Bureau," *Fortune*, March 1953, 135.

34. Interview #26 with General Lucius Clay by Jean Smith, April 1, 1971, New York, DDEPL, 863–864.

35. Oral History Interview with General William H. Draper Jr. by Jerry N. Hess, HSTPL, 8.

36. Smith, *Lucius D. Clay*, 607.

37. Robert J. Donovan, *Eisenhower: The Inside Story* (New York: Harper and Brothers, 1956) 402–403; William R. Conklin, "Eisenhower Picks Lodge for Liaison in Capital Affairs," *NYT*, November 10, 1952: 1.

38. "Letter to Joseph M. Dodge from Dwight D. Eisenhower, November 10, 1952," Box: 1, Folder: Appointment as Director, Bureau of the Budget, JPD.

39. "Eisenhower Would 'Go to Korea,'" *NYT*, October 25, 1952: 1.

40. As quoted in Herbert S. Parmet, *Eisenhower and the American Crusades* (New Brunswick, NJ, [1972] 1999) 143.

41. "'Grandstand Play' Laid to Eisenhower," *NYT*, October 26, 1952: 1.

42. W. H. Lawrence. "Stevenson Says G.O.P. Hurts Efforts to Gain Korea Peace," *NYT*, October 30, 1952: 1.

43. Parmet, *Eisenhower and the American Crusades*, 143; Ambrose, *Eisenhower: Soldier and President*, 285.

44. Charles J. V. Murphy, "The Eisenhower Shift: Part I," *Fortune* (January 1956): 87. Murphy interviewed the participants from the voyage, but kept his quotes anonymous.

45. Ibid., 87.

46. Ibid., 206.

47. Ibid., 87, 206.

48. Ibid., 87.

49. For a discussion of the "New Look," see, among many: Tom Wicker, *Dwight D. Eisenhower* (New York: Henry Hold and Company, 2002) 29–30; and Lawrence Freedman, *The Evolution of Nuclear Strategy*, 3rd ed. (New York: Palgrave Macmillan, 2003) 76–86.

50. George Bookman Papers, 1981–1993, Box: 1, Folder: "Chapter 9," DDEPL, 6.

51. Laurin L. Henry, *Presidential Transitions* (Washington, DC: The Brookings Institution, 1960) 503.

52. In a letter to his brother Milton, who had considerable input in the State of the Union, Eisenhower wrote: "I hope—and pray—that it contains no blunders that will later arise. The only two items in which I think such could happen are the order to the Seventh Fleet and the removal of price controls. In both cases, I believe our contemplated action to be correct; the unpredictable ingredient is public reaction, both here and abroad. In any event, I go on the theory that the Executive of this nation must depend upon the finest set of brains he can mobilize around him. By and large, he must follow the advice of these people or, in the long run, he will so discourage them as to make them useless in a pinch." See "To Milton Stover Eisenhower, February 2, 1953," in *Papers of Dwight D. Eisenhower*, 14:18.

53. Dwight D. Eisenhower, "Annual Message to the Congress on the State of the Union," February 2, 1953, APP, http://www.presidency.ucsb.edu/ws/?pid = 9829.

54. "The Liquidation of Controls," *Los Angeles Times*, February 6, 1953, A4.

55. "An End of Hypochondria," *NYT*, February 7, 1953: 14.

56. "A Farewell to Controls," *WSJ*, February 3, 1953: 10.

57. "CED Upholds Ike's 'Indirect' Controls Plan," *Washington Post*, March 16, 1953: 7.

58. "Prices, 'Watchdog' Urged in Congress," *NYT*, February 9, 1953: 36.

59. "Inflation Threat Seen by Douglas," *NYT*, March 27, 1953: 17.

60. John Gibson, "Economic Controls," *WSJ*, February 2, 1953: 2.

61. Dwight D. Eisenhower, "The President's News Conference," March 5, 1953, APP, http://www.presidency.ucsb.edu/ws/?pid = 9734.

62. The quotation is from Eisenhower, "May 1, 1953," in *The Eisenhower Diaries*, 235; the record of the meeting is found in Eisenhower, Notes on Legislative Leadership Meeting, April 30, 1953, Box: 1, Folder: Legislative Meetings (4) [April–May], Papers as President, Ann Whitman File, Legislative Meeting Series, DDEPL. The dialogue that follows, including the emphasis, comes from these notes except where indicated.

63. Eisenhower, "May 1, 1953," in *The Eisenhower Diaries*, 235–236.

64. "He [Taft] simply wanted expenditures reduced, regardless." Ibid., 235.

65. Ibid., 235–236.

66. "Excerpts From Editorials Commenting on Elections," *NYT*, November 5, 1954: 12.

67. "To Milton Stover Eisenhower (November 6, 1953)," *PDDE*, 14.

68. "Memorandum of Discussion at the 138th Meeting of the National Security Council (March 25, 1953)," *FRUS* 1952–1954: vol. 2: National Security Affairs (in two parts), 1:261.

69. Pearson, "Defense or Economy: Up to Ike," *Washington Post*, September 23, 1953: 43.

70. John G. Norris, "Wilson Sees Defense Cuts Near Limit," *Washington Post*, September 30, 1953: 1.

71. Fiscal Year 1955 Department of Defense Budget, September 30, 1953, Box: 12, Joseph Dodge, 1952–53, Folder: 2, Administrative Series, Presidential Papers of Dwight D. Eisenhower, DDEPL.

72. "Memorandum of Discussion at the 166th Meeting of the National Security Council, Tuesday, October 13, 1953," *FRUS*, 1952–1954: vol. 2: National Security Affairs (in two parts), 1:544.

73.Text of Dulles' Statement on Foreign Policy of Eisenhower Administration," *NYT*, January 13, 1954: 2.

74. J. A. Livingston, "Too Much Anti-Inflation Pressure?" *Washington Post*, May 10, 1953: C16.

75. "Text of Truman Speech in Manchester," *NYT*, October 17, 1952: 22.

76. W. H. Lawrence, "Stevenson Warns '4 Fears' Under G.O.P. Replace Freedoms," *NYT*, December 13, 1953: 1.

77. "Appraisal of Current Trends In Business and Finance," *WSJ*, January 25, 1954: 1.

78. "Text of Truman Speech on Economic Problems Facing the Nation and Administration," *NYT*, May 14, 1954: 14.

79. Dwight D. Eisenhower, *Mandate for Change, 1953–1956: The White House Years* (Garden City, NY: Doubleday and Company, 1963) 307.

80. Ibid., 304–307.

81. "348: To Benjamin Franklin Caffey, Jr., July 27, 1953," *PDDE*, 14:429.

82. Dwight D. Eisenhower, "Annual Message Transmitting the Economic Report to the Congress," January 28, 1954, APP, http://www.presidency.ucsb.edu/ws/?pid=9997.

83. Selma Mushkin, "The Internal Revenue Code of 1954 and Health Programs," *Public Health Reports* 70, no. 8 (August 1955): 791.

84. "In 1952, on the eve of the changes in tax policy that codified the tax subsidy, 63 percent of households had health insurance coverage. In 1957, three years after the implementation of the tax subsidy, nearly 76 percent of American households had health insurance . . . by lowering the after-tax price of health insurance, the change in tax policy led workers to purchase more group health insurance coverage from their employers and encouraged the expansion of employment-based, group health insurance in the United States. In addition, households who already had group insurance, as well as households with high marginal tax rates purchased policies with more generous coverage after the implementation of the tax subsidy. Thus, the tax subsidy increased the amount of health insurance demanded, and extended access to health care. By fostering an increase in the demand for group insurance relative to individual coverage, it also ensured that health insurance in the United States would evolve as a group, employment-based system." Melissa A. Thomasson, "The Importance of Group Coverage: How Tax Policy Shaped U.S. Health Insurance," *American Economic Review* 93, no. 4. (November 2003): 1373–1374.

85. Burton Crane, "U.S. Stockholders Top 10 Million," *NYT*, July 24, 1956: 33, 37.

86. "Annual Budget Message to the Congress: Fiscal Year 1955," *PDDE*, doc. 14, 90–100.

87. *House Report on the Internal Revenue Act of 1954: Minority Views*, US Code, Congressional and Administrative News, vol. 3, 83rd Cong., 2nd sess. (Washington, DC: United States Government Printing Office, 1954) 4601.

88. M. Packman, "Shares in Tax Relief," *1954 Editorial Research Reports*, vol. 1, Washington, DC: Congressional Quarterly Press, http://library.cqpress.com/cqresearcher/cqresrre 1954031600.

89. Ibid.

90. Joint Economic Committee, *Economic Report of the President. Hearings Before the Joint Committee on the Economic Report* (Washington, DC: Government Printing Office, 1954) 80, 102–104.

Chapter 13

1. Mark H. Rose and Raymond A. Mohl, *Interstate: Highway Politics Since 1939*, 3rd ed. (Knoxville: University of Tennessee Press, 2012) 7.

2. Interview with Dr. Gabriel Hauge by Ed Edwin, May 31, 1967, Oral History Research Office, Columbia University, New York City, 77.

3. Leo Egan, "Governors Oppose U.S. Aid for Modernizing Highways," *NYT*, July 14, 1954: 1.

4. Eisenhower, *Mandate for Change*, 548.

5. Interview with General Lucius D. Clay by Ed Edwin, February 20, 1967, New York, Box: 18, Articles, Interviews and Statements 1950–1977, Folder: Oral History Project on Eisenhower Administration, Lucius Clay Collection, GML, 101.

6. Ibid.

7. Rose and Mohl, *Interstate*, 74.

8. "Letter to Sherman Adams from Joseph M. Dodge," January 18, 1954, Box: 13, Folder: 7, Resignations, Bureau of the Budget, JPD.

9. "65—Letter Accepting Resignation of Joseph M. Dodge as Director of the Bureau of the Budget, March 27, 1954," APP, http://www.presidency.ucsb.edu/ws/index.php?pid= 10193&st=dodge&st1.

10. Actually, April 15 did not become "Tax Day" until the following year as a result of the 1954 Internal Revenue Act.

11. John Harriman, "The Budget-Cutter Leaves: Dodge, Ike's Most Feared Aid, Quits Job," *Boston Globe*, April 11, 1954: C68.

12. Rose and Mohl, *Interstate*, 74–75.

13. Interview with General Lucius D. Clay by Ed Edwin, GML, 102–103.

14. "Manion Raps Ike's 'Rush to Social State': Charges Shift from His Earlier Beliefs," *Chicago Tribune*, March 7, 1955: C6.

15. U.S. Congress, Senate Committee on Public Works, *National Highway Program*, 84th Cong., 1st sess. (Washington, DC: Government Printing Office, 1955) 121.

16. Ibid., 497.

17. Hon. Joseph Campbell, "Is The President's New Highway Program Sound? CON," *Congressional Digest*, vol. 34, May 1955: 151.

18. Mark H. Rose, *Interstate: Express Highway Politics, 1939–1989* (Knoxville: University of Tennessee Press, 1990) 81.

19. Interview with Dwight D. Eisenhower by Ed Edwin, July 20, 1967, DDEPL, 100–101.

20. Dennis W. Johnson, *The Laws That Shaped America: Fifteen Acts of Congress and Their Lasting Impact* (New York: Routledge, 2009) 278.

21. Tom Lewis, *Divided Highways: Building the Interstate Highways, Transforming American Life* (Ithaca, NY: Cornell University Press, 2013) 117.

22. Eisenhower, *Mandate for Change*, 548.

23. Eisenhower, "Special Message to the Congress Transmitting Proposed Changes in the Social Security Program.," August 1, 1953, APP, http://www.presidency.ucsb.edu/ws/?pid = 9662.

24. Dwight D. Eisenhower, Middle Way Speech, Boise, ID, August 20, 1952, Box: 1, Folder: July 12, 1952 to Sept. 14, 1952, Ann Whitman File, Speech Series, DDEPL.

25. "Judge the GOP by Its Voting, Sparkman Asks," *Chicago Tribune,* August 14, 1952: 11.

26. See, in particular, Andrew Morris, "Eisenhower and Social Welfare," in *A Companion to Dwight D. Eisenhower,* ed. Chester J. Pach (Malden, MA: Wiley-Blackwell, 2017) 255.

27. "946: To Richard Milhous Nixon, Personal and Confidential," *PDDE*, 13:1366–1369.

28. Interview with Dwight D. Eisenhower by Ed Edwin, July 20, 1967, DDEPL, 101–102.

29. Dwight D. Eisenhower, Radio and Television Address to the American People on the Administration's Purposes and Accomplishments, January 4, 1954, APP, http://www.presidency.ucsb.edu/ws/?pid = 9985.

30. Eisenhower, "Special Message to the Congress on Old Age and Survivors Insurance and on Federal Grants-in-Aid for Public Assistance Programs," January 14, 1954, APP, http://www.presidency.ucsb.edu/ws/?pid = 9874.

31. Wilbur J. Cohen, Robert M. Ball, and Robert J. Myers, "Social Security Act Amendments of 1954: A Summary and Legislative History," *Social Security Bulletin,* September 1954: 16.

32. *Congressional Record—Senate*, August 13, 1954: 14381–14382.

33. U.S. Congress, House Committee on Ways and Means, *Report to Accompany H.R. 9366: Social Security Amendments of 1954,* House Report No. 1698, 83rd Cong., 1st sess., May 28 (Washington, DC: Government Printing Office, 1954), 26.

34. Wilbur J. Cohen, Robert M. Ball, and Robert J. Myers, "Social Security Act Amendments of 1954: A Summary and Legislative History," *Social Security Bulletin,* September 1954, 13.

35. *Congressional Record—Senate*, August 13: 14416.

36. "More Social Security," *NYT,* September 4, 1954: 10.

37. William Leuchtenburg, *In the Shadow of FDR: From Harry Truman to George W. Bush* (Ithaca, NY: Cornell University Press, 2001) 48–49; see also Jason Scott Smith, *Building New Deal Liberalism: The Political Economy of Public Works, 1933–1956* (New York: Cambridge University Press, 2009); John W. Sloan, *Eisenhower and the Management of Prosperity* (Lawrence: Kansas University Press, 1991); Gerard H. Clarfield, *Security with Solvency: Dwight D. Eisenhower and the Shaping of the American Military Establishment* (Westport, CT: Greenwood Publishing Group, 1999) 11; Parmet, *Eisenhower and the American Crusades*, 10. See

also Wicker, *Dwight D. Eisenhower*, 3; Ambrose, *Eisenhower: Soldier and President*, 575; Geoffrey Perret, *Eisenhower* (New York: Random House, 1999) 507; and Steven Wagner, *Eisenhower Republicanism: Pursuing the Middle Way* (DeKalb, IL: Northern Illinois University Press, 2006).

38. Ludwig Erhard, "Prosperity for All, (1957)" in *The Economics of Success*, 194.

39. Chiyoda-ku Hirakawa-cho, *The Constitution of the Liberal Democratic Party and Its Declaration, Basic Principles, Characteristics, Mission Platform* (Tokyo: The Liberal Democratic Party, 1964) 2–7.

40. "1408: To George Magoffin Humphrey, April 26, 1955," *PDDE*, 16:1686–1687.

41. Dwight D. Eisenhower, "288—The President's News Conference," December 2, 1959, APP, http://www.presidency.ucsb.edu/ws/index.php?pid = 11587&st = banker&st1 = .

42. Eisenhower, "Remarks at Meeting of the World Bank and the International Monetary Fund," September 28, 1956, APP, http://www.presidency.ucsb.edu/ws/?pid = 10614.

43. Michael D. Bordo, "The Bretton Woods International Monetary System: An Historical Overview," National Bureau of Economic Research Working Paper 4033 (Cambridge, MA: NBER, 1992), see Table 2 in Bordo's article.

44. Iwan W. Morgan, *Eisenhower versus "The Spenders": The Eisenhower Administration, the Democrats and the Budget, 1953–60* (London: Pinter Publishers, 1990) 129.

45. Christopher A. Preble, " 'Who Ever Believed in the "Missile Gap"?' John F. Kennedy and the Politics of National Security," *Presidential Studies Quarterly* 33, no. 4 (December 2003): 801–826.

46. "Missile 'Penny-Pinching' Denounced by Kennedy," *Atlanta Constitution*, November 7, 1957: 18.

47. George Bookman Papers, Box: 1, Folder: "Chapter 12," DDEPL, 21.

48. Eisenhower, "70—The President's News Conference, April 9, 1958," APP, http://www.presidency.ucsb.edu/ws/index.php?pid = 11346&st = inflation&st1 = .

49. "Democrats Sweep 1958 Elections; Will Have 64 Senators, 283 Representatives, 35 Governors," in *Congressional Quarterly Almanac 1958*, 14th ed. (Washington, DC: Congressional Quarterly, 1959), 11:713–716, http://library.cqpress.com/cqalmanac/cqal58-1340275.

50. Eisenhower, "The President's News Conference," November 5, 1958, APP, http://www.presidency.ucsb.edu/ws/?pid = 11286.

51. Ibid.

52. Dwight D. Eisenhower, *Waging Peace* (Garden City, NY: Doubleday and Co., 1965) 379.

53. Notes of Cabinet Meeting, June 5, 1959, Box: 14, Folder: Cabinet Meeting of June 5, 1959, Cabinet Series, DDEPL.

54. "Fancy Juggling," *WSJ*, October 6, 1958: 12.

55. Eisenhower, *Waging Peace*, 385.

56. Ibid., 387; also ibid., Appendix U.

57. Cabinet Minutes, March 13, 1959, Box: 13, Folder: Cabinet Meeting of March 13, 1959, Cabinet Series, DDEPL, 2–3.

58. William M. McClenahan, Jr., and William H. Becker, *Eisenhower and the Cold War Economy* (Baltimore: Johns Hopkins University Press, 2011) 100.

59. Walter Lippmann, "Money Markets Lack Confidence in President's War on Inflation," *Los Angeles Times*, May 17, 1959: B5.

60. Joint Economic Committee, *January 1959 Economic Report of the President (27 January 1959)* (Washington, DC: Government Printing Office, 1959) 204–205, 209. See also McClenahan and Becker, *Eisenhower and the Cold War Economy*, 108.

61. A. W. Phillips "The Relationship Between Unemployment and the Rate of Change of Money Wages in the United Kingdom 1861–1957," *Economica* 25, no. 100 (1958): 283–299.

62. Paul A. Samuelson and Robert M. Solow, "Analytical Aspects of Anti-Inflation Policy," *American Economic Review* 50, no. 2 (May 1960): 185, 192.

63. "Man of the Year," *Time* 75, no. 1 (January 4, 1960): 11.

64. Joseph Alsop, "The LBJ Congress," *Hartford Courant,* July 8, 1959: 14.

65. Interview with Robert B. Anderson by Herbert Parmet, March 11, 1970, DDEPL, 19–20.

66. Richard E. Mooney, "Nixon Committee Asks U.S. to Bar Inflation," *NYT*, June 28, 1959: 1. See also Gellman, *The President and the Apprentice*, 451–460.

67. "Prosperous 60s Seen by Nixon Panel: Rising Living Level Predicted with End to Price Increases Nixon Panel Predicts Rising Living Levels," *Los Angeles Times,* April 17, 1960: 1.

68. Democratic Party Platforms, "1960 Democratic Party Platform," July 11, 1960, APP, http://www.presidency.ucsb.edu/ws/?pid=29602. See also Collins, *More*, 49–50.

69. When adjusted for inflation and population. See C. I. Jones, "The Facts of Economic Growth," in *Handbook of Macroeconomics*, ed. John B. Taylor and Harald Uhlig (Amsterdam: Elsevier, B.V., 2016) 2:5.

70. Eisenhower, "Annual Message Presenting the Economic Report to the Congress," January 20, 1960, APP, http://www.presidency.ucsb.edu/ws/?pid=11806.

71. Eisenhower, "Telegrams to Vice President Nixon and Henry Cabot Lodge," November 9, 1960, APP, http://www.presidency.ucsb.edu/ws/?pid=12014.

72. Herbert Stein, *Presidential Economics: The Making of Economic Policy from Roosevelt to Clinton* (Washington, DC: American Enterprise Institute for Public Policy Research, 1994) 157.

73. "Directive by the President Concerning Steps to Be Taken with Respect to the United States Balance of Payments (The 1960 Supplement to Title 3 of the Code of Federal Regulations)," Federal Register 25:12221.

74. Eisenhower, "The President's News Conference at Augusta, Georgia," November 16, 1960, APP, http://www.presidency.ucsb.edu/ws/?pid=12020.

75. "To Milton Stover Eisenhower, May 25, 1959," *PDDE*, 20:1492–1493.

76. There are, of course, varying interpretations of Eisenhower's meaning. For a good overview, see James Ledbetter, *Unwarranted Influence: Dwight D. Eisenhower and the Military-Industrial Complex* (New Haven, CT: Yale University Press, 2011) chap. 5 and 6. My own interpretation is similar to Martin J. Medhurst's in emphasizing the notion of balance over the criticism of the military-industrial complex. See Martin J. Medhurst, "Reconceptualizing Rhetorical History: Eisenhower's Farewell Address," *Quarterly Journal of Speech* 80, no. 2 (May 1994): 295–316. For a critical take on Medhurst, see Robert L. Scott, "Eisenhower's Farewell Address: Response to Medhurst," *Quarterly Journal of Speech* 81, no. 4 (November 1995): 496–501.

77. David Greenberg, "Beware the Military-Industrial Complex: Eisenhower's Farewell Address Has Been Completely Misunderstood," *Slate,* January 14, 2011, http://www.slate.com/articles/news_and_politics/history_lesson/2011/01/beware_the_militaryindustrial

_complex.html; see also Will Inboden, "Looking Back on Ike's Farewell Address," *Foreign Policy*, December 17, 2010, http://foreignpolicy.com/2010/12/17/looking-back-on-ikes-fare well-address/.

78. Eisenhower, "Farewell Radio and Television Address to the American People," January 17, 1961, APP, http://www.presidency.ucsb.edu/ws/?pid = 12086.

79. Leonard S. Silk, "Nixon's Program —'I Am Now a Keynesian,'" *NYT*, January 10, 1971: E1.

80. Richard Nixon, "Address to the Nation Outlining a New Economic Policy: 'The Challenge of Peace,'" August 15, 1971, APP, http://www.presidency.ucsb.edu/ws/?pid = 3115.

Epilogue

1. "892: To Bernard Edwin Hutchinson, July 10, 1950," *PDDE*, 11:1217–1218.

2. Summary of Notes of Interview with General Douglas MacArthur by Forrest C. Pogue, January 3, 1961, New York, GML 7.

3. "Commander of Armies That Turned Back Japan Led a Brigade in World War I," *NYT* April 6, 1964: 26.

4. Arthur A. Kimball, Memorandum for Mr. Arthur Minnich, November 1954, Box: 3, Folder: ACW Diary November 1954, Ann Whitman File, Ann Whitman Diary Series, DDEPL.

5. "Eisenhower Mourns Death of J. M. Dodge," *NYT*, December 4, 1964: 39, 1.

6. "Plan to Double Individual Income, December 27, 1960," in *Japan: A Documentary History*, ed. David J. Lu, vol. 2, *The Late Tokugawa Period to the Present* (Armonk, NY: East Gate, 1997) 527–530.

7. "The Honorable Joseph M. Dodge," Box: 1, Folder: 2, Biography, JDP.

8. Nakamura Takafusa, "Ikeda Hayato: The Man Who Created the 'Economic Era,'" in *The Prime Ministers of Postwar Japan, 1945–1995: Their Lives and Times*, ed. Akio Watanabe (Lanham, MD: Lexington Books, 2016).

9. "Obituaries: Ludwig Erhard Guided W. Germany's Recovery," *Boston Globe*, May 5, 1977: 39.

10. John F. Kennedy, "Remarks in the Rudolph Wilde Platz, Berlin," June 26, 1963, APP, http://www.presidency.ucsb.edu/ws/?pid = 9307.

11. Bordo, "The Bretton Woods International Monetary System," 1–2.

12. See, generally, Walter W. Heller, "The Future of Our Fiscal System," *Journal of Business* 38, no. 3 (July 1965): 235–244.

13. J. Bradford De Long, "America's Only Peacetime Inflation: The 1970s," National Bureau of Economic Research, Historical Working Paper 84 (Cambridge, MA: NBER, 1996).

Index

Acknowledgments

I have many people to thank for their help in this long and often arduous process. First, I must thank the Mellon Achievement Fund and Michael and Ling Markovitz for the fellowships they provided during my time at the University of Chicago, along with Freehling and Mann travel grants. The College of Family, Home and Social Sciences at Brigham Young University provided me a Research Grant and the History Department has proven generous in providing time and support for my work. I could not have survived without this help.

Some of the ideas and research found here were originally published as "The International Origins of Dwight D. Eisenhower's Political Economy," in the *Journal of Policy History* 24, no. 4 (Fall 2012); and "Becoming a State-in-the-World: Lessons Learned from the American Occupation of Germany," in *Studies in American Political Development* 26, no. 2 (October 2012). My thanks to Cambridge University Press for permission to reproduce my conclusions here.

Throughout the research phase of this project I benefited tremendously from the help of able archivists at the Harry S. Truman Presidential Library, the Detroit Public Library, the Columbia University Oral History Archives, the Dwight D. Eisenhower Presidential Library (which also provided me its Presidential Library Travel Grant), the George C. Marshall Research Library and the National Archives. The archivists and librarians at each of these institutions helped with insights, suggestions, and an uncanny ability to track down my sometimes obscure requests.

I must thank the many research assistants who have contributed over the years—in particular Christina Baer, Jeremy Cooper, and Elisabeth Loveland—for patiently tracking down and entering a never-ending volume of data. Their attention to detail and dedicated work was extraordinary. My friend Greg Whisenant provided invaluable suggestions for improving the manuscript. I am also grateful to Bob Lockhart at the University of Pennsylvania Press for taking this project under his wings so quickly and seamlessly.

Like many first-time authors, I benefited from the time and attention of dedicated mentors. Bruce Cumings, at a critical juncture, offered a few simple suggestions that dramatically changed the way I saw this project. He encouraged me to think of the American state as something that could exist outside of the borders of the country. In addition, John Cochrane showed a great deal of patience in sharing his insights about the world of economics. When I met him I told him I couldn't "do the math." Nevertheless, he took the time to help me conceptualize the economic world in a way that made much of what follows possible. I have benefited tremendously from his help, support, and example as a scholar. I must also thank Amy Dru Stanley who more than anyone taught me the craft of the historian. Her passion for ideas and her skill at grounding those ideas in history remains my model. In particular, I must thank Jim Sparrow. His knowledge and passion for history have often left me breathless—and given me a notebook full of ideas, books to "look at," and things to think about. At every turn he has offered sage advice and critical support. Most important, at moments when I have doubted myself he always believed in my project and then patiently showed me why I should believe as well. He, too, has been a generous mentor and friend.

Finally, my colleagues at BYU have been extremely supportive as has the university through time and money to research. In particular I am grateful for the help of Aaron Skabelund and Stewart Anderson. Andrew Johns, especially, took time to help me work through intellectual and professional questions.

Finally, throughout these years my family, whether immediate, extended, or in-law, has always remained supportive and never second-guessed my decision to get a PhD or dedicate myself to this book (even when it meant missing events and functions). In particular, my wife Sara has always stayed true to my dream and supported me through this project, despite the obvious challenges that come to the spouse of a professor. To her and our three sons (Spencer, John, and William) I owe much more than I can repay.